SOCIALIST REGISTER 2011

THE SOCIALIST REGISTER

Founded in 1964

To get online access to all Register volumes visit our website

http://www.socialistregister.com

SOCIALIST REGISTER 2011

THE CRISIS THIS TIME

Edited by LEO PANITCH, GREG ALBO and VIVEK CHIBBER

LEFTWORD BOOKS, NEW DELHI
THE MERLIN PRESS, LONDON

First published in 2010 by
The Merlin Press Ltd.

Published in India by
LeftWord Books
12 Rajendra Prasad Road
New Delhi 110001
INDIA

LeftWord Books is the publishing division of
Naya Rasta Publishers Pvt. Ltd.

www.leftword.com

ISBN 978-81-87496-99-1

British Library Cataloguing in Publication Data is available from the British Library

ISSN. 0081-0606

Printed by
Progressive Printers
A 21 Jhilmil Industrial Area
G.T. Road
Shahadara
Delhi 110095

CONTENTS

CONTRIBUTORS

Sam Ashman is a senior research fellow in the School of Economics and Business Sciences at the University of the Witwatersrand, Johannesburg.

Karl Beitel is an independent researcher and scholar living in San Francisco, currently employed by the American Federation of Teachers.

Riccardo Bellofiore is professor of economics at the University of Bergamo.

Johanna Brenner is a founding member of Solidarity, a democratic, revolutionary, socialist, feminist, anti-racist organization, and professor emerita of Sociology/Women's Studies at Portland State University, Portland.

Dick Bryan is professor of political economy at the University of Sydney.

Noam Chomsky is institute professor and professor emeritus of linguistics at the Massachusetts Institute of Technology.

Bryan Evans is associate professor in the Department of Politics and Public Administration, Ryerson University in Toronto.

Ben Fine is professor of economics at the School of Oriental and African Studies, University of London.

Julie Froud is a professor at Manchester Business School and member of the ESRC Centre for Research on Socio-Cultural Change, University of Manchester.

Francesco Garibaldo is president of the international network, Regional and Local Development of Work and Labour, and former director of the Institute for Labour.

Sam Gindin is a former research director of the Canadian Auto Workers and is currently the visiting Packer Chair in Social Justice at York University, Toronto.

Joseph Halevi teaches political economy at the University of Sydney and is also with the International University College of Turin and CRIISEA at the University of Picardie, France.

Doug Henwood is based in Brooklyn, where he edits Left Business Observer and hosts a weekly radio show called Behind the News.

Michael Moran is professor of government in the School of Social Sciences and an affiliate of the ESRC Centre for Research on Socio-Cultural Change, University of Manchester.

R. Taggart Murphy is a professor in the MBA Program in International Business at the Tokyo campus of Tsukuba University.

Susan Newman is a senior research fellow on the Corporate Strategy and Industrial Development (CSID) research programme at the University of the Witwatersrand, Johannesburg.

Adriana Nilsson is a doctoral candidate in politics at the University of Manchester.

Hugo Radice is a life fellow in the School of Politics and International Studies, University of Leeds.

Mike Rafferty is a senior research analyst at the Workplace Research Centre, University of Sydney.

Alfredo Saad-Filho is professor of political economy in the Department of Development Studies, School of Oriental and African Studies, University of London.

Anwar Shaikh is professor of economics at the New School for Social Research, New York.

Susanne Soederberg holds a Canada Research Chair in Global Political Economy in the Departments of Global Development Studies and Political Studies at Queen's University, Canada.

Karel Williams is professor of accounting and political economy at Manchester Business School and director of the ESRC Centre for Research on Socio-Cultural Change, University of Manchester.

PREFACE

Crises have a way of clarifying things. Remember when we were told, again and again, by Wall Street whiz kids and Ivy League economists, that freeing up the economy was the road to stability? That the solution to market instability was – to free up the markets even more? That the obscene salaries and perquisites being handed to CEOs and financial analysts were worth it because they were bringing prosperity to all? To question these nostrums, however mildly, was to invite ridicule and abuse. Then, after those fateful weeks in Autumn 2008, as one Wall Street titan after another came to the brink of collapse or collapsed altogether, we witnessed the impossible. Virtually overnight, the warm embrace of the market turned into a suffocating incubus. As workers lost jobs by the hundreds of thousands, pensions went up in a puff of smoke, life savings vanished, families lost their homes, the grim reality of capitalism, the remorseless logic of the profit motive, became impossible to ignore. The major capitalist economies fell into an abyss, the like of which had not been seen since the Great Depression. And for the first time in decades, the mountainous piles of books, essays, and stories produced to defend the free-market mania started to appear as nothing more than smoke and mirrors.

It has been three years since the crisis began, and there is no clear end in sight. Whether or not we are at the beginning of the first Great Depression of the 21st century remains to be seen. But what recovery there has been is halting and precarious, and we now live with the possibility of long-term stagnation. And make no mistake, for millions of workers across the world it has meant what crises always do – coming face to face with the fact that in capitalism, it is profits that matter, not people.

The Left has always recognized that crises mean, first and foremost, untold suffering by the most vulnerable sections of society, the scars of which remain long after the crises abate. This is why serious socialists have never welcomed economic breakdown. But precisely because of their disruptive effects on business as usual, economic crises also present political opportunities. In previous crises, such as in the Great Depression, and even in the late 1960s and 1970s, economic dislocation became the occasion for massive social explosions and gains for the working people.

Are we positioned now to make comparable – or indeed any – advances? It is possible, but we need to be honest about our capabilities. Over the past decades, it is the Right that has gone from strength to strength. For working people, the grim reality for over a generation has been a steady dismantling of the institutions that they built up in the second half of the twentieth century. Across the developed world, social democracy has morphed from representing working-class interests to becoming the guardian of business profits; in the global South, the visions of national liberation and socialism seem like dim echoes from a distant past. The Left is today the weakest it has been since the defeat of the Paris Commune.

Indeed, since the crisis began, it is the ruling classes, not the labour movements, that have seized the crisis as an opportunity. Even while the public stands disgusted with the speculative orgy that neoliberalism unleashed, even while the mythology of market fundamentalism has been discredited, and even while public sentiment is hostile to the bank bailouts – the response of capitalist states has been to shore up, however they can, the very model that brought the economy to ruins. In the very week in late June 2010 when we were writing this preface, the leaders of the G-20, meeting in Toronto, declared that their holding fast to free markets since the onset of the crisis had been 'the right choice'. And they pledged to 'renew for a further three years… [their] commitment to refrain from raising barriers or imposing new barriers to investment or trade… [and] to rectify such measures as they arise'. They also promised to 'minimize any negative impact on trade and investment of [their] domestic policy actions, including fiscal policy'. It appears we are entering a new age of austerity. This portends a further assault on trade unions and the social entitlements of the working classes.

So in this conjuncture we need to have a sober appreciation of our weakness. Whatever else goes into revitalizing the Left, surely one part of it will be the development of an adequate analysis of the crisis, in its political and economic dimensions. On this score, Marxist political economy stands out as having built the analysis of crisis and instability into its very core. This is precisely why past crises have been the occasion for a 'return to Marx'. It is not altogether surprising that Marx's *Capital* has rocketed up the sales charts, and we see his familiar bearded visage on the cover of such establishment magazines as *Foreign Policy*.

We are devoting two volumes of *The Socialist Register* to analyzing 'the crisis this time'. This one, our 47th, encompasses several themes, including putting the crisis in historical and theoretical perspective, analyzing the centrality of financialization in it and surveying its dimensions in the US, Europe, Japan and South Africa. The volume also examines the impact of the crisis on the working class both socially and politically, while demonstrating that, in spite of its instabilities, 'exit strategies' are geared to revitalizing neoliberal capitalism. Next year's volume will extend the geographical focus to China, the Middle East, Eastern Europe and Latin America, and deepen the analysis of the epicentre of the crisis in the USA. It will further explore the Left's response to the crisis so far, and the linkages between the economic crisis and the ecological crisis and the crisis of the city. This will set the stage for the 49th volume of the Register, which will focus entirely on socialist strategy and organization for our time.

Many of the contributors to our two volumes on the crisis presented drafts of their essays at a highly stimulating workshop at York University in February 2010, and we want to thank Frederick Peters, Khashayar Hooshiyar, Adam Hilton, Aidan Conway, and Tammy Kovich for their role in making this possible. Our associate editor, Alfredo Saad-Filho, made a particularly important contribution in helping us plan both crisis volumes. We want to thank all of our contributors, especially for their responsiveness to our comments on their essays, while pointing out to our readers that neither they nor we necessarily agree with all of the diverse approaches to the crisis in the volume. We thank Louis Mackay for his cover design. And we warmly express our gratitude to Adrian Howe and Tony Zurbrugg, our colleagues at the Merlin Press, and especially to Alan Zuege, now the Register's assistant editor, for their creativity and hard work in the preparation of this volume. The work they all have put into making the Register available online, including the entire Register archive, has been indispensible.

With the publication of his capstone volume, *Morbid Symptoms: Health under Capitalism, The Socialist Register 2010,* Colin Leys stepped down as co-editor to become an associate editor. We are extremely grateful for his tremendous help in editing this volume, which only puts into sharper relief his brilliant editorial skills and intellectual leadership over the past 12 years. Amidst the spread of market-driven politics, Colin's unwavering socialist commitment has been a model for Left intellectuals everywhere. We will continue to count on his guidance over the next phase of the Register's development.

LP
GA
VC
June 2010

CAPITALIST CRISES AND THE CRISIS THIS TIME

LEO PANITCH AND SAM GINDIN

I

Exactly a hundred and fifty years before the current crisis began in August 2007, the collapse of the Ohio Life Insurance Company in New York triggered what became known as 'the great crisis of 1857-8'. As it quickly spread to Europe's main financial centres, Karl Marx 'was delighted and thrilled by the prospects for another revolutionary upsurge on the continent'. As Michael Kratke notes, 'the crisis started exactly as Marx had predicted already in 1850 – with a financial crisis in New York' and the crisis itself led Marx to extend 'the scope and scale of his study' for the *Grundrisse* notebooks he was working on, so as to take account of 'the first world economic crisis, affecting all regions of the world'. In their correspondence, Marx and Engels agreed that 'the crisis was larger and much more severe than any crisis before', viewing the financial crisis as 'only the foreplay to the real crisis, the industrial crisis that would affect the very basis of British prosperity and supremacy'.[1] In October 1857, Engels wrote to Marx: 'The American crash is superb and will last for a long time... Now we have a chance'. And two weeks later: '...in 1848 we were saying: now our moment is coming, and in a certain sense it was, but this time it is coming completely and it is a case of life or death'.[2]

As the crisis abated and began to fade away in mid-1858, Marx tried to understand why it had not turned out as expected. He came to the conclusion that the relatively rapid recovery could be largely explained by the sharp depreciation of capital on a large scale and an equally sharp and major shift in the structure of exports from Europe towards the colonies, with this especially applying to British industry which was then so central to global capital accumulation. This allowed for a return to dynamic capitalist growth, while at the same time reproducing the contradictions which, as Marx wrote in the *Grundrisse*, would lead again to 'crises in which momentary suspension of all labour and annihilation of a great part of the capital violently lead it back to the point where it is enabled [to go on] fully employing its productive powers without committing suicide. Yet, these regularly recurring catastrophes lead to their repetition on a higher scale, and finally to its violent overthrow'. Capitalist production, Marx noted, 'moves in contradictions which are constantly overcome but just as constantly posited'.[3]

Fifty years later – a full century before the onset of today's crisis – the great financial crisis of 1907 that also started on Wall Street and included a stock market crash, accelerating runs on the banks and an 11 per cent decline in US GDP, once again quickly spread to 'an extremely severe monetary and banking crisis such as Europe had not experienced for a long time'.[4] But since this crisis was even more short-lived than 1857-8, it provided little fodder for the theories of crises that had become so prevalent in Marxism in the wake of capitalism's 'first great depression' that began in the mid-1870s, and which led Engels in 1884 to speak in terms of the 'inevitable collapse of the capitalist mode of production which is daily taking place before our eyes'.[5]

II

The Marxist search for a general theory of capitalist crises was intensified in the late 19th century in a context that confirmed deep crisis tendencies in the sphere of production, centred on the contradictions associated with capitalism's constant drive to accumulation. But this begged the question of why the resultant overaccumulation was sometimes readily corrected and other times not. The appeal of Marx's identification of a tendency towards a falling rate of profit (FROP), based on the rising organic composition of capital, was partly that it seemed to offer an answer to this, but aside from empirical controversies there was a basic conceptual problem that revolved around the many 'counter-tendencies' that were adduced, starting with Marx, to explain why the FROP does not always manifest itself. The problem lay in these counter-tendencies being, as often as not, the very substance of capitalism's dynamics: i.e., higher rates of class exploitation, the development of new technologies and commodities, the emergence of new markets, international expansion, and innovations in credit provision, not to mention state interventions of various kinds.

What the FROP offered in terms of theoretical certainty it lost as an expression of historical materialism. Too often its presentation as an economic law tended to be ahistorical and its materialism tended to be mechanical. The recognition of this was why, at least between the first great depression that ended in the mid-1890s and the even greater one that was triggered at the end of the 1920s, the FROP was 'long neglected or rejected by Marxist theorists'.[6] The sense that capitalism had survived the first depression and entered a new stage was 'a decisive factor in the "crisis of Marxism" which erupted at the end of the century'.[7] Labriola's assessment at the time captured the weakness of mechanical theories of economic breakdown: 'The ardent, energetic, and precocious hopes of several years ago – have now come up against the more complex resistance of economic relations and the ingenuity of political contrivances'.[8]

Nevertheless, even though the mid-1890s economic recovery helped foster social democratic evolutionary revisionism, the language of crisis and collapse was never far from earshot in Marxist debates before the First World War. The very prescience with which Marxism in this period theorized inter-imperial rivalry leading to destructive war was now rooted in an expectation that continuing limits to domestic accumulation would drive further the export of capital and the colonization that had come to define the fragmented process of capitalist globalization in the last decades of the 19th century.

It is well known that Marxists theorists were influenced in this respect by Hobson's 1902 classic, *Imperialism: A Study,* while rejecting his notions, anticipating Keynes, that reformist redistributive measures would solve the domestic underconsumption that spawned external expansion. What is less well known is that Hobson himself was influenced by the writings of US business economists who, in the wake of the deep recession of the early 1890s, drew on Frederick Jackson Turner's 'closing of the American frontier' thesis to argue that the domestic market was no longer able to sustain the enormous productive capacity of the newly-emerged corporate form.[9] Their claims were soon to prove wildly wrong. By 1898 the US recession had ended, and home markets continued to dwarf exports. The frontier may have been filled territorially but accumulation within it was only in its very early stages when Turner identified its 'closing'.[10]

Marxist crisis theorists at the time not only seriously misinterpreted the kind of capitalism developing in the United States, they more generally underestimated the long-term potential for domestic consumption and accumulation within the leading capitalist states. This was partly due to their failure to appreciate the extent to which working-class industrial and political organizations then emerging would undermine the thesis of the 'immiseration of the proletariat'. But it was also due to their undeveloped theory of the state, which reduced it to an instrument of capital and underestimated its relative autonomy in relation to both imperial and domestic interventions. This shortcoming was also much in evidence among those Marxist theorists who, unlike Luxemburg, began not with underconsumptionist tendencies but, like Hilferding, with the implications of the concentration and centralization of capital and the consequent fusion of industry and finance. This, they argued, led to limited competition at home alongside the recruitment of the state to aggressively support expansion abroad, and gave rise not only to the export of capital but also to the politicization of competition among the leading capitalist states – the ultimate outcome being cataclysmic inter-imperial rivalry.

As we have argued in these pages before, the penetration and incorporation of the other developed capitalist states by the US imperial state in the second half of the 20th century rendered this old theory of inter-imperial rivalry increasingly anachronistic.[11] And even as applied to pre-First World War capitalism, the political economy of underconsumption on the one hand and finance capital on the other was problematic; the understanding of the capitalist state was reductionist; and the explanation of imperial expansion was at best partial. It was ironic that Hilferding's *Finance Capital* (1910), so highly influential despite mistakenly generalizing from German developments at the time, actually recognized that it was 'impossible to derive general laws about the changing character of crises from the history of crises in a single country… [or from] specific phenomena peculiar to a particular phase of capitalism which may perhaps be purely accidental'.[12]

Many of these limitations in classical Marxist crisis theories have lingered to this day, and helped keep alive the notion that capitalism is in a late, if not quite final, stage. Since the Great Depression of the 1930s, there has especially been a propensity to see a permanent overaccumulation crisis whose consequences have been consistently delayed by special circumstances like war, waste or bubbles. This runs counter to the insight Marx arrived at shortly after the 1857-8 crisis that 'permanent crises do not exist', even while insisting that capitalism would repeatedly throw up new crises.[13] Indeed, insofar as crises are 'turning-points', a very important question for Marxists today, especially given the impasse of the Left in face of the first capitalist crisis of the 21st century, is whether this crisis will also be a turning-point in the way the Left thinks about crises.

III

The term 'crisis' is commonly used to refer to interruptions in the process of capital accumulation and economic growth. To the extent, however, that most such interruptions are either self-correcting (e.g. through the devaluation of 'excess' capital), or their depth and duration are shortened by state intervention (e.g. fiscal stimulus), their social significance is limited.

Of greater significance is that some such interruptions do not simply come and go, but take on a much larger dimension. So we need to ask not just *why* crises occur, but why some crises are *distinct*: why they last so long, are marked by persistent economic uncertainty, and produce significant political and social change.

It is these latter, less frequent but deeper *structural crises* that concern Marxist theory. Three crises of this kind, separated from each other by roughly a generation, have been identified in the modern era of capitalism: the long 'first great depression' of the last quarter of the 19th century, the more concentrated 'Great Depression' of the 1930s, and the decade-long 'stagflation' of the 1970s. The current crisis has exhibited many of the characteristics that would make it the fourth. The weakness of a general theory that tries to encompass each of these crises lies in all that is obscured along the way. As David Harvey has recently cautioned:

> There is no singular theory of crisis formation within capitalism, just a series of barriers that throw up multiple possibilities for different kinds of crises. At one particular historical moment conditions may lead to one kind of crisis dominating, but on other occasions several forms can combine and on still others the crisis tendencies get displaced spatially (into geopolitical and geo-economic crises) or temporally (as financial crises).[14]

This does not mean retreating to an eclectic description of those historical moments designated as crises. It only means recognizing that capitalist development is a contradictory process prone to crises, the genesis, nature and outcome of which are historically contingent, and need to be investigated with the tools of historical materialism.

Of course, we must be careful not to slip into reading the history of capitalism in terms of a series of crises. Crises, however significant, are only moments in the development of global capitalism. While structural crises represent 'turning points' of a certain kind, this should not be extended to imply that such crises alone are what spur on further capitalist development. The concentration and centralization of capital, while accelerated during the crisis of 1873 to 1896, had begun earlier and continued after the great US merger wave at the turn of the twentieth century. The growth of Fordist technology, well in train long before the crisis of the 1930s, continued apace right through the Depression. The roots of the neoliberal era go back to the post-war US project for the making of a global capitalism and the rise of MNCs and growth of financialization through the 1950s and 1960s.

The first requisite of any proper understanding of structural crises that avoids the pitfalls of mechanically unfolding economic laws should be to locate facts about the conditions of accumulation and the general economic situation – profits and wages, credit and interest rates, trade and capital flows, etc. – in relation to the class and state configurations in the particular historical conjunctures in which these crises occur. Crises, as Arrighi brilliantly argued some 40 years ago, are historically specific; they occur within particular periods of capitalist development and must be theorized within the class and institutional matrices of that period.[15] Arrighi's analysis was grounded in the different types of capitalist dynamics entailed in the 'predominantly competitive capitalism' of the late 19th century and the transition to the 'predominantly monopoly capitalism' of the 20th century. Insofar as this carries an implication of a general decrease in competition beyond limiting price competition, it was misleading, since the concentration of capital raised competition from the local and regional level to a continental and international plane and intensified competition based on product differentiation and systemized innovation. But Arrighi was in any case careful not to derive an explanation of crises directly from this. He rather stressed that it was the specificities of capital-labour relations in each conjuncture – especially the degree and nature of proletarianization at a global level – that held the key to determining the nature of each crisis.

In the 'first great depression', skilled workers were as (or more) mobile than industrial capital, and the availability of land for unskilled workers in the Americas was especially important as an outlet for the 'reserve army of labour', especially in Europe. Gabriel Kolko rightly pointed out that 'this escape valve for the human consequences of economic crises in one state by relying on the growth of others is among the central events in modern history'.[16] The option of migration or returning to the land gave individual workers, as Arrighi argued, a strength in the labour market that limited the downward flexibility of wages and this, combined with inter-capitalist price competition, contributed to a profit squeeze. It was in part in response to this that key developments in state capacities – from Bismarck's initiation of the welfare state in Germany to the establishment of the Interstate Commerce Commission and the first merit civil service reforms in the US – emerged during the 1880s.

By the time of the 1930s crisis, the democratic resources that workers had obtained (not only as individually enfranchised voters but also through unionization and party formation) had undermined the ability of states with trade deficits to automatically embrace the austerity policies required by the discipline of the gold standard. This significantly contributed to the policies that led to the collapse of international trade and capital flows in the 1930s.[17] So did the closure in the 1920s of the immigration safety valve that the US and Canada had provided for the reserve armies of Europe, contributing indirectly thereby as well to the repression of democracy in central European states. This also factored into the subsequent ability of the US working class to form industrial unions even in the face of the Great Depression, and act as a major catalyst for the historic development of US state capacity through the New Deal.

The stagflation and profitability crisis of the 1970s was rooted in the basis established for trade union militancy by the achievement of near full employment and the expansion of state expenditures and services in the 1960s. Whether wage demands were chasing inflation or causing it likely varied from country to country, and from economic quarter to economic quarter; the crucial point is that worker militancy was a significant factor in preventing the restoration of both higher profit rates and a higher profit share of national income after their downturn in the second half of the 1960s. This did not immediately lead to lower levels of investment, but these investments proved incapable of eliciting productivity increases adequate to sustain profits, in good part because of the workplace resistance, which was such a defining element, to the reorganization of work of the time.[18] The overall organization of production was still largely based on variations on the technological paradigms developed for industry in the 1930s and 1940s, and by the 1960s these had reached their limits in terms of new productivity growth. The marked productivity growth (and profitability) that resulted from the widespread application of computerization to industry was only reached in the 1990s, by which point workers' capacity for resistance was long broken.

This emphasis on the class dimension is not meant to underestimate the complex factors that lead to structural crises but to view these other factors through the prism of class and state relations. This applies not only to the timing of technological change but also to capital's organizational forms. In the 'first great depression' of the late 19th century the legal corporation was born, but how this affected the course and resolution of that crisis is obviously very different from the way the multidivisional, global, networked corporation – barely a gleam in any capitalist's eye in the 1930s, and still only taking shape via MNCs in the 1970s – will affect the course and resolution of the current crisis. The integrated international production networks embodied in the 21st century corporate form now stand so much at the heart of global accumulation – and are so intimately related to the proletarianization of the Global South – that they effectively rule out extensive protectionism as a state response. Similarly, how the scope of finance and its relation to production is implicated in the current crisis cannot be understood at all in terms of what Hilferding meant by 'finance capital' with its emphasis on the institutional fusion of banks and industry at the national level. Rather, today's financialized capitalism – expressed in the financialization of corporations and the financialization of workers as savers and consumers, as well as in the growth and prominence of financial institutions proper – bespeaks a whole global economy enmeshed in the trading of financial instruments and subjected to their abstract measures of value.

A second requisite for properly understanding structural crises is an appreciation of contingency in relation to their duration and resolution. This is especially important in terms of going beyond the question of why particular interruptions in accumulation occur – these are, after all, not unusual events under capitalism – to ask what contradictions and barriers stand in the way of their relatively quick resolution. The two questions may of course overlap, but they are not necessarily the same. In the midst of an interruption of accumulation, a high degree of uncertainty about its duration and resolution is what characterizes it as a 'crisis'. Such contingency is based on the indeterminacy of whether and how social relations can be modified to accommodate the resumption of accumulation, and whether capital can deploy, and if so how quickly, new technological and organizational forms. This contingency is especially related to whether the state has the capacity to intervene in ways which contain the crisis and can develop the new institutional infrastructure needed to support a regeneration of accumulation.

In this regard, the orthodox fiscal policies of the early 1930s – rooted both in the initial determination by the leading capitalist states to maintain the gold standard and the limited regulatory capacities of state institutions – were critical to the conversion of a recession into the Great Depression. And it was the extensive development of institutional capacity through the New Deal and the Second World War that proved crucial to the sustained revival of capital accumulation. In the crisis of the 1970s, the reluctance of states through most of the decade to impose deflationary discipline on both capital and labour aggravated inflation and made the eventual 'correction' all the greater. When the US Federal Reserve first tried in late 1969 and early 1970 to address gathering inflationary pressures by rapidly raising interest rates, it quickly drew back in the face of the commercial paper crisis this caused for corporations and banks.[19] And despite the fear of unemployment that higher interest rates usually induce, they were greeted at the time by the largest strike wave since the immediate post-war period. It was only a decade later, after the experience of stagflation had undermined the confidence of labour amidst the counter-mobilization of capital and the development of derivatives markets, that Paul Volcker was able to steel the resolve of the Federal Reserve to sustain the even higher interest rates that were so crucial to the capitalist resolution of the crisis of the 1970s.

A third requisite for adequately understanding structural crises relates to how their resolution leads to a different pattern of determination of subsequent crises. Because the resolution of a structural crisis is not simply quantitative but qualitatively affects socio-economic, political and even cultural relations, this changes the terrain for the development of future crises. The resolution of the crisis of the late 19th century opened the door to the kind of concentration of capital that meant that during the Great Depression corporations cut production rather than prices, in direct contrast to the late 19th century, and so aggravated the crisis. The state intervention, from New Deal programmes to military expenditure, that laid the ground for the recovery and the embrace of post-war Keynesianism, would in its turn give rise by the 1960s to the near full employment that gave the working class the confidence and power to raise wages and resist workplace pressures, contributing to the profit squeeze of the 1970s. The resolution of the crisis of the 1970s, unlike that of the 1930s, involved the defeat of trade unionism as well as the regulatory liberalizations which allowed for expanding rather than constricting capitalism's globalizing tendencies.

The nature of the current crisis cannot be grasped if it is not first understood that the way the 1970s crisis was resolved set up the conditions for the sub-prime crisis three decades later. The failure to recognize this obscures the fundamental differences between the 1970s crisis and the present one in terms of the degree of working-class strength; the transformations in finance, technology and the international division of labour; and the institutional learning that has occurred within and among states.

IV

The crisis this time – the first structural crisis of the 21st century – can only be understood in terms of the historical dynamics and contradictions of capitalist finance as they developed in the second half of the 20th century. By the 1980s and 1990s, what Arrighi referred to as the 'predominantly monopoly' capitalism that had succeeded the earlier 'predominantly competitive' capitalism was now giving way to what might be called 'predominantly financialized' capitalism. This term captures the greater mobility of financial capital across sectors, space and time (especially via derivatives) – that is, financial capital's quality as general or 'abstract' capital – which during these decades greatly intensified domestic and international competition at the same time as it brought a much greater degree of financial volatility.

But just as the term 'monopoly capitalism' always had problematic connotations, so does the common connotation that 'financialized capitalism' is merely speculative or parasitic or rentier. To draw this implication from the term is misleading, above all because the spheres of finance and production are linked in significant ways, more so today than ever before. Thus while the phenomenal growth of financial markets since the 1980s led to over-leveraging and excessive risk-taking, this was tolerated and in fact encouraged for reasons that went far beyond the competitive dynamics and power of finance itself. It was accepted because it had become not only functional to, but also *essential* for, the domestic and global expansion of the capital involved in producing goods and nonfinancial services.

The internationalization of finance allowed for the hedging and spreading of the risks associated with the global integration of investment, production and trade with the dollar at its centre. The development of derivative markets provided risk-insurance in a complex global economy without which the internationalization of capital via trade and FDI would have been significantly restricted. Finance also contributed to the restoration of general profitability through the impact of the pursuit of shareholder value, and the mergers and acquisitions it sponsored, on class discipline within firms and the allocation of capital across firms, thereby increasing the rate of exploitation and productivity growth. And the financial sector directly fostered capital accumulation not simply through investments by venture capitalists in high tech, but by developing its own innovations in computerized banking and financial information systems. At the same time, the credit that was provided to more and more working people became especially important in sustaining consumer demand in a period of wage stagnation and growing economic inequality.

The growing significance of finance in the major capitalist economies was already visible by the 1960s. It was strongly registered in the role finance came to play in resolving the economic crisis of the 1970s, especially through the global role of the institutions of Wall Street and its satellite the City of London, and their relationship to the nexus of the US Treasury, Federal Reserve and the other G7 finance ministries and central banks. The predominance of the dollar in global finance reflected and reinforced the global institutional predominance of US financial institutions. Indeed, ever since Bretton Woods effectively established the dollar as the global currency at a fixed price to gold – and especially since the early 1970s when the dollar's detachment from gold demonetized it 'along with copper, nickel, silver, not to mention wampum and clam shells' (as Kindleberger once amusingly put it[20]) – the US Treasury bond market had served as the foundation for all calculations of value in the global capitalist economy. This was the basis for US bonds acting as a vortex for drawing other countries' savings to American financial markets, for the cheap credit that sustained the US as the world's major consumer market, and for US capitalism's broader global successes in the closing decades of the 20th century.

But contradictions in this finance-led capitalism also grew apace. A major motivating factor in the US Federal Reserve's turn in 1979 to using very high interest rates to defeat inflation at home was that it was already starting to behave like a global central bank, with paramount responsibility for protecting the dollar's indispensable role in global capitalism. And from the early 1980s on, the competitive volatility of global finance produced a series of financial crises whose containment required repeated state intervention, not least in the form of pouring liquidity into the system at the first sign of a financial crisis. With more funds flowing into the US, this increased the competition among domestic lenders and tended to lower interest rates and financial profitability. In response, financial companies looked for new markets but also loaned more relative to their deposits and capital base. This in fact amounted to a vast increase in credit and the effective money supply, which however – given the defeat of labour, the low cost of imports, and the increased corporate ability to fund investments with internal funds – now produced asset inflation rather than price inflation. The great asset inflation in stocks and bonds as well as real estate was not itself antithetical to the recovery of corporate profitability, and the development of the dynamic sectors in the 'new economy', let alone the phenomenal growth in the construction industry. But competition and speculation in the financial sector created a series of financial bubbles.

The active role of states in managing successive financial crises, with the American state acting as the chief fire-fighter, was crucial for the confidence of the financial markets. But this invited 'moral hazard' and encouraged future bubbles to form. The idea that states had withdrawn from the economy amidst the globalization of capitalism was a neoliberal ideological myth, as states in the developed capitalist countries at the centre of global finance pumped more money into the banks, while they ensured that in the developing countries crises were generally used to impose financial and market discipline on their populations.

Unlike the other three structural crises of capitalism, the current crisis was not caused by a profit squeeze or collapse of investment due to overaccumulation; in the US in particular profits and investments had recovered strongly by the late 1990s. After a brief downturn at the beginning of the new century, profits were at a peak in the two years before the onset of the crisis in August 2007, and investment was growing significantly. The productive sector was able to readily access the funds it needed for investment (in terms of profits, cash flow and cheap credit), and real non-residential investment, recovering from its lows in the first years of the new century, in fact increased by an average of 6.7 per cent between 2004 and the first quarter of 2008.[21] It was only after the financial meltdown that profits and investment declined.

The roots of the 'Great Financial Crisis' lay in the growing importance of US mortgage finance, a development which cannot be understood apart from the vital role of the state and the effects of the erosion of working-class strength. The state's support for home ownership (through supportive taxes and institutional access to credit) was a long-standing and ever more widespread element in the integration of workers into US capitalism. And the state pressures that contributed to stagnating working-class incomes and the erosion of social programmes reinforced working-class dependence on the rising value of their homes. Alongside this, mortgages figured prominently in the development of financial markets: the decisive role of American state agencies in encouraging the securitization of mortgages was central to the more general explosion of securitization and to the ultimate collapse of domestic and global financial markets.[22]

The close linkages between finance and the state were central both to the making of the US housing bubble and to its profound global impact when it burst. In the context of a highly volatile global financial system, investors gravitated to the safety of US Treasury bonds, despite low US interest rates which reflected a monetary policy designed to prevent a recession in the early 2000s. But the lower yields intensified the competitive search within global finance for higher yields. The historical safety of mortgages, a very large portion of them backed by the US government, reinforced the public's confidence in perpetually rising home prices. This made housing debt especially attractive to investors who could now borrow funds at low interest and put the money into bundles of mortgages offering much higher returns. A broader stratum of the US working class responded to falling wages and increasingly unequal income distribution by taking out second mortgages on the bubble-inflated values of their homes.

The eventual bursting of the housing bubble undermined workers' wealth and effective savings, leading to an overall decline in US consumer spending, producing effects that the bursting of the stock market bubbles had not. Mortgage-backed securities became difficult to value and to sell in any of the financial markets to which they had spread around the world. Taken together with the impact of the housing crisis on mass consumption, and thus on the US economy's ability to function as the consumer of the rest of the world's goods, illusions that other regions might be able to avoid the crisis were quickly dispelled.

An important factor in generating the conditions that led to the greatest financial crisis since 1929 was thus the weakness of the working class, in contrast to the other three crises of capitalism, in which elements of working-class strength were prominent. In the US, in particular, the defeat of trade unionism was linked to the recovery of profitability, which in turn limited the dependence of industrial corporations on financial credit. This contributed to the banks introducing and marketing new consultancy and accounting services as well as financial services to corporations, and to the ever greater importance they gave to developing new credit markets among consumers. As successful as this was, it also brought a new vulnerability to financialized capitalism. Whereas indebted states can raise taxes, and indebted corporations can raise income from bonds or from reorganizing work to increase exploitation, indebted workers and their families can only work so many longer hours, and if this explained the growth of household debt, it left the financial sector more and more vulnerable to workers' inability to pay their debts. Moreover, since some three quarters of household debt in the US was in the form of mortgages, as the housing bubble burst, this had – in contrast to a decline in stock or even bond prices – an immediate impact on the whole economy because of the direct link of mortgages to construction, furniture and appliances. The main assets that workers owned – their homes and their pensions – fell in value and this quickly led to a decline in their capacity and proclivity, to consume, with immediate effects on industry in the US and abroad.

Developments in the auto industry – second only to mortgages in terms of its reliance on consumer credit – were particularly crucial here. In the face of intensive competition from Japanese (and to a lesser degree European) companies, the strategy of the Detroit Three since the late 1980s had been to concentrate on the production of SUVs and pickup trucks with their higher profit margins. They were counting on the continuation of low interest rates, low oil prices, and low unemployment. But as the financial crisis hit in the summer of 2007, financial investors not content with the low returns entailed in the safety of US Treasury securities turned to commodities. The resultant explosion of oil prices (by the summer of 2008 they were, at over $140 a barrel, more than double the pre-crisis level), alongside the credit crunch and increasing employment insecurity, put the brakes on vehicle sales (SUV and pickup truck sales fell by almost half). The Detroit Three had already been rapidly losing market share before the crisis and the added losses moved GM and Chrysler into bankruptcy in the US portion of their operations (Ford survived on its cash reserves), with enormous ramifications for their auto parts suppliers. Since the automobile industry has one of the most significant production multiplier effects on the economy, this dramatically aggravated the crisis in the US, with immediate ramifications internationally, as well.

The crisis at the same time highlighted the continuing centrality of the American state in the global economy. As the crisis unfolded the rise of the US dollar in currency markets and the enormous demand for US Treasury bonds reflected the extent to which the world remained on the dollar standard and the American state continued to be regarded as the ultimate guarantor of value. Treasury bonds were in demand because they remained the most stable store of value in a highly volatile capitalist world. The American state's central role in terms of global crisis management – from currency swaps to provide other states with much needed dollars, to overseeing policy cooperation among central banks and finance ministries – has also been confirmed in this crisis. Even while international tensions surfaced, what was striking was the extent of general cooperation among the capitalist states.

Before the crisis, pundits of every economic persuasion, usually blurring the lines between capitalist crisis and US decline, had been predicting that the 'imbalances' represented by the US trade deficit, combined with the global holdings of 'excess' dollars, would lead to a collapse of the dollar and bring about a severe crash. But it was not, in fact, these imbalances that caused the crisis; on the contrary, global capital rushed into the US as uncertainty increased. In this regard, the notion that foreign states were just doing the US a favour by buying Treasury bonds should finally be dispelled by this crisis.

Although the crisis was not caused by the trade and capital flow imbalances, these imbalances are central to the contingencies surrounding its duration and resolution. It is the maintenance rather than the elimination of the US trade deficit that is in fact an important condition for maintaining global demand in the face of neoliberal pressures for austerity, and thus sustaining a global economic recovery. This is not to say that globalization makes international trade and capital flow imbalances no more meaningful than imbalances between the regions of a domestic economy. This misses the point that the global economy is both nationally asymmetric and class-structured. Because of the central place that the US state and capital occupy in the global economy, the dollar has not been undermined by the trade or fiscal deficits during this crisis. The dispersal of production globally has reflected not a weakening of American capital and empire, but the integration of other economies into a global capitalism led by the American state, finance and MNCs. Capital flows out of and into the US cannot be understood apart from this.

It has rather been the states of the Eurozone – whose new currency was touted as the alternative reserve currency to the dollar – that have taken the hardest hit in this crisis, requiring help from the US directly via dollar swaps and indirectly via the IMF. This finally led the European Central Bank to follow the Federal Reserve's lead in quantitative easing, but only on the condition that fiscal austerity be applied throughout Europe. But this can only make Europe, and the rest of the world, more dependent on the US as the global consumer of last resort. If the US reversed its stimulus policies this would dangerously undermine whatever signs of recovery there have been so far. That the US has not done this reveals again how much responsibility Washington takes for managing the global capitalist economy – in sharp contrast with Berlin or Brussels.

This aspect of the US imperial role will be tested by whether the G20 can really succeed the G7 as the linchpin of crisis management and policy coordination among the finance ministries and central banks of the world's leading capitalist states. Whereas in the series of intermittent financial crises in the 1980s and 1990s it was the developing states that were required to undertake austerity, even as the G7 states poured liquidity into their own financial markets, the prescriptions for a capitalist cure in this structural crisis are being reversed. Now that the large developing states have indeed been integrated into global capitalism, they are being encouraged by the US to stimulate their economies to increase global demand. This cannot be done overnight, precisely because of what it would entail in terms of transforming the wages and working conditions of the newly proletarianized workers of the South. This is why, given Europe's commitment now to fiscal austerity coupled with neoliberal structural reforms, a key question is how much faster mass consumption can develop in the South, and especially in China, and how long the US, as the world's largest consumer, can tide this process over.

V

Here is where we must bring the working class back in. The massive growth of the global proletariat that has been the *sine qua non* of capitalist globalization produces tendencies towards the equalization of wages and conditions at a global level. The continuing travails of trade unionism in the developed capitalist countries have partly been a reflection of this. Today's fiscal austerity which necessitates a sharp assault on public sector unions – the last ones left standing with significant density – will only carry this further.

The full actualization of this tendency in the current global conjuncture depends also on working-class organization and struggles in the Global South, most especially in China. MNCs have been attracted to China for two reasons. First to participate in China's export-based mode of accumulation oriented around low labour cost suppliers and final sales to workers with higher standards of living in the developed capitalist world. But at the same time MNCs have also been attracted by the prospect of mass consumption among a significant portion of the Chinese working class. There are intra-capitalist divisions of interest involved here, sometimes appearing within a single MNC or investment bank, and now also surfacing within the Chinese ruling class. The current conflicts in which Chinese workers are engaged also pose increasingly sharp choices. This was seen in the strike wave of 2010 which yielded some large wage increases but not yet any significant organizational change in Chinese trade unionism.[23] It cannot be known in advance whether the working-class struggles increasingly in clear view in China will lead to the emulation of the West's individualized consumerism or whether they will lead to new socialist definitions of needs, aspirations and capacities.

What is clear is that the outcome cannot but impinge on, and possibly even be affected by, the direction Western working classes take out of the current crisis. It was only through a long and contradictory path that individualized consumerism rather than collective services and a democratized state and economy became the main legacy of Western working-class struggles in the 20th century. Even the trade unions' capacity to sustain this is now in severe doubt, especially when it is put in the context of the ecological limits to capitalist growth. Whether there can be a radical redefinition of what is meant by standards of living in the context of working-class struggles, both in the North and the South, is now on the agenda as never before.

This must begin with people's immediate material needs, but must at the same time be oriented to strengthening popular capacities to act independently of the logic of capitalism.[24] Any forms of resistance in defence of working people's homes or savings, jobs or social programmes, should obviously be actively encouraged and supported. More general demands – like the defence of public health care and its extension to include dental care and drugs for everyone, the development of a truly adequate and universal public pension system, free, accessible and expanded public transportation – would both address popular concerns and carry a broader strategic weight. Winning these kinds of demands would reduce working-class dependence on their employers and markets for their security, facilitate class solidarity because of their focus on universal rights and collective needs, and demonstrate the broader potentials of the public provision of services, such as affordable housing that includes a new sense of community and relationship to the surrounding city.

In terms of how such expanded public services would be financed, it is highly significant that the last time the nationalization of the banks was seriously raised, at least in the advanced capitalist countries, was in response to the 1970s crisis by those elements on the Left who recognized that the only way to overcome the contradictions of the Keynesian welfare state in a positive manner was to take the financial system into public control. Since even conservatives have flirted with some form of bank nationalization through the current crisis, it is very important to contrast temporary bail-out style nationalizations with the fundamental democratic demand for turning the whole financial system into a public utility that allocates national savings on an entirely different basis than that which governs banking and investment today. This would allow for the distribution of credit and capital to be undertaken in conformity with democratically established criteria, and would thus involve not only capital controls in relation to international finance but also controls over domestic investment, since the whole point of the exercise would be to transform the uses to which finance is put. The call for nationalization of the banks therefore provides an opening for advancing broader strategies that begin to take up the need for systemic alternatives to the intractable problems of contemporary capitalism. This highlights the need to transform economic and political institutions so as to foster and sustain democratic planning processes.

The severity of the global economic crisis has once again exposed how states are enveloped in capitalism's irrationalities, and reinforced the need for building new movements and parties to transcend capitalist markets and states. Even as they tried to stimulate the economy, states were impelled to lay off public sector workers or cut back their pay, and to demand that bailed-out companies do the same. And while blaming volatile derivatives market for causing the crisis, states promoted derivatives trading in carbon credits as a solution to the climate crisis. In the context of such readily visible irrationalities, a strong case can be made that – to really save jobs and the communities that depend on them in a way that converts production to ecologically sustainable priorities during the course of this crisis – we need to break with the logic of capitalist markets, rather than use state institutions to reinforce them.

In the same notebook of the *Grundrisse* where Marx reflected, in the wake of the 1857-8 crisis, on the process that allowed capitalism to recover so as to go on 'fully employing its productive powers without committing suicide', he wrote of capital's continuing development becoming itself 'the moving contradiction' by laying the foundation-stone for workers to step beyond their role as the chief actors in production to becoming the chief actors in society. The central condition for this was 'the general reduction of the necessary labour of society to a minimum, which then corresponds to the artistic, scientific, etc. development of the individuals in the time set free, and with the means created, for all of them'.[25]

However deep the crisis, however difficult the problems faced by elites both inside and outside the state, and however widespread the popular outrage against them, any challenge to capitalism that will come out of the crisis this time will certainly require hard and committed work by a great many activists. Among all the good reasons for work-time reduction, not the least of them is the time people need for changing the world. This extends from the time to take up struggles for immediate reforms, to the time to develop the capacities to engage in democratic planning in the future. To clarify that *this* is on the agenda is an essential strategic precondition for creating the new movements and parties, and eventually the new state institutions, that will be needed to make twenty-first century socialism a real possibility.

NOTES

1 Michael R. Kratke, 'Marx's "Books of Crisis" of 1857-8', in Marcello Musto, ed., *Karl Marx's Grundrisse: Foundations of the Critique of Political Economy 150 Years Later*, London: Routledge, 2008, pp. 169-75. Kratke also points out that one of Marx's articles for the *New York Tribune* correctly predicted that the British state's response to the crisis would be to suspend the 1844 Bank Act so banks could issue their own notes to address their liquidity problems.

2 Quoted in Marcello Musto, 'Marx's Life at the Time of the *Grundrisse*: Biographical Notes on 1857-8', in Musto, *Karl Marx's Grundrisse*, p. 153.

3 'Chapter on Capital, Notebook VII' in Karl Marx, *Grundrisse: Foundations of the Critique of Political Economy*, Translated by Martin Nicholas, Harmondsworth: Penguin, 1973, pp. 410, 750.

4 Rudolf Hilferding, *Finance Capital: A Study of the Latest Phase of Capitalist Development*, Brighton: Harvester Press, 1981 [1910], p. 288.

5 Quoted in F. R. Hansen, *The Breakdown of Capitalism: A History of the Idea in Western Marxism, 1883- 1983*, London: Routledge and Kegan Paul, 1985, pp. 36-7.

6 Ibid., p. 64.

7 Lucio Colletti, *From Rousseau to Lenin: Studies in Ideology and Society*, London: New Left Books, 1972, p. 59.

8 Quoted in Ibid, p. 60.

9 See Peter Cain, *Hobson and Imperialism: Radicalism, New Liberalism and Finance 1887-1938*, Oxford: Oxford University Press, 2002, pp. 111-15; and Carl P. Parrini and Martin J, Sklar, 'New Thinking about the Market, 1896-1904', *The Journal of Economic History*, XLIII(3), 1983.

10 As Bruce Cumings has put it: 'The transcontinental railway symbolized the completion of the national territory – by the 1860s America was a linked continental empire. But distant connections to isolated Western towns and farms, Pony Express mail service, and peripheral mudflats like Los Angeles, do not a national market make. Instead for fifty years (roughly from 1890 to 1940) Americans peopled and filled in the national territory. At the same time that the US became the leading industrial power in the world... the dominant tendency was expansion to the coast and exploitation of a vast and relatively new market'. 'Still the American Century', *Review of International Studies*, 25(5), 1999, p. 282.

11 Leo Panitch and Sam Gindin, 'American Empire and Global Capitalism', *Socialist Register 2004*. See also our 'Gems and Baubles in Empire', *Historical Materialism*, 10, 2002.

12 Hilferding, *Finance Capital*, p. 288.

13 Karl Marx, *Theories of Surplus Value*, Part II, Moscow: Progress Publishers, 1975, p. 497.

14 David Harvey, 'Introduction' to Karl Marx and Friedrich Engels, *The Communist Manifesto*, London: Pluto, 2008, pp. 24-5.

15 Giovanni Arrighi, 'Towards a Theory of Capitalist Crisis', *New Left Review*, 111, 1978 (the original version was published in Italian in 1972).

16 As Kolko once brilliantly put it regarding the 'international phenomenon which the emergence of European capitalism created': 'Marx notwithstanding, no national ruling class ever passively allowed an industrial reserve army to emerge to destroy the existing order, and they attempted to rely on imperialism, migration, or whatever to sustain their hierarchical social orders. Nor will all workers wait for socialism to find bread. However reticent they may initially be, many will migrate before starving...'. Gabriel Kolko, *Main Currents in Modern American History*, New York: Harper & Row, 1976, p. 68.

17 See especially, Barry Eichengreen, *Golden Fetters: The Gold Standard and the Great Depression*, New York: Oxford University Press, 1995, as well as his *Globalizing Capitalism: A History of the International Monetary System*, Princeton: Princeton University Press, 1996.

18 This argument is sustained in our *The Making of Global Capitalism: The Political Economy of American Empire*, forthcoming with Verso, but we advanced this position in relation to Marxist debates on the 'profit squeeze' at the time against David Yaffe (Leo Panitch, 'Profits and Politics', *Politics and Society* 7(4), 1977; also ch. 3 of *Working Class Politics in Crisis*, London: Verso, 1986), and more recently against Robert Brenner (Sam Gindin, 'Turning Point and Starting Points: Brenner, Left Turbulence and Class Politics', *Socialist Register 2001*).

In addition to downplaying the effect on productivity of workplace resistance as well as the refusal of workers to accept lower wages to restore profits after the downturn in profitability occurred, those who deny that working-class strength was a factor in causing the 'profit squeeze' fail to appreciate the full impact of compensation costs for capital at the time. Taking benefits as well as wages into account, compensation costs not only kept up with productivity growth but also, once adjusted by the producer price index (which reflects the price corporations get for their product), real compensation costs grew *faster* than productivity, and workers received a growing share relative to capital of the value added in industrial production.

19 See Charles W. Calomiris, 'Is the Discount Window Necessary? A Penn Central Perspective', *Federal Reserve Bank of St. Louis Review,* May, 1994; and Charles D. Ellis, *The Partnership: The Making of Goldman Sachs*, New York: Penguin, 2009, ch. 7.

20 C.P. Kindleberger, *International Money: A Collection of Essays*, London: Allen & Unwin, 1981, p. 103.

21 *Economic Report of the President, 2010,* Washington: US Government Printing Office, 2010, Table B-91. The 2007 *Economic Report to the President* (p. 36) summarized the situation in 2006 as follows: 'Moderate growth in hourly compensation along with solid productivity growth together with strong aggregate demand has driven the share of profits in gross domestic income to its highest level since 1966'.

22 For elaboration of the argument in this and the following paragraphs, see the new Chapter 12 on 'The Political Economy of the Subprime Crisis' to the second edition of Leo Panitch and Martijn Konings, eds. *American Empire and the Political Economy of Global Finance*, London: Palgrave Macmillan, 2009.

23 See Anita Chan, 'Labor Unrest and Role of Unions', *China Daily*, 18 June 2010, available from http://www.chinadaily.com.cn.

24 The following paragraphs draw on the 'ten theses on the crisis' in Greg Albo, Sam Gindin and Leo Panitch, *In and Out of Crisis: The Global Financial Meltdown and Left Alternatives*, Oakland: PM Press, 2010.

25 Marx, *Grundrisse*, pp. 705-6.

CONFRONTING THE CRISIS: A CLASS ANALYSIS

HUGO RADICE

In the summer of 2007, global inter-bank credit markets dried up in response to the growing awareness of massive over-lending, most famously to the so-called sub-prime household mortgage market in the US. Over the following twelve months, financial institutions and monetary authorities struggled to contain the problem through providing emergency loans to rescue particular institutions, taking some into public ownership (notably Northern Rock in the UK), and providing liquidity to financial markets. The full extent of the credit crunch did not, however, become apparent until the collapse of the US mortgage banks Fannie Mae and Freddie Mac and the US insurance giant AIG, and finally the fateful decision by US Treasury Secretary Paulson to allow Lehman Brothers to go bankrupt in September 2008. This in turn triggered a wave of bank insolvencies and rescues around the world, and rapidly led to a general collapse of business and consumer confidence.

In the months that followed, government bailouts of banks and some other financial sector companies were accompanied by the massive provision of liquidity by central banks, which prevented the complete meltdown of global finance, but not the arrival of a global recession. Coordination of policy measures between the governments and central banks of the major economies was conducted mostly through existing channels, such as the International Monetary Fund and the Bank for International Settlements; at the highest level, the regular G8 summits were partly supplanted by an enhanced G20 structure that included the largest emerging economies. Nevertheless, there were sharp falls in output, investment and employment in the US and in Europe through 2009. Elsewhere, the picture was mixed, partly because banking systems in many less advanced economies were much less implicated in the overlending and speculation that preceded the credit crunch, and partly because in China, India and the Asian region more generally, the sheer momentum of accumulation meant that they suffered only a slowdown of growth rather than actual declines in output.

By the end of 2009, a tentative recovery was discernible at the global level. However, despite continuing discussions about the reform of financial regulation, the focus of attention had steadily switched from the solvency and liquidity of the banking system to the massive government deficits caused by bailouts and counter-recessionary spending. Early IMF-led bailouts of a small number of countries, including Latvia and Iceland, took on far greater significance in early 2010, when months of wrangling over a support package for Greece led to large-scale speculative attacks on bond markets in the Eurozone. In Britain, bringing down the public deficit, expected to reach over 12.5 per cent of GDP in 2009-10, became the centrepiece of the Conservative party's campaign in the May 2010 general election. On 9 May 2010 the Eurozone countries, with the involvement of the IMF, agreed a massive 750 billion package of loans and guarantees, intended not only to prevent a Greek default, but also to block speculative attacks on other member states. Despite the convulsions in global bond markets, the economic recovery appeared to be gathering pace, but plans for deep public spending cuts in many countries threatened a new global recession.

Evidently, this has been a massive and global crisis, and the main aim of this essay is to set out a framework for understanding its causes and consequences. Beginning with a preliminary sketch of the various ways in which the term 'crisis' has been understood this time, and the central importance they all attach to 'financialization', we turn to examining the nature of the extraordinary expansion of the financial services sector in recent decades, and argue that it is inseparable from important changes in the institutions and practices of capitalist production. These changes in turn need to be placed in the context of the simultaneous intensification of global integration, affecting not only material production but also the nature of the state and the states-system. Taken together, financialization and globalization are central elements in neoliberalism – the left's critique of which, the essay concludes, needs to be centred on a class analysis, rather than on the conventional 'states versus markets' approach, if we are to develop a socialist alternative based on equality, democracy and sustainable livelihoods.

WHAT SORT OF CRISIS?

While the downturn has been the most severe since the 1930s in terms of conventional economic data, it can still be viewed in all essentials as a cyclical crisis, only exacerbated on this occasion by an egregious credit expansion which delayed the onset of the crisis. Unemployment rose substantially from mid-2008 in the wake of sharp falls in both consumer and business spending, while the consequential decline in tax revenues and increased spending on statutory benefits paid out necessitated the abrupt abandonment of the limits almost universally imposed over the last twenty years on public borrowing as a proportion of national income, with levels of 10 per cent and more becoming commonplace. In this narrative, the primary focus falls on financial sector excesses and the prospects for public regulation to prevent this, coordinated across national jurisdictions.[1] The widespread concern among politicians and the media over the ballooning public deficits, and the case-by-case interventions of the IMF, are also no different in principle from previous cyclical episodes.

A second and broader narrative sees the crisis in the context of the longer-term dynamic of global capitalism. Many Keynesian and Marxist scholars argue that the severity of the recession is the result of the repeated postponement of adjustments that should have been made when the great postwar boom, itself contingent upon specific initial conditions, came to an end in the early 1970s.[2] As these conditions faltered or became exhausted, the embedded concessions won by workers during the boom made it difficult for high profitability and thus rapid economic growth to be sustained. In the narratives of Brenner and others, 'the crisis' today is an extension of the crisis of the 1970s: a crisis of overproduction that has been going on for more than three decades, kept going only by a series of asset bubbles and the expansion of financial speculation at the expense of real investment.[3] From this standpoint, it has merely been a matter of waiting for the inevitable crunch, when the accumulated contradictions of capitalism finally broke through the sticking-plaster of easy money applied by the world's central banks. One common prognosis based on such analyses is that we are entering a long period of stagnation, marked by persistent high unemployment and slow economic growth. On the one hand, this could be the consequence of the successful reassertion of the principles of sound finance: restoring balanced government budgets and cleaning out the 'toxic' debt mountains built up by both households and businesses will lead to a chronic deficiency of demand and sluggish investment in the manner of the 1930s. On the other hand, a more 'political' argument is that governments will find it politically impossible to impose austerity in the classical manner, with the resulting stalemate having much the same outcome of prolonged stagnation.

A third and still broader narrative which more explicitly embraces political and ideological aspects begins from the characterization of the last thirty years as the epoch of neoliberalism. In this view, the deregulation, privatization, financialization and globalization spawned by the Thatcher/Reagan 'neoliberal revolution' spread throughout the world by means of the Third World debt crisis engineered in the 1980s, the refoundation of the EU and its absorption of former Soviet satellites in the 1990s, and the demise of the developmental state with the East Asian crisis in the last years of the century. This was supposed to create a political-economic monoculture, a seamless global economy, and famously an end to 'boom and bust' once markets were truly free to work their magic. Many on the Marxist left and Keynesian centre alike have consistently dismissed this as ideological hype, intended to crush workers' resistance under the banner of 'There Is No Alternative', rather than as a genuine alternative path for capitalism: each of the elements listed above has been seen as riddled with contradictions and incapable of generating sustained growth. Accordingly, the 2007-08 credit crunch and current recession are seen as a crisis of neoliberalism, exposing its pretensions and necessarily ending the thirty-year experiment, with some commentators predicting renewed state interventionism. The need for greater regulation of money, credit markets and banking, above all, lie at the heart of this third narrative, if only for their apparently central role in the aetiology of the crisis.[4]

Finally, a fourth perspective on the crisis is significant by its general absence, namely whether it presages a crisis of capitalism as such. From 1917 until the demise of the USSR in 1991, Marxists for the most part had this prospect at least at the back of their minds when discussing economic crises in any of the previous three senses, although all but the most simple-minded were always reluctant to predict capitalism's endgame once the post-First World War upsurges of the trade union and socialist movements subsided in Europe and elsewhere. In the current crisis, it is clear that the self-defined 'revolutionary' left has not only little public presence in debating its causes and consequences, but also little clear idea as to whether and how capitalism might be ended. The challenge of this political absence – the crisis of socialism – remains to be answered.[5]

A NEW AGE OF FINANCE

The first three perspectives set out above all give pride of place to the financial sector as the epicentre of the crisis. In the cyclical view, the boom that began around 2001 after the so-called dot-com crisis was characterized by easy credit conditions that led to a rapid expansion of household debt; the financial sector found new ways to generate and sell on mortgage debt in particular, which served to conceal the growing fragility of the 'debt mountain' until it was undermined by rising interest rates and commodity speculation. In the long downturn approach, much the same argument is developed in a reading of the entire period since the end of the postwar boom as a sequence of such cycles, each more intense and fragile than the one before. This perspective brings into play the secular growth of the financial sector, fuelled by the gradual breaking-down of the legal and regulatory constraints initially established in the 1930s and enshrined in global norms under the 1944 Bretton Woods agreement. Finally, in the neoliberalism narrative, the liberalization of finance is seen as closely connected to the demise of the Keynesian order that prevailed during (or even was responsible for) the postwar boom. The story of financialization rests on the notion that initially, capitalism centres not on finance, but on the 'real' economy, the production of goods and services to meet the needs of households and businesses; through time, financial activities expand to the point where they displace real production as the driving force in capitalist accumulation.[6]

The evidence that finance has become more salient, say from the 1960s to the present, is substantial. In advanced capitalist economies, especially the US and UK, the financial sector's share of GDP, employment, stock market capitalisation, tax revenues, profits, etc., has increased through time across the sequence of trade cycles and the expansion of public sector deficits since the 1970s. Deregulation – whether as cause, effect or both – has extended alongside the financial sector's expansion, as banks diversified into the management of investment funds, the provision of insurance products, and trading in securities, currencies and commodities, and new institutions such as private equity and hedge funds have also emerged as significant players. On the other side of the credit markets, the continued spread of consumer durables and home ownership in many countries has led to a long-term trend increase in household indebtedness. The (real) business sector, meanwhile, rediscovered the potential for making profits out of restructuring, mergers, leveraged buyouts, takeovers, and the like, rather than the simple production of goods and services, and in the course of it all, ended up with generally higher levels of debt. Banks and other financial companies also began to take on more debt, and to find new ways of concealing their real debts from the weakened regulators.

In the 1990s, the rise of finance spread from the core advanced capitalist countries into the 'emerging markets' of East Asia, Latin America and Eastern Europe, enshrined in the Washington Consensus so vigorously promoted by the newly-neoliberal World Bank and IMF. This peripheral financialization included the establishment of many new stock and bond markets, moves towards currency convertibility and the liberalization of capital flows, and the rapid development of modern banking systems, including rural microcredit initiatives.

All this was closely related to the process of securitization, whereby banks sold packages of loans to far-flung investors around the world; the pooling of risk which traditionally was undertaken by the banks now became the investors' own responsibility, and it was the growing awareness of this risk that lay behind the sub-prime mortgage crisis and credit crunch of 2007. Liberalization also contributed to the extraordinary growth in the marketing of derivatives, a form of financial asset through which third parties with no direct interest in the underlying assets could speculate on future price movements.

What has made these developments so problematic for global capitalism has been the sequence of speculative 'bubble' crises, starting with the Japanese property bubble of the late 1980s, and proceeding through Mexico 1994, East Asia 1997, Russia 1998, dot-com 2000 and Argentina 2001, and culminating in the global 2007 credit crunch. Major corporate and financial bankruptcies, notably the hedge fund Long Term Capital Management in 1998 and Enron in 2001, were also characterised by high leverage and risky investment strategies. The connection between financialization and speculative crises seems confirmed by the intellectual justification for deregulation provided by mainstream economics: freed from the 'financial repression' of the 1930s to the 1970s, market forces could take their natural course towards inevitably efficient outcomes. If the mainstream said that the growth of finance was the result of deregulation, the critics could only agree: the same cause, but with a radically different consequence.

But why has financialization happened? David Kotz has taken to task those who see the process as one in which the financial sector itself drives deregulation, promoting neoliberal ideology and policies with the express purpose of increasing its power vis-à-vis the 'real' economy.[7] He argues, instead, that neoliberalism has created opportunities for the growth of finance, but originated in the crisis that brought the postwar boom to an end in the early 1970s. For capitalists, the key to resolving that crisis was to break the alliance with labour established after the war, and to block any further expansion in state expenditure and taxation, all in the context of intensifying international competition. The monetarist economic philosophy of Friedman and Hayek provided the basis for a broad assault on the claims of labour and the state, by restoring the legitimacy of private property rights and the freedom to trade. Privatization, globalization and deregulation then created new and expanding markets for financial products and services, and this was supported by big business in general, not just the financial sector.

This raises the crucial question of how 'finance' is constituted in relation to capitalists and to capitalism as a whole. Kotz cites Hilferding's *Finance Capital* (1910) as the foremost analysis of this question within the Marxist tradition,[8] but he points out that Hilferding's concept of finance capital was based on the particular model of direct bank ownership and control of industrial corporations in that era, which was particularly prevalent in Germany. The modern form of financialization shows more continuity with the development of the corporation in the US and UK, which allowed the fusion of private capitals into the limited liability company based on share ownership. What characterizes the recent expansion is the sector's ability to create and market legal claims on 'shares' in all manner of future income streams, such as repayment of student loans, rents on scarce natural resources, or future tax revenues.

In some important respects, the 'production' of financial instruments should be seen as no different from the production of any other goods and services. The financial capitalist (meaning a capitalist who invests in the production of financial products, *not* Hilferding's more specific concept) establishes a business which hires workers to make and sell these particular commodities. Like all capitalists, financial capitalists seek to create and preserve competitive advantages so that the above-average profits obtained from innovation can be protected from new entrants. With financial instruments, the capitalist's advantage may be based, as with industrial products, on proprietary production technologies or more cost-effective management methods, but the most importance source of advantage is privileged knowledge of the future prospects for the revenue streams obtained from the given instrument. On this basis, financial capitalists engage in continuous innovation, usually more apparent than real, in order to replenish regularly their flow of above-average profits. It is this, when coupled with the feverish speculation that accompanies the final stages of a credit boom, that explains the extraordinarily high stock-market capitalization achieved by banks like the Royal Bank of Scotland in the run-up to the present crisis.

But it is vital to look just as closely at the purchasers of financial services. One major market for the financial sector consists of businesses. This has traditionally divided into (a) commercial banking services such as trade credit, revolving overdrafts, payments, etc., and (b) investment (or merchant) banking services such as securities issuance, advice on mergers and acquisitions, and the purchase and sale of financial assets. The erosion of barriers between the two, which was confirmed in the US by the repeal in 1999 of the Glass-Steagall Act of 1933, is seen as a major source of recent innovations in the relations between finance and business, with the 'passive', very cheap retail deposits (by both businesses and households) being once again deployed in the more lucrative if risky investment-related activities.

It is important to see this in relation to changes in capitalist enterprise as a whole, and especially in big business, that have largely been ignored in discussions of the neoliberal era.[9] Forty years ago, it was widely held that big business had undergone a managerial revolution, in which shareholding owners had been displaced by a combination of the dispersal of share ownership, the shift to disinterested institutional shareholders, and the monopoly of technical and business knowledge accumulated by full-time executive managers. This view was shared by mainstream economists (then still broadly Keynesian), institutionalists like Galbraith, and Marxists like Baran and Sweezy.[10] Apart from the direct evidence on ownership and control of large firms, their sheer size and power appeared to insulate them from effective competition. Well-known firms of the day such as GM and Ford in the US, or ICI and Dunlop in the UK, had been dominant in their respective sectors for decades, and had reached comfortable accommodations with unions and governments alike; the rapid growth of foreign direct investment in the 1960s seemed merely to extend their dominance across the globe in the form of the transnational corporation.

However, already by the early 1970s the rapid growth of international trade and investment was disrupting the cosy world of postwar big business.[11] Sharper competition in world markets led to the beginnings of world-wide sourcing: US firms set up 'runaway shops' to undertake labour-intensive production segments at greatly reduced cost in Mexico and East Asia, and their European and Japanese competitors responded quickly. Equally important were the much bigger flows of cross-investments between core states, often by takeover, which dramatically undermined the complacency of dominant national firms. Coupled with the effects of the sequence of economic, financial and political shocks from 1968 to 1973, by the mid-1970s even the biggest corporations found themselves in a new world of irreducible uncertainty. The result was a massive shareholder counter-revolution, in which size was no protection against management failure and consequential takeover or break-up. The loss of power among the corporate élites was sweetened by the rise of stock options, tying managers to shareholder interests. The credit squeeze that accompanied the early Thatcher/Reagan years merely accelerated this process.

The financial sector benefited enormously from the demise of managerialism and the return of 'shareholder value'. On the one hand, the purchase or dismantling of big firms generated massive fees for financial advice and new issues of stocks and bonds, as well as great opportunities for speculation. On the other hand, the relentless pressure on corporate profits led to a revolution in management practices and culture within big business. The multi-divisional structures pioneered in the 1920s by GM and DuPont to deal with the complexity of running giant diversified companies became once again the basis for internal financial management systems that in effect reproduced stock market discipline within the firm: top management focused on making money, not particular products. Thus it was that General Electric, building on its early investments in consumer finance, became eventually a giant of the financial sector. Hence, too, the extraordinary phenomenon of Enron which, while ostensibly in the energy business, was essentially making its profits from financial manipulations. More commonly, corporations no longer just held their liquid funds 'in the bank', but demanded that the bank actively sought to maximize the return on them. The imbrication of non-financial businesses and the financial sector makes it questionable to argue, as Kotz and so many others do, that during this period 'the financial sector became, not dominant over the nonfinancial sector as it had been in J P Morgan's day, but independent of it'.[12] On the contrary, the symbiosis has returned, but in a new form.

At the same time, important changes have taken place in the engagement of households with the financial sector. Rising prosperity for upper- and middle-income households, first within advanced capitalist countries and more recently even in emerging markets, has substantially increased the savings capacity of the sector. Through collective or individual pension plans, household savings are directed to financial institutions for long-term investment, a flow that has expanded greatly in recent years with the restriction or outright privatization of state pension schemes. At the same time the acquisition of assets, especially home ownership, provides collateral against which households can borrow, whether to rebalance further their lifetime income and expenditure, or simply to engage in discretionary financial speculation aimed at increasing their wealth. In this respect, while poorer households have evidently been the victims of overselling by sub-prime mortgage providers, their richer counterparts are active and willing participants in the housing price bubble. More generally, from the early hire purchase system that fuelled consumer durable sales in the US in the 1920s, through to today's multiple credit-card holding, the amassing of debt has become a normal practice for so-called 'middle-class' households, creating behavioural norms that are emulated by lower-income groups and by aspirant consumers in less developed countries.[13] Meanwhile, the super-rich have been as important as institutional investors in directly driving demand for new forms of financial intermediation such as hedge funds.[14]

Finally, the government sector has itself fuelled the hypertrophy of finance, not only by actively deregulating the financial sector, but by its own direct engagements with the financial sector. In the last two decades, privatization has spread from its original simple form of the sale of public enterprises (mostly in utility sectors) through stock markets, to the 'new public managerialism',[15] whose 'value for money' approach within government departments provided easy profits for private providers from out-sourcing public services, and more recently to the wide range of collaborative ventures such as Public Private Partnerships (PPPs). These forms of collaboration are designed to take public investments off the state's own balance sheet, thereby keeping debt/GDP ratios down, but at the cost of transferring wealth to financiers and investors through transaction fees and higher yields.[16]

The new world of financial power and influence is thus emphatically not one in which the financial sector has become 'detached' from the real economy. Rather, it is one where the so-called real economy of businesses, households and governments has been thoroughly 'financialized'. We all make money now, not things.[17]

GLOBAL CRISIS – OR CRISIS OF GLOBALIZATION?

What is more, financialization in this sense has become universalized, as a constitutive element in the growing economic interdependence of capitalist economies in recent decades. On the face of it, global financial integration meant that the 'contagion' of credit market failure spread across the world in 2007-8 with unprecedented rapidity. It did not take long to realize that the collapse of the US sub-prime mortgage market was threatening banks not only in the US, but all over the world, especially in continental Europe where the search for higher yields had been even more pressing than in Anglo-Saxon economies. All kinds of new financial products were being bought whose riskiness could not easily be understood, given the longer chains of financial intermediation and the persistence of cultural differences between national financial systems. It seemed clear in late 2008 that globalization had exacerbated and intensified the credit crisis, and that effective governmental efforts to address the resulting downturn would require a significant degree of 'deglobalization'. This breathed new life into campaigns for financial transfer taxes as well as against tax havens. The 'globalization consensus' was shaken, if not shattered, and it seemed that national solutions needed to be sought, rather in the manner of Keynes in the early 1930s.[18] In this vein, Grahame Thompson has argued that the financial system is not in fact global, but 'supranationally regional', and that the crisis was really a North Atlantic crisis with spillovers to the rest of the world. In the absence of effective global monetary governance, the regulatory response both has been, and should be, national in character.[19]

But how have governments actually responded? Of course, they have sought to shore up their political support, at least within democracies, by presenting their decisions as motivated by the desire to preserve jobs, restore financial stability, punish the guilty, and so forth. But across all the range of responses it is hard to find any evidence of an about-turn with regard to the salience of global interests. Rather, reviewing the experience of the last three years, the network of central bank coordination, both informal and through the formal activities of the Bank for International Settlements and the IMF's Financial Stability Forum, has continued to function effectively by consensus. There was, initially, universal *de facto* support for dramatic increases in government debt and deficits in response to the crisis, and some willingness of central banks (the Federal Reserve much more than the European Central Bank) to provide as much money as required to fund these deficits, e.g. through 'quantitative easing'.[20]

It is certainly true that by 2010, there was a sharp about-face regarding the acceptability of fiscal deficits. As the Eurozone countries grappled with the fiscal crisis facing its weaker members, the vacillations of German Chancellor Merkel seemed to reflect a need to respond to domestic political and economic interests. However, this did not in the end prevent the agreement of an IMF-backed rescue package, as even the ECB finally followed along the 'quantitative easing' path. Although there is as yet no clear way forward, there is universal acceptance, too, that the Basel II accords on bank capitalisation levels were a major if unanticipated contributor to the 'irrational exuberance' of banks before the crunch. And even amidst minor skirmishes over Germany having jumped the gun on the practice of short selling bonds, no major central bank or finance minister has broken ranks to pursue an overall 'national' solution.

In terms of broader relations between the world powers, the continuing growth of India and China – assisted in the latter case by a massive fiscal stimulus – has helped to sustain demand for industrial goods and commodities; trade tensions have been, if anything, lower than earlier in the decade; and the G8 has been replaced in remarkably short order as the main global inter-governmental forum by the G20. It remains to be seen, however, whether such global solidarity will be maintained as the clamour grows from business and financial leaders for substantial cuts in public spending.

Why has the response of governments been to deepen global coordination rather than retreat from it? The answer is very simple: for big business the world over, it would be catastrophic for them to take any other course. There is not a single large firm anywhere that can see anything other than a fleeting advantage to a return to protectionism, because *effective* protectionism in 2009 would require not merely rebuilding the apparatus of tariff and non-tariff barriers that the world has spent sixty years dismantling, but the reconstruction of the immensely complex global chains of supply and demand in which they are enmeshed. Furthermore, the maintenance of an integrated global financial sector is especially important to big business, because its activities underpin global production and trade in so many ways, not least in terms of their dependence on the financial market for hedging of risks in foreign exchange and interest rates. Indeed, the new wave of business mergers and acquisitions since late 2008 has provided a lifeline to global investment banks in generating revenues from which they can rebuild their capital, alongside the fees earned by marketing the flood of new government bond issues.

For those who still see globalization as reversible, however, the clinching argument is the global trade imbalances that supposedly plague the world economy. These imbalances are seen as a major factor in holding back economic growth, in maintaining wasteful currency speculation, and in perpetuating tensions between the great powers. In Brenner's narrative,[21] two key moments in the last thirty years were the 1985 Plaza accord, in which the US persuaded the main surplus countries (especially Japan) that the relative value of the dollar should fall; and what he terms the reverse-Plaza accord of 1995, where it was agreed that the dollar should rise in value. His critique is reminiscent of the 1970s critique of 'dirty floating', when free-marketeers and diehard Keynesians joined forces in condemning the practice of government intervention in currency markets following the abandonment of the fixed-rate Bretton Woods currency system. Violent swings in currency values are seen as creating great uncertainty, which encourages investors to engage in short-term speculation rather than long-term investment. In this view, the way to avoid both large currency movements, and the payments imbalances which accompany them, is ideally to return to Keynes' original pre-Bretton Woods proposals for addressing imbalances, under which surplus countries as well as deficit countries would be required to make adjustments in their domestic macroeconomic policies in order to restore equilibrium.

This viewpoint epitomizes the deep-rooted methodological nationalism within contemporary political economy.[22] This is an ontological position in which the world economy is constituted necessarily as a set of competing nation-states, without any underlying unity: in this view, the phenomena of global integration are historically contingent, rather than immanent in the unbounded character of capital accumulation. Much of the objection to trade imbalances is that they are inevitably offset by imbalances on the capital account; most visibly, the vast trade deficits of the US with East Asia are covered by the equally large return flows of investments to the US, both indirect (in government and corporate securities) and direct (through the establishment or purchase of businesses, real estate, and other business assets). Despite all the evidence that it is US businesses and US governments that have directed the relentless assault on US workers' living standards over the last thirty years, it appears to be still widely believed among progressives that inward investment is a bad thing; and that because it contributes to the weakening of the US economy, and threatens the value of the dollar, the Chinese, and many others, will one day want to sell their dollar assets. Therefore, the US administration should seek to correct the trade imbalance so that the Chinese stop investing in the US and are no longer able to hold the US to ransom.[23]

There is however a radically different way to understand the trade imbalances. They have persisted over the last 50 years or so *precisely because capitalism has become globally integrated.* We do not concern ourselves with the fact that, within one country, some regions or population groups have 'surpluses' and others have 'deficits' – that is, some save and some borrow – for the simple reason that the resulting contractual obligations are considered to be legally enforceable. Whatever may have been the case regarding post-colonial expropriations in the 1960s and 1970s, over the last thirty years a dense network of multi- and bilateral interstate treaties, including effective arbitration practices, has extended this to most parts of the world. In any case, the history of the capitalist world economy is one of almost universal trade imbalances offset by capital flows, in some cases (e.g. Canada) for a century or more, and even if in certain places and times there have been massive defaults on international debts, the capital flows that fuel global accumulation quickly resume. In addition, today the global distribution of assets and liabilities of most corporations (including banks) is managed, with the help of currency hedging, to reduce almost to vanishing point any serious risk to their liquidity or solvency from currency fluctuations. In the interwar period, the extent and depth of global integration was far less; after the breakdown of repeated efforts to achieve an international solution, the response of turning towards autarchy was still feasible, as the liberal Keynes reluctantly recognized.

In short, globalization has indeed gone hand in hand with financialization, because the geographical extension of the production and trade networks of the 'real economy' has entailed the parallel extension and integration of financial services provision. In the course of this double transformation, the greater interdependence of economic activities and economic policies across national borders has been matched by a growth in the coordination and management, both public and private, of that interdependence. The actual effectiveness of that coordination and management depends, however, on how the interests and capabilities of actors are shaped by the uneven and contradictory path of the crisis. If we are to arrive at a realistic assessment of that path, we need to place the arguments on financialization and globalization within the framework of a deeper account of the unfolding of neoliberalism since the 1970s.

NEOLIBERALISM AND THE CRISIS

As already noted, it is widely held that neoliberalism arose as a reaction to the many problems that emerged in the later 1960s and early 1970s and brought the postwar boom to an end. Although there are many disagreements about the details, the common story is that after the war, a Keynesian welfare-state capitalism emerged with three important features: a high-wage mass-production industrial economy that included an alliance between capital and organised labour; a massive growth in state intervention, especially through public ownership and welfare/warfare public spending; and a renewal of the liberal ideal of free trade within a framework of managed currencies under the Bretton Woods agreement. All three features came under challenge in the 1970s with the demise of the postwar boom, and by the mid-1980s it was clear that a new form of political economy was emerging. As progressive scholarship grappled with the nature and significance of the changes, a wide range of terms were deployed reflecting particular areas of change such as forms of production (post-Fordism), macroeconomic policy (monetarism), political practice (Thatcherism), and development (the Washington Consensus). By the mid-1990s, the term neoliberalism had increasingly become the portmanteau term of choice, contrasted with the forms of capitalism that preceded it – Keynesian welfare-state capitalism in the North and dependent development in the South.

How then is neoliberalism, this new and seemingly ubiquitous form of capitalism, to be understood? In mainstream social science, and also in many Marxist analyses, the market/state relation is central both to diachronic stories of capitalism's evolution through distinct stages, and synchronic stories of comparisons between different varieties of capitalism. From such a perspective, therefore, the issues that arise in any major economic crisis centre on the balance between the public and private, that is between the market and state as regulatory mechanisms; and in the historically given conditions of multiple territorial states, that entails also the question of relations between states. The simultaneous presence of different varieties of capitalism within a common global context may also then be seen as offering a menu of choices for changing the existing order in response to the crisis.[24] If the market/state relation is the key axis of variation, then this menu will consist of either a return to a more state-based order, or a reassertion of the market, or a combination of the two that somehow contains and stabilises the contradiction between the two. This approach is surely helped by the substantial continuities in capitalist institutions and practices, not only between the Keynesian and neoliberal eras, but also across the earlier (and very much more traumatic) change from liberalism to Keynesianism.[25]

However, for socialists seeking to uncover the reasons for the rise of neoliberalism, the market/state approach has difficulty in answering questions of agency – how were these changes actually effected and by whom? It proves to be remarkably difficult to distinguish between the role of powerful market actors, such as major transnational businesses, and that of the political régimes that direct the actions of states.[26] Part of the reason for these difficulties is that there is constant confusion between the publicly-articulated *ideology* of neoliberalism, and its actual *practices*. As Ferguson puts it: 'Neoliberal policy is thus much more complicated than a reading of neoliberal doctrine might suggest'.[27] The sharp contrast posited between the Keynesian and neoliberal eras encourages the view among progressives that the present crisis can be mitigated by a return to the earlier system, thereby marginalizing any more radical alternative.

An alternative approach in the Marxist tradition is to treat the *class relation* between capital and labour as the fundamental contradiction of capitalism, shaping both the market and the state. In this approach, the standpoint set out by Marx in *Capital Volume I* remains both analytically powerful and politically effective. However, 'actually existing' Marxist political economy has repeatedly slid back from Marx's standpoint, both through the misinterpretation of Marx's critique of political economy, and through the seductive attractions of a political practice oriented first and foremost to the state.[28]

In the critical alternative, class as a relational concept centred on wage labour not only explains the origin of surplus value (and thereby of capital and its accumulation and reproduction), it also provides the key to understanding the historical specificities of capitalism as a mode of production, including the transformation of the absolutist state into the modern bourgeois state.[29] From this starting point, a historical sociology of capitalism[30] can be constructed, within which the transition to neoliberalism in the 1970s does not appear only as an offensive to roll back the state and the material gains of workers after 1945, and at an international level to cope with a more integrated global economy, important though such motives undoubtedly were to particular powerful actors within the system. Instead, we can point to certain developments towards the end of the postwar boom which much more seriously threatened to provide the foundations for transcending capitalism.

First, the fiscal crisis of the state was not just a matter of the financial burden that 'excessive' state spending placed upon capital, but rather that democratic politics could not establish a firm boundary between the public and the private. The key response was not cuts in public spending or even privatization, but the *depoliticization* of economic policy, e.g. through central bank 'independence', fiscal rules and devolution to executive agencies.[31]

Secondly, the postwar period saw the steady growth of upper layers of the working class which tended to pursue their own interests within the system, either by adopting the objectives and methods of militant trade unionism, or by pushing for the economic and social status of the independent professional vis-à-vis the capitalist class. Either way, both of these types of class solidarity came under severe assault under neoliberalism, through attacks on the representation and bargaining rights of trade unions, and through the increasing subordination of professionals in many fields to capitalist employers.[32]

Thirdly, neoliberalism was also a militant capitalist response to the threat that rising real wages in core capitalist states posed to labour markets through the pursuit of shorter working hours and earlier retirements, and to the simultaneous threat that the growing savings capacity of workers might lead to 'pension fund socialism'.[33] Under neoliberalism, the worker tendentially becomes a self-exploiting citizen with the mentality of a capitalist, investing in his/her 'human capital',[34] as well as in assets both material and financial, on the basis of a logic of monetary profit rather than particular material need. Cuts in state pensions and the encouragement of boundless consumerism are among the phenomena that complement this development.

Fourthly, the era of neoliberalism also needs to be understood in terms of relations between the first and third worlds. With the end of colonial rule national bourgeoisies came to power in most of the Third World in a wide variety of regime forms, and ostensibly pursued national development strategies through forms of economic protectionism, notably import-substituting industrialization (ISI). In the disorder of the 1970s, the unity of the Third World took the form of calls for a 'new international economic order', challenging at the same time US hegemony, Western imperialism as a whole, and the Cold War split in international society. The global debt crisis of the 1980s radically separated the Third World into regional and sectoral groupings which pursued their divergent interests in competition with each other; this allowed the emergence of new forms of imperial governance that culminated in the Washington Consensus. What is most important in this remarkable transformation is not so much the changing strategy of the great powers, but the emergence of 'denationalized' bourgeoisies throughout the less developed world which enthusiastically adopted the new strategy as junior partners.[35]

Lastly and related to this is the problem, already well recognized by the end of the postwar boom, of natural resource limits on production and accumulation. This required a determined effort to demolish the idea that such resources 'belonged' to the people of whatever country they happened to be in, and therefore should be exploited by them however and to what extent they wished. Many of the changes in law, diplomacy and business practice under the general rubric of globalization have been geared to this end, for example the proliferation of bilateral investment treaties that enshrine the private property rights of foreign investors.[36] More recently, the push to extend the existing system of global governance is stimulated by the desire to address the pressing problem of anthropogenic climate change without doing anything about the existing grotesque inequalities of wealth and power in the world.[37]

CONCLUSION: A CLASS RESPONSE TO THE CRISIS

Because neoliberalism is a project of class hegemony, the current economic and financial crisis is only a crisis *of* neoliberalism if there is a working-class challenge to that hegemony.[38] As long as the policy focus was on rescuing the banking sector from 'meltdown', and this was funded largely through borrowing from willing lenders, governments were for the most part able to win popular support. By autumn 2009, it seemed that recovery was under way, and the prognosis was business as usual. But since then, the politics of the crisis has entered a new and more uncertain phase in which capital is fighting to protect the gains made under neoliberalism from any challenge from below. The declaration of fiscal war on states, which surfaced in the Greek crisis at the end of 2009, is designed to ensure that governments are not tempted to retain the substantial powers that they exercised in 2008-09, and that the costs of adjustment fall on the working classes – hence spending cuts not tax rises, and further and deeper privatization.[39] The longer-term purpose is to restrict regulatory reform to the more egregious forms of high finance, preserving the primary role of finance of directing global corporate restructuring and investment. For this purpose the normal *modus operandi* is blackmail: make the cuts and protect big finance, or we stop lending.

But as has been loudly and rightly proclaimed by the unexpectedly resuscitated Keynesians, the global savings pool is in fact large enough so that a quick return to balanced budgets is not actually needed: that is, the threat by investors of withholding funds is a hollow one. Furthermore, public spending cuts across Europe and North America are likely to lead to a double-dip recession, meaning an end to the recovery in sales and profits, and especially a collapse in investment: among other undesirable effects for capital, this will hit the earnings of investment banks – and is already doing so.

In relation to regulatory reform, market/state theorists are concerned about finding the appropriate methods of mitigating financial market failures, while protecting the market economy – essentially technical issues of adjusting institutions and practices. Operating with the postulate of a general interest in 'prosperity' and 'good governance' both nationally and globally, they are preoccupied with the question of how reforms will be agreed given the well-known differences in economic policies and institutions in different countries and regions. This reform debate is focused on transparency, market access and information flows, seeking to address the complexities of risk management in globalized financial circuits in isolation from the realm of production.[40]

For class theorists, on the other hand, regulatory reform conceals the class nature of a project that is mainly about protecting the gains made by capital in the last thirty years, and facilitating its continuing extension into the heart of the state and into the global periphery. At all costs, the 'common sense' of neoliberalism must be protected from any suggestion that collective public provision of livelihood is feasible or desirable. The imposition of austerity, furthermore, is not just a question of 'paying for the cuts', but of permanently lowering workers' living standards. The mantra of international competitiveness is wheeled out again: if we Greeks/Canadians/French/Irish do not accept 'reality', we will lose our livelihood to those who do. In addition, the focus on excessive public spending as the newly-discovered ultimate cause of the crisis is framed so as to divide public sector workers (wasteful, unproductive – except of course the valiant 'front line' nurses, firemen, soldiers, etc.) from private sector workers (efficient, productive, overtaxed – apart from a few bad eggs in the financial sector). Among the key supposed ways of reducing public spending is to further pursue 'value for money' through accelerating the outsourcing of public provision: this is now the predominant form of privatization in both current consumer services and public infrastructure, opening new fields of investment for capital.

Where does this leave the working class? For those who have swallowed neoliberalism, there is of course no such thing any more: the 1970s and 1980s broke the stranglehold of organized labour on the prosperity of the developed world, and also subordinated peripheral workers and peasants to new forms of comprador capitalism. In place of class, the neoliberals have successfully promoted the idea of social inclusion/exclusion: the excluded being the failed financial subjects in the Northern working classes, and failed states and societies in the global South.[41]

Effective resistance starts by repudiating this world-view. Solidarity among workers of the world is based upon the universal experience of wage labour, and upon the complex webs of interdependence in the material provision of livelihood. Fighting the cuts, in workplaces and communities, exposes the false logic of competitiveness. Cutting public services will not of itself create more private sector jobs, but it will certainly reduce the provision of services essential to creative work and active citizenship. And German car workers need prosperous Greek consumers, just as Greek leisure workers need German holiday-makers.

Communities at all levels from local to global need to be re-imagined.[42] In workplaces, unions have over the years seen their capacity to mobilize collective resistance eroded by hostile legislation, the denial of access to the media, and the seductive promise of servicing the career and even financial needs of individual members. Fighting redundancies, closures and cuts in pension rights requires a dramatic change in thinking, centred on the demand for economic security as a human right. The discourse of sustainability can be reconfigured around the issue of economic security, as the demand for sustainable livelihood rather than sustainable finance. The new debt peonage of households and public authorities alike represents an opportunity to repudiate the sanctity of private property (can't pay, won't pay!). Under neoliberalism, politics has been reduced to electoral competition between different teams of professionals all dedicated to serving capital. We have to escape from this trap. Building a broad alliance around resisting the cuts by demanding economic democracy and justice can provide a basis for challenging this, laying the ground for the rebuilding of the missing socialist dimension of the crisis this time.

NOTES

For advice and suggestions I am grateful to Pinar Bedirhanoglu, Dick Bryan, Sam Gindin, Jim Kincaid, David Kotz, Huw Macartney, Tom Marois, Bill Tabb, Jan Toporowski and Robert Wade.

1 Good narrative accounts of the genesis and development of the crisis in the financial sector can be found in: Gillian Tett, *Fool's Gold*, London: Little,

Brown, 2009; John Lanchester, *Whoops! Why Everyone Owes Everyone and No One Can Pay*, London: Allen Lane, 2010; Andrew Ross Sorkin, *Too Big to Fail: Inside the Battle to Save Wall Street*, London: Allen Lane, 2009; and Paul Mason, *Meltdown: the End of the Age of Greed*, London: Verso, 2009.

2 Among these conditions were the clearout of excess capacity through depression and war; the delayed implementation of pent-up technological advances; the massive expansion of state expenditure maintained in the transition from war to peace; the new dynamism of trade and foreign investment under the Bretton Woods dispensation; and the unchallenged hegemony of the US.

3 Robert Brenner's well-known line of argument is continued in relation to the crisis this time in his 'What is Good for Goldman Sachs is Good for America: The Origins of the Present Crisis', available at http://repositories.cdlib.org. A broadly similar analysis is offered by John Bellamy Foster and Fred Magdoff, *The Great Financial Crisis: Causes and Consequences*, New York: Monthly Review Press, 2009; and Graham Turner, *The Credit Crunch: Housing Bubbles, Globalisation and the Worldwide Economic Crisis*, London: Pluto Press, 2008.

4 This is the context in which the crisis is analysed by Andrew Gamble, *The Spectre at the Feast: Capitalist Crisis and the Politics of Recession*, London: Palgrave 2009. For a prescient analysis written before the credit crunch see Anastasia Nesvetailova, *Fragile Finance: Debt, Speculation and Crisis in the Age of Global Credit*, London: Palgrave Macmillan, 2007. See also Elmar Altvater, 'Postneoliberalism or Postcapitalism? The Failure of Neoliberalism in the Financial Market Crisis', *Development Dialogue*, 51, 2009, and other articles in the same issue; and John Gray, 'After the Gold Rush', *New Statesman*, 23 April 2009, available at http://www.newstatesman.com.

5 See Hugo Radice, 'The Idea of Socialism: from 1968 to the Present-Day Crisis', *Antipode*, 41(S1), 2010.

6 For discussions of the concept of financialization, see Gerald Epstein, ed., *Financialization and the World Economy*, Cheltenham: Edward Elgar, 2005; and Andy Pike and Jane Pollard, 'Economic Geographies of Financialization', *Economic Geography*, 86(1), 2010.

7 David Kotz, 'Neoliberalism and Financialization', to appear in Gary Teeple and Stephen McBride, eds., *Relations of Global Power: Neoliberal Order and Disorder*, Toronto: University of Toronto Press, forthcoming 2010. The idea that finance has 'decoupled' from the real economy is also a premise of Edward LiPuma and Benjamin Lee, 'Financial Derivatives and the Rise of Circulation', *Economy and Society*, 34(3), 2005.

8 Rudolf Hilferding, *Finance Capital: A Study of the Latest Phase of Capitalist Development*, Brighton: Harvester Press, 1981 [1910]. Within Marxism there has been remarkably little new thinking on the subject since Hilferding prior to the current crisis; but see Costas Lapavitsas, 'Financialized Capitalism: Crisis and Financial Expropriation', *Historical Materialism*,17, 2009.

9 A striking very recent exception is Susanne Soederberg, *Corporate Power and Ownership in Contemporary Capitalism*, Abingdon: Routledge, 2010.

10 See John Kenneth Galbraith, *The New Industrial State*, London: Deutsch, 1972, and Paul Baran and Paul Sweezy, *Monopoly Capital: An Essay on the American*

Economic and Social Order, New York: Monthly Review Press, 1966.

11 For critical analyses of TNCs in that period, see Hugo Radice, *International Firms and Modern Imperialism*, Harmondsworth: Penguin Education, 1975.

12 Kotz, 'Neoliberalism', p. 16.

13 See Paul Langley, 'Financialization and the Consumer Credit Boom', *Competition and Change*, 12(2), 2008, and Johnna Montgomerie, 'The Pursuit of (Past) Happiness? Middle-Class Indebtedness and American Financialization', *New Political Economy*, 14(1), 2009.

14 Photis Lysandrou, 'The Root Cause of the Financial Crisis: The Structure of Inequality versus the Structure of Finance', Conference Paper, CRESC, University of Manchester, Manchester, April, 2010.

15 See e.g. Rod Rhodes, 'The Hollowing-Out of the State: The Changing Nature of Public Service in Britain', *The Political Quarterly*, 65(2), 1994, and Michael Power, *The Audit Society: Rituals of Verification*, Oxford: Oxford UP, 1997.

16 For a comparative international study of these new forms see Dexter Whitfield, *Global Auction of Public Assets*, Nottingham: Spokesman Books, 2010.

17 For an interesting recent anthropological study of this change in the US working class, see E. Paul Durrenberger and Dimitra Doukas, 'Gospel of Wealth, Gospel of Work: Counter-Hegemony in the US Working Class', *American Anthropologist*, 110(2), 2008.

18 Compare Robert Wade, 'Is the Globalization Consensus Dead?', *Antipode*, 41(S1), 2010 with John Maynard Keynes, 'National Self-Sufficiency' [1933], in Keynes, *Collected Writings*, Volume XXI, London: Macmillan, 1982.

19 Grahame Thompson, '"Financial Globalization" and the "Crisis": A Critical Assessment and "What is to be Done?"', *New Political Economy*, 15(1), 2010. The method of argument is to contrast 'reality' with an ideal model of a fully-globalized financial system with one currency and homogenous market structures; for a critique of his earlier use of this method, see Hugo Radice, 'The Question of Globalization', *Competition and Change*, (2)2, 1997.

20 This supposedly radical intervention, under which central banks offer to purchase financial assets from banks in order to provide cash that can be lent to businesses and households, is merely a more extensive version of the practice of 'open-market operations' traditionally used by central banks to influence the money markets.

21 Brenner, 'What is Good for Goldman Sachs'.

22 See Charles Gore, 'Methodological Nationalism and the Misunderstanding of East Asian Industrialization', *European Journal of Development Research*, 8(1), 1996.

23 For a good example of this thinking see Martin Wolf, 'Grim truths Obama should have told Hu in Beijing', *Financial Times*, 18 December 2009, p. 15.

24 See Gamble, *The Spectre at the Feast*, ch. 6. The best introduction to the varieties of capitalism debates is David Coates, ed., *Varieties of Capitalism, Varieties of Approaches,* London: Palgrave Macmillan, 2005. For a methodological critique see Hugo Radice, 'Comparing National Capitalisms', in Jonathan Perraton and Ben Clift, eds., *Where are National Capitalisms Now?* London: Palgrave Macmillan, 2004.

25 For a full account of the history of the concept of neoliberalism, see Jamie Peck, 'Remaking Laissez-Faire', *Progress in Human Geography*, 32(1), 2008. On its modern use see Jamie Peck, Nik Theodore and Neil Brenner, 'Postneoliberalism and its Malcontents', *Antipode*, 41(S1), 2010.

26 See for example the comparative analysis of recent change within Western Europe in Vivien Schmidt, *The Futures of European Capitalism*, London: Oxford University Press, 2002.

27 James Ferguson, 'The Uses of Neoliberalism', *Antipode*, 41(S1), 2010. See also Chris Harman, 'Theorising Neoliberalism', *International Socialism*, 117, 2007.

28 The arguments that follow are developed more fully in Hugo Radice, 'Political Economy and the Revolutionary Subject', *Critical Sociology*, forthcoming.

29 See, for instance, Benno Teschke, *The Myth of 1648: Class, Geopolitics and the Making of Modern International Relations*, London: Verso, 2003.

30 In the sense of Derek Sayer, 'The Critique of Politics and Political Economy: Capitalism, Communism and the State in Marx's Writings of the mid-1840s', *Sociological Review*, 33(2), 1985.

31 On depoliticization see Peter Burnham, 'The Politics of Economic Management in the 1990s', *New Political Economy*, 4(1), 1999. This depoliticization also extended, importantly, to the international arena with the transfer of policy debate to unelected expert commissions and intergovernmental bodies such as the Organization for Economic Cooperation and Development and the Bank for International Settlements. On the consequences of this for global responses to the current crisis, see Paul Cammack, 'The Shape of Capitalism to Come', *Antipode*, 46(S1), 2010.

32 On deprofessionalization in the legal profession, see Stephen Ackroyd and Daniel Muzio, 'The Reconstructed Professional Firm: Explaining Change in English Legal Practices', *Organization Studies*, 28(5), 2007. On academia, see the special issue on 'Universities, Corporatization and Resistance' of *New Proposals: Journal of Marxism and Interdisciplinary Inquiry*, 3(2), 2010, and Chris Shore, 'Audit Culture and Illiberal Governance: Universities and the Politics of Accountability', *Anthropological Theory*, 8(3), 2008.

33 The only serious threat of this kind was the Meidner Plan, whose defeat heralded the end of social-democratic rule in Sweden. See Stuart Wilks, 'Class Compromise and the International Economy: The Rise and Fall of Swedish Social Democracy', *Capital and Class*, 58, 1996.

34 See Ben Fine, *Social Capital versus Social Theory: Political Economy and Social Science at the Turn of the Millennium*, London: Routledge, 2001.

35 On the postwar trajectory of global developmentalism see *Socialist Register 2004: The New Imperial Challenge*; Hugo Radice, 'The Developmental State under Global Neoliberalism', *Third World Quarterly*, 29(6), 2008; and Gillian Hart, 'D/developments after the Meltdown', *Antipode*, 46(S1), 2010.

36 The Latin American case is explored in Ronald Cox, 'Transnational Capital, the US State and Latin American Trade Agreements', *Third World Quarterly*, 29(8), 2008.

37 On the interrelations between the financial and environmental crises, see Ulrich Brand, 'Environmental Crises and the Ambiguous Postneoliberalising of

Nature', *Development Dialogue*, 51, 2009, and Noel Castree, 'Crisis, Continuity and Change: Neoliberalism, the Left and the Future of Capitalism', *Antipode*, 46(S1), 2010.

38 See Peck et al., 'Neoliberalism', and Greg Albo, 'The Crisis of Neoliberalism and the Impasse of the Union Movement', *Development Dialogue*, 51, 2009.

39 See Hugo Radice, 'Cutting Public Debt: Economic Science or Class War?', *The Bullet*, 350, 4 May 2010, available at http://www.socialistproject.ca.

40 Critical analyses in this field do not always escape this problem; see for example Duncan Wigan, 'Credit Risk Transfer and Crunches: Global Finance Victorious or Vanquished?', *New Political Economy*, 15(1), 2010, and Yuval Millo and Donald Mackenzie, 'The Usefulness of Inaccurate Models: Towards an Understanding of the Emergence of Financial Risk Management', *Accounting, Organizations and Society*, 34(5), 2009.

41 On social exclusion as a substitute for class subordination see Radice, 'Political Economy and the Revolutionary Subject'; on failed states see Shahar Hameiri, 'Failed States or a Failed Paradigm? State Capacity and the Limits of Institutionalism', *Journal of International Relations and Development*, 10(2), 2007.

42 For a promising case see Hilary Wainwright, with Mathew Little, *Public Service Reform… But Not As We Know It*, Hove: Picnic Publishing, 2009.

THE FIRST GREAT DEPRESSION OF THE 21ST CENTURY

ANWAR SHAIKH

The general economic crisis that was unleashed across the world in 2008 is a Great Depression. It was triggered by a financial crisis in the US, but that was not its cause. This crisis is an absolutely normal phase of a long-standing recurrent pattern of capitalist accumulation in which long booms eventually give way to long downturns. When this transition occurs, the health of the economy goes from good to bad. In the latter phase a shock can trigger a crisis, just as the collapse of the subprime mortgage market did in 2007, and just as previous shocks triggered general crises in the 1820s, 1870s, 1930s and 1970s.[1] In his justly famous book, *The Great Crash 1929*, John Kenneth Galbraith points out that while the Great Depression of the 1930s was preceded by rampant financial speculation, it was the fundamentally unsound and fragile state of the economy in 1929 which allowed the stock market crash to trigger an economic collapse.[2] As it was then, so it is now.[3] Those who choose to see each such episode as a singular event, as the random appearance of a 'black swan' in a hitherto pristine flock,[4] have forgotten the dynamics of the history they seek to explain. And in the process they also conveniently forget that it is the very logic of profit which condemns us to repeat this history.

Capitalist accumulation is a turbulent dynamic process. It has powerful built-in rhythms modulated by conjunctural factors and specific historical events. Analysis of the concrete history of accumulation must therefore distinguish between intrinsic patterns and their particular historical expressions. Business cycles are the most visible elements of capitalist dynamics. A fast (3-5 year inventory) cycle arises from the perpetual oscillations of aggregate supply and demand, and a medium (7-10 year fixed capital) cycle from the slower fluctuations of aggregate capacity and supply.[5] But underlying these business cycles is a much slower rhythm consisting of alternating long phases of accelerating and decelerating accumulation. The various business cycles are articulated into these basic waves.[6] Capitalist history is always enacted upon a moving stage.

After the Great Depression of the 1930s came the Great Stagflation of the 1970s. In that case the underlying crisis was covered up by rampant inflation. But this did not prevent major job losses, a large drop in the real value of the stock market index, and widespread business and bank failures. There was considerable anxiety at the time that the economic and financial system would unravel altogether.[7] For our present purposes, it is useful to note that in countries like the US and the UK the crisis led to high unemployment, attacks on unions and on institutional support for labour and poor people, and inflation which rapidly eroded both real wages and the real value of the stock market. Other countries, such as Japan, resorted to low unemployment and gradual asset deflation which stretched out the duration of the crisis but prevented it from sinking to the depths it did in the US and the UK.

Regardless of these differences, a new boom began in the 1980s in all major capitalist countries, spurred by a sharp drop in interest rates which greatly raised the net rate of return on capital, i.e. raised the net difference between the profit rate and the interest rate. Falling interest rates also lubricated the spread of capital across the globe, promoted a huge rise in consumer debt, and fuelled international bubbles in finance and real estate. Deregulation of financial activities in many countries was eagerly sought by financial businesses themselves, and except for a few countries such as Canada, this effort was largely successful. At the same time, in countries such as the US and the UK there was an unprecedented rise in the exploitation of labour, manifested in the slowdown of real wages relative to productivity. As always, the direct benefit was a great boost to the rate of profit. The normal side effect to a wage deceleration would have been a stagnation of real consumer spending. But with interest rates falling and credit being made ever easier, consumer and other spending continued to rise, buoyed on a rising tide of debt. All limits seemed suspended, all laws of motion abolished. And then it came crashing down. The mortgage crisis in the US was only the immediate trigger. The underlying problem was that the fall in interest rates and the rise in debt which fuelled the boom had reached their limits.

The current crisis is still unfolding. Massive amounts of money have been created in all major advanced countries and funnelled into the business sector to shore it up. But this money has largely been sequestered there. Banks have no desire to increase lending in a risky climate in which they may not be able to get their money back with a sufficient profit. Businesses such as the automobile industry have a similar problem because they are saddled with large inventories of unsold goods which they need to burn off before even thinking of expanding. Therefore the bulk of the citizenry has received no direct benefit from the huge sums of money thrown around, and unemployment rates remain high. In this respect, it is striking that so little has been done to expand employment through government-created work, as was done by the Roosevelt Administration during the 1930s.

This brings us to the fundamental question: how is it that the capitalist system, whose institutions, regulations and political structures have changed so significantly over the course of its evolution, is still capable of exhibiting certain recurrent economic patterns? The answer lies in the fact that these particular patterns are rooted in the profit motive, which remains the central regulator of business behaviour throughout this history. Capitalism's sheath mutates constantly in order for its core to remain the same. A full explanation of the theoretical dynamics is beyond the scope of this essay, but we can get a good sense of its logic by examining the relation between accumulation and profitability. In what follows I will focus on the United States because this is still the centre of the advanced capitalist world, and this is where the crisis originated. But it must be said that the real toll is global, falling most of all on the already suffering women, children and unemployed of this world.

ACCUMULATION AND PROFITABILITY

'The engine which drives Enterprise is ... Profit.'[8] (J.M. Keynes)
'Sales without profits are meaningless.'[9] (Business Week)

Every business knows, at the peril of its extinction, that profit is its *raison d'être*. The classical economists argued that it is the difference between the profit rate (r) and the interest rate (i) which is central to accumulation. The reason is that profit is the return to active investment, while the interest rate is the return to passive investment. A given amount of capital may be invested in producing or selling commodities, in lending money, or in active speculation. The rate of profit in each case is its return, fraught with all the risks, uncertainties and errors to which such endeavours are subject. As business people come to learn, '[t]here are known knowns. There are ... known unknowns...But there are also unknown unknowns'.[10] On the other hand, the same amount of capital could just as well be invested in a savings account or a safe bond, earning interest in quiet and relative safety. The interest rate is the benchmark, the safe alternative, to the rate of return on active investment. Marx argues that it is the difference between the two rates, which he calls the rate of profit-of-enterprise ($r - i$), that drives active investment. Keynes says much the same thing: he calls the profit rate the marginal efficiency of capital (MEC), and focuses on the difference between it and the interest rate as the foundation for viability of investment. Neoclassical and post-Keynesian economics also focus on this same difference, albeit in a roundabout manner: production costs are *defined* to include an 'opportunity cost' comprising the interest equivalent on the capital stock, so that 'economic profit' is the amount of profit-of-enterprise and the corresponding rate of profit is simply the rate of profit-of-enterprise $(r - i)$.[11]

Consider the following illustration. Suppose that the firm's annual profit is \$100,000. Suppose the current interest rate is 4 per cent and the firm's beginning-of-year capital stock is \$1,000,000. Then the firm's capital could have instead earned \$40,000 if it had been put into a safe bond. From a classical point of view, we can think of the firm's total profit as having two components: \$40,000 as interest equivalent and \$60,000 as profit-of-enterprise. Neoclassical economics disguises all of this by treating the hypothetical interest equivalent as a 'cost' on a par with wages, materials, and depreciation. As a consequence, its definition of economic profit is already profit-of-enterprise (\$60,000). Post-Keynesian economics typically adopts many neoclassical concepts, of which this is one.

The rate of profit is the ratio of annual profit to beginning-of-year capital stock, i.e. $r = \dfrac{\$100,000}{\$1,000,000} = 0.10$. The corresponding rate of profit-of-enterprise (*re*) is the amount of profit-of-enterprise divided by the capital stock, which yields $re = \dfrac{\$60,000}{\$1,000,000} = 6\%$. It is easy to see that the rate of profit-of-enterprise equals the difference between the profit rate and the interest rate: $re = r - i = 10\% - 4\% = 6\%$.

Two further considerations become important at an empirical level. First, profit as listed in national accounts is neither total profit (*P*) nor profit-of-enterprise (*PE*) but something in between. National accounts define economic profit as actual profit net of actual interest paid. So if the firm under consideration had *borrowed* half of its total capital (\$500,000), it would have to pay out \$20,000 in actual interest payments (4 per cent of its total debt of \$500,000). Hence the national accounts measure of profit ($P' =$ \$80,000) is actual profit ($P =$ \$100,000) *minus* actual interest paid on actual debt (\$20,000). Therefore in order to measure actual profits we need to add actual monetary interest paid to the profit figure listed in national accounts. We can then calculate the level and rate of profit-of-enterprise in the previously discussed manner.[12]

Secondly, it is important to note that all rates of profit will be *real* rates, i.e. inflation-adjusted, if we use current-dollar profit flows in the numerator and the current-cost capital stock (capital measured in terms of its current-price equivalent) in the denominator. In this way both the numerator and the denominator reflect the *same* set of prices, which is the essence of a real measure.[13] This is obvious in the case of the profit rate (r) when both P and K reflect current prices. But it also applies to the rate of profit-of-enterprise (re) whose numerator is excess of current profit over the current interest equivalent on the beginning-of-the-year current-cost capital stock (P - iK). Measured in this manner, the rate of profit-of-enterprise $re = r - i$ is a real rate.[14] Further details, derivations and considerations of the specificity of national account measures of profit and capital are presented in the Appendix: Data Sources and Methods.

With this in hand, we turn to the analysis of the events which led to the current crisis. First and foremost are the movements of the rate of profit.

POSTWAR PATTERNS IN US ACCUMULATION

The general rate of profit

Figure 1 displays the rate of profit for US nonfinancial corporations, which is the ratio of their profits *before* interest and profit taxes to the beginning of year current cost of their plant and equipment. Also displayed is the trend of the rate of profit (see the Appendix for details). As previously explained, we need a measure of profits before interest payments because we will subsequently compare this amount to the interest equivalent on the same capital stock in

Figure 1: Actual and Trend Rate of Profit, US Nonfinancial Corporations 1947-2010
(Profit = Earnings Before Interest and Taxes)

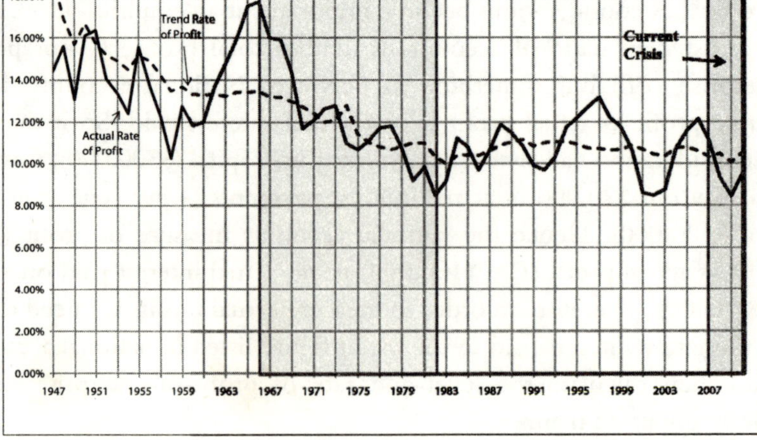

order to derive profit of enterprise. Since published profits of nonfinancial corporations are net of actual interest payments, we add this latter amount back to their published profits. This expanded measure of nonfinancial corporate profit captures a part of the profits of financial corporations, since the latter firms derive their revenues from interest payments.

We see that the actual rate of profit is subject to many fluctuations, and can be greatly influenced in the short run by particular historical events. For instance, the big run-up of the profit rate in the 1960s reflects the corresponding escalation of the Vietnam War. Wars are generally good for profitability, at least in the early stages. The fitted trend of the rate of profit also displayed in Figure 1 is designed to distinguish between structurally driven patterns in the rate of profit and short run fluctuations arising from conjunctural events such as the Vietnam War. We see that the trend rate of profit drifted downward for thirty-five years, but then stabilized. The question is: what happened to reverse this pattern?

Productivity and real wages

Figure 2 provides the central clue. It depicts the relation between hourly productivity and hourly real compensation (real wages) in the US business sector from 1947-2008. Real wages tend to grow more slowly than productivity, i.e. the rate of exploitation tends to rise. But beginning with Reagan in the 1980s, real wage growth slowed down considerably. This is made evident by comparing actual real wages since 1980 to the path they would have followed had they maintained their postwar relation

Figure 2: Hourly Real Wages and Productivity, US Business Sector 1947-2010 (1992=100)

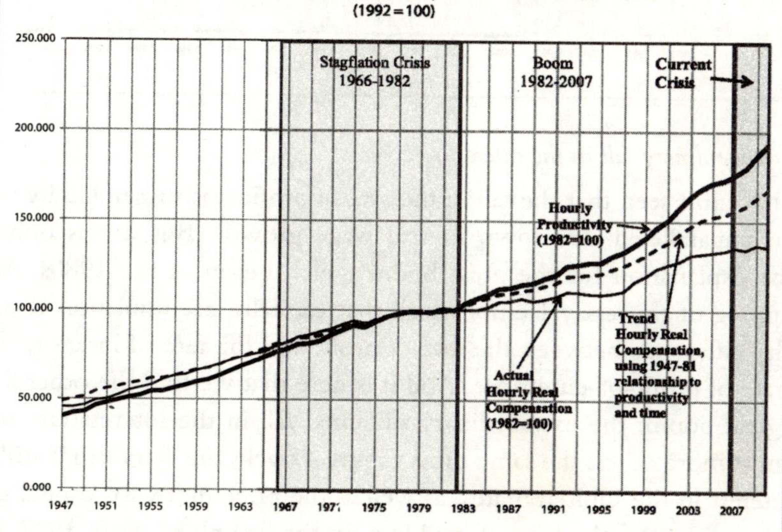

to productivity. This departure from trend was brought about through concerted attacks on labour in this era. We will see that its impact on the profit rate was dramatic, because employee compensation is large in relation to profit.

Impact on profitability of the suppression of real wage growth

Figure 3 depicts the great impact that the suppression of real wage growth had on profits. It shows the actual profit rate as well as the counterfactual path it would have followed had corporate nonfinancial real wages maintained their postwar relation to corporate nonfinancial productivity. The repression directed against labour beginning in the Reagan era had a clear purpose: it fuelled the boom of the latter part of the twentieth century.

Figure 3: Actual and Counterfactual Rate of Profit of US Nonfinancial Corporations 1947-2009
(Counterfactual path if real wages had continued on their postwar trend)

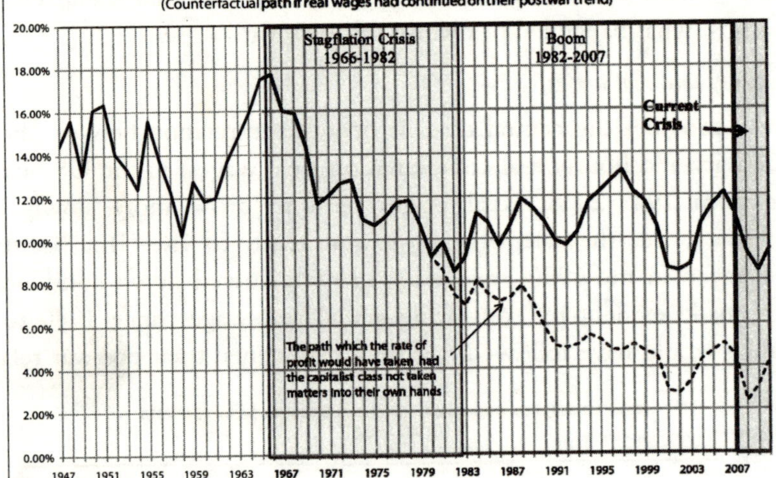

The extraordinary fall in the interest rate

We have just seen that the fall in the rate of profit was suspended by means of an unparalleled slowdown in real wage growth. But this is only part of the explanation for the great boom which began in the 1980s. At the beginning of this essay I emphasized that capitalist accumulation is driven by the difference between the rate of profit and the rate of interest, i.e. by the rate of profit-of-enterprise. And it is here that we find the other key to the great boom: the extraordinary sustained fall in the interest rate which began at more or less the same time. Figure 4 tracks the 3-month T-Bill rate of interest in the United States, as well as the price index for capital goods (p_k) shown on the chart as a dotted line. In the first phase, from 1947-1981, this interest rate rose twenty-four fold, from 0.59 per cent in 1947 to 14.03 per cent in 1981. In the second phase, from 1981 onward, it fell equally dramatically, going from 14.03 per cent to a mere 0.16 per cent in 2009. In order to separate market influences from policy interventions it would be necessary to discuss the theory of competitively determined interest rates –

Figure 4: The Rate of Interest (3 Mo. T-Bill), US 1947-2008

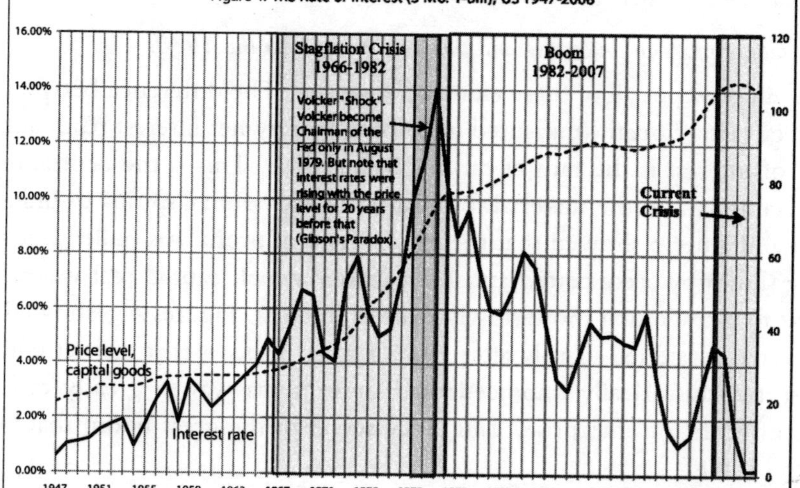

Figure 5: US and World (US Trading Partners) Nominal Interest Rates

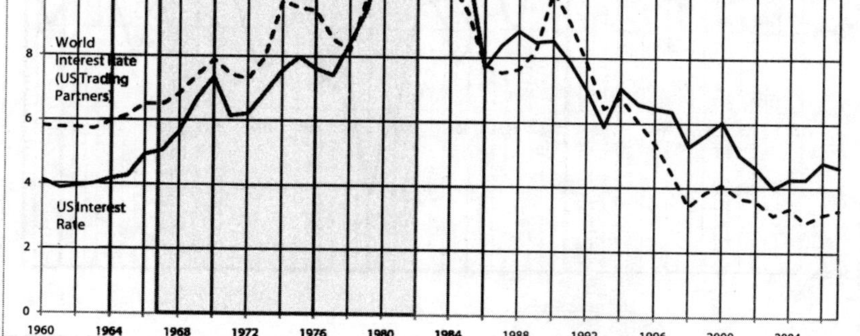

which is not possible within the scope of this essay.[15] In any case, whatever the relative weights of market factors and policy decisions, the long rise and subsequent long fall in the interest rate was also evident in most major capitalist countries. Figure 5 shows this by comparing the US interest rate to the average interest rate of US trading partners. Among other things, this demonstrates that the dynamics we observe in the US were characteristic of the capitalist centre as a whole.

The rate of profit-of-enterprise and the great boom after the 1980s

We can now put all of these elements together. The difference between the general rate of profit (measured gross of monetary net interest paid) and the rate of interest is the rate of profit-of-enterprise. This is the central driver of accumulation, the material foundation of the 'animal spirits' of industrial capital. Figure 3 showed that the general rate of profit was pulled out of its long slump by a concerted attack on labour which caused real wages after 1982 to grow much more slowly than in the past. Figures 4-5 showed that the interest rate fell sharply after 1982. Figure 6 shows that the net effect of these two historically unprecedented movements was to greatly raise the rate of profit-of-enterprise. *This* is the secret of the great boom that began in the 1980s.

The great boom was inherently contradictory. The dramatic fall in the interest rate set off a spree of borrowing, and sectoral debt burdens grew

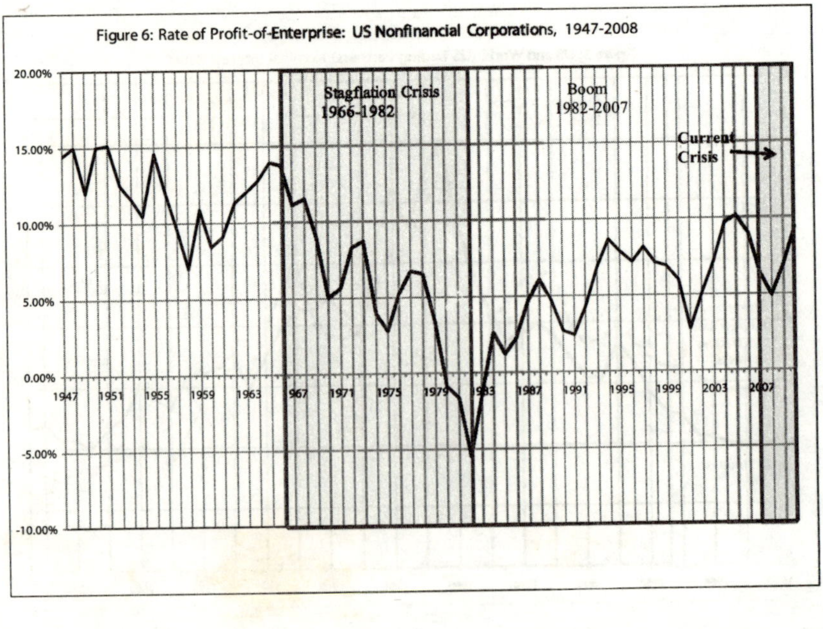

Figure 7: Household Debt-to-Income Ratio

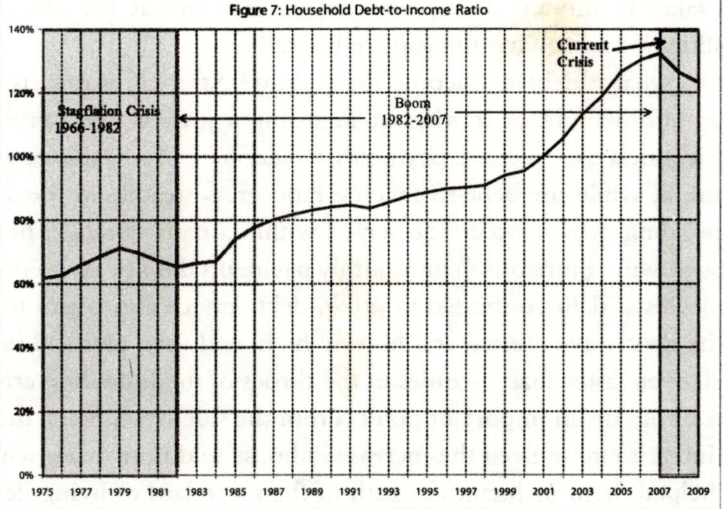

Figure 8: Household Debt Service Ratio

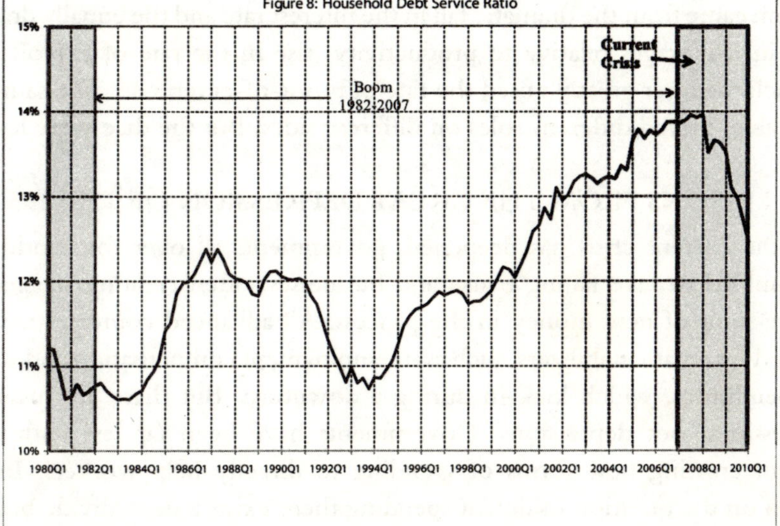

dramatically. Households, whose real incomes had been squeezed by the slowdown in real wage growth, were offered ever cheaper debt in order to maintain growth in consumer spending. In consequence, as shown in Figure 7, household debt-to-income ratios grew dramatically in the 1980s. Secondly, once the rate of interest has been lowered to zero (it is 0.0017, i.e. 0.17 per cent, at this very moment), there is nowhere else to go on that score. Yes, the gap between this base rate and the rate at which businesses or consumers borrow (the prime rate, the mortgage rate) can still be squeezed by the state. But this gap is the source of the profit of the financial sector, which takes in money at one rate and lends it out at the other. So the possibilities for narrowing the gap are limited.

But so what if debt-to-income ratios grow? After all, if debt is cheaper, one can afford more of it without incurring a greater debt-service (ratio of amortization and interest payments to income). And indeed, as shown in Figure 8, while the debt-to-income ratio grew steadily in the 1980s the corresponding debt-service ratio stayed within a narrow range: households were borrowing more but their monthly payments did not go up much. But in the 1990s as debt continued to grow, debt-service also began to rise. By 2007 the debt wave crested at a historic high, and then plunged in 2008 as debt fell even faster than incomes in the throes of the unfolding crisis.

This brings up an important point. From the side of workers, the decline in the interest rate spurred the increase in household borrowing which for a while helped them maintain the path of their standard of living despite the slowdown in real wages. From a macroeconomic side, the resultant surge in household spending *added* fuel to the boom. The primary impetus for the boom came from the dramatic fall in the interest rate and the equally dramatic fall in real wages relative to productivity (rise in the rate of exploitation), which together greatly raised the rate of profit-of-enterprise. The same two variables played different roles on different sides. But the dice were loaded.

LESSONS FROM THE GREAT DEPRESSION OF THE 1930s

As the current crisis has deepened, governments all over the world have scrambled to save failing banks and businesses, often creating staggeringly large sums of new money in the process. All advanced countries have so-called automatic stabilizers, such as unemployment compensation and welfare expenditures, which kick-in during a downturn. But these are meant for recessions, not depressions. Governments have been far less enthusiastic about creating new forms of spending to directly help workers. Indeed, even on the question of deficit spending there exists a deep divide between two different policy camps.

These divisions were clearly visible at the recently concluded G-20 meetings in Toronto in June 2010. On one side was the orthodoxy, which pushed for 'austerity', this term being a code word for cutbacks in health, education, welfare and other expenditures which support labour. Jean-Claude Trichet, head of the European Central Bank said at these meetings that 'the idea that austerity measures could trigger stagnation is incorrect'. 'Governments should not become addicted to borrowing as a quick fix to stimulate demand.... Deficit spending cannot become a permanent state of affairs,' said German Finance Minister Wolfgang Schauble. Part of the motivation for this stance arises from a faith in the orthodox economic notion that markets are near perfect and quick to recover. After all, the nonfinancial corporate rate of profit-of-enterprise in Figure 6 shows a decided upturn in 2010. And for some investment banks, money has been like oil in the Gulf of Mexico: just waiting to be skimmed off the top. In 2010, Goldman Sachs' first-quarter earnings were $3.3 billion, double that of the year before, making it the second most profitable quarter since they went public in 1999. In the optimistic light of orthodox theory, this suggests that happy days are almost here again. European central bankers also retain a searing memory of the deficit-financed German hyperinflation of the 1920s and its subsequent devastating social and political consequences. Finally, there is the practical question of the potential benefits for European capital of austerity programmes. European labour survived the neoliberal era in better shape than US and British labour and, as Reagan and Thatcher showed, a crisis provides the perfect cover for an attack on labour. From this point of view the possibility that austerity may make things much worse for the bulk of the population is an acceptable risk if it weakens a hitherto resistant labour force.

The American side at the G-20 meetings expressed a different set of concerns. In the US alone, household wealth has already fallen by trillions of dollars and new housing sales are now below 1981 levels. Moreover, the International Labour Organization has recently warned that a 'prolonged and severe' global job crisis is in the offing – something which must be taken very seriously by an imperial power already tangled in multiple wars and global 'police actions'. Finally, here too there is a critical matter of history. President Barack Obama urged EU leaders to rethink their stance, saying that they should '*learn from the consequential mistakes of the past* when stimulus was too quickly withdrawn and resulted in renewed economic hardships and recession'.[16] The 'consequential mistakes' to which Obama refers had to do with events in the 1930s. The Great Depression triggered by the stock market crash in 1929 led to a sharp fall in output and a sharp rise in unemployment from 1929-32. But over the next four years output grew by almost 50 per cent, the unemployment rate fell by a third and government spending grew by almost 40 per cent. Indeed, by 1936 output was growing at a phenomenal 13 per cent. The rub was that the federal budget went into deficits of almost 5 per cent over these same four years. So in 1937 the Roosevelt administration increased taxes and sharply cut back government spending.[17] Real GDP promptly dropped, and unemployment rose once again. Recognizing its mistake, the government quickly reversed itself and substantially raised government spending and government deficits n 1938. By 1939 output was growing at 8 per cent. It was only then that the US began its build-up for a possible war, and only in 1942 that it was fully engaged. Figure 9 depicts the growth rate of GDP during these critical years.

There are several lessons that can be taken from these episodes. First, cutting back government spending during a crisis would be a 'consequential mistake'. This is Obama's point. Second, it is absolutely clear that the economy began to recover in 1933, and except for the administration's mis-step in cutting government spending in 1937, continued to do so until the US build-up to the Second World War in 1939 and its full entry in 1942 (Pearl Harbor being December 7, 1941). It is therefore wrong to attribute

Figure 9: Real GDP Growth in the Great Depression, 1929-1942

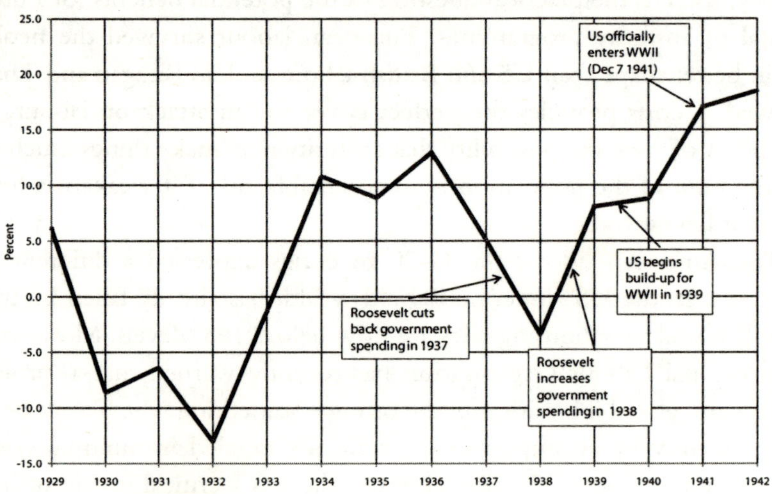

the recovery, which had begun *nine* years before the war, to the war itself. The war itself *further* stimulated production and employment. Third, it is nonetheless correct to say that (peacetime) government spending played a crucial role in speeding up the recovery. Fourth, the government spending involved did not just go towards the purchase of goods and services. It also went toward direct employment in the performance of public service. For instance, the Work Projects Administration (WPA) alone employed millions of people in public construction, in the arts, in teaching, and in support of the poor.

SOME POLICY IMPLICATIONS FOR THE PRESENT PERIOD

Government spending can greatly stimulate an economy. This is evident during times of war, which are most often accompanied by massive, deficit financed, government spending. In the Second World War, for instance, in 1943-1945 the US ran budget deficits averaged *25 per cent*. By contrast, the budget deficit today, in the second quarter of 2010, is less than 11 per cent. In any case, it is important to note that a war is a *particular* form of a social mobilization which serves to increase production and employment. In such episodes, some part of the resulting employment is derived from the demand for weapons and other supporting goods and services and the demand for other items which this in turn engenders. But another part is direct employment in the armed forces, government administration, security, maintenance and repair of public and private facilities, etc. So even during a war we have to distinguish between two different forms of economic stimuli: direct government *demand* which stimulates employment provided that businesses do not hold on to most of the money or use it to pay down debt; and the direct government *employment* which stimulates demand provided that the people so employed do not save the income or use it to pay down debt.

The same two modes could equally well be applied to peacetime expenditures in a social mobilization to tackle the crisis. In the first mode government expenditures are directed towards businesses and banks, with the hopes that the firms so benefiting will then increase employment. This is the traditional Keynesian mode: stimulate business and let the benefits *trickle-down* to employment. In the second mode the government directly provides employment for those who cannot find it in the private sector, and as these newly employed workers spend their incomes, the benefits *rise-up* to businesses and banks. The requirement that monies received be re-spent is a crucial one. Huge 'bailout' sums have been directed in recent times towards banks and nonfinancial businesses in every major country of the world. Yet these funds have most often ended up being sequestered there: banks need them to shore up their shaky portfolios and industries need them to pay off debts. Quite correctly, neither sees any point in throwing this good money after bad in a climate in which there is little hope of adequate return. Thus not much of the massive bailouts have trickled down. But if the second mode were to be employed, the matter is likely to be very different. The income received by those previously unemployed has to be spent, for they must live. The second mode therefore has two major advantages: it would directly create employment for those who need it the most; and it would generate a high rise-up effect for businesses who serve them.

What then prevents governments from creating programmes for direct employment? The answer of course is that stimulus of business is the preferred mode for capital. Indeed, since the direct employment of labour subordinates the profit motive to social goals, it is correctly seen as a threat to the capitalist order – as 'socialistic'. Moreover, it would interfere with the neoliberal plan to make further use of cheap global labour, whose existence not only allows for cheaper production abroad but also helps keep real wage growth in check at home. So the question of our time is whether we can have social mobilization to combat the consequences of a Great Depression without being tricked into wars. This is a global question, because unemployment, poverty, and environmental degradation are entirely global. But mobilizations, by their nature, begin locally. The goal is to make them spread, against the resistance of powerful interests and craven states.

APPENDIX: DATA SOURCES AND METHODS

This appendix details the sources and methods of the variables displayed in Figures 1-9. Most of the data is from the US Bureau of Economic Analysis National Income and Product Accounts (NIPA) and Fixed Asset (FA) tables available online at http://www.bls.gov. Other sources are listed below.

Figure 1: $r = \frac{P}{K(-1)}$, and the trend value of *r* (*rtrend*)

P is the sum of nonfinancial corporate profits from NIPA Table 1.14, line 27, up to the first quarter of 2010; and nonfinancial corporate net monetary interest paid from Table 7.11, line 11 *minus* line 17, which is only available annually up to 2008 and was extended to 2010 using trends of the individual components. Corporate profit as listed in NIPA is net of actual net monetary interest paid, so we need to add the latter item back in order to get profits before interest. This gives us the NIPA equivalent of the familiar business accounting measure 'Earnings Before Interest and Taxes' (EBIT). This step is necessary because we will subsequently subtract the interest *equivalent* on all capital (not just actual net interest paid on borrowed capital) in order to get the mass and rate of profit-of-enterprise (see the calculations for Figure 6 below).

The denominator of the profit rate is the capital advanced for the year. Since NIPA lists the capital stock at the end of the year, it is necessary to use the current-cost nonfinancial corporate capital stock of the *previous* year (*K(-1)*). The end of year capital stock is listed in FA (Fixed Assets) Table 6.1, line 4. The FA data was available annually until 2008, and was extended to 2009 using its log trend.

rtrend was calculated by running a LOESS regression in Eviews 5 on *P* and *K(-1)* with bandwidth = 0.50. LOESS is a nearest-neighbour type of regression with a polynomial of degree 1 (linear) and local tricube weighting. This technique is not sensitive to short run fluctuations in the data, which makes it useful for estimation of trends. *rtrend* was generated by dividing the fitted (trend) value of *P* by *K(-1)*.

Figure 2: Business sector hourly productivity and actual and counterfactual hourly real compensation.
Hourly productivity and actual real compensation are available from the US Bureau of Labor Statistics (BLS), under the heading of 'Major Sector Productivity and Costs Indexes', at www.bls.org. The 2010 figure was for the first quarter. The ratio of productivity (*y*) to real employee compensation (*ec*) follows a steady trend in the postwar 'golden age' 1960-1981, which was captured by regressing ln(ec) on ln(*y*) and a time trend (the latter was not significant). This trend was then forecast over 1982-2009 to estimate the (counterfactual) path that *ec* would have followed if the previous trend had been maintained (*ecc*). Using 1960-1981 yields a more modest counterfactual wage path than the one derived from using the whole period from 1947-1981. I chose the more modest option so as to avoid overstating the benefit to profitability of the real wage slowdown beginning in the Reagan-Thatcher era.

Figure 3: The actual rate of profit (r) compared to the counterfactual rate of profit (rc)
The previously calculated variables were used to create the ratio of hourly counterfactual employee compensation to actual hourly compensation (*z* = *ecc/ec*). Beginning in 1982, actual total nonfinancial corporate employee compensation (*EC*) was multiplied by *z* to estimate the total compensation that employees would have received (*ECCc*) had wages remained on their pre-1982 path. The difference (*ECc* – *EC*) represents the profit that has been gained from the real wage slowdown. Adding this to actual profit gives estimated counterfactual profit, and dividing the latter by the lagged capital stock *K(-1)* then gives an estimate of the counterfactual rate of profit.

Figure 4: The interest rate and the price level
The interest rate is the 3 month T-bill rate, available in Table 73, first data column in *The Economic Report of the President* published by the BEA on http://www.gpoaccess.gov/eop/tables10.html. The price level used is the price of new capital goods, since that is the relevant indicator the purchasing power of profit. This is available in NIPA Table 1.1.9, line 7 (fixed investment deflator).

Figure 5: The US and US-Trading Partner interest rates
The US interest rate has been described above. US trading partner weights taken from the Federal Reserve Board Indexes of the Foreign Exchange

Value of the Dollar (http://www.federalreserve.gov/releases/h10/Weights) were used to derive a weighted average of interest rates taken from the International Financial Statistics (IFS) of the International Monetary Fund (IMF). I am greatly indebted to Amr Ragab for these calculations.

Figure 6: $re = r - i$, where both r and i have been previously described.

Figures 7-8: Debt-to-Income and Debt-Service ratios
Figure 7 is the ratio of household debt to personal disposable income. The former is obtained from the Federal Reserve Bank's *Flow of Funds* Table D3, line 2; and the latter from NIPA Table 2.1, line 26.
Figure 8 is the ratio of debt service (amortization and interest payments on outstanding mortgage and consumer debt) to personal disposable income, which is listed as the variable DSR in *Flow of Funds* table called 'Household Debt Service and Financial Obligations Ratios' available at http://www.federal reserve.gov/releases/housedebt/default.htm.

Figure 9: Real GDP growth during the Great Depression, 1929-42
Real GDP growth is directly available from 1930 onward in NIPA Table 1.1.1, line 1. The growth rate for 1929 was calculated using data for 1928-1929 (794,700, 843,334) available in *The World Economy: Historical Statistics*, OECD Development Centre, Paris 2003.

NOTES

1 The Crisis of 1825 has been viewed as the first real industrial crisis. The Crisis of 1847 was so severe that it sparked revolutions throughout Europe. Maurice Flamant and Jeanne Singer-Kerel, *Modern Economic Crises*, London: Barrie & Jenkins, 1970, pp. 16-23. The nomenclature 'The Long Depression of 1873-1893' is from Forrest Capie and Geoffrey Wood, 'Great Depression of 1873-1896', in D. Glasner and T. F. Cooley, eds., *Business Cycles and Depressions: An Encyclopedia,* New York: Garland Publishing, 1997. The Great Depression of 1929-1939 is well known. The timing of the Great Stagflation of 1967-1982 is from Shaikh, 'The Falling Rate of Profit and the Economic Crisis in the U.S.', in R. Cherry et al., eds., *The Imperiled Economy*, New York: Union for Radical Political Economy, 1987. Both the name and the timing of the worldwide economic crisis which erupted in 2008 remain to be settled.

2 John Kenneth Galbraith, *The Great Crash, 1929*, Boston: Houghton Miflin, 1955, chs. I-II, and pp. 182, 192. Galbraith was ambivalent about the possibility of a recurrence of a Great Depression. As a historian, he was only too aware that financial 'cycles of euphoria and panic ... accord roughly with the time it took people to forget the last disaster'. John Kenneth Galbraith, *Money: Whence It Came, Where It Went*, Boston: Houghton Mifflin Company, 1975, p. 21. He noted that these cycles are themselves the 'product of the free choice and decision of hundreds of thousands of individuals', that despite the hope

for an immunizing memory of the last event 'the chances for a recurrence of a speculative orgy are rather good', that 'during the next boom some newly rediscovered virtuosity of the free enterprise system will be cited', that among 'the first to accept these rationalizations will be some of those responsible for invoking the controls ... [who then] will say firmly that controls are not needed', and that over time 'regulatory bodies ... become, with some exceptions, either an arm of the industry they are regulating or senile'. Galbraith, *The Great Crash, 1929*, pp. 4-5, 171, 195-96. Yet as a policy maker he continued to hope that none of these events will come to pass.

3 Floyd Norris, 'Securitization Went Awry Once Before', *New York Times*, 29 January 2010.

4 David Smith, 'When Catastrophe Strikes Blame a Black Swan', *The Sunday Times*, 6 May 2007.

5 Shaikh, 'The Falling Rate of Profit'; J.J. van Duijn, *The Long Wave in Economic Life*, London: Allen and Unwin, 1983, chs. 1-2.

6 E. Mandel, *Late Capitalism*, London: New Left Books, 1975, pp. 126-27.

7 Shaikh, 'The Falling Rate of Profit', p. 123.

8 John Maynard Keynes, *A Treatise on Money*, New York: Harcourt, Brace and Company, 1976, p. 148.

9 Lewis Braham, 'The Business Week 50', *Business Week*, 23 March 2001.

10 Donald Rumsfeld, 'DoD News Briefing – Secretary Rumsfeld and Gen. Myers', United States Department of Defense, 12 February 2002, available from http://www.defense.gov.

11 Eckhard Hein, 'Money, Credit and the Interest Rate in Marx's Economics: On the Similarities of Marx's Monetary Analysis to Post-Keynesian Analysis', *International Papers in Political Economy*, 11(2), 2004, pp. 20-23; Karl Marx, *Capital, Volume III*, New York: International Publishers, 1967, ch. XXIII; Shaikh, 'The Falling Rate of Profit', p. 126n1.

12 I have previously argued that current-cost *gross* stock is the appropriate measure of capital. Shaikh, 'Explaining the Global Economic Crisis: A Critique of Brenner', *Historical Materialism*, 5, 1999, pp. 106-7. But this measure is no longer estimated by most national accounts, because they have recently switched to the assumption that capital goods depreciate geometrically over an *infinite* lifespan. This assumption 'is widely used in theoretical expositions of [neoclassical] capital theory because of its simplicity', despite the fact some regard it as 'empirically implausible'. Charles R. Hulten, 'The Measurement of Capital', in E. R. Berndt and J. E. Triplett, eds., *Fifty Years of Economic Measurement: The Jubilee of the Conference of Research on Income and Wealth*, Chicago: University of Chicago Press, 1990, p. 125. The 'infinite tail' which it assumes also causes many problems. Michael J. Harper, 'The Measurement of Productive Capital Stock, Capital Wealth, and Capital Services', BLS Working Paper No. 128, US Bureau of Labor Statistics, 1982, pp. 10, 30. The infinite-life assumption makes it impossible to calculate gross stock measures because these rely on the use of the specific life spans of individual capital goods. In a forthcoming work I will show how gross stock measures can be calculated by combining previously available information on the useful lives of specific

capital goods with newly derived rules for the behaviour of chain-weighted aggregate capital stocks. These new capital stock measures change the observed patterns of the rate of profit from 1947-1982, but have only a limited impact on the patterns from 1982 onward which are the focus of this paper.

13 A rate of profit is by definition the ratio of money magnitudes. Thus we can write it as $r = P/K$ where both profit P and capital K are measured in current prices. Alternately, we can deflate the denominator by the price index of capital p_K to turn current-cost K into $K_R \equiv K/p_K$, the real (inflation adjusted) capital stock. To preserve dimensional homogeneity in the ratio we then must also deflate the numerator by p_K to turn nominal profit P into $P_R \equiv P/p_K$, the real mass of profit measured in terms of its purchasing power over capital. The ratio of the two real measures is once again r.

14 In measuring the rate of profit-of-enterprise we are making no assumption about the determination of the nominal interest rate. The standard neoclassical Fisher hypothesis is that the real rate of interest (i_r) is *defined* as the difference between the nominal interest rate (i) and some rate of inflation expected by the representative investor (p^e). Under the further assumption that the real rate of interest is exogenously given, this implies that the nominal interest rate follows the (expected) rate of inflation. But under rational expectations, the expected inflation rate will track the actual rate of inflation. So the argument boils down to the hypothesis that nominal interest rates track the *rate* of inflation – a proposition which has been so widely disproved that it only survives in textbooks. Pierluigi Ciocca and Giangiacomo Nardozzi, *The High Price of Money: An Interpretation of World Interest Rates*, Oxford: Clarendon Press, 1996, p. 34. The opposite finding, known since the times of Tooke and Marx, rediscovered by Gibson, and remarked upon by Keynes, is that interest rates mostly track the price level rather than its rate of change. This observation has proved so disconcerting to the orthodoxy that it is now embalmed under the heading of 'Gibson's Paradox'. J. Huston McCulloch, *Money & Inflation: A Monetarist Approach*, New York: Academic Press, 1982, pp. 47-49.

15 In order to assess the extent to which the remarkable movements in the interest rate were policy driven, it would be necessary to develop an adequate theory of the competitive determinants of this variable. Such a theory is possible, but its presentation is beyond the scope of the present paper. Suffice to say that it would link the interest rate to the price level *and* to the costs of banking. On the price side, it would explain the pattern which dominates the 1947-1981 phase, in which the nominal interest rate rises alongside the price level (as in 'Gibson's Paradox'). It would also allow for explicit policy interventions, such as the so-called 'Volcker Shock' which increased the interest rate from 10.4 per cent in 1979 to 14.03 per cent in 1981. It is worth recalling that Paul Volcker became Chairman of the Federal Reserve Bank of the United States only in August 1979, whereas interest rates had been rising along with the price level for three decades prior to that. On the cost side, such a theory would explain how the interest rate could fall relative to the price level when banking costs were falling, and could even fall absolutely despite a rising price level – as was the case from 1981 onward. Only then could we judge the relative influences

of market forces and policy on the postwar path of the interest rate.

16 Emphasis was added to the Obama quote. All quotes are from the report: 'G20 Summit: An Economic Clash of Civilizations', *The Christian Science Monitor*, 25 June 2010.

17 'Roosevelt and the inflation hawks of the day were determined to pop what they viewed as a stock market bubble and nip inflation in the bud. Balancing the budget was an important step in this regard, but so was Federal Reserve policy, which tightened sharply through higher reserve requirements for banks… During 1937, Roosevelt pressed ahead with fiscal tightening despite the obvious downturn in economic activity. The budget … was virtually balanced in fiscal year 1938… The result was a huge economic setback, with GDP falling and unemployment rising'. Bruce Bartlett, 'Is Obama Repeating the Mistake of 1937?', *Capital Gains and Games Blog*, 25 January 2010, available from http://www.capitalgainsandgames.com.

CAUGHT IN THE WHIRLWIND: WORKING-CLASS FAMILIES FACE THE ECONOMIC CRISIS

JOHANNA BRENNER

The great recession has no doubt punctured American celebration of the unregulated market and generated anger at wealth disparities and shock at the loss of the American dream. Yet three decades of conservative dominance and political drift to the right have taken their toll. With the cooptation/destruction of vehicles for working-class resistance (especially unions, civil rights and community-based organizations), most working-class families are not engaged in collective action but are instead fending for themselves, desperately seeking ways to avoid the brunt of this crisis. Reliance on (and continued possibilities for) individual survival strategies tends to reproduce existing social divisions; these, in turn, undergird the prevailing populist response to the crisis. In this political discourse, where 'Main Street' confronts 'Wall Street', deserving Americans (aka 'working families') are caught between an irresponsible, self-serving elite and a dependent, parasitic (of colour) 'underclass'. There are more and less conservative versions of the 'Wall Street/Main Street' discourse; however, they all share the assumption that self-sufficient family households are both sign and substance of the American ideal. Although the male breadwinner family is no longer the unitary standard for 'good' families, the hard-working family that takes care of its own remains central to the actual survival strategies on which the vast majority of working-class people rely and, therefore, also remains at the centre of hegemonic definitions of citizenship, virtue and the good life.

The ideal of the self-sufficient family is of course a myth obscuring the many private and public subsidies that allow successful families to maintain standards of living, protect their children from harm, and transmit class and race privilege from one generation to the next. This ideal also justifies the continuing dependence of family households on the extensive exploitation of women's labour. Women have kept working-class family households afloat by increasing their participation in waged work in addition to their unpaid labour, freeing both male partners/spouses, corporations, and government from fully supporting the work of social reproduction. Further, although some family households headed by women are able to make it financially, single motherhood is more often a ticket to poverty than to independence.

Yet, insofar as single mothers survive even in impoverished circumstances, they often do so by relying on social networks that include their children's fathers and other kin. Familial connections, in other words, are crucial to the reproduction of people and social class. They are also a narrow form of solidarity that, in ordinary circumstances, reinforces rather than challenges the competitive striving endemic to capitalist economy and society. Family networks are not inevitably or always conservatizing. When embedded in broader communities of resistance, they can be mobilized for collective action expressing expanded boundaries of solidarity. Outside such circumstances, however, because familial networks tend toward socio-economic and racial/ethnic endogamy, working-class survival strategies organized through family networks also tend to reinforce rather than transcend existing social divisions.

In the short run, then, we can expect these divisions to retard the development of radical, anti-capitalist movements in response to what promises to be a long-lived slide, if not a continuing acute crisis, in working-class standards of living and conditions of work. On the other hand, the family survival strategies that have so far allowed a large part of the working class to weather the recent crisis and the decades-long attack on male workers' wages as well as the dismantling of the 'private welfare state' comprised by employer-based pensions and health insurance, will inevitably run into their limits. Like the earth's resources, there is a limit to the carrying capacity of the human body.

Of course, distress does not automatically lead to resistance. But increasing strain on what had been relatively successful survival strategies will surely open some opportunities for the left. In thinking about how to take advantage of these opportunities, the left should carefully consider both the kinds of reforms we support and the language we use to defend and justify those changes. If we intend to use the fight for reforms to prefigure alternatives to capitalism, then we need to develop alternatives to gendered and racialized familistic political discourses, while at the same time acknowledging and respecting the emotionally laden and materially based commitments that give those discourses such power.

PRELUDE TO THE CRISIS

The rise of a new capitalist regime of flexible accumulation, global restructuring of the economy and a one-sided class war extending over the past thirty years have reshaped the living and working conditions of the US working class. One fundamental consequence of capitalist victory in this war has been the precipitous decline in men's wages and their access to secure employment; this decline undermined the material basis of the working-class male breadwinner family household.[1] Married couples maintained their standard of living by sending mothers into the labour force and by taking on enormous amounts of debt, while single parents drifted ever deeper into poverty.

Women keep families afloat

Between 1972 and 2005, the labour force participation rate for men aged 25-54 declined from 95 per cent to 90 per cent. This overall decline was driven primarily by a reduction for men with a high school education or less. Meanwhile, women in the same prime working age group increased their labour force participation from 51 to 75 per cent, the most significant change being the entry of married mothers with young children into wage work.[2] Although there is no doubt that a good portion of this increase reflects the declining employment and earning opportunities of working-class men, even mothers who work out of necessity appreciate their paid working lives and express a preference for reducing their work-family conflicts rather than leaving paid work altogether. More women than ever are doing a double day and the gender division of labour within family households persists. While a majority of mothers juggle paid and unpaid work, professional managerial-class women and working-class women confront this issue with distinctly different resources.

Between 1979 and 2007 the real wages of men aged 25 years and older with less than a college education declined, for some groups precipitously: by 28 per cent for men with less than a high school education, by 16 per cent for high school graduates and by 7 per cent for men with some college education. At the same time, with the exception of women who did not graduate from high school, women's wages *increased.* Most spectacularly, the real earnings of women with a bachelor's degree or higher skyrocketed by 33 per cent. (Real earnings of men with the same education increased, but less – by 18 per cent.)[3] College-educated women reaped the benefits of the feminist movement, breaking into what had been the exclusive male preserve of upper managerial and professional occupations.

A gender wage gap remains within all educational groups, since men started out with earnings substantially higher than those of women. Nonetheless, the gender gap has been narrowing, while the class gap is widening.

In 1979 a woman with at least a bachelor's degree working full time earned *less* than a man with either some college or a high school education (86 per cent of the earnings of men with a high school education and 80 per cent of the earnings of men with some college or an AA degree). By 2007 this pattern had been reversed: men with a high-school education earned 74 per cent of the incomes of college educated women, while men with some college education earned 87 per cent of the earnings of women with at least a college degree.[4]

Such large income gains by professional/managerial men and women inevitably increased income inequality among families. Between 1979 and 2000 household incomes of married-couple families with children grew generally, but exponentially more for those in the top 20 per cent, who saw their income jump by 66 per cent. By comparison, income in the middle quintile rose 24 per cent and in the bottom quintile only 7.4 per cent. With the exception of families in the richest 20 per cent, married mothers' incomes were crucial to this growth in household income, because working-class men's wages were falling or stagnating over the period. Wives' earnings accounted for about half the income growth in the next richest fourth quintile among families, 78 per cent of income growth in the middle quintile, and for *all* of the growth experienced by the worst off bottom two quintiles. In the six years leading up to the crisis, from 2000-2006, when married-couple family incomes were declining or barely growing, wives' earnings made all the difference, reducing the decline in family income which occurred across the bottom three quintiles of all married-couple families with children (and allowing for small increases in real family incomes in the top two).[5]

Indeed, the impact of the capitalist class assault on men's wages (that is, on the wages of the better paid sections of the working class) can be charted also by the increasing importance of wives' earnings to total family income. Throughout the 1970s, the contribution of wives' earnings to family income hovered around 26 per cent, but began to climb after 1980, increasing from that point to 31 per cent in 1991. Remaining fairly steady during the growth years of the 1990s, when the decline in men's wages levelled off, wives' share of family income began to rise again after 1999, reaching 36 per cent in 2007 – an historic high.

The proportion of wives in dual-earner families who earned more than their husbands by the time the crisis hit in 2007 was 26 per cent – an increase from 18 per cent in 1987.[6] Although some of these are professional/managerial families benefiting from the sharp rise in college-educated women's earnings, many are families in which husbands are low-paid or sporadically employed. A 2007 study of native born men and women aged 25-34 found that while 18 per cent of married male college graduates had wives whose income was higher than theirs, nearly 25 per cent of men in lower education groups earned less than their wives.[7]

Of course, once we chart the changing family fortunes of *all* prime-age men and women, which include, in addition to married-couple families, families where parents living together are not married, single parents with a cohabiting partner, parents living with a relative or other adult, and solo parents, the picture darkens even further. For all families headed by adults aged 25-54, the last thirty years have seen median family income plummet by 29 per cent in the lowest income families – the bottom 30 per cent of all families – and by 13.2 per cent for families in the middle 50 per cent of the income distribution. Meanwhile, rather than losing ground, median income rose for families in the top 20 per cent.[8]

Borrowing to keep up

In addition to increasing women's hours in paid labour, families also survived through taking on debt. Although media and pundit excoriation of 'profligate and irresponsible' borrowing is widespread, household debt, at least for families, reflected efforts to simply maintain their standard of living when housing and healthcare expenses were climbing and employment increasingly unstable.[9] Between 1972 and 2000, due to both deregulation of the mortgage industry and rising housing prices, monthly mortgage payments of families with children increased 69 per cent. By 2001, among 'middle-income families' who owned homes (those making between $20,000 and $100,000 annually), the proportion defined as 'house poor' (spending more than 35 per cent of their income on housing) had climbed to 13.5 per cent.[10] Over the last twenty years, average family expenditures for health care increased 74 per cent.[11]

As savings rates plummeted, (in 2006, personal savings averaged 0.04 per cent of disposable income – its lowest level since 1934), credit card debt increased – between 1989 and 2005 by 315 per cent in real dollars. A 2005 survey of 'low and middle' income households with credit card debt found that almost one in three had used credit cards in the last year to pay for basic expenses including, rent or mortgage, medical care, groceries, utilities or insurance.[12]

Credit card debt also partially drove the rise in mortgage debt. Homeowners who borrowed on their homes did so to pay off their debts rather than for conspicuous consumption. A 2005 survey of households with credit card debt found that half of these households used home equity loans to pay down credit card debt.[13] For those homeowners targeted by predatory lenders, refinancing was primarily through ultimately disastrous subprime mortgages.[14]

In 2006, 61 per cent of subprime loans went to people who could have qualified for loans with better terms.[15] Women were 32 per cent more likely than men to receive a subprime loan and 41 per cent more likely to receive a high-cost subprime mortgage. The gap between men and women became greater as incomes rose: women earning over twice the area median income were 46 per cent more likely than men with similar incomes to receive subprime mortgages. Women of colour were more likely than white women to be subprime borrowers. This over-representation of women in the subprime mortgage pool exists for all types of mortgages, but is especially true of refinance and home improvement loans, which are more likely to be subprime and predatory mortgages.[16] Foreclosure rates are higher among women of colour than among any other group, partly because they were targeted for subprime mortgages and also because of the racial wealth gap which meant that women of colour were less able to use savings to cover house payments when they ran into financial trouble.[17]

As debt rose, so did the number of personal bankruptcies, increasing 400 per cent between 1980 and 2002.[18] Again, while pundits and politicians cited consumer irresponsibility to justify restrictive changes in the bankruptcy laws, overspending was not leading families into financial ruin. In 2001 'trouble managing money' or 'credit card overspending' accounted for less than 6 per cent of family bankruptcies; nearly ninety per cent of families were driven into bankruptcy by a job loss, a medical problem, a family breakup or some combination of all three.[19]

Who takes care?

Although the last thirty years have seen profound changes in gender relations, timing of marriage and first birth, life expectancy, and household formation, the core answer to this question is still the family household and kin networks. Throughout the life cycle, families and family households provide a private safety net within which kin share unpaid care work, living space and income. The first and most important point here is that care remains largely a private responsibility of the family household and takes significant amounts of time. It is only by pooling their time and incomes that individuals are able to deliver the care that children, injured and ill adults, and elders need. In families where women and men work full time, men do more housework and care giving than in families where women work part time or not at all. Still, across the increasing variety of family arrangements, women's care work provides the bedrock of family survival.

The expansion of mothers' working hours relies on the availability of goods and services that substitute for their unpaid labour in the home. The same forces of capitalist globalization that have shifted the balance of power between capital and labour so sharply in capital's favour have also created the conditions for mothers of young children to work. The '24-7' economy with inexpensive goods and services based on the low-wages of a non-unionized, contingent labour force makes a double day possible. Immigrant women, driven to the US by the destruction of their livelihoods at home, supply the nannies, sitters, childcare centre workers and housecleaners whose very low-paid labour enables professional/managerial women to do career jobs and working-class women to have barely affordable childcare. But if the commodification of household labour allows mothers to work for pay, families still have much work to do.

Just in caring for household members, married couples with children under 18 together put in from almost 7 to almost 9 and one-half hours *every day* on average just in caring for household members.[20] In addition, close to one in five adults are providing unpaid care for a person 50 years of age or older, spending an average of 19 hours per week.[21] Mothers have made room for paid work by cutting back on hours spent in housework and by getting help from male partners. Between 1965 and 2000 married fathers doubled the time they spend in housework (from 4.4 to 9.7 hours a week), while married mothers' time decreased by 44 per cent. [22] Yet women's total unpaid labour time did not decrease commensurately, because some of the time saved on housework was devoted to increased hours caring for children.[23]

Caring for children

Men do more childcare and housework than they used to, but fathers in many dual-earner families still specialize in paid work, while mothers shoulder more responsibilities for care. Among dual-earning married couples with children under eighteen, full-time working fathers worked more hours per day than full-time working mothers (fathers' workdays were 16 per cent longer). Mothers employed full-time performed 52 per cent more housework and childcare than their full-time working husbands. Not surprisingly, fathers had 28 per cent more time for leisure and sports than did mothers. Full-time working mothers work many more hours (in paid and unpaid work combined) than mothers who are employed part time or not employed.[24] In other words, dual-earner strategies rest on an extension of women's total working hours.

Although men and women are moving closer in terms of time spent in unpaid labour, on another dimension they remain far apart: women's engagement in paid work is still profoundly shaped by the ages of their children – in stark contrast to men. In 2007, before the recession hit, the labour force participation rate for fathers with children 6–17 was 93.2 per cent and for fathers with children under 6, 95.7 per cent; almost all of these fathers worked full time. On the other hand, the labour force participation rate for mothers of children 6–17 was 77.2 per cent and 63 per cent for mothers with children under 6 and only some three-quarters of these mothers worked full time. Almost half of married mothers with children under 18 either did not work (31 per cent) or worked part time (18 per cent), compared to 9 per cent of married fathers. Mothers with very young children are especially unlikely to work full time. Among married mothers with children 3 years old or younger in 2007 the majority either did not work (43 per cent) or worked part time (17 per cent). This was also true for single mothers with very young children – 36 per cent did not work at all and 16 per cent worked part time. However, more single mothers work full time than married mothers and, in addition, their unemployment rate was quite high at 8 per cent.[25]

Given that welfare reform has substantially ended ongoing income support for single mothers, their relatively low levels of labour force participation are surprising. Part of the explanation may be that at least some of these mothers are not reporting income earned under the table. Additionally, the classification of family households in the labour force participation data obscures some of the shared income support arrangements of non-traditional family households. The labour force participation and employment information provided by the US Bureau of Labor Statistics only compares married parents to parents of 'all other marital statuses'. However, included in this latter group are unmarried mothers living with their child's father, mothers living with another adult (most commonly a relative), and mothers living with a cohabiting partner. In other words, some of these mothers, like married mothers who are not employed or employed part-time, may be exchanging unpaid carework for income support. In 2007, 6 per cent of households with children under 18 were maintained by two unmarried parents and over one-third (35 per cent) of mothers not living with their child's father lived with another adult.[26]

Kin networks have always been important sources of support for working mothers and they remain so today. One-third of working-class families rely on relatives for childcare. Nearly 20 per cent of working mothers with young children use the children's grandparents for childcare. Single mothers are much more likely to rely on grandparents than married mothers. But one study found that almost a quarter of professional/managerial families rely on relatives for childcare.[27] On the other hand, professional/managerial families were three times more likely than other families to hire sitters/nannies, in part because of the longer work hours their jobs require. They also use centre care more frequently and rely on spouses/partners less frequently than working-class families. Working-class families that use centre care spend a much higher proportion of their total incomes on childcare than do professional/managerial families.[28]

Caring for adults

In 2009, an estimated 61.8 million people provided unpaid care to an adult relative – on average for more than 20 hours a week. About 43.5 million people (19 per cent of all adults) care for a family member or friend who is age 50 or older; two-thirds of these caregivers are women. [29] Although most families will care for adult members at some point, professional/managerial families bring many more resources to this task. Low-income families are more than twice as likely as higher-income families to provide more than 30 hours of unpaid assistance a week to parents or parents-in-law and fully 20 per cent of poor families do so. The burden of caring for ill and disabled people is higher in working-class families because they tend to have more serious health problems.[30] About three-quarters of caregivers to adults also have worked for pay while providing care. Difficulties at work are common for these caregivers, and especially so for working-class caregivers who have less control over their work activities and schedules than do those in professional/managerial occupations. Nor can they afford to buy their way out of work/caring conflicts as professional/managerial families do.[31]

Among adults aged 25, the proportions living with parents between 1970 and 2000 increased 48 per cent for white men, 66 per cent for Black men, 72 per cent for white women, and 73 per cent for Black women. By 2007, 20 per cent of men and 16 per cent of women aged 25-29 lived with parents.[32] The increase in young adults living with parents was most dramatic in the 1980s – when economic restructuring eliminated many living-wage blue-collar jobs. The proportion of adults aged 25-34 living with their parents increased 32 per cent between 1980 and 1990.[33] The share of married couples aged 25 living with parents also rose sharply between 1970 and 2000. As college-educated men and women are least likely to marry in their mid-twenties, married couples in this group are much more likely to be low-wage earners unable to establish independent residence, especially if they have children.

Black men and women were more likely than white men and women to live with parents; and Black men were far more likely to live with parents than any other group, reflecting their exclusion from secure employment and living wage jobs.[34]

The capitalist accumulation strategies that came to define the US economy over the last 30 years have increased class inequalities among young adults. Contrary to popular perception, college education has not become more widespread over the past three decades. In 2007 only 25 per cent of young adults aged 25 to 34 had a bachelor's degree and only 5 per cent had graduate degrees.[35] Meanwhile, the life chances of children not born into professional/managerial families have shifted dramatically. As already noted, men without a college degree have lost ground in wages and employment since 1980; and although the real wages of the women they are likely to marry or partner have risen somewhat, they remain far below the levels that these less educated men used to earn. In the professional/managerial class, postponement of marriage and childbearing in favour of education and savings supports occupational success; for the working class, postponement represents the challenges of establishing an independent household on working-class wages. These differences are also, of course, aggravated by institutionalized racism.

Financial support from parents to adult children has generally increased over the past twenty years and is significant even beyond the substantial investments many parents make in their children's education.[36] One study found that at age 29-30, 13 per cent of respondents received at least some economic support (covering living expenses) from a parent. Another estimated the amounts received on average to be about $1,600.[37] Here again, income inequality among families has powerful effects. A survey of parents aged 41-50 with at least one child aged eighteen or older found that almost one-half of parents earning $75,000 or more were providing primary support for a child, compared to one-quarter of those earning less than $50,000.[38]

FAMILIES IN THE CRISIS

The crisis has accelerated all the trends described above and revealed the fragility as well as the importance of these family survival strategies. Women's wages are even more crucial sources of household income, young adults are turning to parents for financial support and housing, intergenerational families are growing, marriage and fertility rates are declining.[39] Existing divisions within the working class are widening as some families manage to hold on, while others – solo mothers, low-wage couples, the long-term unemployed – plunge even further into financial disaster. And for many families, the strategies that worked in the past are reaching their limits – there are simply not enough hours in the day, nor enough jobs, nor people available to help care.

Shelter from the storm

Where women's earnings once kept families afloat, now they are cushioning families with unemployed men from total disaster. Women's unemployment rates are lower than men's because the hardest hit sectors of the economy, construction and manufacturing, employ many more men than women.[40] Although women have lost jobs, their unemployment rate in 2009 was 8.1 per cent, compared to 10.3 per cent for men.[41] Between 2007 and 2009 the proportion of families with an unemployed member almost doubled (from 6.3 per cent to 12 per cent, the highest level since this data began being collected in 1994). In two-thirds of married-couple families with an unemployed husband, the wife remained at work.[42]

The proportion of married-couple families with children in which the mother was the only job holder rose dramatically – from 4.9 per cent of all such families in 2007 to 7.4 per cent in 2009.[43] In response to fathers' unemployment or wage reductions, more mothers have been seeking employment, although not necessarily getting it. Whether women's expanded hours in paid work will extend their total working day depends on their household resources. There is some evidence from previous recessions that unemployed married fathers increase their involvement in housework and childcare and decrease it when they return to work.[44] Mothers not living in a married couple household are faring very badly in the crisis; between 2007 and 2009 their unemployment rates skyrocketed from 8 per cent to 13.6 per cent.[45]

When the crisis hit, many adult children turned to parents for help. A survey of unemployed adults found that 50 per cent had borrowed money from friends or relatives, predominantly from parents.[46] Even college educated young adults have needed extensive support from their parents, about 40 per cent of whom have drawn money out of savings to help their children, with one in six parents taking out a loan.[47] A survey of low- and middle-income families in 2008 found that credit card debt among people over 65 was 26 per cent higher than it had been in 2005.[48]

The recession caused a significant spike in the proportion of young adults living with parents. In just twelve months between 2007 and 2008, the number of Americans living in a multi-generational family household increased by 2.6 million. The proportion of adults aged 25-34 living in multigenerational households grew 6 per cent.[49] In 2009, 13 per cent of parents reported that an adult child had moved in with them. Although these were most likely to be young adults whose unemployment rates have increased dramatically, older adults have also been forced to go back home. Eleven per cent of those aged 25-34 said they had moved in with their parents because of the recession.[50] The proportion of people of this age living in the home of a parent was 10 per cent higher in 2009 than in 2007. What is more, fully 11 per cent of people in what is considered the prime working years, aged 35 to 44, had moved in with parents or in-laws.[51]

Uneven impacts, uneven resources

The effects of the crisis on families are widespread – a December 2009 survey found that 44 per cent of families had experienced the job loss of one or more members, a reduction in hours, or a cut in pay over the past year.[52] But they are also very uneven. Some families are managing much better than others and these differences map along familiar lines – single parent households, workers who are not part of the professional/managerial class, families of colour, are much more likely to experience unemployment, to be ineligible for unemployment benefits, to have given up looking for work, to have lost health coverage, to be in foreclosure, to be renters pushed out of their homes by foreclosure. In 2009, the unemployment rate for college educated Black workers was double the rate for whites. Before the crisis hit, between 2000 and 2007, Black employment *decreased* by 2.4 per cent and incomes declined by 2.9 per cent. One third of Black children lived in poverty. Those years were already a recession for Black communities; today, what the crisis has wrought for them can only be described as the Great Black Depression.[53]

Resources to deal with the crisis are also unevenly distributed. For example, although one in four homeowners owe more than their properties are worth, most US homeowners still have some equity and nearly 24 million owner-occupied homes don't have any mortgage.[54] College-educated people caring for disabled, ill, or elderly adults have more paid help and are much less likely to be the person providing most of the care. In contrast, many working-class families have had to increase the amount of unpaid labour they provide to ill, disabled or elderly family members. The use of paid aides, housekeepers, or other services to care for adults declined from 41 per cent in 2004 to 35 per cent in 2009.[55] Households which were able to afford paid help in 2004 were less able to do so in 2009.[56] Access to the public safety net is uneven as well. Only 30 per cent of unemployed contingent workers (low-wage, part-time and temporary workers who are more likely to be women and men of colour) receive unemployment benefits compared to 55 per cent of unemployed non-contingent workers.[57]

The uneven impact of the crisis on families and the skewed distribution of resources (savings, home equity, adequate pensions, income) among families, have political effects. For now, among many sectors of the working class, it is possible for family networks to offer significant shelter from the storm. Yet, the crisis, unlikely to end quickly or with a new burst of economic growth, will ratchet up the pressures on families, as savings are depleted, as joblessness extends month after month, as mothers seek to re-enter paid work or extend their hours, and as women's employment comes under new attack – a consequence of the fiscal crisis in state and local government, paired with the conservative drumbeat demanding deficit reduction at the federal level. Without serious infusions of cash from the federal government, state and local spending is slated for slashing cuts.

While some of the cuts will be taken through reduction in public workers' pay (direct cuts and unpaid furloughs), decreasing employment in the public sector is quite likely. Since women workers are over-represented in the public sector, these shifts will increase their unemployment rate, removing some of the cushion that women's employment has provided to families thus far in the crisis. Public sector cuts will also worsen the conditions under which families provide unpaid care work. Shorter school days or school years, cuts in public transportation, cuts in spending on home care, reduction in subsidized childcare, all increase unpaid labour time that the household must deliver. Single mothers are more likely to rely on all these services, but women in two-parent families will also be forced to spend more hours on care work.

Developing a politics of care

Misery of course does not create resistance. But as current family survival strategies run up against their limits, openings for organizing will appear. Meanwhile, the accelerating drumbeat of opposition to public sector workers is forcing their unions into a last-ditch battle. If the unions are ready to embrace strategies for building community-labour alliances that offer more than lip-service, it might be possible to overcome the growing hostility directed at public sector workers and build an effective movement around the politics of care. This politics of care will challenge the devaluation of carework and careworkers as well as create links between those who use care services and the workers who provide them.

We are not likely to make gains very quickly; but in fashioning our strategies, the basis can be laid for a new politics of care that challenges capitalism's animating principles and embodies a vision of social solidarity and participatory democracy.

Three themes might be useful in making the case for reforms in a way that promotes a broader anti-capitalist politics:

From private to public: In defending and even demanding the expansion of public services, we want to emphasize the inequality and insecurity that pervades marketized provision of care. For example, the fight for single-payer health insurance highlights the injustice of relying on family resources to access health care.

From hierarchy to democracy: One of the most effective neoliberal political discourses is the demand that government be made more accountable by contracting out government services to private and non-profit organizations that are supposedly more flexible and responsive to those who depend on their services. We can effectively counter this neoliberal agenda by building on the experiments in democratizing government that have been won through popular and trade union struggles; these creative initiatives offer alternatives to bureaucracy far more compelling than phony involvement and superficial accountability.[58]

From exclusion to inclusion: The campaigns for immigrant rights and the rights of lesbian, gay, bisexual and transgendered (LGBT) people have posed, in different ways, the question of social citizenship – who belongs to the 'we' that cares for and about each other. Rather than emphasizing, as these campaigns often do, that immigrants and LGBT families are 'hard-working' – 'like us' – and, therefore, deserving, we could demystify the self-sufficient family ideal, expose the important, but now too limited, ways that we collectively support each other, and demand that these helping hands be extended to all.

Might we say from each according to ability and to each according to need?

NOTES

I would like to thank Mary C. King for sharing her work with me and Barbara Laslett and the editors of *Socialist Register* for their very helpful editorial comments.

1 In 2008, 20.7 per cent of all families with children were male breadwinner families, compared to 44.7 per cent in 1975. Heather Boushey, 'The New Breadwinners', in Heather Boushey and Ann O'Leary, eds., *A Woman's Nation Changes Everything,* Washington: Center for American Progress, 2009, p. 35.

2 Explanations for the decline for working-class men include a decrease in available jobs, declining wages, expansion of the federal disability program (between 1980 and 2004 the number of beneficiaries rose from 2.9 to 5.2 million), and

the negative impact of rising incarceration rates on the employability of men, especially men of colour. Abraham Mosisa and Steven Hipple, 'Trends in Labor Force Participation in the United States', *Monthly Labor Review,* 129(1), 2006, pp. 49-51. Richard A. Settersten Jr. and Barbara Ray, 'What's Going on with Young People Today? The Long and Twisting Path to Adulthood', *The Future of Children*, 20(1), 2010, p. 18. In 1975, 39.6 per cent of mothers with children under 6 worked for pay, by 2008 64.3 per cent did. Boushey, 'New Breadwinners', p. 35.

3 US Bureau of Labor Statistics, *Highlights of Women's Earnings in 2007*, Washington: US Department of Labor, October 2008, Chart 3, p. 5.

4 Ibid., Table 17, p. 72.

5 Lawrence Mishel, Jared Bernstein, and Heidi Shierholz, eds., *State of Working America 2008/2009,* Ithaca: Cornell University Press, 2009, Table 1.22.

6 In families where wives have earnings, but husbands may not, wives were much more likely to earn more than their husbands. Wives in one-third of these families did so compared to 26 per cent in families in which both wives and husbands have earnings. US Bureau of Labor Statistics, *Women in the Labor Force: A Databook*, Washington: US Department of Labor, 2009, Tables 24 & 25.

7 Richard Fry and D'Vera Cohn, *Women, Men and the New Economics of Marriage,* Washington: Pew Research Center, 2010, pp. 15-16. The proportion of wives making as much or more than their husbands doubled between 1967 and 2008. However, increases were much greater for women with less than a college degree than for those with a college education. In 1967 30 per cent of college educated wives made as much or more than their husbands; in 2008 41 per cent did so – an increase of around 33 per cent. In contrast, the proportion of wives earning as much or more than their husbands grew 152 per cent for wives with a high school education and 88 per cent for those with some college. Boushey, 'New Breadwinners', p. 38.

8 Heather Boushey and Joan C. Williams, *The Three Faces of Work-Family Conflict,* Washington and San Francisco: Center for American Progress and Center for WorkLife Law, 2010, p. 6.

9 The incidence of job loss was 28 per cent higher in the 1980s than in the 1970s. Johanne Boisjoly, Greg J. Duncan, and Timothy Smeeding, 'The Shifting Incidence of Involuntary Job Losses from 1968 to 1992', *Industrial Relations*, 37, April 1998, Figure 4, p. 217.

10 Elizabeth Warren and Amelia Warren Tyagi, *The Two Income Trap: Why Middle Class Parents are Going Broke,* New York: Basic Books, 2003, p. 230n33

11 Jose A. Garcia, *Borrowing to Make Ends Meet: The Rapid Growth of Credit Card Debt in America,* New York: Demos - A Network for Ideas and Action, 2007, p. 2.

12 Garcia, *Borrowing to Make Ends Meet,* pp. 1-3; Cindy Zeldin and Mark Rukavina, *Borrowing to Stay Healthy: How Credit Card Debt is Related to Medical Expenses,* New York: Demos - A Network for Ideas and Action, 2007, p. 2.

13 Garcia, *Borrowing to Make Ends Meet,* p. 3.

14 Most subprime loans were not made to home buyers but to home owners.

Nicolas P. Retsinas and Eric S. Belsky, eds., *Building Assets Building Credit: Creating Wealth in Low-Income Communities*, Washington: Brookings Institution, 2005, p. 210.

15 Rick Brooks and Ruth Simon, 'Subprime Debacle Traps Even Very Credit-Worthy As Housing Boomed, Industry Pushed Loans To a Broader Market', *Wall Street Journal*, 3 December 2007.

16 Allen J. Fishbein and Patrick Woodall, 'Women are Prime Targets for Subprime Lending', Consumer Federation of America, Washington, December, 2006.

17 For example, median wealth for single black and Latina women is $100 and $120 respectively, while their same-race male counterparts have $7,900 and $9,730. The median wealth of single white women is $41,500. Insight Center for Community Economic Development, *Lifting as We Climb: Women of Colour, Wealth, and America's Future,* Spring 2010, p. 5, available at http://www.insightcced.org.

18 From $291,000 in 1980 to $1.5 million 2002. Warren and Tyagi, *Two Parent Trap*, p. 215.

19 Ibid., p. 132. This contrasts with all households filing for bankruptcy, where credit card overspending or trouble managing money was cited in 55 per cent of the cases (p. 230n28).

20 The range here reflects differences between families where mothers work part-time or not at all (more likely to have young children and therefore a higher total demand for hours of care) and those where they work full time. Calculated from Bureau of Labor Statistics, 'Married Parents' Use of Time, 2003-06', News Release, Bureau of Labor Statistics, Washington, 8 May 2008, Table 2.

21 National Alliance of Caregiving, *Caregiving In The U.S.: A Focused Look at Those Caring for Someone Age 50 or Older*, November 2009, pp. 11, 13, available at http://www.caregiving.org.

22 Suzanne M. Bianchi, John P. Robinson and Melissa A. Milkie, *Changing Rhythms of American Family Life*, New York: Russell Sage, 2006, pp. 91-94. Possible reasons for this decrease are smaller family size, lower standards of cleanliness, and increased marketization (employment of housecleaners and other services, availability of prepared foods, inexpensive fast food as an alternative to meals at home, etc.).

23 Ibid., ch. 4. This trend has occurred in both working-class and professional/managerial families, although the increase among college-educated parents was twice that for other parents. The upward trend was most marked from the mid-1990s and is apparently accounted for by increases in time spent with children six years and older. Reasons for this trend remain debated. See pp. 87-8 and Garey Ramey and Valerie A. Ramey, 'The Rug Rat Race', Brookings Papers on Economic Activity, Spring 2010, available from http://www.brookings.edu.

24 Calculated from Bureau of Labor Statistics, 'Married Parents' Use of Time', Table 2. Fathers with wives employed part time or not at all do more hours of paid work than do fathers whose wives work full time. Averages of course hide subgroups of dual-earner/dual-carer couples – for example, 'tag teaming'

parents who work different shifts so one parent can be at home with children. Fathers in service occupations (higher paid such as protective services and lower paid such as janitorial work) are twice as likely to tag team as professional/managerial fathers.

25 Calculated from Bureau of Labor Statistics, 'Employment Characteristics of Families 2007', News Release, Bureau of Labor Statistics, Washington, 30 May 2008, Table 5.

26 Almost all fathers living with their own children were living with the child's mother (94 per cent) or with another adult. Only 3.4 per cent of fathers living with their children were actually solo parenting compared to 17 per cent of mothers. Rose M. Kreider and Diana B. Elliott, *America's Families and Living Arrangements: 2007*, US Census Current Population Reports, P20-561, Washington: US Department of Commerce, September 2009, pp. 6 and 12.

27 Boushey and Williams, *Three Faces*, p. 18.

28 Ibid., p. 9.

29 National Alliance of Caregiving, *Caregiving In The U.S.: Executive Summary*, pp. 4-7, available at http://www.caregiving.org.

30 Boushey and Williams, *Three Faces*, pp. 11-12.

31 National Alliance of Caregiving, *Executive Summary*, p. 17.

32 Settersten Jr. and Ray, 'What's Going on with Young People', p. 25.

33 In 1980, 8.7 per cent of adults 25-34 lived with parents; by 1990, 11.5 per cent did so. US Bureau of the Census, *Family Arrangements Historical Time Series*, Table AD-1 Young Adults Living at Home: 1960 to Present.

34 Settersten Jr. and Ray, 'What's Going on with Young People', pp. 25 and 27.

35 Ibid., p. 27.

36 A 2005 survey found that 37 per cent of adults ages 60 and older whose grown children were financially independent (i.e., not receiving their primary financial support from their parents) reported giving money to one such child in the past year. Paul Taylor, Cary Funk and Courtney Kennedy, *From the Age of Aquarius To the Age of Responsibility Baby Boomers Approach Age 60*, Washington: Pew Research Center, 2005, p. 10.

37 Settersten Jr. and Ray, 'What's Going on with Young People', p. 40n47. See also, Karen Fingerman, 'Giving to the Good and the Needy: Parental Support of Grown Children', *Journal of Marriage and Family*, 71(5), p. 1220.

38 Paul Taylor et al, *From the Age of Aquarius*, p. 17.

39 Gretchen Livingston and D'Vera Cohn, *US Birth Rate Decline Linked to Recession*, Wassington: Pew Research Center, 2010; Alex Roberts, *Marriage and the Great Recession*, available at stateofourunions.org.

40 Between 2007 and 2009, employment dropped 23.3 per cent in construction, 16 per cent in manufacturing, 7.6 per cent in trade transportation and utilities, and 7.8 per cent in professional and business services, while increasing or staying steady in education and health services which employed 1/3 of all women in 2007 but less than 10 per cent of all men. Rebecca M. Blank, 'The Impact of the Recession on Women', presentation sponsored by Women's Policy, Inc, 21 January 2010, available at http://www.womenspolicy.org.

41 Black and Latino women are more likely to be unemployed (13.4 and 11.3 per cent respectively) than white or Asian women (7.2 and 7.7 respectively) – and this is also true among men. Heidi Hartmann, Ashley English, and Jeffrey Hayes, *Women and Men's Employment and Unemployment in the Great Recession*, Washington: Institute for Women's Policy Research, 2010, pp. 28-9.

42 Black and Latino families were more likely to have an unemployed member (17.4 per cent and 16.9 per cent) than were white and Asian families (11 per cent). Bureau of Labor Statistics, 'Employment Characteristics of Families 2009', News Release, Bureau of Labor Statistics, Washington, 27 May 2010, p. 1.

43 *Understanding the Economy: Working Mothers In The Great Recession*, Washington: US Congress Joint Economic Committee, May 2010, p. 3.

44 Lynne M. Casper, *My Daddy Takes Care of Me! Fathers as Care Providers*, US Census Bureau, Current Population Reports, P70-59, Washington: US Department of Commerce, September 1997, pp. 3-5.

45 The unemployment rate for single mothers with children under six was even higher – 17.5 per cent in 2009. *Understanding the Economy*, p. 4. At least one third of these mothers were cohabiting with their child's father or living with a relative. Given that these mothers are more likely to be low-earning and younger, the chance that other adults in the household are also unemployed is comparatively high.

46 Michael Luo, 'Jobless Turn To Family For Help', *New York Times*, 30 January 2010.

47 Joyce Wadler, 'Caught in the Safety Net', *New York Times*, 14 May, 2009

48 Jose Garcia and Tamara Draut, *The Plastic Safety Net: How Families are Coping in a Fragile Economy*, New York: Demos-A Network for Ideas and Action, 2007, p. 4.

49 Paul Taylor, Jeffrey Passel and Richard Fry, *The Return of the Multi-Generational Family Household*, Washington: Pew Research Center, 2010, p. 1 and Table 1, p. 22.

50 Paul Taylor, Richard Fry and Wendy Wang, *Home for the Holidays…and Every Other Day*, Washington: Pew Research Center, 2010, pp. 2-3.

51 US Bureau of the Census, *Family Arrangements Historical Time Series*, Table AD-1 Young Adults Living at Home: 1960 to Present; Wadler, 'Caught in the Safety Net'.

52 Valerie Adrian and Stephanie Coontz, 'The Long-Range Impact of the Recession on Families', A Report Prepared for the 13th Annual Conference of the Council on Contemporary Families, Augustana College, Rock Island, 16-17 April 2010.

53 Deepak Bhargava et al., *Battered by the Storm: How the Safety Net is Failing Americans and How to Fix It*, Washington: Institute for Policy Studies, Center for Community Change, Jobs with Justice, and Legal Momentum, December 2009.

54 Ruth Simon and James R. Hagerty, 'One in Four Borrowers is Underwater', *Wall Street Journal*, 24 November 2009.

55 National Alliance of Caregiving, *Executive Summary*, p. 12.

56 In 2009 almost 2/3 of users of paid services had $50,000 or more in household income, compared to less than half in 2004. Ibid., p. 13.

57 US Government Accountability Office, *Unemployment Insurance: Low-Wage and Part-Time Workers Continue to Experience Low Rates of Receipt,* Report to the Chairman, Subcommittee on Income Security and Family Support, Committee on Ways and Means, House of Representatives, September 2007.

58 Hilary Wainwright, *Reclaim the State: Experiments in Popular Democracy*, Revised Edition, London: Seagull Books, 2009; Johanna Brenner, 'Democratizing Care', in Janet C. Gornick and Marcia K. Meyers, *Gender Equality: Transforming Family Divisions of Labor*, London: Verso, 2009.

BEFORE AND AFTER CRISIS: WALL STREET LIVES ON

DOUG HENWOOD

My assignment for this volume was to write about Wall Street before and after The Crisis. My first thought was, that's easy. Before The Crisis, Wall Street was the most powerful economic, political, and social force in the US. After The Crisis, Wall Street is the most powerful economic, political, and social force in the US. Ok, next essay.

Actually I must confess to being a little surprised at this outcome. I've never been one to believe – and I do mean believe, in the sense that it's often a faith for which supportive arguments are mobilized after the fact rather than a logical conclusion following an evaluation of the evidence – in the fragility of the capitalist order or the tenuousness of US imperial power. The left is full of crisis mongers who've seen one coming every day for the last thirty years. But I did think that Wall Street was, to turn its own jargon back on itself, in for a bit of a haircut after the financial crisis and the ensuing recession. I'd assumed that its power, prestige, income, and freedom to manoeuvre would be scaled back, if not to the levels of the early 1950s, at least to something less than the lordly dominance it's enjoyed since the bull market in stocks took off on the afternoon of August 12, 1982.

But that seems not to have happened. Wall Street has used the crisis, if not to enhance its power at least to demonstrate it. Also striking, though a bit off-topic, was the inability of all the death-agony Marxists who'd been waiting for something like this since 1929 to make any political hay with it.

There are several dimensions to Wall Street's rise to pre-eminence over the last few decades. One can simply be measured in money. For example, in almost every year since the US national income accounts begin in 1929, securities and commodities brokers have been the highest-paid of the almost 90 industries reported by the Bureau of Economic Analysis.[1] The only exceptions were in the late 1940s and early 1950s, when they were beaten by their industrial cousins in holding companies and investment offices. But the securities industry's premium has grown enormously over time. From 1929 through 1939, it was 237 per cent of average pay. It fell during the Second World War and the immediate postwar decades, at just under 180 per cent of average pay. But with the takeoff of the bull market in 1982, the premium began to swell, crossing 300 per cent in 1992 and 400 per cent in 2006. It fell back some in 2008, to a mere 409 per cent. It fell further in 2009, to 366 per cent, which may look like a substantial decline, but is still higher than any year before 2004. These numbers refer to the royalty of the financial sector, of course, but the story for the sector as a whole is very similar, if less dramatic.

Or take profits. As the bull market was about to take off in 1982, the financial sector claimed 12 per cent of pretax profits in 1982; that nearly tripled to 34 per cent at the 2008 peak. It fell by more than half in the heat of the crisis, to 15 per cent at the end of 2008 – but as of the beginning of 2010, it was back up to 34 per cent.

Or take the proliferation of assets. Financial assets of all kinds – not just debt, but equities and everything else the Federal Reserve counts in its flow of funds accounts – were equal to 462 per cent of GDP in 1982. That measure rose steadily for the next 25 years, more than doubling to a peak of 1,058 per cent of GDP in 2007. The ratio came down a bit with the early stages of the financial crisis, but bottomed in the first quarter of 2009 and has risen ever since. It is substantially higher than in 2006, what seems like near the peak moment of the bubble.

So here's the story the numbers tell us: whereas from the 1930s through the 1950s, Wall Street was something of a not very visible back office for capitalism (whose denizens lived well, but not large), since the 1980s especially, they've accumulated an enormous amount of wealth, and with it, more and more power and prestige. I will address below what led to this, but here are some personal anecdotes to support the numbers. Until the 1980s, a few people would migrate from Yale to the financial sector on graduation – I did, actually, but it was a brief, low-paying diversion – but it was hardly a flood. Only one of my undergraduate friends came out of a Wall Street family; they lived well, but not all that differently from everyone else. They had a house in the Hamptons, but it had been passed down through the family. The patriarch who first bought it went bankrupt in the Great Depression and moved out there as a low-cost refuge. Now, there's no data on that house, but the neighbouring property is valued by Zillow.com at $22 million.

As Kingman Brewster, Yale's genteel upper-crust president in the early 1970s put it in my freshman facebook (back when that was a document on paper), the days when people rolled like bowling balls from Wall Street in New Haven to Wall Street in New York were past. 'Enjoy the privilege of doubt', he further counselled us. The year before, in 1970, Brewster, who could count two passengers on the *Mayflower* among his ancestors, had said: 'I am appalled and ashamed that things should have come to such a pass in this country that I am sceptical of the ability of black revolutionaries to achieve a fair trial anywhere in the United States'. It is impossible to imagine the president of Yale saying anything like that today. Nor is it possible to imagine any Yale president cutting back on the number of 'legacies' – undergraduates admitted largely because their parents went to Yale and gave it lots of money – as Brewster did. The US bourgeoisie has changed substantially in the last 40 years.[2]

When Brewster encouraged incoming students to doubt, Yale's endowment was worth less than $500 million.[3] Just fourteen years later, Yalies were indeed rolling like bowling balls from one Wall Street to the other: one-third of Yale's graduating class applied for a job at First Boston[4] – not much doubt there.[5]

SO WHAT EXACTLY DOES WALL STREET DO?

Let's be generous and concede that it does provide some financing for investment. But an enormous apparatus of trading has grown up around it – not merely trading in certificates, but in control over entire corporations. I think it's less fruitful to think of Wall Street as a financial intermediary than it is to think of it as an instrument for the establishment and exercise of class power. It's the means by which an owning class forms itself, particularly the stock market. It allows the bourgeoisie to own pieces of the productive assets of an entire economy. So, while at first glance the tangential relation of Wall Street, especially the stock market, to financing real investment might make the sector seem ripe for tight regulation and heavy taxation, its centrality to the formation of ruling-class power makes it a very difficult target.

On the whole, the financial sector has surprisingly little to do with raising money to finance real corporate investment.[6] It rarely has. That's especially true of the stock market. Even in the boomiest moments of the late 1990s dot.com bubble, IPOs financed only a small fraction of corporate investment – about 5-6 per cent – and initial offerings were far outweighed by stock buybacks. Between 1995 and 2000, corporate stock buybacks were 3.5 times as large as IPOs.

Or, looked at another way, if you combine net equity offerings (which, given the heavy schedule of buybacks over the last quarter century, have been negative most of the time since 1982), takeovers (which involve the distribution of corporate cash to shareholders of the target firm), and traditional dividends into a concept I call transfers to shareholders, you see that corporations have been shovelling cash into Wall Street's pockets at a furious pace. Back in the 1950s and 1960s, nonfinancial corporations distributed about 20 per cent of their internal funds (profits plus depreciation allowances) to shareholders. In the 1970s, that fell to 15 per cent, which helped create the sour mood on Wall Street in that decade. (That's the decade average. It fell below 8 per cent in 1976.) After 1982, though, the shareholders' share rose steadily. It came close to 100 per cent in 1998, fell back to a mere 25 per cent in 2002, and then soared to 126 per cent in 2007. That means that corporations were actually borrowing to fund these transfers to shareholders. This fell during the crisis, bottoming at 21 per cent in mid-2009, but as of the beginning of 2010 it had recovered to 47 per cent.

Businesses do get outside financing, but the most important source of that is old-style banks, with so-called commercial and industrial (C&I) loans. C&I loans began contracting in nominal terms at the end of 2008, and fell an average annual rate of 21 per cent in the first five months of 2010.

For a long while, shareholder ownership was more notional than active. After the 1929 crash, Wall Street sort of receded into the background, giving us the Golden Age of Galbraith's managerial capitalism. But when economic performance faltered in the 1970s, when the Golden Age was replaced by Bronze Age of rising inflation and falling profits, Wall Street, meaning shareholders, finally asserted itself. They unleashed what has been dubbed the shareholder revolution, demanding not only higher profits but a larger share of them. The first means by which they exercised this control was through the takeover and leveraged buyout movements of the 1980s. By loading up companies with debt, they forced managers to cut costs radically and ship larger shares of the corporate surplus to outside investors rather than investing in the business or hiring workers. This cost-cutting mania helped drive the outsourcing movement.

The 1980s debt mania came to a bad end, as highly leveraged companies found themselves unable to cope with the early 1990s recession. So the shareholder revolution recast itself as a movement of activist pension funds, led by the California Public Employees Retirement System (CalPERS). The funds lobbied management, drew up hit lists of badly run companies, and generally pushed the idea that firms should be run for their shareholders. It had some successes. Compensation structures were rejiggered to emphasize stock over direct salaries; the idea was to get managers to think and act like shareholders, since they were materially that under the new regime.

But pension fund activism sort of petered out as the decade wore on.

Managers still ran companies with the stock price in mind, but the limits to shareholder influence have become very clear since the financial crisis began. Managers have been paying themselves enormously while stock prices languished. If the stock price wasn't cooperating, well, options could always be back-dated. The problem was especially acute in the financial sector: Bank of America, for example, bought Merrill Lynch because its former CEO, Ken Lewis, coveted the firm, and if the shareholders had any objections, he could just lie to them about how sick the brokerage firm was. It was as if the shareholder revolution hardly happened, at least in this sense.

THE FINANCIAL REVOLUTIONARY

It is worth a closer look at the financial revolution that began in the 1980s. To concentrate the inquiry, one could do little better than study the intellectual evolution of one of its prime theorists, Harvard Business School professor Michael Jensen.

To set the scene, the financial world of the 1970s was, from an elite point of view, a nightmarish thing. Economic growth was weak, labour productivity was sagging badly, and the stock and bond markets were disaster areas. So was real wage growth, but that's not the kind of thing that bourgeois pundits worry about. They did worry about the fact that stocks, as measured by the S&P 500 index, lost almost 3 per cent of their real value in the 1970s. A portfolio of long-term Treasury bonds lost 32 per cent of their value. Corporate profitability, which was 7.6 per cent in 1969, fell by half to 3.8 per cent in 1980.[7] This was nothing less than a social emergency. Deregulation, by stimulating competition and disciplining workers, would, it was assumed, turn this mess around.

Along with those transformations in the political realm came major transformations in the relationship between stockholders and management, between Wall Street and the Fortune 500. After the crash of 1929, Wall Street was in deep disrepute, and shareholders were mostly passive creatures who quietly collected their dividends and hoped for the best. The post-Second World War boom was kind to them, and rewarded their passivity; managers ran firms with little outside interference. As economic and financial performance deteriorated in the 1970s, Wall Street and the people who are paid to think for the owning class began scheming.

Prominent among the schemers was Michael Jensen, who developed a finance-based theory of corporate governance that would become exceedingly influential in the 1980s. As I put it in my book *Wall Street*: 'Though it took some time to evolve to full ripeness, Jensen's argument is, in a phrase, that stockholders can't trust the managers they've hired to run their corporations, and a radical re-alignment is in order'.[8]

Starting with a 1976 paper co-written with William Meckling, Jensen began what would amount to a fifteen-year rethink of the modern corporate form.[9] In the first paper of the series, Jensen and Meckling wonder why it is that shareholders entrust the companies they own to a bunch of managers they don't know, a slate of people with their own interests and agenda. Managers would prefer a comfortable, well-compensated life without a bunch of shareholders breathing down their neck. It would be much more pleasant to buy a corporate jet than pass the cash along to shareholders. Or it might be ego-gratifying for a CEO and his inner circle to expand aggressively even if the effort isn't likely to be all that profitable. Shareholders, who should come first, often came last. But having identified the problem, Jensen and Meckling really didn't have much of a solution, though they did suggest that managers be required to hold both the stock and the debt of their firms so they weren't tempted to screw either class of outside financial interests.

A few years later, though, Jensen thought he'd found the magic bullet: the leveraged buyout (LBO). Firms, especially older ones in mature industries that generate more cash flow than they can profitably reinvest, should join with an investment boutique like Kohlberg Kravis Roberts (they were the stars of the 1980s – today's counterpart would be a group like Blackstone), borrow gobs of money from institutional investors, and take their public firms private. The large debt load would assure that outside investors got plenty of cash, and assure that managers, facing huge interest bills, wouldn't waste money on perks or bad investments. Managers would be paid mostly in stock options rather than cash, which would inspire them to great feats of creativity and make them think like stockholders and not high-end welfare queens. After an appropriate course of slimming – meaning reduced investment, layoffs, outsourcing, speedup – firms would go public again, lean, mean, and massively efficient. Managers' options would turn wonderfully profitable.

Things didn't work out as planned. Though a few early deals went well, at least for investors, as the 1980s progressed, the deals got more bloated and inappropriate, and the increase in indebtedness drove a lot of firms to the wall with the advent of the early 1990s recession: there just wasn't enough cash to cover the interest bill and keep the doors open.

Despite the institutional evolution from the standard public corporation to the LBO'd firm, Jensen always held shareholder rights to be sacrosanct. Why the shareholder, and not workers, customers, or society, should be the ultimate constituency of the corporation is something Jensen never addressed.

He did, however, direct considerable vitriol at those nonshareholder interests in response to a critique of his work – the enemies of economic progress were 'striking Eastern Air Lines pilots, Pittston Coal miners, [and] New York Telephone employees, who seem perfectly content to destroy or damage their employer's organization while attempting to serve their own interests. Ralph Nader's consumer activist organization is another example'.[10]

A few years later, Jensen came around to celebrating failure, though failure of a certain kind: if firms can't make it, they should go. If they're too big, they should shrink. If they're too weak to go it alone, they should merge.[11] This is in some sense a development of his earlier themes, but with far more emphasis on managing the exit of capital from dying sectors or enterprises than on the revival of sagging ones.

Jensen was rather quiet during the late 1990s, but after the corporate scandals of the early 2000s, like Enron and WorldCom, he began thinking publicly again about the complexities of running large joint-stock companies.[12] While still holding to the centrality of the stock market, he did allow that managers paid in equity had an interest in manipulating the books to get and keep the stock price up. But, on the other hand, responsible managers had a duty to 'just say no' to Wall Street's pressure for quick profits; their real duty should be to maximize a firm's market value over the long term. How, or why, managers should say 'no' to their alleged overseers, isn't clearly revealed.

In the wake of WorldCom and the rest, Jensen also discovered that there were costs to 'overvalued equity'. Managers and boards would do anything, even committing crimes, to maintain an inflated stock price. (Jensen meant accounting crimes, of course. Interestingly, one of the sponsors of his 2004 work was BP, a firm that would later become famous for committing crimes far more serious than cooking the books.) Jensen professed to be mystified as to why short-sellers couldn't cure the problem of overvaluation – surely these profit-seeking sharks could find overvalued firms and sell their stock aggressively in the hope of making money on their collapse. Since the shorts couldn't do it, and managers have no interest in doing it, the task of managing down an inflated stock price falls to the board of directors – who should think about talking openly to the short-selling community to get the job done. Why boards should do this is another undisclosed detail of Jensen's argument – or, for that matter, how a group that meets about one day a month can know what's going on inside the corporation they're supposed to run. Perhaps aware of the tightness of the corner he's painted himself into, Jensen is reduced to an almost prayerful demand: 'We must stop creating and consuming the heroin', the heroin being all the gaming that surrounds an overvalued stock price.

Given Jensen's history, the notion of an overvalued stock price is rather strange: thirty years earlier, he declared the efficient market hypothesis (EMH) the best-established principle in the social sciences. If the EMH were true, sustained overvaluation would be impossible, since wise market players would see through accounting tricks and pummel the inflated shares back to earth. To followers of the EMH, the stock market was the best real-time grading system for corporate performance that could be imagined. Add that to the faith in the paramount position of the stockholder in the economic hierarchy and you have a perfect theoretical rationale for the financialized capitalism that has evolved over the last three decades. Of course, the slump of the early 1990s was proof that Jensen's prescription of heavy debt loads was a potentially fatal one, and the slump of the early 2000s was proof that loading up managers with stock also had its problems. And the bust of the late 2000s is proof that the whole strategy of financialization hasn't worked out as planned.

I recently emailed Jensen for his thoughts on recent financial history, since he's published nothing since 2006. The response of one of the prime intellectual architects of financial and corporate policy over the last few decades had nothing to say: 'I have not been working directly on the financial crisis since I have been devoting my time to leadership, integrity and a value-free approach to values. My time is totally committed to these matters and I do not have the time or interest in discussing the crisis'.

A value-free approach to values, which presumably means more than shareholder value. Being hegemonic means never having to say you're sorry.

RESTRUCTURING US CAPITALISM

Of course, to review this history isn't to suggest that Jensen was personally responsible for the course of the last three decades; not even an esteemed professor at the Harvard Business School is that powerful. There were many other personalities and impersonal forces that shaped it. But it should serve to remind us that the crash of 2008 had a long pedigree.

And Jensen was dealing throughout, if not productively, with some real problems. Who should own and run a capitalist enterprise and how? What is the role of non-owners, if any? How do all the various actors keep each other in check in a system that reveres and unleashes self-interest? What to do with companies, sectors, and regions that have fallen on hard times?

Rather than being purely parasitical – which it often is – Wall Street was also at the centre of the restructuring of US capitalism since the early 1980s.

You could even date the origin of Wall Street's top-down revolution to the New York City fiscal crisis of 1975, when a cadre of bankers essentially took over city government and began the long campaign of austerity for the poor and subsidized gentrification that has characterized urban policy ever since. All the financial machinations theorized by Jensen helped lubricate the aggressive restructuring of US industry and labour relations since the early 1980s – decreased job security, disappearing benefits, outsourcing, the whole familiar package. These transformations do a lot to explain the 90 per cent rise in productivity between 1982 and 2010, nearly three times the increase in real compensation, 34 per cent. No wonder profitability rose so dramatically.

Of course, a system based on high levels of mass consumption – both to sustain aggregate demand and perform political legitimation – had to do something to compensate for the squeeze on mass purchasing power that delivered the increase in profitability and the rise in elite incomes. (A measure of the latter: average real incomes of the bottom 90 per cent rose 13 per cent between 1982 and 2007 – that's a cumulative total, not an annual average – compared with 407 per cent for the richest 0.01 per cent.[13])

Wall Street was very helpful in squaring that circle by providing truly heroic doses of credit to US households. With so much money accumulating at the top in need of profitable outlet, and so much need accumulating below, the financial sector was there to mediate. Between the first quarter of 1983 and the peak in the second of 2008, residential mortgage debt increased by $9.6 trillion, and consumer credit by another $2.2 trillion. That brought total household debt from 65 per cent of after-tax income to 134 per cent. Debt, measured both in nominal dollars and relative to income, fell in the two years after the bubble burst, but remains extraordinarily high. Right now, it doesn't look like the debt creation machinery can be fired up to anything like its former pace – but how will the circle remain squared? The only option for capital might be a massive austerity plan for the working class – wage cuts, tighter credit, and lower levels of consumption – but will that be economically or politically sustainable? Few people in US public life are asking this question.

Certainly not anyone on Wall Street, where it looks like the good old days are back (for Wall Street, that is), with profits surging and bonus packets bursting at the seams. How have they done that? Not by financing an economic recovery, that's for sure. Commercial and industrial lending, as was pointed out earlier, has been contracting hard. Overall, borrowing and lending have contracted markedly. The swing in credit flows is truly remarkable. At the peak of the bubble in the third quarter of 2007, there was

$5.4 trillion in new borrowing and lending throughout the US economy. In the last quarter of 2009, that had contracted to -$841 billion (the negative number meaning that more old debt was paid off or written off than new loans were extended).[14] But almost all the borrowing was by the US government, and almost all new lending by the Federal Reserve. Outside those two public entities, new borrowing and lending was close to -$2 trillion (again, meaning more old debt disappeared than new debt was created).

The residential mortgage sector is entirely a ward of the state now; almost all new mortgage lending as of early 2010, what little there was, was underwritten by Washington. So with so little normal financial activity going on, how is Wall Street making money? In part by underwriting its own rescue – many big banks have been floating stock and bond issues to rebuild their capital base, and the investment banks have been taking their usual cut. And they've been trading for their own accounts and that of their customers. Not all that long ago it seemed like the hedge fund industry, if not exactly a goner, was going to be on a radical weight reduction regime. No longer. Though some funds blew up, the survivors look to be doing quite well for themselves.

Wall Street demonstrated its immense political power during this crisis. In July 2010, after enormous amounts of dickering, Congress passed and the president signed a bill, now nicknamed Dodd-Frank, creating a new regulatory architecture.[15] While Dodd-Frank will change the way Wall Street does business to some extent, bankers headed off the biggest threats, and security analysts estimate that the hit to profits will be less than 10 per cent. Banks will be required to boost their capital – though this is part of an international effort through the Basel Committee, coordinated through the Bank for International Settlements. Banks will be forced to stop trading on their own account (the so-called Volcker Rule, named after former Federal Reserve chair Paul Volcker), and will also be required to spin off part of their derivatives business into separately capitalized subsidiaries. But regulators will have to devise specific rules based on the legislation, an activity in which bank lobbyists will no doubt figure prominently. And the rules won't go into full effect for four to five years. The hodge-podge of regulators – the Fed, the Securities and Exchange Commission, the Commodity Futures Trading Commission, the Comptroller of the Currency, just to name a few – will be left largely intact, though they will be encouraged to consult more closely. That is less than Bush's Treasury Secretary Henry Paulson wanted to do: in a Treasury paper issued late in his term, Paulson proposed creating a single overarching regulatory authority. Insurance will still be regulated at the state, and not the federal, level.[16]

Regulators will be given the power to wind down large, system-threatening institutions before they go under instead of during or after their failure. But a $19 billion levy on the banks to prepay the costs of such resolutions was dropped – the same day that the House killed an effort to extend unemployment benefits, amidst the worst outbreak of long-term unemployment since the 1930s. Dropped as well was Obama's original proposal for an independent and powerful consumer financial protection agency; instead, a new body will be created inside the Fed, an institution not previously known for its attentiveness in protecting consumers from hungry bankers.[17]

Soon after the House passed the bill, Treasury Secretary Timothy Geithner went on Lawrence Kudlow's TV show to correct the perception, common in the so-called business community, that the administration is anti-business.[18] The choice of outlet is interesting: Kudlow, a former Reagan administration budget official, is a militant supply sider and all-around right-winger with a one-dimensional worldview. Geithner appealed to that dimensional singularity by assuring Kudlow and his CNBC audience that the administration plans to keep a lid on the favourable tax treatment of capital gains and dividends, and emphasizing that 'this president understands deeply that governments don't create jobs, businesses create jobs'. The administration has a 'pro-growth agenda', which is a phrase that Kudlow loves to use himself. But despite all these efforts to placate capital, capital remains fairly hostile to the administration and its modest regulatory efforts – which will, no doubt, prompt further efforts by Obama & Co. to placate business, efforts that will never satisfy, and will so have to be repeated … and repeated.

So in return for hundreds of billions of dollars in public funds used to keep the financial system from going under, the banks will emerge from this crisis largely unscathed. One reason for this is Wall Street's skill at lobbying, and its ability to spread huge amounts of cash around Washington. As Public Citizen documented, between 1998 and 2008, Wall Street spent $5 billion in campaign contributions and deployed 3,000 lobbyists across Capitol Hill to get its way.[19] While $5 billion sounds like a lot, it was less than a third of the Goldman Sachs bonus pool for 2009, and spread out over a decade. Wall Street has a lot of money, and Congress can be bought on the cheap.

But, as I argued earlier, Wall Street also represents the commanding heights of the economy, the central mechanism by which ruling-class economic power is formed and exercised. It's only surprising to people who don't understand this that Washington dances so faithfully to the bankers' tunes.

WE THE PEOPLE

Alas, it's not just about ruling class power. We must be honest with ourselves, though, and recognize the deep conservative streak in much of the US population. In February, for example, Gallup released a poll showing that over half – 57 per cent to be precise – of Americans are more worried that there's too much regulation of business by government than too little; just 37 per cent believe the reverse. Not quite a quarter, 24 per cent, think that government should be more involved in regulating business; more than twice that many, 50 per cent, think it should be less involved.[20] This comes after three decades of experience with deregulation, in which finance has repeatedly blown up, electricity has gotten more expensive, *E. coli*-infested hamburgers have sickened hundreds of thousands of people, and the airline industry has, on balance, lost more money than it's made throughout its entire history as a commercial enterprise.

Of course, there are contradictions. When you ask people specific questions about regulation, such as about finance, you get friendlier responses. But the more general poll taps into the common sense or gut reaction of the American popular mind, which is what makes it so easy for the right to shoot down even specific attempts at regulation.

On a somewhat cheerier note, Gallup also recently reported that 36 per cent of Americans have a positive image of socialism.[21] But 95 per cent have good feelings about small business, 86 per cent about free enterprise, 64 per cent about capitalism, and 49 per cent about big business. It may be that every time Fox News labels Obama a socialist, that improves collectivism's image among Democrats. Sadly, this means that handing out buckets of money to Wall Street to restore the *status quo ante bustum* is now synonymous with socialism in the popular mind. Maybe not. So this poll suggests that the prospects for the left in America aren't completely hopeless – just partially so.

The recession probably ended, at least in some formal sense, in mid-2009, and the economy has been stabilizing ever since. But the recovery, such as it is, is likely to be weak and stumbling. and it could take five years or more to recover the 8.4 million jobs lost in the recession. Indeed, the long-term employment picture in the US is remarkably bad. Because the weakest expansion in modern history was followed by the worst recession since the 1930s, total employment in June 2010 was 2 million below the peak reached in 2001. Barring an unlikely major acceleration of job growth in the second half of 2010, the first decade of the 21st century will be the first decade in which employment contracted since 1900, when accurate statistics first became available. In the face of this, the radical left, much of which has been angling for a crisis as some sort of *deus ex machina* event that would cause the scales to fall from the eyes of the masses and embrace socialism, has been unable to make any political headway in the US at all. In fact, most of the radical political energy in the US so far is coming from the right. This actually isn't all that uncommon. Economic troubles generally increase the vote for far-right parties in European elections but not far-left parties.[22] The rise of the Tea Partiers in the US, reminiscent of the rise of militias and Ross Perot during the economic troubles of the early 1990s, not to mention the election of Ronald Reagan in 1980 after the stagflationary crises of the 1970s, only shows that a similar pattern operates in the US.

Maybe years of stagnation will change the political landscape in ways friendlier to the left. But as this is written, three years after the onset of a financial crisis, Wall Street looks to have consolidated its power. Stranger things have happened, no doubt, but it's hard to think of one at the moment.

NOTES

1 The count of industries and their exact names have changed four times over the years, with breaks in 1948, 1987 and 1998. The ratios reported in the text are based on splicing the series together.

2 Eric Pace, 'Kingman Brewster Jr., 69, Ex-Yale President and U.S. Envoy, Dies', *New York Times,* 9 November 1988, available at http://www.nytimes.com.

3 The Yale Endowment, 2008, available at http://www.yale.edu/investments.

4 Harper's Index, *Harper's,* July, 1986, available at http://www.harpers.org/index/1986/7/11.

5 By 1985, the endowment had doubled in nominal terms – which sounds nice, but that was well behind the pace of inflation. That real underperformance didn't last for long. The endowment was soon on a tear, beginning the transformation of Yale into a university attached to a hedge fund. It passed $5 billion in 1997, $10 billion in 2000, and $20 billion in 2007. It too has fallen back, to $16 billion at the end of the last fiscal year, which takes it back to its 2005 level, when the university was practically begging for quarters on the street. Yale now feels very poor, and is cutting the budget and laying off staff.

6 I make this argument at considerable length in my book *Wall Street*, New York: Verso, 1997. The book is available for free download at http://www.wallstreetthebook.com.

7 The computations are my own. The nominal values of the S&P 500 index are deflated by the Consumer Price Index; the return excludes dividends. The bond return measure is based on a notional 8 per cent coupon Treasury bond whose value is adjusted according to market interest rates; it assumes that interest payments are reinvested in the mythical portfolio. Because of timing, taxes and fees, actual returns for real investors would be lower than

this theoretical value. Corporate profitability is defined as profits before taxes from the national income accounts divided by the value of the tangible capital stock from the Federal Reserve's flow of funds accounts, both for nonfinancial corporations.

8 For more on Jensen, see Henwood, *Wall Street*, pp. 265-77. The complete works of Jensen can be found at http://www.people.hbs.edu/mjensen.

9 Michael C. Jensen and William H. Meckling, 'Theory of the Firm: Managerial Behavior, Agency Costs and Ownership Structure', *Journal of Financial Economics* 3(4), 1976, available at http://papers.ssrn.com.

10 Michael C. Jensen, 'The Evidence Speaks Loud and Clear', *Harvard Business Review* 89(6), 1989, pp. 12-14. Jensen does not include this delight on his website.

11 Michael C. Jensen, 'The Modern Industrial Revolution, Exit, and the Failure of Internal Control Systems', *Journal of Finance*, 48(3), 1993, available at http://papers.ssrn.com.

12 Some recent papers that take up the issue: Michael C. Jensen, Kevin J. Murphy, and Eric G. Wruck, 'Remuneration: Where We've Been, How We Got to Here, What are the Problems, and How to Fix Them', Harvard NOM Research Paper No. 04-28, July 2004 and ECGI-Finance Working Paper No. 44, 2004; Michael C. Jensen, 'Agency Costs of Overvalued Equity', Harvard NOM Research Paper No. 04-26, May 2004 and ECGI-Finance Working Paper No. 39, 2004. Both available at http://papers.ssrn.com.

13 Data from Tony Atkinson, Thomas Piketty and Emmanuel Saez, 'Top Incomes in the Long Run of History', Revised January 2010, *Journal of Economic Literature*, (Forthcoming), available at http://elsa.berkeley.edu/~saez.

14 The calculations are my own, from the Federal Reserve's flow of funds accounts.

15 Dodd for Connecticut: Senator Christopher Dodd, whose state is home to a good deal of the hedge fund industry, and Frank for Massachusetts: Representative Barney Frank, whose state is home to a number of large mutual fund and money management firms.

16 Francesco Guerrera, Tom Braithwaite and Justin Baer, 'Financial Regulation: A Line is Drawn', *Financial Times*, 30 June 2010. Howard Davies, 'Wall Street's New Double Act Comes Up Short', *Financial Times*, 1 July 2010. Both available at available at http://www.ft.com.

17 For the original Obama proposal, see US Department of the Treasury, *Financial Regulatory Reform: A New Foundation*, available at http://www.financialstability.gov. Obama has shown none of the toughness in dealing with Congress that earlier presidents have shown in pushing their agenda. Even with a large Congressional majority, Obama has been more timid with the legislative branch than his predecessor was with a slim majority. And next to a master like LBJ, Obama is a piker. By this, I don't mean to imply that Obama is some sort of closeted radical – he isn't. But his weakness in fighting for what is supposedly his own agenda, and his eagerness to compromise with the opposition party, is striking in purely partisan political terms. For an interesting speculation on what Lyndon Johnson would have done to pass Obama's alleged domestic

agenda written by a veteran of the Johnson White House, see Tom Johnson, 'What LBJ Would Do', a special commentary written for CNN, available from http://www.cnn.com.

18 Ben White, 'W.H. Works to Flip Anti-Business Rep', *Politico.com*, 8 July 2010, available at http://www.politico.com.

19 Public Citizen, *Sold Out,* March 2009, available at http://www.wallstreetwatch.org.

20 Frank Newport, 'Americans Leery of Too Much Gov't Regulation of Business', Gallup Poll, 2 February 2010, available at http://www.gallup.com.

21 Frank Newport, 'Socialism Viewed Positively by 36 per cent of Americans', available at http://www.gallup.com.

22 See Markus Brückner and Hans Peter Grüner, 'Economic Growth and the Rise of Political Extremism', Centre for Economic and Policy Research Discussion Paper 7723, March 2010, available from http://www.cepr.org.

OPPORTUNITY LOST: MYSTIFICATION, ELITE POLITICS AND FINANCIAL REFORM IN THE UK

JULIE FROUD, MICHAEL MORAN, ADRIANA NILSSON AND KAREL WILLIAMS

The greatest banking crisis in the UK since before 1914 produced a brief 'might have been' democratic moment: when elected politicians, in both the executive and in Parliament, could see the powerful financial interests of the City of London disadvantaged, and when wider popular forces could have seriously challenged financial elites. Yet the outcome so far has failed entirely to match this opportunity. This gap between the potential opportunity for radical change presented by the crisis and the timid reforms enacted is especially puzzling since the combination of such a severe crisis with unprecedented government rescue and intervention was immediately demystifying. In Britain, as elsewhere, it discredited the economic grand narrative of Bernanke and others about the 'Great Moderation' – a narrative about how capitalism had discovered a durable combination of growth, low inflation and low unemployment. In retrospect, this 'Moderation' was revealed as a credit led, asset price bubble inflated by shadow banking which had been camouflaged by another narrative about the benefits of financial innovation.[1] This discovery immediately raised questions about whether finance was a pro-cyclical destabilizing activity and created an opening for radical critique which argued that UK finance had fed a transaction economy rather than supporting sustainable circuits of material transformation.[2]

More broadly, the first phase of the crisis in Britain – from the 2007 failure of Northern Rock to the post Lehman systemic crisis of autumn 2008 – was a demystifying moment, when finance sector alibis, technocratic expertise and the assumptions of the political classes were tested and found wanting under pressure of unanticipated events. The banking rescue of 2007-8 amounted to the socialization of banking losses at a cost to the UK taxpayer of up to £1,000 billion or more (if we include contingent liabilities and exclude quantitative easing).[3] British taxpayers got very little in return. The challenge of a brief democratic moment was met by the restatement of old pre-crisis narratives about the importance of 'flexible', market responsive regulation, and about the social value of finance. Familiar tropes and memes like shareholder value were redeployed to neutralise intervention such as the part nationalisation of the banking system: public ownership, as we shall show in this essay, was defined as an interim arrangement driven by private sector imperatives.

All this narrowed the social definition of banking problems and solutions, while it also closed or discouraged discussion of how the behaviours and structures that failed were embedded in mainstream banking business models. The financial structures that failed were not so much a 'system' as a bricolage of long, fragile chains which were smart at the moneymaking links but dumb through the long chains where they were dependent on values or behaviours that would certainly change over the conjuncture.[4] The incidental and unforeseen consequence of these chains was catastrophic liquidity and solvency problems for markets and banks which were too interconnected to fail and could pass the costs of bail out onto the taxpayer. The bricoleurs of investment banking were incentivised to create a lattice-work of chains by the 'comp ratio' business model which made wholesale banking a lucrative joint venture between shareholders and the senior workforce. Under the 'comp ratio' convention, senior investment bankers expected a fixed share of turnover which they could then increase at will because the financial innovation of derivatives allowed the tiering of transactions in a way that was not possible in other sectors of the economy.

But in the absence of this kind of analysis, technocrats and elite politicians have failed to find points of intervention or to turn the crisis into an intelligible and politically actionable reform story. Instead, as we will demonstrate, various old constitutional and economic narrative mystifications were recycled to create a fog of confusion which inhibited reform. The result so far is marginalisation of left and radical forces (or no change on the past twenty-five years). Against this background, this essay has two interlinked aims. First, it presents an analysis of political obstacles to democratic control and reform of the finance sector that caused the financial crisis of 2007-8; a crisis that, after extreme intervention to save banks and support markets, has by 2010-11 become a fiscal crisis for individual states and a sovereign debt crisis for the eurozone. Second, it addresses (in this context) the role of 'ideology' within the socio-political process by examining how discourses format the world through what is now called 'performativity'. And it shows how this new kind of discursive description can be developed and integrated with more established kinds of institutional analysis so as to generate new insights into the political obstacles to reform.

The end result is an argument about how elite power has worked politically to frustrate post-crisis reform in the British case through mystification, as constitutional and economic story telling has narrowed debate and participation in ways that promote regulatory closure and safeguard the status quo. Such mystification works by mobilising narratives which are fragile and contestable so that outcomes, in terms of reform, are open and uncertain. Our use of the notion of mystification is entirely conventional: by it we mean the elaboration of narratives (about governing and about markets) that are designed to convey coherent stories about how social processes are conducted, but which function – by their silences, their gaps and their contradictions – to serve economic interests. Our empirical material is drawn from the UK, and is mostly concerned with the first phase of response to the crisis, which culminated in the anticlimax of the British government's White Paper of July 2009 – a document that avoided major reform of banking and finance. We also show below that, while the White Paper eventually resulted in the timid and limited reforms of the Banking Act of 2010, it did not entirely succeed in closing off debate. On the contrary, it opened a new, and continuing, phase of struggle for reform initially led by dissenting elite technocrats.

The argument below is illustrated with UK evidence and our aim is to provide an analysis of national peculiarities, but the issues raised are relevant to other jurisdictions (national and supra national). We hope to raise broad questions about the mechanisms of elite power in present day capitalism where the importance of narrative has intensified since Reagan and Thatcher. We also aim to encourage reflection on how narrative power could be challenged so as to deliver a more democratic reform of finance.

THE PUZZLE OF OPPORTUNITY LOST

If financial bricolage and banking business models survive unreformed, why be surprised and why conceive of the outcome as a puzzle? While crises are inherently threatening and disruptive, their resolution usually depends on the balance of forces prevailing before the crisis and this often favours the restoration of the status quo. The marginalization of left and radical forces, in and after the crisis, only continues a well established historical trend which we examine in the next section. A British labour movement that had been in retreat and disarray for three decades was hardly likely to be reconstituted as an arbiter of outcomes by one moment of crisis. Capitalist democracy is nevertheless robust partly because of its capacity for reform, with or without the pressure from organised labour, by virtue of the space it allows for political 'reflexivity': market failings are publicly interrogated and reforms introduced in the light of evidence and values. As we show towards the end of this essay, such robust interrogation was belatedly supplied by elite technocrats in the regulatory agencies, like the Bank of England and the Financial Services Authority (FSA) as they tried to reclaim the reform initiative. Elsewhere, in the immediate aftermath of the crisis, mainstream politicians from all parties (and trade unionists of all persuasions) willingly substituted the scapegoating of individual bad bankers for a credible reform programme.

The puzzle of so little reflexivity in the immediate aftermath of the crisis must be related to a more fundamental paradox. Since Reagan and Thatcher, social scientists have increasingly preferred not to talk about ideology (or ideologies) as the false knowledge of the bourgeoisie; while, paradoxically, capitalism has in this same period been enveloped in mystifications which greatly strengthen capitalist power against democratic challenge. In particular, 'storytelling' has become an important weapon in the armoury of economic elites. If Noel Coward celebrated the potency of 'cheap music' in *Private Lives,* political and business elites have discovered the potency of cheap stories in public life. This potency is considerable because these stories have a performative as much as a narrative dimension: as we shall see, the new economic stories, like the old constitutional stories, provide templates for the design and redesign of old and new institutions and regulatory regimes.

The issue of performativity has been approached recently through case studies by authors like Donald Mackenzie who have moved from science and technology studies (STS) into the study of finance.[5] But the typical result is a scholarly, narrowly focused, historical case study of technicality which is a poor guide to the large scale dynamics of financial innovation and crisis. And, more specifically, the STS approach has encouraged a narrow preoccupation with the performativity of formal knowledge like the algebraic finance theory of Black and Scholes in economic markets, and that has gone along with neglect of informal stories in political contexts. Such informal stories matter because they are part of a struggle to impose 'closure' which narrows political agendas in ways that consolidate elite power. We explicitly reject the idea of capture promoted in public choice economics which supposes that selfish, rent seeking special interests usually win at the expense of an indifferent public. As analysts of closure, we envisage a more complex and cultural world with uncertain outcomes. Here stories are used to motivate political action and inaction but different narratives often compete and much is outside the stories, so that closure is a kind of temporary special case not an inevitable permanent result. From this point of view, normal capitalist politics can be defined as the activity of interfering with (another's) narrative so as to enforce the limits on performativity and secure action or inaction. Institutions then matter because they provide location and partition which set limits on the circulation of stories in a world where sectional agendas usually compete: where you stand then often depends on where you sit.

The story has been an important device of elite power since the beginning of formal mass democracy in Britain around 1918. There is a venerable tradition of constitutional mystification about 'arms length control' and such like which justifies the unaccountability of elites by implying that the delicate functioning of our institutions would only be upset by the intrusion of majoritarian democratic forces.[6] Political developments after 1979 gave business narratives a new impetus in economic affairs. If the end of British style corporatism under Mrs Thatcher displaced organised labour, it also threatened organised business and the traditional trade association in a world where the Tory or New Labour default in favour of the market did not automatically deliver sector friendly regulation and tax regimes. Big business, especially in finance and pharmaceuticals, increased its spending on 'do it yourself' lobbying by individual firms.[7] Single firm efforts were backed up by organising loose distributive coalitions of firms which did not so much negotiate as legitimate their sectional demands for business-friendly regulation with stories about their activity's social value. This value was defined opportunistically as industry contribution to whatever the political classes thought they wanted by way of jobs, tax revenue, a green or knowledge-based economy etc.[8]

The new economic mystifications about private equity as a better form of ownership, or about the social value of a large finance sector, like the old political mystifications about arms length control, owe very little to intentionality or conscious manipulation by elite insiders. While recognising the importance of new financial elites,[9] we do not suppose that such elites have an executive committee of the plutocracy which meets in the boardroom at Goldman Sachs to decide the industry line for Davos. Cheap stories allow business elites to operate in loose coalitions distinguished mainly by an absence of much imagination and the ever present support of many PR functionaries and lobbyists. Their work on and with stories is rather like mass TV advertising with its endless repetition and simple updating of the same message in search of a suggestible but amnesiac target audience.[10] All this is capable of being routinised because the cheap story works by selection of evidence and assertive identifications which simplify matters in the hope of gaining political intelligibility and acceptance. But most industry stories can then be unpicked by resourceful critics, who do not find it difficult to develop better evidenced alternative stories. The business 'story' as a mystifying device is subject to interference and often vulnerable, as when the NGOs successfully attacked big pharma's story about innovation and R and D.[11]

THE PREHISTORY OF THE CRISIS

After the late 1980s finance became a domain of high politics where agendas were set by industry leaders, sympathetic technocrats and supportive elite political sponsors. If political participation narrowed, so did intellectual debate as two mystifications supplied what Wright Mills called the 'vocabulary of motivation' for elite economic and political practices in finance. The first mystification was a variation on the venerable laissez-faire narrative about self-regulation that helped legitimise a particular regulatory order by conferring on financial markets the right to run their own affairs. The second mystification was a more contemporary narrative about the social and economic value of finance in the wider economy. That narrative helped politically empower finance as a sector by emphasising the importance of an economic regime and a 'light touch' regulatory regime tailored to the needs of financial markets.

The first of these mystifications about 'light touch regulation' was a kind of ghostly return framed by the peculiarities of British historical development. The City is the oldest, and the most distinctive, part of the business community in the UK. Key city markets and institutions – the Bank of England, the stock exchange and Lloyds in insurance – can be dated back to the creation of what Cain and Hopkins call the 'military fiscal state' at the end of the 17th century. Britain's early entry into industrialism, preceding as it did the development of any democratic political forces, created a politically privileged and broader business elite which promoted regulation without the law or public controls. The expression of this was in doctrines of self-regulation and cooperative regulation – the latter a doctrine that any public regulation should only be conducted with the cooperation of regulated enterprises.[12] The doctrine was peculiarly well embedded in financial markets, dominated as they were by the oldest, most entrenched of business elites. The doctrine of self-regulation in financial markets was structurally reinforced after the First World War by the reorganisation of the Bank of England so that it functioned as the voice of the City in government; and by the reorganisation of City markets – mostly into cartels – so that, under the eye of the Bank of England, markets could regulate participants.

Before or after the rise of the labour movement, the appearance of formal democracy after the First World War, and the rise of an interventionist state, the City represented regulation as a matter of flexible control by market actors with practical experience.

The decline of the industrial spirit in metropolitan England in the later 19th century led to a fusion of metropolitan political, administrative and financial elites which was memorably described at the start of the 20th century by Hobson in *Imperialism*.[13] In this process, financial occupations experienced collective upward mobility. For much of the 19th century the stock jobbers' trade, for example, occupied the same twilight moral world as that of the bookie; by the end, stock jobbing became a respectable occupation for public schoolboys – the first old Etonian jobber dates from 1891.[14] Marital and business alliances connected financial, aristocratic and political elites.[15] The growth of financial markets through the twentieth century (leading finally to the City of London's 'Big Bang' in the 1980s and the growth of proprietary trading in the 1990s) led to the emergence of new and more numerous financial elites who claimed meritocratic provenance and whose world was European or global as much as national. But the political representatives of the new elites were incorporated into a national reworking of the old style British alliance of the post-industrial elites. This reworking was personified by David Cameron, as Tory opposition leader in the first phase of crisis, and coalition prime minister from May 2010. An old Etonian with an aristocratic wife, family wealth of more than £30 million and a curriculum vitae including a stint in corporate PR, Cameron described his father – senior partner in Panmure Gordon – as 'a fourth or fifth generation stockbroker'. As leader of the opposition in 2007, he endorsed utterly conventional views about 'innovative financial services … (as) important industries of the future'.[16]

The mystification of self-regulation proved hard to sustain in the age of globalised markets, financial innovation and the new business models that developed from the 1980s onwards.[17] Big Bang was accompanied – in the Financial Services Act 1986 – by the reconstruction of regulation around a Securities and Investments Board (SIB). This reconstruction was designed simultaneously to provide a more robust system of controls while preserving the autonomy of markets from the 'usual suspects', such as lawyers and democratically elected politicians. That is why the SIB was a complex half public, half private body, and why it presided over the institutionally convoluted system of 'Self Regulatory Organizations' (SROs) that were supposed to supervise separate markets – and why the Bank of England continued to control banking supervision.[18] It was these arrangements that were discredited by successive regulatory failures, and above all by the massive failure of light touch regulation to foresee and forestall the crash of the House of Baring in 1995.[19] The subsequent creation in 1997 of a new regulatory body, the Financial Services Authority, with considerable formal power, did represent an inching towards a more formal, publicly controlled, system. But the strength of the historically entrenched regulatory ideology, and the strength of the interests in the markets, ensured, we now know, that the new FSA was rapidly colonised by that old ideology; so the FSA until 2007 practised market friendly, light touch regulation in the belief that this regulatory style promoted innovation and guaranteed London's place as a leading global financial market place.[20]

Why was so much invested in the reinvention of an old regulatory style for a new order? If it was explicitly designed to enhance London's competitive advantage, why was it so important to have a globally leading financial centre? And why were the conventional views of narrowly based metropolitan elites so widely accepted? One answer lies in the bureaucratic politics of international financial diplomacy. By the 1980s the UK was a declining military and diplomatic power with a palsied manufacturing sector. But its financial regulators punched above their weight in the networks of international financial regulators: the Bank of England, for instance, regularly provided the chairs (including the founding chair) of the key Basel committees concerned with banking regulation. And they punched above their weight because London was a financial centre of an importance well beyond the scale of the wider UK economy. Possessing a leading global financial centre was thus the equivalent, in international financial regulatory politics, of a permanent seat on the Security Council or possession of an independent nuclear deterrent.

There was also a new supporting economic narrative about the social value of finance which, from the 1980s onwards, legitimised the objective of strengthening London's comparative advantage. In this narrative, finance became the goose that laid the golden egg, so that what was good for the global financial centre in London was also good for the UK economy. The old constitutional mystifications that legitimised market-friendly regulation did have some (contestable) evidential foundations because it could be argued that regulatory systems more based on the law and adversarial regulation, like in the US, were also prone to regulatory failure. But the new narrative about the social value of finance to the wider economy was more or less pure fantasy. Crucially, through 15 years of finance-led boom from the early 1990s the finance sector never employed more than one million workers directly; demand from finance maybe employed another half million indirectly out of sector though numbers employed did not increase as finance sector output grew and profits boomed.[21] These profits were disproportionately captured by foreign owned investment banks and financial services conglomerates who had by the mid 1990s taken over British owned firms, who treated the City as one arena of their trading system and who recruited a cosmopolitan workforce. As a sector built on tax avoidance, the tax contribution of the City was always limited and over the five years 2002-7 averaged just over 6.5 per cent of government receipts, or less than half what British manufacturing contributed.[22]

The fantastic new mystification about the social value of finance exerted a powerful hold over the minds of participants in financial markets, financial regulators and economic policy makers by the 1990s. It was powerful because it was promoted by the heft of a new lobbying and PR machine and because it re-motivated an old political pattern of alliance amongst metropolitan elites which was part of their historic lineage. The narrative about the social value of finance was so potent because it served to align the calculations of different elites (in markets, the core executive and the regulatory agencies) about the benefits of financial innovation; and because it was congruent with the historically engrained culture of consensus amongst (old and new) metropolitan elites who were once again in the saddle during the years of Thatcherite triumphalism. Thatcher's control of the state rested on the way the electoral system gave power to a party supported by only a minority of votes concentrated in the metropolitan south east – in the very England sketched so memorably by Hobson almost a century earlier.

The mystification involved here was more fundamentally potent because it was consonant with the new economic rhetoric about enterprise and rewards which was part of the post-Thatcher settlement. The regulatory narrative in the decade after the return of Labour to government in 1997 was couched in new language about 'light touch' regulation. The City was viewed by the new Labour government as both a tax cash cow, and as an engine of growth, job creation and innovation in the UK economy. But the City was also pictured – and pictured itself – as operating in an international climate of ferocious competitiveness in which comparative advantage accrued to the financial centre which most effectively pursued market friendly regulation.

Why was New Labour, after 1997, overpowered by this ghostly return where a new kind of neoliberal rhetoric about competitiveness hybridised with the self-serving historical excuses for regulation of the City by the City? Why did they go along with all this? An answer turns on both the long term regulatory history of the City of London, and the tactical contingencies that faced Labour in the years of Conservative ascendancy. The decline of class based political parties with mass membership opened the way for the hijacking of the Labour Party by a small clique who saw that centrist swing voters were the key to electoral success and delivered three election victories in a row. The New Labour four (Blair, Brown, Campbell and Mandelson) succeeded and failed in much the same way as any rock band because their over-sized egos led them to believe their own publicity about novelty; rather peculiarly they also believed Mrs Thatcher's publicity about economic transformation and private sector enterprise thanks to flexibilised labour markets and lower income and corporation taxes.

Politically, New Labour distanced their party from the trade unions and thereby made Labour financially dependent on, and sympathetic to, City donors who had converted to the Murdoch style of politics whereby business supports not the centre right but whatever side is winning, in the hope of sympathy after the election. Economically, they did not (maybe could not) question the success of the experiment in economic management which originated in the Thatcher response to the economic crisis of the 1970s, and which had never changed the incapacity of the British private sector to create jobs. Instead New Labour made policy framework changes like independence for the Bank of England and then boosted the role of such changes in ending 'boom and bust'. Thus Labour, in a confused way, tried to claim the credit for a fifteen year boom which was actually sustained by equity withdrawal from appreciating house prices, and by increasing public expenditure which one way or another accounted for more than half the job creation from 1997-2007.[23] The continuing decline of the manufacturing base was accepted on the assumption that compensation would come from paradigm change to knowledge or creative industries and from building the City's positioning of the financial services industry.

Like other bands which succeed by playing mood music for the decade, New Labour was bound to look foolishly out of style when times changed. But the problem with New Labour was more fundamental than one of style and personnel because the financial crisis exposed New Labour's fundamental incapacity for economic analysis and prescription. After Gordon Brown had resigned as party leader in May 2010, none of the candidates had serious policies for banking reform or any sense of what to do next economically if the crisis marked the end of a thirty year long experiment in encouraging enterprise.

BUSINESS AS USUAL

The power of mystifying narrative was demonstrated in the wasted year between the downfall of Lehman Brothers in September 2008 and the summer of 2009, when popular hostility to bankers was strong but the impetus for banking reform was deflected and dissipated. The interim result was a timid British government White Paper on financial reform published in July 2009 which promised to change very little; and a Banking Act which, in April 2010, enacted more or less exactly the timid original proposals.[24] All this becomes intelligible if we consider how financial and allied elites quickly recovered from the traumas of 2007-08 by closing ranks and recycling the old mystifying narratives. The old constitutional mystifications and the shareholder value trope were together deployed to ensure it was to be business as usual in newly nationalised banks. Meanwhile, the newer story about the social value of finance was deployed to deflect demands for radical structural reform, such as breaking up banks that were 'too big to fail'.

Extreme intervention to prop up the banking system resulted in *faute de mieux* nationalisation of banks like Northern Rock and Royal Bank of Scotland, which passed into public ownership; just as the state also acquired a substantial minority stake in Lloyds. Public ownership is not, of course, democratic control, but it did represent a democratic threat to elite power. A major part of the banking system was now state owned and controlled so that elected politicians could, in principle, always ask what state-owned banks were doing and instruct them to do something different by way of lending or pay. At this point the fusion and interpenetration of elites became important. The challenge of democracy was headed off by a few key figures at the Treasury, notably the civil servant John Kingman (who has since left to work for Rothschild) and Paul Myners the ex-fund manager who had been brought in by Labour as a junior Treasury minister. Their institutional creation was United Kingdom Financial Investments (UKFI) a new holding company for government majority and minority stakes in banks, where City grandees in the chairman role worked alongside Kingman as chief executive.

This kind of social defence by closing elite ranks requires a narrative justification to motivate anti-democratic practice. In the case of UKFI, this was provided by combining an old constitutional mystification with newer tropes about shareholder value. Kingman repeatedly insisted that UKFI operated at 'arms-length' from government.[25] The new agency was thereby inserted into an old pattern of institutional arrangements between agencies and the democratic state in Britain. As Flinders' recent study shows, the doctrine of the 'arms-length' relationship has been a central feature of constitutional rhetoric in Britain and a key device to insulate the workings of agencies with delegated functions from the accountability pressures of the democratic state.[26]

This was backed up by invoking the tropes of shareholder value and constructing the citizen/ taxpayer as a shareholder in failed banks which should be first managed, and then sold off, in a way that maximised shareholder value. UKFI's Framework Document of March 2009 insisted on the one 'overarching objective of protecting and creating value for the taxpayer as shareholder'.[27] Within this discursive frame UKFI acquired the identity of an engaged, responsible, large institutional investor whose relations with state-owned bank managements were formally subordinated to familiar private sector investment objectives. Democratic interference with day-to-day management decisions or second guessing of business strategy then became unthinkable; just as high pay, for example, remained justifiable if linked with 'performance' as defined inside the shareholder value model. As UKFI elaborated its role and mandate, it increasingly represented, not the nationalisation of the banks, but the privatisation of the Treasury as a new kind of fund manager.

Demands for more broad based structural reform of (non-nationalised) banks and markets were then deflected by updating the old narrative about the social value of finance in the Bischoff and Wigley reports.[28] These reports arose out of the pre-crisis high politics of financial lobbying and were ostensibly about the competitiveness of London as an international financial centre (not about the causes of crisis or the solution of re-regulation). Commissioned before the crisis but published afterwards, they represented a striking intervention against reform by financial elites in the first year after the crisis, when their defensive and negative task was simply to prevent substantial re-regulation and restructuring.

Sociologically, the reports represent more fusion of the metropolitan elites and the deliberate exclusion of other voices, so that finance could report on finance. The first report was co-chaired by Win Bischoff, former chairman of Citigroup, and the Chancellor of the Exchequer. The second report was commissioned by the Mayor of London from a group headed by Bob Wigley, European chair of Merrill Lynch. In their working methods Bischoff and Wigley provide a stark contrast with those of earlier generations of reports on the City, such as the Macmillan Committee of 1931, the Radcliffe Committee of 1959 and the Wilson Committee of 1980. These inquiries, for all their biases, included in their memberships prominent critics of the City, and gathered evidence likewise from sceptics. By contrast in the cases of Bischoff and of Wigley, non-City groups were not included or consulted in the information gathering, problem-defining phase or subsequently in the drafting of the two reports about the benefits of finance. There was no speaking part for non-financial businesses and their trade associations, or for trade unions, despite the unionisation of retail finance workers, or for NGOs representing consumers or pressing social justice agendas, or for mainstream economists or heterodox intellectuals.[29]

Again, the social combination of financial and political elites worked through narrative framing. Both the Bischoff and Wigley reports acted out a kind of discursive two step: in a first step, the reports updated the pre-2007 lobbyist's story by adding up the many contributions of financial services to the national economy; and then in a second step, the reports identified the conditions necessary to maintain this socially valuable activity which incidentally included something like the regulatory status quo. As with most cheap stories, the intellectual substance behind this story was meagre. The method, for example, was to add benefits but not subtract any offsetting costs of finance. Thus Bischoff added up taxes paid and collected by finance without considering the costs of bailing out the financial system.[30] These stories were nevertheless good enough to secure political buy-in by Treasury politicians and civil servants who retained the dominant role in directing reform.

First, leading politicians explicitly bought into the syllogism about the social value of finance and made a commitment to nurture the sector. Thus, in his foreword to the Bischoff Report, the Chancellor of the Exchequer wrote that 'financial services are critical to the UK's future'.[31] In a press release accompanying the Wigley Report, the Mayor of London said: 'Bob's team have identified what needs to be done and I will pull out all the stops to protect London's position as the world's premier financial centre'.[32] Second, the claims about the social value of finance from the Bischoff Report were copied out as a framing device in other official reports, especially the July 2009 White Paper on *Reforming Financial Markets*. In its first chapter, the White Paper begins by reviewing not the causes of crisis but 'the importance of financial services and markets to the UK Economy and the pre-eminence of the UK as a global financial centre'.[33] Claims and evidence from Bischoff were simply copied out and dropped into the text of the White Paper, which reproduced the story and unsurprisingly ended by proposing nothing radical.

City elites went for closure in the Bischoff and Wigley reports and immediately got what they wanted in the White Paper of July 2009, whose title reference to 'reform' did not accurately describe the contents of the report. The White Paper made no proposals for reforming industry structure by, for example, breaking up large complex financial conglomerates or segregating proprietary trading activities. Even the architecture of regulation was to be changed only marginally: the FSA would continue with the addition of a Financial Stability Committee dominated by regulatory insiders. All this was faithfully enacted in the 2010 Banking Act, which demonstrates the power of stories in shaping outcomes to the crisis. But, if political stories are performative, they seldom close things down definitively. So it was with UK financial reform in the aftermath of the crisis. Democracy had been sidelined because the executive and their Treasury advisors would do nothing; and populist politicians were more concerned with electoral advantage than with making banking safe. The resistance to doing nothing was then led by technocrats who re-formed as a kind of dissident elite section operating independently of the rest.

THE TECHNOCRATIC DISSENT

If the twentieth century had reinvented capitalism as rule of experts, the first major crisis of the twenty-first century was profoundly threatening for the technocrats in the regulatory agencies – the FSA and the Bank of England – who had dominated policy on finance in the era of the Great Moderation, after previously redefining central banking as a matter for those with economics PhDs. The crash destroyed much of their intellectual capital. The politicians were forced to improvise intervention in the vortex of the crisis. Then the City and its Treasury allies hijacked rescue management and financial reform. But, from summer 2009, the technocratic elite responded to this challenge by forcibly reopening the argument about the regulation of finance which had apparently been closed down. In the next phase, the technocrats took the leading role in trouble-making but, crucially, failed to form an alliance with senior politicians and democratic forces.

The most important source of technocratic dissent has predictably been the Bank of England, which is neither hostage to the City nor an institution of practical men, as originally envisaged by Montagu Norman. The Bank's relative autonomy from City interests is culturally shaped by a group of technocrats like Governor King and his financial stability director, Andrew Haldane, whose intellectual capital comes from academic economics rather than market experience. From summer 2009, their dissent was actively backed up by Adair Turner as chair of the FSA, who represented not institutional culture but British elite self-assurance. Turner is a well networked fixer who parlayed a first career with McKinsey into a series of elite posts in banking and public life and after the crisis quickly wrote his own FSA report on what went wrong with the financial system.[34]

Papers and speeches by senior Bank of England officials are never the result of individual reflection; they are the result of continuing internal debate within a small group of elite technocrats. In 2009, a series of related papers by Andrew Haldane and speeches by Mervyn King together mounted a radical critique of pre-2007 policies and the subsequent piecemeal reform. They argued that: the benefits of financial innovation had been greatly exaggerated; the UK economy was distorted and over-dependent on a large financial sector and the City; structural reforms were needed to segregate retail banking from banking that rested on proprietary trading; and probably also to dismantle 'banking on the state', where serious moral hazard problems were created by banks that were 'too big to fail'[35] in a system that was guaranteed by the taxpayer. This was ably backed up by Adair Turner who combined fluent McKinsey- style analysis of the banking industry with headline catching phrases about 'socially useless' finance.

If all this was brave and independent, it also represented a narrowing of the technocratic imagination. Andrew Haldane is not J. M. Keynes or William Beveridge because he has no discernible politics beyond hostility to socialisation of private banking losses, and his world view is marked by a naïve scientism. Consider, for example, Haldane's major attempt to rebuild technocratic capital by 'rethinking the financial network' in ways which would give the technocrats a new role in explaining the financial crisis and making the world safe. He boldly proposed a paradigm shift into epidemiology and ecology as ways of relating financial crisis to other kinds of system failure and disaster.[36] This gambit is intellectually radical because it focuses potential solutions on whole system mapping and reconstruction; but it is also politically ambiguous because Haldane's gambit would insulate expert-led banking reform from democratic politics, and do this long before the experts have developed a workable new practice of macro-prudential regulation based on any new paradigm.

If we consider these technocrats as a group, they are a break-away elite splinter whose radicalism is driven by their disruptive commitment to evidence (which had never figured much in other, earlier stories about the economic and social value of finance). The elite technocrats' currency of debate is – in a way that Montagu Norman would have found incomprehensible – systematically assembled economic data. It is their shared commitment to economic arithmetic (rather than a specific theoretical problematic or algebraic method) which ties them together. Thus Haldane has explained ballooning bank balance sheets before 2007 by producing elegant, forensic analysis of how the banks trashed return on assets for evaluating firms, so as to maintain return on equity which kept the stock market happy.[37] Likewise Turner, in his Cass lecture, took the long view of historical changes since 1945 in bank lending and bank balance sheets which led the banks far from any role of intermediation between saving households and borrowing firms.[38] But their faith in numbers has not so far re-energised the (national) reform process because the technocrats are bureaucratically divided and not acting in alliance with senior politicians and outside democratic political forces.

Bureaucratic politics is a primitive force which divides Bank and FSA technocrats who can otherwise happily cite each others papers. In the original reforms that created the now discredited system in 1997, the Bank was the big loser when it was obliged to surrender its jurisdiction over bank supervision to the newly created FSA. The post-2007 Bank agenda for reform now offers the possibility of reclaiming some of that lost 'turf' at the expense of the FSA. The Financial Services Authority was the kingpin of the regulatory system after 1997. It suffered correspondingly from the crisis which discredited light touch regulation and has since tried to reinvent itself as a more adversarial, intrusive regulator.[39] The 2009 White Paper and the 2010 Banking Act disappointed many but they were, from the point of view of the FSA, a highly effective damage limitation exercise because the FSA would remain the kingpin of regulation despite the effect of the crisis on its reputation.

Apart from bureaucratic internal divisions, the British technocrats are weakened by the absence of any high level alliances with politicians who hold power and can mobilise democratic forces for change. The technocratic attempt to redress the inactivity of elected politicians only reproduced a disconnect between technocracy and politics which Beveridge or Keynes would have seen as disabling. Thus the general election campaign of 2010 was conducted almost as though Haldane, King and Turner did not exist and had never intervened. In the adversarial politics of a general election, it was the third and smallest of the main British parties which, under the influence of one man (Vince Cable) advocated the structural reform of breaking up the banks. New Labour offered continuity: its manifesto commended the marginal reshaping of the regulatory system in the White Paper and the Banking Act, and even repeated, virtually verbatim, the UKFI commitment to sell off the public holdings in banks at a price that would maximise return to the taxpayer. The Conservative Party put its trust (once again) in the wisdom of new regulators by proposing to abolish the FSA and transfer jurisdiction over banking regulation to the Bank. If we consider not manifesto programmes but policy initiatives, the two largest British parties have both tended to default on to populist banker bashing as a substitute for banking reform as, classically, with Labour Chancellor Darling's one-off tax on bank bonuses or the Osborne bank levy.

FINANCIAL REFORM AFTER MAY 2010

The general election of 6 May 2010 had a politically sensational outcome: Labour lost but the Conservatives, after failing to win a majority of Parliamentary seats, were obliged to conclude a formal coalition agreement with the Liberal Democrats which included a concordat on policy issues and cabinet seats for the Lib Dems.[40] In the area of banking and financial reform, this outcome represented fundamental continuity because the DemCon coalition was, like its New Labour predecessor, a strong executive which could impose reform policies on the legislature but had no urgent, radical plans for banking and financial reform.

It is interesting to draw the contrast with the United States, where the executive is frustrated by a legislature of independent politicians building independent bases and winning individual struggles as the banking industry lobbies fiercely and contributes generously. US centre-left critics grumble with some justification about loopholes in the US legislation which insists derivatives be exchange traded (but exempts 'customised' derivatives) or proposes a ban on proprietary trading by banks (instead of breaking up the giant conglomerates).[41] But the fact remains that President Obama has managed to get through the Senate a bill that greatly strengthens monitoring of 'systemic risks' by creating a new council of regulators; the President has also tightened the control of failing institutions by creating new procedures for orderly bankruptcy; while the ban on bank proprietary trading attempts to resurrect at least the spirit of the Glass-Steagall separation of retail from investment banking. The last provision was pressed by Paul Volcker from outside the administration. But the US results so far are consistent with Tim Geithner's 2009 white paper on *Financial Regulatory Reform*[42] where the US executive did not so much announce a reform programme as reserve the right to press for as much banking reform as it can get through the system.

The position in the UK was different under New Labour and is now different under the Coalition, whose will to reform has been comprehensively undermined by the narrative mystifications and institutional divisions which we have analysed. With the new coalition, consider what has been fast tracked for action and what has been kicked into the long grass. The most rapid measure on which the coalition partners agree is the need to cut public spending in order to reassure financial markets that the hole in the public finances is being shrunk. Indeed, within a few days of the publication of the programme for government the new coalition had made a down payment of £6 billion in cuts, and its emergency budget of late June 2010 announced 25 per cent spending cuts across most activities plus a welfare benefits freeze. The coalition is moving speedily to ensure that taxpayers and public employees quickly pay down the cost of socialising bank losses.

Meanwhile, banking reform is postponed. The Liberal Democrats fought the election on a commitment to separate retail from investment banking but the coalition agreement remitted this issue to an 'independent commission' of inquiry. This was to investigate and 'be given an initial time frame of one year to report'.[43] It took several weeks of horse trading inside the coalition to settle the membership of the commission which delegates judgement to pro-competition economists incapable of understanding how pathological banking business models were encouraged as excessive competition led to declining return on assets and free current accounts. One mildly heterodox financial journalist (Martin Wolf of the *Financial Times)* is no counterweight to John Vickers and Clare Spotttiswoode, who built their careers as fellow travellers and enforcers of Thatcher's utility privatisation. The one unambiguous loser in the early stages of coalition bargaining has been the Financial Services Authority: the Chancellor's Mansion House speech of June 2010 announced that it would be dismembered and its most important supervision functions transferred to the Bank of England. That result represented not so much effective reform as a bureaucratic political victory for the Bank, which had originally lost responsibility for bank supervision in 1997.

Structural reform of banking and regulation has been complicated as a result of political manoeuvring in the process of coalition formation. A Conservative became Chancellor of the Exchequer (Finance Minister) while a Liberal Democrat became Business Secretary; and the cabinet committee concerned with the banking system is to be chaired by the Chancellor, not the more radical Business Secretary. This victory for the Treasury represents an enduring structural legacy of the Brown years as Chancellor. In terms of government machinery, Mr Brown greatly strengthened the Treasury as an institution in the core executive.[44] (That helps explain why so much of the banking rescue of 2007-8 in the UK was managed from within the Treasury rather than from within the central bank.) Thus the Treasury's ongoing dominance of the banking reform agenda reflects a long term rise in its influence in the field of banking politics. That long term rise in influence ensures that any 'independent commission' will be allowed to contemplate structural reform of the banking system only within limits acceptable to the Treasury.

Against this background, willingness to press structural reform by 'breaking up the banks' remains the key political test of serious reforming intent in the UK. This test is also paradoxical, because intellectual analysis suggests that 'breaking up the banks' is neither a necessary nor sufficient condition of reform. Serious reform should instead focus on curbing volume-driven banking business models, limiting long chain bricolage and redesigning circuits of credit and debt so as to obtain a safer, simpler, smaller and more socially responsible finance sector. The first immediate objective should be to prevent banks being run as a money pot for insiders taking a clip, and help recompense taxpayers for the cost of bailing out banks and markets. The second objective should be to try to reduce risk, both indirectly by taxing all financial transactions (along the lines of the Tobin tax) to encourage shorter transaction chains; and, more directly, via rules about short chain and transparent securitisation of residential mortgages. But in the longer term what is needed is to develop a programmatic strategy for steering capital allocation towards social ends instead of the present system of boom and bust in asset prices followed by reparations from society. A more socially responsible finance would allocate capital to create sustainable circuits between credit and debt which were geared to job creation in a low carbon economy. Other major problems about security in old age could be addressed by switching funds out of the secondary shares market and channelling savings directly into lower yielding infrastructure projects and low carbon technologies (with state guarantees of return).

This kind of reform programme would represent a more comprehensive and radical variant on the kinds of reform already advocated by technocrats like Haldane and Turner, whose problem is that they cannot win politically against the Treasury, City lobbyists and all the other metropolitan elites. The biggest obstacle to reform is not economic confusion about what is to be done but the political status quo under which nothing will be done. So the problem is to find or create significant political actors who could press a radical reform agenda. In the UK, as elsewhere, the problem is that old political forces are weakened but the new political forces have not moved on to finance related issues. Class-based organisation is in decline. The front benches of the leading parties – Conservative, Labour or Liberal Democrat – are in thrall to the City (and its financial contributions) partly because their mass membership is dying. After three decades of retreat, unions, especially in the private sector, are weak: according to the WIRS survey, two thirds of UK workplaces now have no unions at all.[45] However much civil society groups may have secured a strong presence on issues of development, climate change or ethical drug pricing, their expertise and lobbying on finance is weak.

Yet banking after the crisis could be the rallying point for a coalition of taxpayers, customers and the retail banking workforce, who have all been the losers from shareholder value driven banking. There are imaginative possibilities of putting together coalitions of old and new organisations.

Unite, which organises one third of the retail workforce, could join forces with NGOs (in the UK including possibly even Oxfam and the Consumers' Association) on issues like the 'high street' banks' pay incentives for retail advisers to 'sell to' consumers. A new kind of politics of leafleting and boycotts outside high street branches (playing on the vulnerability of their 'brands' to direct action) could start to raise broader democratic issues in relation to finance. At the very least, such actions would diminish a little – we put it no more strongly – the likelihood that coalition government in the UK will delay and obstruct necessary reform of finance.

NOTES

1 For the pre 2007 narrative about innovation, see E. Engelen, I. Erturk, J. Froud, A. Leaver and K. Williams, 'Re-conceptualizing financial innovation: frame, conjuncture and bricolage', *Economy and Society*, 39(1), 2010, pp. 33-42.

2 This argument is elaborated in the Alternative Banking Report of 2010 to which we were contributors: CRESC, *An Alternative Report on UK Banking Reform: A Public Interest Report from* CRESC, Manchester: University of Manchester Centre for Research on Socio Cultural Change, 2009, available at http://www.cresc.ac.uk.

3 M. Horton, M. Kumar and P. Mauro, *The State of Public Finances: a Cross Country Fiscal Monitor,* Washington: IMF, 2009, p. 28n12.

4 For an overview of these arguments, see E. Engelen et al., 'Re-conceptualizing financial innovation', pp. 42-6.

5 See D. Mackenzie, *An Engine Not a Camera*, Cambridge: MIT Press, 2006.

6 This argument is elaborated in: M. Moran, *The British Regulatory State: High Modernism and Hyper Innovation*, Second Edition, Oxford: Oxford University Press, 2007; and M. Flinders, *Delegated Governance and the British State: Walking Without Order,* Oxford: Oxford University Press, 2008.

7 For the rise of 'do it yourself' (individual firm) lobbying see M. Moran, 'The company of strangers: defending the power of business in Britain, 1975-2005', *New Political Economy*, 11(4), 2006.

8 See 'GlaxoSmithKline: keeping it going', in J. Froud, S. Johal, A. Leaver and K. Williams, *Financialization and Strategy,* London: Routledge, 2006.

9 For a developed argument see M. Savage and K. Williams, eds., *Remembering Elites,* Oxford: Blackwell, 2008.

10 See A. Davis, 'Public relations, business news and the reproduction of corporate elite power', *Journalism*, 1(3), 2000; and *Public Relations Democracy: Politics, Public Relations and the Mass Media.* Manchester: Manchester University Press, 2000.

11 This can especially be seen in the case of big pharma's story about the significance of research and development. J. Froud et al., *Financialization and Strategy,* pp. 158-68.

12 The argument is elaborated and documented in Moran, 'The company of strangers' and Moran, *The British Regulatory State.*

13 J. A. Hobson, *Imperialism: A Study*, New York: Cosimo Publishing, 2006 [1902].
14 D. Kynaston, *The City of London, Volume 1, A World of Its Own 1815-1890*, London: Pimlico, 1995, pp. 318-25.
15 M. Lisle-Williams, 'Merchant banking dynasties in the English class structure: ownership, solidarity and kinship in the City of London, 1850-90', *British Journal of Sociology*, XXXV(3), 1984.
16 D. Jones, *Cameron on Cameron*, London: Fourth Estate, 2008, p. 292.
17 I. Erturk and S. Solari, 'Banks as Continuous Reinvention', *New Political Economy*, 12(3), 2007.
18 The argument is elaborated and documented in M. Moran, *The Politics of the Financial Services Revolution*, London: Macmillan 1991.
19 For the evidence on Barings, see M. Moran, 'Not steering but drowning: policy catastrophes and the regulatory state', *Political Quarterly*, 72(4), 2001.
20 The best documented account is in House of Commons Treasury Select Committee, *The Run on the Rock, Fifth Report Session 2007-8*, Volume 1, HC 56-1.
21 CRESC, *Alternative Banking Report*, pp. 28-51.
22 For discussion see M. Moran, S. Johal and K. Williams, 'The financial crash and its consequences', in N. Allen and J. Bartle, eds, *Britain at the Polls*, London: Sage, 2011 (forthcoming).
23 For analysis of the sources of job creation, see J. Buchanan, J. Froud, S. Johal, A. Leaver and K. Williams, 'Undisclosed and unsustainable: problems of the UK national business model', CRESC Working Paper No. 75, Centre for Research on Socio-Cultural Change, University of Manchester, Manchester, 2009.
24 We have documented this in J. Froud, A. Nilsson, M. Moran and K. Williams, 'Wasting a Crisis? Democracy and Markets in Britain after 2007', *Political Quarterly*, 81(1), 2010.
25 See P. Hampton and J. Kingman, 'A precise mandate to protect taxpayers' interests', *Financial Times*, 14 November 2008; House of Commons Treasury Select Committee, *Banking Crisis, Volume 1, Session 2007-8, HC 114-I*, Oral Evidence, q.2572ff.
26 Flinders, *Delegated Governance and the British State*.
27 UK Financial Investments Limited, *Shareholder Relationship Framework Document*, London, UKFI, 2009, p. 13.
28 W. Bischoff and A. Darling, *UK International Financial Services – The Future: A Report from UK Based Financial Services Leaders to the Government*, London: HM Treasury, 2009; B. Wigley, *London: Winning in a Changing World*, London: Merrill Lynch Europe, 2008.
29 Detailed in CRESC, *Alternative Banking Report*, pp. 23-6.
30 The figures are scrutinised in Ibid., pp. 28-38.
31 Bischoff and Darling, *UK International Financial Services*, p. 2.
32 See CRESC, *Alternative Banking Report*, p. 22.
33 HM Treasury, *Reforming Financial Markets*, CM 7667, London: HM Treasury, 2009, p. 17.

34 Adair Turner, *The Turner Review: A Regulatory Response to the Global Banking Crisis*, London: Financial Services Authority, 2009.

35 A. Haldane, 'Small lessons from a big crisis', Remarks at the Federal Reserve Bank of Chicago 45th Annual Conference 'Reforming Financial Regulation', Chicago, 8 May 2009; 'The debt hangover', Speech given at a Professional Liverpool dinner 27 January 2010, available at www.bankofengland.co.uk.

36 A. Haldane, 'Rethinking the financial network', Speech delivered at the Financial Student Association, Amsterdam, April 2009, p. 3, available at http://www.bankofengland.co.uk.

37 P. Alessandrini and A. Haldane 'Banking on the State', Bank of England paper, November 2009, available at http://www.bankofengland.co.uk.

38 Adair Turner, 'What do banks do, what should they do and what public policies are needed to ensure best results for the real economy', Lecture at Cass Business School, London, 17 March 2010, available at http://www.fsa.gov.uk.

39 See Turner, *The Turner Review*, pp. 88-9.

40 The programme, 'The Coalition: Our Programme for Government', London: Cabinet Office, 2010, is downloadable at: http://programmeforgovernment.hmg.gov.uk.

41 See, for example, R, Reich, 'The senate finance bill merits two cheers', *Financial Times*, 24 May 2010.

42 Department of the Treasury, *Financial Regulatory Reform: A New Foundation*, Washington: Department of the Treasury, 2009.

43 See the section on 'Banking' in 'The Coalition: Our Programme for Government'.

44 C. Thain, 'Treasury Rules OK? The Further Evolution of a British Institution', *British Journal of Politics and International Relations*, 6, 2004.

45 B. Kersley, C. Alpin, A. Bryson, H. Bewley, G. Dix and S. Ovenbridge, *First Findings from the 2004 Workplace Employment Relations Survey*, London, Department of Trade and Industry, 2005, Table 4.

THE GLOBAL CRISIS AND THE CRISIS OF EUROPEAN NEOMERCANTILISM

RICCARDO BELLOFIORE,
FRANCESCO GARIBALDO AND JOSEPH HALEVI

The global financial crisis that erupted in, and spread out from, the United States in 2007-8 has highlighted long-standing structural faults within European capitalism, especially its neomercantilist dimension. By neomercantilism we mean the pursuit of economic policies and institutional arrangements which see net external surpluses as a crucial source of profits.[1] The solution to the problem of effective demand is seen as lying above all in a positive trade balance. Moreover, the current account surplus is seen as increasing the private sector's ability to operate on international capital markets. This outlook on the part of capitalist institutions and firms – and in Germany, Holland and Scandinavia, also on the part of unions – relegates the domestic level of employment and of wages to a subordinate role compared with external expansion. Profits accruing from net exports reduce firms' dependence on a relatively small or slow-growing domestic market, and Europe's surplus countries are well aware that were it not for their export strategy domestic investment, profits and employment would be lower. Persistent export surpluses, especially from large economies, are tantamount to exporting unemployment.

Since the Second World War European neomercantilism has been institutionalized in the phases that, from the founding of the Common Market in 1957, led to the creation of the European Union (EU). The largest neomercantilist countries of the EU operate from within the European Monetary Union (EMU), formed in 1999 and known also as the Eurozone. Throughout the wrongly termed 'Golden Age of capitalism' (1950-1973), the countries with the highest growth of exports were, in rank order, Japan, Italy and Germany. The latter two, together with France, define the essence of European neomercantilism. Holland and Belgium have had to adjust their trade strategies to the German and – to some extent, in the case of

Belgium – French trade patterns. Austria's strategy gravitates mostly towards Germany's, as does the greater part of the extra-Scandinavian trade of the Northern countries. Spain, Portugal and Greece could not, and cannot, join the neomercantilist club; they have always and systematically had negative external balances, a position also reached permanently in the 1970s by the United Kingdom.

This is where the specifically European problems begin. In a context where intra-European trade accounts for the greatest part of each country's trade, the absence of an intra-European mechanism for redistributing surpluses requires the deficit countries to undertake the adjustment by going into recession. The surplus countries will therefore suffer negative repercussions on their exports and on the related level of employment. They may still maintain their net position with a trade surplus, but at a reduced overall level of activity, with, thus, higher levels of unemployment, as Germany has today. In the last three decades the severity of the intra-European adjustment has been mitigated by net European exports to the United States. Yet the role of the US market has been declining because of the shift in US trade towards Asia.

The European deficit countries could in principle correct their imbalances by devaluing their currencies. When such a step is barred, either because all currencies are linked by a fixed exchange rate mechanism allowing only occasional changes, as under Bretton Woods and the moderately adjustable exchange rate mechanism of the European Monetary System from 1979 to 1992, or because of a single currency as in the EMU, the only non-disruptive adjustment must be a fiscal redistribution from the surplus to the deficit countries. Insofar as this is blocked by political or institutional factors, the deficit countries have no other alternative but to go through a recession, which then drags down the whole regional economy. Indeed, after the end of the Bretton Woods system in 1971, each phase of intra-European economic relations ended with solutions that worsened the internal contradictions of the system, as they systematically avoided the cooperative route, precisely for neomercantilist reasons.

Crucially, the United States functions as the market where the net neomercantilist position of Europe is consolidated. From 1958 onwards the US external surplus was whittled away by Europe and Japan. Germany had already emerged as the main European surplus country, obtaining its net exports essentially from intra-European trade. For the European countries, the deficits with Germany weigh heavily on their overall external account balance. Thus attaining a surplus with the United States has become a necessity, to compensate for those persistent deficits as well as for the deficits with dollar-based raw materials and energy-exporting countries. The US has remained the largest, richest, and most durable market for the realization of net surpluses for the EU, and for the Eurozone in particular. As we shall see, this was directly related to the transformation of the US into a globally importing economy when the new, debt-driven phase of US capitalism gathered momentum in the Reagan era. This emerged at a time when Europe was mired in internal stagnation, straitjacketed by the European Monetary System, and when, as a result, net exports beyond the Eurozone became a vital factor in the leading firms' search for profits. The drive for external surpluses has ever since been the main policy and institutional stance of EU bodies and individual countries alike, except those with unbridgeable external deficits: namely, the United Kingdom, Spain, Portugal, and Greece. This policy stance helps to explain the notable passivity exhibited in the Eurozone towards the US during the dotcom bubble of the 1990s, as well as during the much more lethal real estate bubble of the 2000s.

At the same time, because of the long-term tendency to stagnation in the EU produced by the internal contradiction described above, European financial surpluses were being invested in toxic securities issued in the United States. By deliberately nurturing stagnation through wage deflation the European institutional and economic system gave financial firms an incentive to place the proceeds of the export surpluses in 'structured vehicles' and derivatives connected to the US subprime market. Even European banking institutions that were legally mandated to lend to the network of medium and small industrial enterprises took the toxic securitized path, without knowing what they were buying, simply because real investment demand was not forthcoming. This was the case with the German *Landesbanken*: born as facilitators of productive activities, they could borrow from the capital markets at subsidized rates – a facility annulled by Brussels' reregulation policies. Hence instead of easing the financing of investment to small and medium sized firms, the Landesbanken invested in securitized papers, thereby becoming an important conduit of the contagion which spread from the USA to Europe with the eruption of the US financial crisis in 2007. After a few months the crisis spread beyond the financial sector and soon engulfed the whole economy, especially as the collapse of US demand towards the so-called BRIC countries (Brazil, Russia, India and China) impacted on Germany through a decline in its exports of capital goods, and then spread to the whole of Europe. The *impossibility of de-linking* from the US as the 'provider of last resort' of effective demand became transparent, while at the same time exposing the extent to which the practice of neomercantilism within the EU constitutes the most important factor in generating the EU's internal crisis.

THE 'NEW' US CAPITALISM: THE LINCHPIN OF EUROPEAN NEOMERCANTILISM

With the turn to neoliberalism in the US at the beginning of the 1980s, the widely-expected great Keynesian crisis of effective demand did not eventuate, for two reasons. One was the rise of what Hyman Minsky defined as 'money manager capitalism',[2] which had already spawned a pension-fund-driven form of capital accumulation in the 1970s, when the crisis of the improperly-termed Golden Age started to be tackled by curtailing the social role of the public sector and by so-called financial deregulation.[3] The management of pension funds is based on getting the maximum returns within a short time horizon, especially in the light of a weakening stream of contributions due to sagging wages and the need to cover growing claims in the near future of aging populations. The placement ('investment') of these funds in securities, shares and titles of various types creates a link between the interests of the managers of financial institutions and those of the productive firms, with the former having a large say in determining the governance criteria for the entire system of firms.

The other reason was that the officially-stated monetarist goals that inaugurated the neoliberal era in the US were quickly jettisoned.[4] Reagan's military-driven budget deficit, even when still combined with tight monetary policies, reignited the US economy, revalued the US dollar and led to a growing external deficit which became embedded in the economy. The unsuccessful attempt to rebalance the US economy led to the Wall Street crash of 1987. At this point the 'Greenspan put' came into being: the Federal Reserve supported the rise of stock and capital asset values with large amounts of liquidity and lower interest rates. This policy signal was then incorporated into the expectations of financial market operators. From this time onward, the Fed intervened so actively as the guarantor of the banks and other financial intermediaries at any sign of a financial crisis that it effectively became, as Marcello De Cecco brilliantly put it, a lender of *first resort*[5] – and eventually, in 2007, the only lender.

Consequently, markets were becoming more liquid and the supposed quality of collateral assets was thought to be regularly improving, though this was simply a mirage caused by asset price inflation, and in turn led to a perceived increase in the margin of safety.[6] It is for these reasons that the increase in indebtedness was chiefly due to borrowing by financial companies and households, rather than to borrowing by non-financial firms for physical investment. The latter felt a lesser need to use the banking system which, in turn, had to change its frame of reference. From being institutions which selected and monitored industrial firms as their main debtors, banks looked increasingly for returns from consumers' credit and the fees they could earn from arranging securitization packages – the 'originate and distribute' model of banking.

Capital asset inflation[7] goes a long way towards explaining the 'irrational exuberance' that gripped, first, the stock market and, later, the real estate market. Here we may introduce the leading characters in the drama of the 'new' capitalism: traumatized workers, manic-depressive savers and indebted consumers – all performed by the same actor. The traumatized worker, beset by the continuous attack on labour on the shopfloor amidst the deregulation of the labour market, and persistent policies designed to curtail wage demands, was expected to follow a script that involved living under increased insecurity, accepting the intensification of work to keep a job, and chasing after rising health insurance and education costs by working longer hours. The manic-depressive saver and the increasingly indebted consumer represent the other side of the coin. The bubble in asset prices, especially of houses, allowed the expansion of consumption on credit. Savings out of disposable income fell next to zero or even became negative because of the stagnation in real weekly earnings. For the bulk of the population the dynamics of consumption and the growth of effective demand became autonomous from earned income, while the 'originate and distribute' practices of the banks and mortgage lenders produced the perceived wealth effects associated with home ownership and pensions.

Wage deflation, capital asset inflation and the increasingly leveraged position of households and financial companies were complementary elements in a perverse mechanism whereby real growth was crippled by the most toxic aspects of finance. The traditional view of a conflict between industrial and financial capital no longer held. Any easy demarcation between rents and profits, or between productive and unproductive activities, was no longer convincing. At the same time the pressure on the workers came from the same factors that led to the expansion of 'bad jobs' amidst the transformation of the United States into a globally importing economy, while production and retail services were increasingly organized in line with global value chains and outsourcing activities (Walmart is a glaring example). The multiplication of financial companies that accompanied deregulation facilitated the process, as new financial intermediaries sought returns by enhancing peoples' expectations of rising stock and asset values. The more successful corporate cost-cutting and outsourcing measures were, the more stock values rose. Corporate managers – their remunerations linked to stock values – wholeheartedly embraced these policies, with an eye to the short-term, indeed quarterly, maximization of 'shareholder value'. The United

States became the trailblazer of a new form of expanded accumulation entailing *centralization without concentration*.[8] Big mergers and acquisitions occurred in key sectors without leading to a wave of large-scale vertically integrated industrial companies. This model would soon be followed by the European countries, albeit in the context of neomercantilist export objectives.

The integration of East Asia and most recently, and especially, China, as much earlier with Mexico, into the financial and import circuits of North American capitalism enabled a dynamic synergy which was – for a while – unhampered by the US's ballooning deficit. The multiplication of financial companies coincided with China's policy of facilitating the creation of as many new enterprises as possible. To be sure, endemic overproduction ensued in many sectors, engendering a persistent downward pressure on export prices, thus reducing imported inflation not connected to raw material prices. Rising US stock and asset values went hand in hand with rising imports which, by competing against the products of US industrial companies providing well-paid jobs, helped wage deflation. But the process could not have been sustained for such a long time without engineering new sources of effective demand. The interaction between monetary policy and the stock market contributed to the rise in consumption demand through the rise in the value of assets.

The whole two-decade long Greenspan period at the head of the Federal Reserve thus defined a new post-monetarist phase of neoliberalism which can be described as a sort of a 'privatized financial Keynesianism'.[9] Aggregate demand was pulled up because households borrowed against their assets, and the Federal Reserve validated the process by expanding credit at interest rates that helped further rises in asset values. Under these conditions the Federal Reserve could aim at a non-Keynesian type of full employment, in which the increase in the number of jobs sustained consumption and import demand, but where employment was organized on an increasingly precarious basis, resembling full underemployment.[10] From the mid 1990s the argument was advanced that this model was unsustainable since it was predicated on rising personal debt, begetting an expanding external deficit.[11] Yet the 'new' US capitalism – based on the Trinity of the financialization of capital, the fragmentation of labour via value chains and outsourcing, and the increasing focus of economic policy on the monetary dimension – proved longer-lasting than was expected. Indeed, although the 'new' capitalism collapsed with the dotcom crisis in 2000, it was revived by ultra-Keynesian economic and military policies and by the asset bubble driven financial Keynesianism led by the housing and subprime markets. Consequently we witnessed, over a number of years, a rather dynamic capitalist development, highly unequal in terms of income and wealth distribution, centred on consumer credit. If the indebted consumer was the locomotive of US growth, the United States was, in turn, the final buyer of the exports of the neomercantilist economies of Japan, Germany and other significant countries of Europe – and, most of all, of China.

It all finally started to come apart because of the inherent instability of US growth feeding upon the wealth effect that, under a permanent cost cutting regime, favoured China's exports and overall accumulation, thereby increasing the demand for raw materials, the prices of which began to rise again in 2004 outside of the Federal Reserve's target range for inflation. The 'new' capitalism had been based on preventing price inflation except in the case of asset values. Now the Federal Reserve could only generate another round of domestic wage deflation, via an increase in interest rates, in order to offset the domestic impact of a rise in commodity prices. Yet raising interest rates would hurt the main policy objective of sustaining a rise in capital asset values. The hope of financial companies was that the higher cost of borrowing could be offset by a further hike in asset values, thereby expanding the value of the collateral for loan applications. The rapid proliferation of subprime mortgages, enticing poor households to step into the financial swamp, was an attempt to keep the real estate bubble going by all possible means. Meanwhile the US authorities put their faith in two miracles, neither of which occurred: that more complex and obscure securitization packages would distribute risk and thereby reduce the potentially dangerous effects of defaults; and that the same magical financial instruments would draw in the surpluses and savings of the emerging economies to fill the deficits of the United States, Britain, Australia and Spain (the countries which generated the greater part of the world's deficits). To understand why this was in fact no longer possible we need to turn to the growing contradictions of European neomercantilism.

EUROPEAN NEOMERCANTILISM: FROM SUCCESS TO THE PRESENT CRISIS

The root causes of stagnation are to be found in the evolution of neomercantilism within Europe as it unfolded after 1945. In order to put it into perspective we must note that in the inter-war years France's answer to the likelihood of renewed German economic dominance was a financial and economic *entente* based on a cartelized vision of Europe, similar to the then ruling International Steel Cartel. It essentially entailed an institutionalised arrangement between the central banks, aimed at sustaining the respective currencies in a joint effort to accumulate gold bullion.[12] In the postwar period, under US hegemony, the cartelized conception of Europe mutated into the creation of a common economic space for European oligopolies. The Common Market (1957), heralded by the Economic Community of Coal and Steel (1952), was the first substantial step in that direction. Objectively, the push towards a renewed intra-European neomercantilism came from the constraint represented by the persistent German surpluses. Initially, the working of the European Payments Union (1949-1959), set up with Washington's financial contributions, and the counterpart funds of the Marshall Plan, allowed intra-European deficits to be smoothed out. But with the return to convertibility and the end of EPU in 1959, balance of trade constraints became the chief factor governing European economic policy.[13] The policy of prioritizing exports over domestic demand in order to secure a positive trade balance characterized the whole of the 1960s, during which France (in 1963-4), Italy (in 1963-5), and Germany (in 1965) all adopted stop-go policies in order to attain export surpluses.[14]

The undoing of the fixed exchange rate regime in the 1971-72 biennium and the oil- and wage-induced inflationary processes that followed, caused heavy currency fluctuations within Europe which threatened Germany's net trade surplus. In the 1970s the main danger to Germany and France came from Italy, which, by riding inflation, implemented a policy of differentiated exchange rates adjustments. The Lira was made to devalue relative to the D-Mark, boosting exports, and to revalue relatively to the US dollar, thereby reducing the cost of energy imports. The dynamic of Italy's exports was the strongest in Europe, including in its bilateral trade with Germany. The relatively important role of the French financial sector prevented Paris from gambling on inflation. But given the similarities between France and Italy in the consumption goods industries, the more the latter succeeded at its game, the more France was being hurt on its own turf, and in other European markets. A French surrender to Italy, by following the same policy, would have put an end to German surpluses and to the Bundesbank's objective of obtaining them through a strong nominal exchange rate for the D-Mark, counting on controlling wages and on the technological prowess of German industry to secure large productivity gains. The German response to the dangers arising from competitive devaluations was the formation of the European Monetary System (EMS) in 1979. It consisted of an exchange rate mechanism (ERM) which, ultimately, would make European currencies arrive at a fixed parity. Throughout the convergence phase the most inflation-prone countries (Italy, and, upon joining the European Community, Spain and Portugal too) would actually revalue their currencies in real terms.

The ERM established a 'band' setting limits to both upward and downward currency fluctuations. Italy, having in 1979 a much higher rate of inflation than the other would-be member states, negotiated a wider band. The purpose of the ERM was to eliminate inflation-induced currency fluctuations, so that the band acted in a disinflationary manner. This meant that although Italy continued with devaluations in the first half of the 1980s (in the second half the ERM achieved fixed parities), they were less than the rate of inflation, causing a real revaluation of the Lira; and sure enough, the export dynamics of the country began to deteriorate. The EMS was a German preoccupation strongly favoured by Holland and Belgium, which always searched for a niche within German neomercantilism. But the EMS could not, however, be established in 1979 without France, whose government and financial sector preferred to gain export shares through reducing imports via a drastic recession in domestic demand and employment, as had already been demonstrated in the years preceding the launching of the EMS by the government of Raymond Barre.

Under the EMS regime, at least until the absorption of East Germany in 1990, Germany piled up unprecedented surpluses as a proportion of GDP, surpluses surpassed only in 2007-8. The EMS made Europe a rock-solid area of profitable demand for German exports, whereas the deficit with Japan was growing and US imports from Europe were very sensitive to the gyrations of the dollar. Except for the period 1988-1991, the German economy was in a neomercantilist stagnation mode, being one of the slowest-growing countries in Europe, so that its demand for imports was anaemic compared with the rest of Europe's. Given the distribution of income between profits and wages, Germany's rapidly expanding trade surpluses meant sharply rising external profits for its firms. But whereas Germany's intra-European net trade surpluses grew across the board, Italy's declining surpluses did not help French capital accumulation through trade: throughout the 1980s France's deficit grew in both its trade and its current accounts, and as a share of GDP, and the rate of unemployment was 10 per cent. The German-centred ERM pushed Italy into a negative current account position and put the country's budget deficit in the hands of the capital markets. In order to maintain the ERM parities with a deteriorating current account, Italy resorted to financing its external deficit by attracting capital through paying higher interest rates on its bonds, thereby swelling the level of public debt with non-productive financial commitments. It was a deliberate policy by the Bank of Italy aimed at putting pressure on firms so as to force them to restructure and break labour's back. Spain and Portugal were in an even worse state, since in no way could their economies be made into net exporters. They couldn't therefore generate a flow of exports to prevent a credibility crisis arising from financial companies engaged in short-term trading in government bonds and foreign exchange.

The whole EMS phase, including the way it ended in 1992-3, brings us to a clear conclusion. Profit accumulation through net exports was the main objective of the German government and of big business. Large corporations wanted European price stability in order to plan their mark-ups and retain as much as possible of their productivity gains relative to wage costs. The financial sector, which is fully integrated within industrial firms, shared the same objectives, with the additional bonus that price stability and cost-cutting increased the value of financial assets. Between 1988 and 1991 Germany experienced strong growth rates. In 1992, however, when growth was resulting from a Keynesian expansion connected with the costs of German reunification, the Bundesbank scuttled the EMS. The very buoyancy of domestic demand was deemed to be a threat to net exports. A high level of domestic demand was seen as likely to result in higher wages, which would reduce international competitiveness. With the end of the EMS – directly caused by Germany increasing its interest rates for fear of inflation – the Deutschmark was revalued and the Italian Lira sharply devalued, while the French and the German government joined forces to defend parity between their own respective currencies. The high value of the D-Mark hurt German exports for an unexpectedly long time. From 1992 to 2000 export surpluses were not sufficient to finance the international expansion of German capital. In the same decade the low value of the Lira brought Italian net exports to the highest absolute level in the OECD.

The EMS/ERM had crystallized the split of the European neomercantilist trading system into two spheres. On the positive-balance side, with consistent trade surpluses, stood Germany and its neomercantilist satellites, most notably Holland; and with them stood Italy which experienced trade deficits but whose trade surplus could skyrocket at any time if the Lira were allowed to 'dance' (as happened after 1992), and if wage contracts were decoupled from inflation (as happened earlier in 1991). On the other side stood Spain and Portugal, with consistent trade deficits. French political and business leaders saw their country as standing next to Germany as a surplus country, but for most of the years preceding the 1992 crisis of the EMS, the economic reality was just the opposite. Thus to stave off the risk of sliding to the negative-balance side of the neomercantilist trading system – and having no economic means to prevent it – France's leaders shifted their focus to *la construction européenne*. Already in 1988 the formation of the Delors Commission for a single European market started President Mitterrand's push for a single currency in order to prevent France from becoming de facto part of the D-Mark area, and hopefully to allow France to join Germany's control over European monetary policy and prevent further competitive devaluations. The post-1992 crisis in the German current account had convinced France's leaders that German neomercantilism was in a long-term crisis. They thought France would become the new European pivot, in a hegemonic alliance with Germany, provided that a new order could be brought about between the European currencies and the Bundesbank policy of high interest rates could be reversed. The French view stemmed from the fact that, despite having kept parity with the D-Mark, the French economy accumulated large trade surpluses and, unlike Italy, large current account surpluses as well. It appeared as if there was a synergy between France's net merchandise balances and the net financial balances. The high interest policy pursued by the Bundesbank was tackled by delegating to Valéry Giscard d'Estaing the task of threatening to decouple the French Franc from the D-Mark. Under Chancellor Kohl's pressure the Bundesbank relented and in 1996 Germany's interest rates were lowered. The Lira immediately revalued, and so did the Peseta and the Escudo. These were the values on which the lock-in exchange rates for the Euro currency in 1999 were based.

A closer inspection of the period 1992-2001 reveals that the German current account crisis only partly opened up space for the Italian *contropiede*-style neomercantilism, and France's arrogant version. Given Europe's unbridgeable deficits with East Asia – first with Japan, South Korea and Taiwan, and then, overwhelmingly, with China – Europe's net exports benefited in the 1990s from the asset-stripping-induced consumption bubble in Russia, and from the consumption bubbles in Brazil and Argentina whose currencies were pegged to the US dollar. But the Russian and Latin American 'miracles' soon went under when, after 1998, these bubbles were pricked. By the turn of the century the peg to the dollar had gone and the countries concerned were in deep recession, returning to their role as net exporters of raw materials and of energy products, and thereby having a trade surplus with Europe. Thus the overall European external accounts were ever-more dependent on the continuation of the 'new' capitalism in the United States.

But by 2001 the US dotcom bubble was over. The ensuing downturn affected European exports more than could be counteracted by the initial decline of the Euro against the Dollar. However, and very importantly, in 2001 Germany regained its overall net surplus position, and this would expand at an increasing rate, reaching almost 8 percent of GDP in 2007 (it still stood at 6.6 per cent in 2008 when the world crisis had already begun). Net surpluses within Europe were the crucial factor in Germany's performance, in the context of stagnation in Europe as a whole. But before we turn to examining the implications of this for the current crisis of European neomercantilism, we must first address the crucial question of how German capitalism managed to sustain its unchallenged oligopolistic dominance in the European Union.

THE CHANGING STRUCTURAL BASIS OF GERMAN HEGEMONY

The structural basis of Germany's hegemony is well known: the dominance of its capital goods and technology sectors. Historically, at least since 1945, Germany's capacity to orient European policies towards its neomercantilist objectives always depended upon the capital goods sector's ability to generate new machines and new technological complexes, in combination with the oligopolistic position of Germany's corporations in Europe and the wider world. These twin factors also allowed Germany to outsource and relocate production to Eastern Europe, cutting jobs in the process while further expanding its net export position. The Maastricht Treaty of 1992, and the French-inspired Delors Plan launched in 1993, provided the formal ideological and legal framework for the new competitive neomercantilist European playing-field. This was based on the following logic: (a) investment versus consumption, the latter being associated with higher wages; (b) new technologies for greater competitiveness aided by a planned one per cent gap between the growth of productivity rates and the growth of wages; (c) a single tightly-managed Euro-currency to avoid inflation and competitive devaluations. Macroeconomic stability would also require small and diminishing public sector deficits, lest economic expansion rekindle inflation. Both the Maastricht Treaty and the Delors Plan made employment levels a very indirect outcome of economic growth, rather than an explicit policy objective. Hey presto: the whole apparatus of the European Union in Brussels pushed the member countries to strive for a high-tech investment strategy linked to high profits and to cost-cutting financialization under free intra-European capital mobility.

All this encouraged a process of heightened 'destructive' competition in Europe, which culminated in record levels of mergers and acquisitions in the two years immediately before the start of the current crisis in 2007. Greater centralization was dictated by the oligopolistic strategy of controlling larger market shares. Yet the merger movement jeopardized the existing oligopolistic structure in many industrial branches, so that some of the big players increasingly were themselves at risk. The opening up of Eastern

Europe to Western European capital after the fall of the Berlin Wall in 1989 accelerated the industrial restructuring which had begun in the late 1970s, while an additional powerful stimulus came from China's entrance into the global manufactures market. To widen market shares new plants were built in Eastern Europe, prompted by the wish to exploit the wage gap between Eastern and Western Europe. However, the productive capacity of the new plants competed with that of the same firms in the Euro-15 countries, leading to a state of endemic overproduction.[15]

Consider the cases of household appliances and the automotive sectors. In 2007 the appliances industry employed some 200,000 people, mostly in Germany and in Italy. The largest four producers controlled 53 per cent of the European market, and the first seven 71 per cent. This high level of centralization is the result of mergers and acquisitions. From 2002 to 2007 the sector's employment in the EU-15 countries fell by 23 per cent. The decline in employment in this sector for the whole of the 27 countries of the EU has been smaller, because the share of Eastern European production rose to 30 per cent of the total. But the increased volumes of output in Eastern Europe were largely unconnected with East European demand. Hence the new plants competed with the productive capacity of plants in Western Europe. A drastic restructuring process followed, with the end result of curtailing the sector's overall level of employment within Europe.

In 2007, the European automotive industry employed 2 million people, half of them by the major auto assemblers, and half in the direct supply chain. By including other activities connected with the automotive sector (including services) the total goes up to 12 million people; i.e., at that time, 7 per cent of total European employment.[16] If only automobile producers are taken into consideration, the biggest five controlled 65 per cent of the European market and the biggest three 41 per cent. In this case, too, there has been a shift of volumes to Eastern Europe. For the automobile industry the gap between the productive capacity of the new member states and their consumption of automobiles has been estimated in 2007 to be up to a million cars per year. The strategy of shifting production to Eastern Europe has thus compounded the pre-existing problem of European overcapacity in the sector, which is now hovering at around 30 per cent of potential output.

The centralization process through acquisitions and mergers did not lead to concentration in the classical manner of vertically-integrated firms. Instead, productive networks or *filières*, based on the outsourcing of upstream production activities, and made up of many small and medium enterprises, have been set up by the main automative producers (OEM). Each chain is segmented in tiers, each one with a different value-adding capacity, depending on productivity. For instance, in all industries the producers of modules or complex components are stronger than companies producing simple parts. The overwhelming majority of these networks/chains are organised in both tiers and poles; the poles are the key players of each tier.[17] At the bottom of this ladder we find the 'last', the companies just supplying an output of a certain amount of simple manufacturing/processing activity or simple services; these units just struggle to survive.

Given the present weakness of unions, working conditions largely depend on the relative positioning of each company in the supply and value chains/*filières*. These *filières* are now more integrated than in the past. The companies engaged in the upstream activities are not only on the buying side of the option make-or-buy; they are under the authority both of the key players of the *filières*, that is the OEMs, and of the other key players in each tier. The key players decide for the other companies how to plan output quantities in a given period of time, the speed at which to complete and deliver each batch, how to arrange a mix of different items in sequences, etc. They have the classical prerogatives of managers. For highly specialised companies, such as module suppliers, the degree and the nature of the integration in the *filière* is such that the borderlines between companies are blurred and new ways of co-operation begin with new corporate governance schemes. As for working conditions, conditions at the bottom of the chain are very precarious, very close to the grey and black areas of the economy. In this new industrial organisation the companies in the grey and black areas are no longer considered free agents, but, in many industries, are rather seen as functionally dependent parts of the system.

Thus two main closely interrelated and reinforcing processes have profoundly changed European and global 'industrial capital': centralization without concentration, and a model of competition based on the pursuit of a never-ending expansion of all kind of consumption, engendering therefore the necessity to seek new markets. This struggle has been fought by adding new productive facilities when the existing ones already carried significant unused capacity. The new system has also been built on the functional integration into a single framework of many subsystems of companies with different regimes, the overall effect of which has been the squeezing of wages and working conditions in Western Europe. This dire situation has been worsened by the doubling of the global workforce since the end of 1990s.[18]

THE GERMAN STRATEGY'S CONTRADICTIONS

In France in the mid 1990s, especially under the Socialist Government of Lionel Jospin, whose Finance Minister was Dominique Strauss Kahn, Paris thought that the German crisis would enable France to implement the cartelized plan for Europe from a hegemonic position. Yet it was Germany, essentially because of the structural features of its expanded reproduction, and Holland as a service and financial area supplying it, which were able to make the most of the new framework established by the Maastricht Treaty and the Delors Plan. It took nine years, but the German surplus came back with a vengeance, all the more so since the countries in structural deficit could no longer devalue, nor could they develop their own independent fiscal policies.

Let us analyze how the process worked in Germany. The export boom has been based on big productivity gains, without providing a spin-off for employees' general conditions (wages, working conditions and social provision). Instead, with the shrinking of the domestic market, there has been wage moderation and a reduction of social provision.[19] This situation has been compounded by the off-shoring of production to lower-cost countries, including European ones, in order to implement a very aggressive export strategy. Employers' policies on how to overcome the perceived barrier of the traditionally relatively high wages of post-war Germany changed dramatically in the nineties. There was a large shift from the automation strategy of the seventies and the eighties, to the off-shoring of upstream activities, mainly to Eastern Europe and partly to areas in the old EU-15, such as northern Italy. There has been a simultaneous large shift of investments towards East Europe, on a scale that led Sinn to state: 'Current net investment abroad is 50 per cent higher than domestic net investment. German firms are currently engaged in an investment strike [at home]'.[20]

The rationale of this strategy is that high-tech investments can give Germany an advantage over new competitors such as India and China, making the medium-high layers of their mass markets available for German exports. In Germany nowadays the discussion centres on mapping out a trajectory from 'made in Germany' to 'enabled in Germany'.[21] These markets are so big that even if only the richest parts of them become accessible they will suffice to guarantee an adequate return on investment, as is the case with Volkswagen in China. But even if this benefits certain German capitalists operating in China, it may not benefit the German economy. China licences FDI requiring technology transfers. It has also undertaken massive educational and research programmes in industrial know-how.[22] China is therefore increasingly able to supply its home markets with productive processes whose upstream and downstream activities are domestically-based. The overall effect has been, and still is, to add more over-capacity in many industries at the global level, creating new financial risks and, on the long run, new deflationary pressures.

It should have been clear for some time that the German European algorithm is untenable for Europe, and would eventually mercilessly tear the Union apart. The idea that substituting low skilled labour for highly-skilled jobs will generate more jobs for the exporting country is pure wishful thinking. Indeed, during the past ten years German employment has fallen by 1.36 million people.[23] The German growth in the stock of capital in the last 20 years is among the lowest in the EU. It is only the main German export-oriented corporations and financial companies that benefit from the country's macroeconomic stagnation, thanks to wage deflation and the profits they derive from their exports.

With the formation of the EMU in 1999 Germany's neomercantilism hardened. From 2000 to 2008 national income grew more slowly than the Eurozone average, but German labour productivity outpaced the average by more than 35 per cent, while the rise in compensation per employee was half of the Eurozone average.[24] These outcomes emanate from a deliberate deflationary policy aimed at keeping wages in check while extracting productivity increases. These were made possible by the technological transformation of Germany's capital stock which, unlike that of Italy and even France, never lost its structural, intersectoral coherence. It is precisely the coherence of the country's productive apparatus which enabled firms located in the *Bundesrepublik* to farm out production to Eastern Europe while retaining the productivity gains which, combined with domestic stagnation, boosted export performance. Germany's business leaders explicitly stated that the country can remain a low growth area provided it keeps all the capital goods sectors needed to feed exports, FDI projects in Asia and outsourcing to Eastern Europe. Previous attempts to engineer an iron-clad area of protection for this model of accumulation failed because of their ad hoc nature. With the Maastricht Treaty and Stability and Growth Pact, however, now taken up by the EMU, Germany does not have to carry fiscal-institutional responsibility for the deficits that emerge elsewhere in Europe, while its export sectors benefit from the single currency, thereby exacerbating the intra-European divide.

THE CURRENT CRISIS: THE WORSENING EUROPEAN DIVIDE

The present state of affairs in the Eurozone and in the EU reflects the partition of the European Union into three groups. The first is a group of neomercantilist countries centred on Germany and including Holland, Belgium, Austria and Scandinavia. Their neomercantilism can be defined as strong, because of their persistent export surpluses – realized mostly within Europe, since the trend of rising deficits with Asia is not being offset by their fluctuating surplus with the USA. The group's external net balances rests on the combined effect of maintaining a powerful capital goods industry, linked to global oligopolistic corporations, while having a very low long-run domestic growth rate. Germany is not the locomotive of Europe. From the 1970s onwards the rest of Western Europe systematically had much higher rates of growth, thereby stimulating imports from Germany and its economic satellites. Hence the neomercantilist group epitomizes a classical monopoly capital situation, turned into an institutionalized macroeconomic regime by the very process of *la construction européenne* that was wanted by France.

In the past Germany aimed at stable exchange rates to avoid competitive devaluations. In the context of a single currency, competitive devaluations mutate into a competitive widening of the productivity-wage gap. Domestic stagnation ensures that German wages grow less fast than productivity. The country's industrial relations system, based on a neomercantilist entente between capital and the trade unions, allows the gap between productivity and wages to be more favourable to capital than in the rest of Europe. All this leads to low growth in Germany, reinforcing its export competitiveness by means of wage deflation. The end result is that while Europe cannot do without German machinery and technology inputs, Germany is not a fast-expanding importer and so does not contribute to net European demand. It thereby accumulates very large external surpluses that are partly used to finance FDI and joint ventures as far afield as China, as we have seen, as well as elsewhere in Europe, including in its deficit countries. But the 2007-8 crisis of the *Landesbanken* also revealed the more toxic financial consequences of Germany's search for external surpluses.[25]

The second group of countries is the European inner periphery, headed by Italy with France being a case on its own. Firms in Portugal, Spain and Greece would like to generate net exports but they can't because, their export growth notwithstanding, they have weak domestic capital goods sectors, so that any sustained expansion in national income has a rising import content. The import dependency of their technology and durable goods sectors is such that previous, pre-Euro, devaluations did not improve the external balances of these countries. Both Spain and Greece, though not Portugal, experienced higher than the EU's average growth rates. Spain's growth was due to the insertion of the country into the international real estate market via London. In the case of Greece the fiscal deficit enabled it to sustain an import-oriented growth. In both instances the growth of domestic demand led to higher activity, entailing yet more imports per capita. Spain, Portugal and Greece are permanent deficit countries and represent net profitable export areas for Germany, France and Italy, by absorbing 7, 10 and 9 per cent respectively of their total exports. Given the productivity-driven dominance of German export production, the current account deficits of Greece, Spain and Portugal could not be reined in and had be financed by capital inflows obtained by issuing government bonds (in the case of Greece) and/or by capital transfers, such as those resulting from sales of Spanish real estate in London.

Italy symbolizes a weak form of neomercantilism, which in the past depended upon real currency devaluations, especially towards the Deutsche Mark. However, after the dotcom crisis of 2000, the country witnessed a significant capitalist transformation stemming from the so-called 'fourth' capitalism of small and medium-sized multinationals which have successfully crossed over into high value-added productions. With the adoption of the Euro, Italy's net external position deteriorated sharply, turning negative in 2005. On balance the Euro has restricted the European space of Italian capitalism. Since the mid-1990s, under the centre-left government, Italy has implemented a savage wage deflation, while outsourcing apparel and footwear production to Romania and Albania. But whereas for Germany the same outsourcing policy in the automotive and household appliances sectors has been consistent with a juggernaut advance of net exports, Italy has seen its external accounts deteriorate sharply. The 'made in Italy' model is affected by an inherent fragility, and can survive only at the price of a continuous restructuring. Worse still, Asian imports into European markets compete neck and neck with Italy's.

This leaves the major economies of the UK and France. As for the former, were it not for its world financial sector, it would belong to the persistent deficit countries of the inner periphery. France, above all, stands in a peculiar position as a very special case between the surplus and deficit groups: as we have seen, it has a pronounced neomercantilist posture but it seldom achieves the goal of running a net surplus, not least because it is the largest net export market for Germany and increasingly so for Italy; but it tried to avoid the route of competitive devaluation, because of the weight of its financial sector. And just as upon the Euro's establishment, Italy began to lose its surpluses, so did France. The new more favourable currency position that the Euro provided did not help France, and by 2005 it joined Italy in hitting negative territory in both their trade and their current accounts.

Meanwhile Spain, Portugal and Greece saw their deficits double and then treble within a few years. From the mid 1990s until 2008 the growth rates of Spain and Greece were significantly higher than the EU average. Yet the weak capital goods sectors of their economies implied that growth involved net imports and financial inflows. For quite a while EU structural funds for less-developed regions contributed significantly to the expansion of Spain and Greece, as well as of Portugal and Ireland. Brussels' money is estimated to have sustained 1/3 of Spain's growth, and Madrid's budgetary position was not characterized by large deficits or debt: down to 2008 its public debt-to-GDP ratio was well below the 60 per cent established by Maastricht, and the budget deficit was 2 per cent, well below the Maastricht limit of 3 per cent. But the strong integration of Spain into the international real estate financial circuit, while attracting money, caused an immediate contagion when the subprime bubble collapsed in 2007-8. In just a few months unemployment jumped from 11 per cent to 19 per cent, the largest rise in Western Europe. Obviously, the formerly negligible budget deficit also shot up, reaching 12 per cent of GDP by 2010. On top of this the 'new capitalism' put the financing of the budget deficits of weak countries in the hands of capital markets and the (officially despised) rating agencies. Perceptions about the unsustainable nature of Spain's deficit were catapulted into the spread between the interest rate on German bonds and the supposedly riskier ones of Spain.

A similar fate befell Greece, where the capital goods sector's power to generate capital accumulation is even weaker than in Spain. Its high growth rate was entirely Keynesian – but this would eventually prove disastrous in a non-Keynesian world. The country's economy grew on account of its effectively high deficit public spending, plus the usual EU structural funding. The thin productive basis of Greece's economy meant that such a high rate of growth also caused an ever-widening current account deficit. With the onset of the global crisis the European Central Bank ceased to be willing to accept Greek bonds as collateral for lending to Athens, following German pressure and France's surrender to it. Rating agencies made the spread on Greek bonds shoot up to the point where the financing of current government operations was jeopardised. At this point the Socialist Pasok government also surrendered to Berlin, whose sole objective was to save the value of Greek bonds held by German banks.

The predicament of Southern Europe highlights how the crisis is aggravating the divisions within Europe, and especially within the Eurozone. When it comes to its own situation Germany does not always take the same dogmatic view that it holds in relation to the deficits of other Eurozone countries. Shortly after the start of the Euro in 2001 Germany, together with France, let its budget deficit go well beyond the 3 per cent limits set by Maastricht and the Stability Pact. A significant part of this budget deficit helped German companies to undergo the restructuring needed to mount the new export offensive. With the success of the latter and the resulting increase in tax revenues, Berlin advocated once more the need to return to fiscal conservatism, and the Bundestag even passed a law requiring the domestic budget to be balanced. Suffering a fall of 5 per cent of GDP in the current crisis, Germany could not but violate the Maastricht criteria again, while making it clear, however, that not a single German Euro should be transferred to the weaker areas of the Eurozone. Convinced that its industry will successfully fight the crisis through export-oriented restructuring at home and relocation in Eastern Europe, Berlin is adamant that its own public moneys should go to facilitate these tasks, and not be 'squandered' on Greece, which is an example to be noticed by – whom? Portugal and Spain?

Yes; but their situation is self evident. It is France that must take notice, since Paris's budget deficit is rising fast, beyond 8 per cent of GDP, far above Germany's. Paris has taken notice by capitulating on the Greek issue and by itself reverting to a German-style fiscal Protestantism. Hence the most relevant intercapitalist outcome of the crisis so far is the extreme weakening of France's position, burying the idea of a cartelized entente acting as the joint power hub of Europe – the idea so long, and so much, cherished by the French ruling class. Chancellor Merkel is enforcing the legal features of the EMU, the key weakness of which was explained, early in 2010, by one of its German founders, Otmar Issing, as follows:

> The monetary union is based on two pillars. One is the stability of the euro, guaranteed by an independent central bank with a clear mandate to maintain price stability. The other is fiscal solidity, which has to be delivered by individual member states. Member countries are still sovereign. Emu does not represent a state; it is an institutional arrangement unique in history. In the 1990s, *many economists – I was among them – warned that starting monetary union without having established a political union was putting the cart before the horse.* [26]

By May 2010, in the wake of the so-called Greek crisis, the conflict between Germany and France was being narrowed to two competing, yet similar, budgetary rules for the European Union. But both the German plan, based on its own terrifying balanced budget law, and the brand new French proposal of a trajectory towards balanced budgets, are both bound to crash on the rocks of intra-Eurozone asymmetries and a worsening social crisis produced by further state responses to large losses of tax revenue. Each country is taking austerity measures that will make recovery problematic at best.

The race to the bottom generated by this crisis misleadingly bears Greece's name, even though it was a German creation. In a crisis situation such as exists today the inconsistency of the European construct multiplies its structural faults. Europe finds itself in a classical Marxian overproduction crisis whose foundations lie in the stagnation of the last three decades. Overcapacity and the stagnation of working-class incomes compelled countries to find other markets for their outputs, to choose between neomercantilism and an economy based on debt. This, in turn, has created enormous room for manoeuvre for financial capital. In reality the neomercantilist approach has made Germany even more exposed to the crisis; it is not by chance that in 2009 it has registered the highest percentage fall in production among the EU-15 countries. Chancellor Merkel rejected all criticism of this pattern of development, and expressed her conviction of the need for Germany to have a strong export performance in order to maintain its social standards, although up to the summer of 2009 the government took measures defying its own rhetoric. On the whole, the objective of net export has been a factor, among many others, contributing to the political implosion of the European Union, unable to find common industrial and labour policies to face up to the crisis and giving way, instead, to nationalistic attempts to defend each country's status quo, as seen in the Opel-General Motors quarrel.

The mercantilist approach chosen by Germany, Italy and France, in this hierarchical order, which for a long time appeared to be successful, has brought Euroland to a dead end. Since the 1970s Germany has had a deliberate and successful policy to keep its own growth rate well below that of the rest of Europe with the precise objective of piling up financial surpluses. France, too, has not been very keen on sustained growth because successive governments (including Mitterrand's) feared wage demands. And, once public sector spending ceased to support Italy's growth already in the late 1970s, its economy could only grow if favourable exchange rate conditions prevailed. Under these circumstances it is hardly surprising that growth rates in Western Europe declined during every single one of the last four decades.

Europe has fallen more and more into the grip of German surpluses, the only bright spot being net exports to the United States which, however, hardly compensated for the growing deficits with Asia. The formation of the Euro completely crystallized the situation, enabling Germany to reach unprecedented surpluses amidst deepening European stagnation. When the US outlet ceased to function in the wake of the subprime crisis – which cascaded onto the derivative papers held by the Landesbanken – Germany hardened its neomercantilist stance and unilaterally decided to rewrite the rules of the game.

The Greek crisis is just the route chosen by Berlin to modify the EU's code of conduct, to the detriment of France. There is no genuine problem of an excessive Greek deficit. It can easily be handled at the European level by devising common policies to revamp European, and specifically Greece's, growth, which is also the only cure that will not kill the patient. Drastic cuts in public expenditure, while disarticulating the whole system of services and infrastructure on which a modern society rests, reduce the debt ratio only marginally, if at all. But from Berlin's neomercantilist perspective a cooperative growth option is not even remotely contemplated, for the following reasons.

Germany continues to see the Eurozone as a fixed exchange rate system whose function is only to prevent competitive devaluations (which in the past were chiefly indulged in by Italy). For Germany the essential role of Western Europe is to provide net effective demand for Germany's exports. As Wolfgang Münchau recently reported in the *Financial Times*: 'Rainer Brüderle, economics minister, said last week there was nothing the government could do about demand because consumption was a decision by private individuals. A senior Bundesbank official even compared the Eurozone to a football league, in which Germany proudly held the number one slot'.[27] The comparison is patently false: to compete with Germany, Eurozone countries would have to reduce their own growth rates well below Germany's, which means that they would have to be zero or even negative.

The hardening of the German stance towards Greece and the Iberian countries was also due to Berlin's focus on its own outer periphery in Eastern Europe, involving the Baltic countries, which are in a total depression, and the deeply recession-hit Slovakia and Hungary. It is an open secret that, although refusing to confirm it, the ECB has been buying their bonds as collateral for loans, thus rescuing Austrian and Swedish banks from the consequences of their reckless lending to these countries. This was done with the full support of Berlin. Germany's opposition to helping out Greece was the counterpart of its policy of allocating funds to areas that are Berlin's satellites zones, and to the areas where German companies have been pursuing their restructuring strategies, as is the case with Eastern Europe.

It is this 'gestalt' that pushed Sarkozy to confront Merkel (though he did it much too late), compelling Berlin to accept a 750 billion euro fund. Some prominent figures, like Romano Prodi in the *Financial Times*, mistakenly hailed the decision as a step towards European fiscal federalism.[28] It is nothing of the sort. At best it is an emergency fund for German and French banks, structured in a special investment vehicle the content of which is unknown. This explains why the new fund, however massive, did not have a great deal of effect in placating the markets. It underscored the inadequacy of existing European institutions since the new fund is placed outside their framework.

Moreover, the whole 'Greek' episode has underscored the fatal weakness in the role of the European Central Bank. When, in the fall of 2009, on Berlin's insistence, the ECB ruled that Greek government bonds were no longer acceptable as collateral for loans, it pushed the Greek crisis to the point of no return. The decision enhanced the power of the credit rating agencies, whose influence Germany and France both officially wished to curb, allowing the public debt of the inner European periphery to be evaluated by what are themselves the most opaque of all financial companies. A game of Russian roulette began, with the downgrading in quick succession of the Spanish and Portuguese debt, which in turn dragged down the derivatives related to this debt. In this respect the ECB initiated a process similar to the market-driven subprime crisis in the United States. The contagion spread through the derivative products and by mid-May, in tandem with the creation by the EU of the special fund, the ECB made an about-face by starting to purchase Greek, Portuguese and Spanish bonds hand over fist.

The nature of the institutional failure represented by the behaviour of the ECB becomes clear when the events of the November 2009-May 2010 in Europe are compared with those of 2008 in the United States. There, the Federal Reserve inundated the banking system with liquidity and was supported by the US Treasury which, in turn, launched expenditure programmes, no matter how limited and inadequate. Nothing of the kind can happen in Euroland where, instead, the ECB strongly supports the imposition of balanced budgets throughout the zone. The ECB's policies do not stem from a 'wrong' perspective. They are the outcome of *la construction européenne*, in which there is no place for a European Treasury, while the national treasuries are reduced to the role of mere tax collectors, even in times of falling demand and employment. At the same time the ECB is compelled by necessity to contradict itself by purchasing government's debt while opposing active fiscal policies.

PROSPECTS

Meanwhile the prospects for Europe can be sketched out as follows. The EU lacks the internal social and institutional bodies to counteract the current crisis and the stagnationist forces at work. Hence hope is placed in the unlikely possibility of a wave of Schumpeterian, epoch-making innovations, or in new external markets. Yet the latter are few and far between. The US, where households are in debt-deflation mode while the government is trying to stimulate exports, can no longer consume imports from the EU as it did before. The EU is running a deficit with China and Japan, and with Latin America, whose imports are, in any case, now coming more from China. In this context some European countries have deficits with China and Asia that are not hampering their overall surplus position: they are Germany, Holland and Scandinavia. Indeed their surpluses, obtained mostly within Europe, are a necessary means of financing their FDI in China and Asia, and their joint ventures with Chinese and other Asian companies. Against these countries we have France, Italy, Spain, Portugal and Greece. They are a crucial source of surpluses for Germany and the other Northern countries while at the same time their own exports and domestic markets are being penetrated by China's exports. Barring a Euro-centred Schumpeterian miracle, the intra-European structural faults are bound to worsen.

In relation to today's crisis, too, US monetary policy based on the unlimited creation of liquidity at rock-bottom interest rates is highly inadequate. First, because under conditions of acute crisis the money can just stay within the banking system, as indeed has been happening – a sort of liquidity trap, in economists' jargon. Second, because flooding the system with liquidity is sustainable only if the institutions receiving the money at zero cost will employ it somewhere. But with real effective demand falling, or remaining flat, with collateral of a dubious and largely unknown value, unwillingness to lend is a given. It follows that the only way to use the money received gratis is by chasing after risk in order to generate returns. And not just chasing, but actually engineering new forms of structured investment vehicles, creating risk out of thin air. Under these circumstances the restructuring of labour processes which is occurring in companies plagued with excess capacity is leading to unemployment, both directly and also indirectly, through productivity increases. Given that the collapse in labour's bargaining power brought about by the now defunct 'new' capitalism has been made worse by the present crisis, it is unlikely that wages will rise with productivity.

Hence both existing unemployment and productivity growth will reinforce wage deflation which, in the absence of other forces, will worsen the Great Recession, turning it into a Great Stagnation. Expansionary fiscal policies cannot be fully relied upon to lift the system up. The Japanese case is there to teach us a lesson regarding a blind faith in deficit spending.

The challenge is to devise targeted interventions by integrating stimuli to demand with structural reforms aimed at the *socialization of investment*, as a permanent and not a temporary solution, and in such a way that the socialization of investment turns into the *socialization of employment*, with no separation between the two policies. Both presuppose a *socialization of banking*, which turns banks into public utilities.[29] Considering also that with the financialization of capitalism and its new forms, the infrastructural network has been allowed to decay in favour of capital asset values (the state of US infrastructure is there for all to see, but the same can be said about the United Kingdom, Italy and Australia), the socialization of finance is also a crucial instrument for undertaking public spending programmes to rebuild public infrastructure. A structural economic policy is needed, which does not separate intervention in relation to demand from that in relation to supply. Not to be idealist, all this presupposes a renewed strength of labour struggles in production.

The necessity of this kind of intervention is paramount because continental European leaders, both political and business, see the way out of the crisis in a mythical extra-European export boom. Therefore their focus is on productivity increases without any accompanying increase in wages. For the same reason they are refraining from any positive measures. The existing budget deficits are essentially a passive outcome of the crisis. Active policies have been few and uncoordinated, adopted only to prevent the collapse of the system, and have been rapidly removed when the most dramatic phase of the downturn slowed down. Indeed there is now strong pressure from Germany to enforce budgetary deflation on the Iberian countries and Greece, although their impoverishment will hurt the absolute volume of exports from Germany, France and Italy. Most ominously, in France the present government is pushing for a renewed wave of financially-driven privatization in the public services, and is planning the relaxation of minimum wage legislation.

With the end of the neoliberal cycle we can hardly bask in the illusion – typical of left-wing Keynesians – that it all boils down to 'better' economic policies, and not to the evolution of some of the deepest features of the very modus operandi of capitalism. It is impossible to address possible ways out of the crisis without facing the issue of the changes that have occurred in the capitalist labour process, together with the changes in finance affecting demand and inequality. No policy or imagined project for beneficial change can flourish without an organic relation with the social movements that challenge the present state of things.

NOTES

1 This aspect of modern capitalism was already pointed out by Rosa Luxemburg. See her *The Accumulation of Capital*, London: New York: Routledge, 2003, originally published in 1913; and Riccardo Bellofiore, ed., *Rosa Luxemburg and the Critique of Political Economy*, London: Routledge, 2009.

2 Hyman Minsky, 'Finance and Stability: the Limits of Capitalism', Working Paper No. 93, Levy Economics Institute of Bard College, New York, 1993.

3 The rhetoric about 'deregulation' is mostly superficial, as convincingly argued in Leo Panitch and Martijn Konings, *American Empire and the Political Economy of Global Finance*, Basingstoke: Palgrave Macmillan, 2009.

4 Riccardo Bellofiore and Joseph Halevi, 'Deconstructing Labor. What is "new" in contemporary capitalism and economic policies: a Marxian-Kaleckian perspective', in C. Gnos and L.P. Rochon, eds., *Employment, Growth and Development. A Post-Keynesian Approach*, Cheltenham: Elgar, 2010 (forthcoming).

5 Marcello De Cecco, 'The Lender of Last Resort', CIDEI Working Paper 49, Università di Roma La Sapienza, Rome, 1998.

6 Jan Kregel, 'Minsky's cushions of safety. Systemic risk and the crisis in the U.S. Subprime mortgage market', Public Policy Brief Highlights No. 93A, Levy Economics Institute of Bard College, New York, 2008.

7 Jan Toporowski, *The End of Finance: The Theory of Capital Market Inflation, Financial Derivatives, and Pension Fund Capitalism*, London: Routledge, 2000.

8 This same phenomenon is christened by Bennett Harrison a concentration without centralization, thus inverting Marx's terminology. Harrison, *Lean and Mean*, New York: Basic Books, 1994, p. 8.

9 Riccardo Bellofiore and Joseph Halevi, 'A Minsky moment? The subprime crisis and the new capitalism', in Gnos and Rochon, eds., *Credit, Money and Macroeconomic Policy*.

10 Joan Robinson, *Essays in the Theory of Employment*, London: Macmillan, 1937.

11 The most perceptive of these arguments were advanced by Wynne Godley in 'U.S. Foreign Trade, the Budget Deficit and Strategic Policy Problems: A Background Brief', Working Paper No. 138, Levy Economics Institute of Bard College, New York, 1995; and 'Seven Unsustainable Processes', Special Report, Levy Economics Institute of Bard College, New York, 1999.

12 Alain Parguez, 'The Tragic and Hidden History of the European Monetary Union', unpublished paper, Université Franche Comptée, Besançon, November, 2009.

13 Riccardo Bellofiore and Joseph Halevi, 'Is the European Union keynesian-able? A sceptical view', in E. Hein, A. Heise and A. Truger, eds., *European Economic*

Policies. Alternatives to Orthodox Analysis and Policy, Marburg: Metropolis Verlag, 2006, p. 329-45.

14 Stop-go policies meant slowing down domestic demand and relying on export growth.

15 James R. Crotty, 'Structural Contradictions of the Global Neoliberal Regime', *Review of Radical Political Economics*, 32(3), 2000, 361-68. The Euro-15 needs to be distinguished from the EU-15 since the latter includes Britain which is not of the Eurozone group.

16 Francesco Garibaldo, Philippe Morvannou and Jochen Tholen, eds., *Is China a Risk or an Opportunity for Europe? An assessment of the Automobile, Steel and Shipbuilding Sectors*, Frankfurt am Main: Peter Lang, 2008.

17 Francesco Garibaldo and Andrea Bardi, eds., *Company Strategies and Organisational Evolution in the Automotive sector: A Worldwide Perspective*, Frankfurt am Main: Peter Lang, 2005

18 Richard Freeman, 'The Great Doubling: The Challenge of the New Global Labor Market', 2006, available via http://www.econ.berkeley.edu/econ/.

19 Stephan Danninger and Fred Joutz, 'What Explains Germany's Rebounding Export Market Share', IMF Working Paper WP/07/ 24, International Monetary Fund, Washington, 2007.

20 Hans-Werner Sinn, 'The Pathological Export Boom and The Bazaar Effect. How to Solve the German Puzzle', CESifo Working Paper No. 1708, CESifo Group, Munich, April, 2006.

21 See the project: http://www.internationalmonitoring.com.

22 Francesco Garibaldo, Oscar Marchisio and Volker Telljohann, 'The automotive industry', in Garibaldo, Morvannou and Tholen, eds., *Is China a Risk*, pp. 27-51.

23 Sinn, p. 14.

24 *OECD Economic Outlook*, 86, November, 2009.

25 The *Landesbanken* are owned by the German states with the specific task of lending to small and medium industrial firms. For their operations they could also borrow at officially subsidized rates. This facility was annulled by an EU directive which branded it uncompetitive.

26 Otmar Issing, 'A Greek bail-out would be Disaster for Europe', *Financial Times*, 16 February 2010 (emphasis added).

27 Wolfgang Münchau, 'Gaps in the Eurozone "Football League"', *Financial Times*, 21 March 2010.

28 Romano Prodi, 'A big step towards Fiscal Federalism in Europe', *Financial Times*, 21 May 2010.

29 Leo Panitch, 'Rebuilding Banking', *Red Pepper*, 3 January 2009, available at www.redpepper.org.uk.

A LOYAL RETAINER? JAPAN, CAPITALISM AND THE PERPETUATION OF AMERICAN HEGEMONY

R. TAGGART MURPHY

Sixty five years ago, the United States emerged from the Second World War as the undisputed hegemon of world capitalism. But within a generation, neither the American will nor the American ability to continue managing the global capitalist order could be taken for granted. This essay will argue that the key to understanding the repair and continued re-enforcement of American hegemony since the system-shaking tremors of the 1970s can be found in the postwar experience of Japan and its neighbours. Within that experience lies a paradox: it was precisely Japan's deviations from orthodox capitalist methods – the distinctive marks that characterize its political economy – that help explain the continuation of an American-centred world capitalist system long after one might have expected its manifest contradictions to bring it down.

Perry Anderson has recently written: 'In Japan, Korea and Taiwan, the post-war states were creatures of American occupation or protection, on a front-line of the Cold War. Strategically, they remain to this day wards of Washington – planted with US bases or ringed by US warships – without real diplomatic or military autonomy. Lacking political sovereignty, yet needing domestic legitimacy, their rulers … compensated with policies of economic self-development, keeping foreign capital at bay with one hand, promoting domestic corporations with the other'.[1] In other words, for reasons that go directly to the core political legitimacy of their power structures, these states have deliberately flouted neoliberal development doctrine with its emphasis on the free movement of goods and capital. Had Japan's power-holders, in particular, not felt compelled for political and historical reasons to eschew 'liberalization' of their economy – had they allowed capital markets, for example, to determine corporate control while arranging the incentive structure of their system to enshrine financial return as the pre-eminent goal of asset-management – their ability to support US hegemony could have been fatally compromised. Today's global economic system would be a very different animal.

The era of American hegemony has added another contradiction of capitalism to those already identified by Marx, such as tendencies towards overcapacity and a declining rate of profit, as capitalists attempt to defend and enlarge market share. Since the emergence of the dollar as capitalism's dominant currency, we have seen a secular decline in its relative value. Unlike sterling, which maintained its purchasing power through most of the 19th century and was disseminated via British capital exports, the global supply of dollars originates in American current account deficits – raising the possibility of an erosion of confidence in the dollar that ultimately could lead to a crisis of confidence in capitalism itself. This contradiction – first noted by the economist Robert Triffin in 1956 (he called it a 'dilemma') – was resolved or postponed by a Japan that had adopted an export-led growth model partly to forestall the full transforming power of capitalist relations. Among other things, relying on export proceeds and domestic savings rather than foreign direct investment to finance development helped ensure that economic and political outcomes were determined by domestic power holders rather than impersonal market forces. But the export-led growth model brought with it its own contradictions in the form of a build-up of dollars that were not adequately translated into domestic purchasing power. To resolve this contradiction, the authorities deliberately created and fostered asset bubbles. The bubbles, once ended, could not be re-inflated, but the attempts to jolt the economy back into growth with waves of credit creation supplied much of the credit that fuelled bubbles abroad – first in Southeast Asia, and then in the United States itself. And it has also been this Japanese credit that provided the crucial support the dollar needed to survive the bursting of those bubbles and maintain its position as the dominant world currency.

The very market-thwarting mechanisms that the Japanese put in place domestically have repeatedly been pressed into service in managing the biggest contradiction of them all: the rescue of a global capitalist order by a country that had attained wealth and power at least in part through non-capitalist means. But while the methods Japan employed may not have been fully capitalist, they depended for their success on their embedding within a global capitalist order pivoting around the financial hegemony of the United States. And when Japan's methods began to threaten that order, Japan would move to preserve it while doing its best – not always successfully – to limit capitalist liberalization at home. Japan's very resistance to the full transforming power of capitalist relations forms a crucial explanation for both Japan's willingness and its ability to support the global capitalist order.

THE 1950s ORIGINS OF 'THE JAPANESE MIRACLE'

The thirteen crucial years between 1955 and 1968 would see Japan vault from a poor struggling country just beginning its climb out of war's devastation to a position as the world's second largest non-Communist economy (in retrospect, its economy was probably already larger in 1968 than that of the Soviet Union). Japan seized global leadership in a series of industries beginning with textiles and moving up the value-added chain through shipbuilding, motorcycles, a range of consumer electronics, and steel. Dominance of colour television, machine tools, and automobiles was just around the corner. These were all established industries with global markets adequately served by existing capacity when Japanese competitors suddenly arrived on the scene. It is crucial to understanding what subsequently happened both in Japan and to the global capitalist system that one keeps in mind that Japan targeted existing industries and existing capacity rather than attempting to launch new industries. In a nutshell, Japan's strategy for economic recovery from the devastation of war required first that foreign companies be booted out of the domestic market in carefully chosen sectors. The domestic champions that then emerged from a protected home base exported torrential surges of goods to wrest market share abroad from Western companies and establish dominant global positions. For the strategy to work, the exports had to be of equal or higher quality than those available from Western competitors, and offered at lower prices.

In the 1950s, Japan's power-holders stumbled onto a formula for economic growth and capital accumulation that surpassed anything the world had seen until that time. Much of their success stemmed from the way they turned to their advantage the peculiar parameters of that decade: a United States unwilling to restore real sovereignty to Occupied Japan, but also ready to buy anything Japan could sell without demanding reciprocal access to Japan's market. At the beginning of the decade, the United States accounted for close to half the purchasing power of the planet while Japan had barely begun to recover from the devastation of war. So one-way trade with Japan hardly seemed much of a sacrifice to Washington, particularly when it formed part of a broader package that included a string of American bases throughout the Japanese archipelago and put Japan firmly in the Western/capitalist 'camp' – never mind that many of Japan's methods were hardly capitalist. Indeed, Japan's power-holders had no real blueprint for what they were doing, capitalist or otherwise. Mainstream economics, whether of the

Keynesian or, later, neo-classical variant, did not constitute much of their mental furniture. Trained largely in administrative law[2], their economic outlook was informed partly by the Marxian thought that pervaded the upper reaches of Japan's academic establishment at that time.

But the men who led Japan's march to the first rank of the world's industrial powers were not Marxists as such, and even if they had been, the terms on which the United States formally ended the Occupation and restored to Tokyo a limited degree of sovereignty did not allow them to experiment either with Stalinist autarkic industrialization or the self-sufficient import substitution being implemented at the time by such followers of dependency theory as Jawaharlal Nehru's India or Juan Peron's Argentina. Instead, Japan's power-holders reconfigured institutions inherited from the war economy in order to direct scarce capital towards companies that held the promise of becoming internationally competitive exporters in order to accumulate for Japan the key global currency of the day: US dollars. These dollars could then be used to purchase the capital equipment needed for investment in the next targeted industry. Success involved careful identification of the right industry for targeting and access to the patient financing necessary to seize and hold global market share. That meant predictable costs for key inputs – labour, land, money, capital equipment – which in turn required central control over their prices.

The priority given to economic reconstruction in itself required no political discussion, since it was taken as a given by all levels of society at the time. But the Japanese left had both the capacity and the will to make trouble if the interests of working people were not sufficiently attended to. Marginalizing the left was thus essential to the predictability required by the economic strategy Japan came to adopt. Strikes were broken, trade unions largely emasculated[3], and the possibility of a left electoral triumph precluded by a semi-rigged electoral system that favoured conservative rural districts over urban areas. The merger in 1955 of conservative forces into a single Liberal Democratic Party virtually assured the LDP of a parliamentary majority, even if it rarely commanded more than a plurality of the popular vote.

But the social compact that evolved out of the labour struggles of the 1950s also helped sideline the left into a ritualistic, empty sideshow. Under this compact, established companies would see to the economic security of male heads of households in return for complete management discretion over work assignments and job content. While this so-called 'lifetime employment' extended only to core male employees in established companies, it became a norm to be striven for by all forms of enterprise, public and private.

Companies essentially could not fire a permanent employee (*sei-shain*) while the bureaucracy ensured that bankruptcies among major companies in established industries did not occur. Major companies were pressured to keep their suppliers on life support even in difficult times. Banks were loathe to cut off credit either to an established, first-tier company or to any of its recognized principal suppliers. And the Ministry of Finance issued what amounted to a blanket guarantee that no financial institution under its purview would ever be allowed to go bankrupt.

One could argue that these arrangements represented a real achievement by the Japanese left since they did result in the fulfillment of a core left demand: near-universal economic security. But they also provided industry with predictable labour costs by preventing labour markets from taking root. Wages and salaries at all levels from the entry level factory worker through the CEO of a major company were established and coordinated through negotiations between a handful of key company unions and managers acting in consultation with industrial federations and the economic bureaucracy. Annual wage increases could thus be aligned with general economic growth levels. Job-hopping was unheard of among leading companies; a well-established firm would not hire someone who had worked for a direct competitor.

Just as there were no labour markets to speak of, there was no real financial market and certainly no market in corporate control. Established Japanese companies ensured that most of their shares were held by other major companies in reciprocal shareholding arrangements. What actually traded on Japanese 'equity' markets was not pro-rata ownership or pro-rata shares in residual corporate profits, but simply the present value of future dividend streams that bore scant relationship to corporate profitability. Meanwhile, banks provided the overwhelming percentage of financing to industry while their own cost of funds and the rates they charged borrowers were centrally determined. There was nothing resembling credit analysis as a Western banker would understand the concept. Well-connected companies received credit in whatever amounts they needed; the poorly connected need not bother to apply.

It is difficult to see how these arrangements, when viewed as a totality, can properly be termed 'capitalist' without destroying the term's analytical utility by reducing it to a simple label for any economy that is post-feudal but non-Leninist. Although Japan, did in the years between 1955 and 1968, certainly experience 'relentless and systematic development of the productive forces', to quote from Robert Brenner's definition of capitalism,[4] Japan's 'economic units' did not 'depend on the market' for what they needed. The labour and money they required were allocated to them through centrally coordinated methods. Meanwhile, the peculiar Japanese institution of the *sogo shosha* or general trading companies were responsible for delivery of supplies of commodities in the quantities and at the prices required by industry.[5] And, to continue with Brenner's terms, while 'economic units' did respond in a fashion to 'demand with respect to supply for goods and services', the demands that were given priority originated from overseas.

THE EMERGENCE OF CONTRADICTIONS

In 1968, Japan's economic methods began visibly to alter both the political and economic global ecology in which they had flourished. An American presidential election was affected and possibly determined for the first time in the postwar period by trade issues with Japan.[6] Meanwhile, at home, the monetary effects of Japan's methods were beginning to pose a policy challenge.

The Korean War had provided Japan with a temporary surfeit of dollars, thanks to US military procurements. But ever since the war ended, Japan had run its monetary policy in a fashion familiar to many developing countries: using its holdings of US dollars as the principal variable in establishing its money supply, with the domestic money supply targeted at some three times total dollar holdings. All other macroeconomic variables were by necessity subordinated to this objective. In the mid-1960s, however, Japan had begun to run a structural current account surplus, leading to a relentless rise in Japan's US dollar holdings. Dollars that are simply held as reserves without any intention ever to be exchanged or redeemed for imports begin to have perverse monetary implications once they are no longer needed to provide credible backing for domestic currency.[7] If an economy is to avoid inflation – i.e., if domestic money supply is no longer allowed to grow in tandem with increasing reserves – ways must be found to offset the growing reserves. This challenge is being faced today to a greater or lesser degree by all the export-oriented East Asian economies, most particularly China, but Japan has been coping with this structural by-product of its economic methods since the late 1960s.

That was an era when, for the first time ever in its history, Japan had begun to enjoy a degree of prosperity that extended to virtually all its people. Thus understandably the reaction to the emergence of contradictions was to recreate in every way possible the postwar certainties: a stable, undervalued exchange rate and unlimited access to the American market. A new prime minister, Tanaka Kakuei, came to power on the basis of his skill at balancing the demands of textile exporters with the need to mollify an angry Nixon administration. Nixon believed he had been double-crossed by a Tokyo that had promised a reduction in the exports in return for restoration of Okinawa to nominal Japanese sovereignty, but had then failed to deliver. After repairing relations with Washington, Tanaka went on to oversee and re-enforce the political mechanisms necessary for the economic experiments in coping with the build-up of dollars – experiments that would lead to the deliberate creation of asset bubbles. Tanaka understood that widespread prosperity would bring new pressures from relatively less well-off parts of the country; he demonstrated genius in organizing rural construction executives, farmers, and small business owners to extract public works spending and other deliberate allocations of credit from the central bureaucracy.[8] These simultaneously bought off pressure groups that might otherwise have disrupted power balances while providing for a build-up of deposits in Japan's banking system that served to offset the growing dollar horde.

The ascendancy of Tanaka seemed to represent a fundamental power shift. Unlike his predecessors, he hailed from a regional backwater, never went to university, and presented himself as an earthy populist in contrast to Tokyo's effete elites. But his administration helped Japan cope with its emerging contradictions without fundamentally threatening the postwar political order, while leaving the cluster of power-holders in Japan's bureaucracies, major corporations, and leading banks with continued control over economic decision-making.

But before the policy makers clustered around the Tanaka cabinets could finish the groundwork for the deliberate creation of asset inflation, the Bretton Woods system broke up and OPEC producers seized control of global petroleum markets. Japan found itself with other and far more pressing priorities than managing the contradictions of success. Forced into accepting a rise in the exchange value of the yen at the Smithsonian negotiations of December, 1971, Tokyo's economic mandarins were, by late 1973, coping with a currency in free fall as both foreign and domestic players assumed Japan was finished. It was not a stupid assessment. Not only was Japan absolutely dependent on imported energy, it had flourished within a global monetary, trade, and security regime that seemed by that year on the verge of collapse. The Smithsonian negotiations had been intended to resurrect the Bretton Woods system with exchange rates reset to reflect contemporary economic reality. But the agreements floundered on the absence of political will to enforce the new rates. The world found itself with a monetary system – if one can call it a 'system' – which initially seemed based on nothing but the whims of frightened central bankers. Meanwhile, a United States that had served for nearly three decades as the guarantor of Japan's security and its market of first and last resort was enduring with the Watergate affair a political crisis of unprecedented magnitude while suffering its first ever defeat in war.

The pessimists about Japan's future had not reckoned on the country's formidable institutions of control – the same institutions that had brought about the spectacular rush to growth of 1955-1968. Again, the economic bureaucracy set about rationing dollars and energy, establishing and policing domestic cartels, and maintaining dogged control of the yen in the new floating rate world. The results were, for the time, astounding. Japan pushed inflation down from over 20 per cent (as measured by the consumer price index) in 1974 to 3 per cent in 1975. While the rest of the world struggled through the 1970s with the novel phenomenon of 'stagflation' – simultaneous inflation and high unemployment –Japan's recession was over by the end of 1975. In the teeth of the worst global slowdown since the 1930s, Japan again grew briskly, racking up not only healthy GDP numbers but also substantial increases in exports thanks in part to deliberate market interventions to keep the value of the yen lower than it otherwise would have been. Indeed, something like half the total increase in global exports in 1976 came from Japan.

Japan's triumphant return from the economic graveyard to which it had been assigned after the break-up of Bretton Woods would see the country emerge as the key supporter for a reconfigured global monetary order still revolving around the US dollar. Japan would play a central and defining role in the most important American political realignment since the New Deal: the success of the so-called Reagan Revolution. And Japan would serve as a tacit model for the rest of East Asia – most importantly for China in the wake of the death of Mao Zedong.

JAPAN AND THE RESTORATION OF DOLLAR HEGEMONY

Following the Bretton Woods collapse, Saudi Arabia and the Gulf Emirates had contemplated billing their customers in a currency other than the dollar. But their ultimate decision to stick with the American currency was not driven by any evidence that Washington had either the will or the ability to halt the rapid erosion in the purchasing power of the dollar after 1973. Rather, they needed American military protection and no other currency circulated in the quantities required to replace the dollar as a global medium of exchange. The OPEC cartel could compensate for the continued decline in the dollar's value by periodically boosting prices, but no such option was available for anyone else. And as the decade proceeded, inflation accelerated and the exchange value of the dollar continued to plummet.

Events culminated in the summer of 1978 with a full-fledged dollar crisis. The incoming Carter administration had blamed Japan for America's escalating trade deficits, accusing the country of 'dirty floating' – unannounced interventions to suppress the exchange value of the yen. Under pressure, the Japanese abandoned 'dirty floating'. The yen predictably rose to previously unimagined heights, breaking the psychologically critical Y180/$1 barrier. The Americans had gotten what they asked for, but instead of the reduction in the bilateral trade deficit with Japan that they expected would follow a clean float, found themselves instead staring into the abyss of a dollar collapse. Japan joined Switzerland, Saudi Arabia and West Germany in a four-country rescue mission for the dollar, while Carter's hand was forced into engineering the appointment of hard money man Paul Volcker as Chairman of the Federal Reserve.[9] Owing no political debt to Carter, Volcker set about halting the slide in the dollar's purchasing power with steep hikes in interest rates and a concomitant deep recession that would doom Carter's re-election chances.

It is at this point that Japan stepped out from being a supporting actor to assuming the starring role in the resurrection and restructuring of American hegemony over global finance and the global economy – and thus the survival and recovery of global capitalism from its worst systemic crisis to that date since the 1930s. Ronald Reagan won the 1980 American presidential election with what amounted to a mandate to destroy what was left of the liberal Keynesian order that had prevailed since the New Deal and the Second World War; his campaign had succeeded in blaming this order for the inflation and other economic ills of the 1970s. 'Government is not the solution to our problems. Government is the problem', is the way he famously put it. Once in office, Reagan intended to launch direct attacks on the institutions that provided for the economic security of the American working and lower middle classes. And with the breaking of the 1981 air controllers strike, his administration did succeed in dealing labour a crippling institutional blow from which it has never recovered.

But the administration lacked the political stamina to roll back directly the social welfare programs that formed the core of the New Deal legacy. A handful of 'supply side' gurus had seized the limelight with the notion of tax cuts purportedly so stimulative that tax revenues would rise even as rates fell. Savvier Republicans used this 'voodoo' economics as a cloak for their true intentions, believing that the prospect of financial disaster in the wake of the tax cuts would force the government to reduce spending. They counted on this indirect means of 'starving the beast' to gut the welfare state. Meanwhile, Democratic leaders such as Speaker of the House Tip

O'Neill lacked the political support to withstand the administration's tax-cut offensive, particularly after the assassination attempt against Reagan in April 1981. They caved to White House pressure, anticipating that events would force the administration to reveal its unpopular hand when it came back to Congress to negotiate spending reductions in order to forestall financial catastrophe.[10]

These events never occurred: the deficit would indeed snowball, but it would be smoothly financed without a political or market crisis. With the sole exception of economist Robert Mundell (who however thought it would be 'the Saudis' who would finance the deficit[11]), no observer saw that this would happen. The public sector deficit soared to levels few had thought could be sustained over time without ruin. The United States emerged from the enactment of a structural Federal deficit with a robust economy that played to the country's emerging comparative advantage in the design and packaging of complex bundles of high-value added manufactures and services. And a permanent Federal deficit would greatly enhance the power and wealth of the American ruling class at the direct expense of the working and lower middle classes.

It is critical to note here that the structural Federal deficit that forms the most enduring financial legacy of the so-called 'Reagan Revolution' was not a Keynesian deficit intended to plug the gap between capacity and utilization opened up by a temporary cyclical decline in private demand. For the Reagan deficits were not used to fill otherwise idle capacity; instead they financed the radical restructuring of the heavily unionized sectors of US manufacturing as well as the infrastructure of the emerging globalized economy: Wall Street, Silicon Valley, the aerospace and defence industries. Classic cyclical Keynesian deficits are prescribed as emergency measures when low interest rates are insufficient to stimulate an economy – when monetary policy has become an exercise in pushing the proverbial string. The Reagan deficits, by contrast, were launched in an era of historically high interest rates. The policy mix seemed so odd that one Japanese newspaper described it as equivalent to running a heater and an air conditioner at the same time.

The key enabler was Japan. The Japanese economy emerged from a shallow slow-down brought on by the so-called Second Oil Crisis of 1979 with its high household savings rate intact, but with a permanent reduction in Japanese industry's funding needs for domestic plant and equipment investment. By the simple rules of balance of payments accounting, therefore, much of the country's savings would necessarily be deployed abroad. A US Treasury scouring the world for funds to finance the Reagan deficits would take the lion's share. The restructuring of the American economy – and the concomitant realignment of American class power – would be financed with barely a hitch.

While the Japanese may have stumbled without deliberate political choice into their role as America's enabler, the contradictions – political, financial, and social – would become increasingly burdensome. Japan's response to events in the decade that followed the collapse of Bretton Woods had been almost entirely reactive.[12] There was never any real debate over what the country should do. Even the financing of the Reagan Revolution had not been a thought-through, conscious political decision, but simply a reaction to existing financial circumstances. True, 1980 saw the revision of the Foreign Exchange Control Law, speeding the ability of Japanese financial institutions to deploy assets abroad by eliminating the need to obtain clearance from the Ministry of Finance for each transaction, but this was simply an acknowledgement of reality – the recycling of Japan's growing surpluses needed to be an efficient process.

There was one problem. A steep rise in the value of the yen against the dollar would wipe out all yen-equivalent profits from Japanese investments in US Treasury securities. Japanese insurance companies, after all, must settle claims in yen, not dollars; if they paid 240 yen per dollar for a Treasury bond on issue but got back 200 yen or less when the bond matured, the interest income would be wiped out by the exchange loss. But asset managers in the early 1980s calculated they would have to get back fewer than 180 yen on the dollar for these investments to become money-losing propositions for them. That 180 number was the rate that had been breached briefly during the peak of the 1978 dollar crisis. Japan's asset managers interpreted the events as proof that the US and Japanese governments together had the capacity to ensure the crisis would not be repeated.

Indeed, as the 1980s wore on, fears of another dollar crisis seemed remote as global demand for dollar securities drove the American currency to post Bretton Woods highs. Enjoying the advantage of a cheap yen, Japanese manufacturers embarked on a kind of second golden age as industry after industry fell to the Japanese onslaught: automobiles, earth moving equipment, colour film, machine tools, and a whole range of consumer electronics from the recently introduced VCRs through portable listening devices. Japan would even set its sights on the hot new industry of semiconductors.[13] But while Japan's manufacturers may have been basking in unprecedentedly favourable conditions, the country's politicians found themselves pulled into the early stages of the desperate late 20th century struggle within the American ruling class between the avatars of the 'new economy' of Wall

Street and Silicon Valley and the champions of older industries. The Reagan revolution would succeed in destroying the political power of the American white working class by its assault on unions and by the economic devastation its deficits would wreak on that class's traditional employers in the so-called 'rust belt' manufacturing industries. (Working people of colour had little political power to destroy.) But substantial factions of American capital derived their wealth and power from these industries and they reacted with fury to what they saw as 'unfair' Japanese assault on their industries – fury that manifested itself in pressure on Washington and waves of hostile sentiment aimed at Japan.

The ideological constraints within which received opinion operated – the fetishization of 'free trade' and 'free markets', the deliberate blindness to the power and class struggles that inevitably accompany economic transformation – meant that the only acceptable way conceptually to frame the crisis was to ascribe it to currency manipulation. Japan must be 'manipulating' its currency in order to grant its exporters an 'unfair' advantage. (If this sounds like an echo of the charges levelled today at China, that is not a coincidence.) Even standard neo-classical economics would teach that a strong dollar was an inevitable outcome of the success of Volcker and Reagan in halting the erosion of the dollar's purchasing power, re-affirming the dollar's role at the centre of global finance, and then exploiting that role to run up large, politically painless deficits. But a direct challenge to free market orthodoxy was inconceivable in American ruling circles; instead business leaders such as Caterpillar's Vice President Donald Fites hunted about for evidence that the Japanese were engaged in various supposedly sneaky practices to keep the yen undervalued. They hoped to give the US government an ideologically acceptable excuse to intervene in foreign exchange markets.[14] And they believed their own notices: that the loss of so much of the American manufacturing base to Japanese competition was due to currency manipulation and could be fixed if dollar/yen rates were realigned. 'There isn't anything wrong with the US-Japan trade balance that a Y180/$1 rate wouldn't solve', was a widely repeated remark in the Washington of the time.[15]

Japan's power holders may have felt like canoeists caught in the unforeseen torrents of a raging river; all they had consciously done, after all, was buy the Treasury securities on offer and export well-made products at low prices. But they did start paddling furiously once they understood the extent of the potentially destructive power of the American political currents and eddies. Competing factions of Japan's political elite put aside their differences to engineer the removal of a woefully inadequate Suzuki Zenko as prime minister and replace him with Tanaka disciple Nakasone Yasujiro. Nakasone worked with key bureaucrats in the Ministry of Finance to signal Washington that Tokyo would not be amiss to a coordinated effort to bring the dollar down a bit. And he helped prepare the country for the adjustments necessary when the yen would begin to rise again, assuring Japanese industry that, one way or another, their loss of an exchange advantage would be made up to them.

The realization that Japan would have to do something to avoid being dashed on the rocks of American hysteria was accompanied by an awakening on the part of Japan's elite to the potential for accidents inherent in the country's growing financial power. On May 10, 1984, a mistranslated report that surfaced in the Japanese business press about the supposed problems of the Continental Bank of Illinois led Japanese fund managers to pull their deposits from the bank without notifying the Japanese authorities or, in some cases, their own senior executives. The Japanese had become so important to Continental's funding that the bank had to go to the Federal Reserve for an emergency bailout the next day. The Japanese had sparked a full-scale bank run without the slightest intention of doing so.[16] The Continental Illinois bailout may have been a relatively minor incident, but it underscored two new realities: that whatever Japan did would move markets. And that events could very quickly get out of control.

This became more and more evident in the aftermath of the Plaza Accord of September, 1985 – the piece of theatre jointly staged by Washington and Tokyo at New York's Plaza Hotel with a supporting cast from London, Paris, and Bonn to demonstrate their collective disapproval at the dollar's strength. The players intended to induce traders in the foreign exchange markets to bid the dollar down. Narrowly speaking, the Accord was a great success in that the dollar did fall – and farther than anyone expected it to, or even wanted it to. The Y180/$1 rate that had been seen for close to a decade as the ceiling beyond which the yen could not possibly rise was breached for good, never to return. But Japan's trade surplus continued to climb, the US current account deficit to worsen, and the restructuring of the American economy to pick up steam. In 1986 as the dollar was steadily sinking, Microsoft would go public, the historic Homestead Steel Works in Pittsburgh would close its doors, and 'junk bond' house Drexel Burnham Lambert would report net profits of over $500 million, the most money that a Wall Street firm had ever earned to that point.

For despite the impressive campaign mounted by the world's leading central banks in the wake of the Plaza Accord to lower the exchange rate of the dollar, no one in Tokyo or Washington actually wanted to see the dollar dethroned as the universal settlements and reserve currency. And until that happened, the United States would continue to run trade deficits that were automatically financed by its trading partners. But in the sudden and seemingly unstoppable rise in the yen, the Japanese had to contend not only with an extra burden on their exporters but what in retrospect was quite obviously the end of the benefits flowing directly to Japanese households from the export-led growth model. To compensate Japanese industry for their strong currency burdens and to keep the good times rolling at home, the Japanese authorities took out of the closet the tools that had first been forged during the break-up of Bretton Woods in order to blow bubbles in asset markets.

PIONEERING 'BUBBLENOMICS'

It is perhaps appropriate that the Japanese were the pioneers of 'bubblenomics', to use Brenner's term, since the Japanese economic strategy had involved the deliberate creation of excess capacity in global industries. The late 1980s Japanese bubble represented an attempt to resolve the contradictions of that strategy that had finally caught up with Japan. Brenner has argued that at this critical juncture the Japanese economic authorities 'pioneered' a 'remedy' for the 'long term weakening of capital accumulation and of aggregate demand (that) has been rooted in a profound system-wide decline and failure to recover of the rate of return on capital, resulting largely – though not only – from a persistent tendency to over-capacity, i.e., oversupply, in global manufacturing industries'. That remedy involved 'titanic bouts of borrowing and deficit spending, made possible by historic increases in ... paper wealth ... enabled by record run-ups in asset prices'.[17] Brenner was writing specifically of what happened in the United States in the mid 1990s when 'corporations and households, rather than government' would 'propel the economy forward' through the heavy borrowing, but he was right to draw attention to the way in which the Japanese had pioneered things.

The contradictions stemmed directly from Japan's economic methods: methods that made it harder and harder for the United States to exchange goods of real value for what the Japanese wanted to sell. 'You Americans just don't make anything that we Japanese want to buy anymore' was a commonly heard refrain in late 1980s Japan. But if that was truly the case, then the only way to keep Japanese sales going was to transfer purchasing power to the customer – i.e., the United States – which is what happened. And the ultimate source of that purchasing power was Japan's domestic households. To rephrase things, Japan's aggregate demand was being deliberately sent to the United States in order to keep Japanese factories running.

The contradiction here goes to the heart of Brenner's contention that the 'persistent tendency to over-capacity in global manufacturing industries' is at the root of the growing severity and frequency of financial crises that have beset the world since the collapse of Bretton Woods. Individual Japanese companies did not treat profit-making as a *raison d'être*. The economic system in which they were embedded and the incentive structure of that system rewarded technological progress, gross revenues, cost-reductions on the assembly line, and market share. Profits were incidental and could be shameful if excessive; certainly no Japanese CEO would hold out profits as an overriding corporate goal. Even the recovery of fixed investment costs was largely a peripheral concern; as long as established Japanese manufacturing companies generated enough revenue to cover their variable costs, they were essentially protected from the risk of bankruptcy and they received the financing necessary to make whatever plant and equipment investments were required to capture and hold market share. Japanese management did not face pressure from equity markets for return. Financing was almost entirely in the form of short-term bank loans (themselves financed by household deposits) that were regularly rolled over as a matter of course; thus the fixed costs incurred from capital investment were essentially socialized since Japanese companies faced no existential risk from capital investments that did not pay for themselves.

Japanese companies could thus survive and even thrive at rates of return on invested capital (ROI) and rates of return on equity (ROE) that would spell takeover or bankruptcy for at least their American counterparts, if not their European ones. But that did not spare the Japanese system as a whole from the consequences of anaemic returns on its aggregate invested capital. Japan's postwar economic structure had been, as we have seen, configured not to generate high rates of return but to generate *high rates of dollar holdings*. Since these dollars over time were increasingly used simply as a form of consumer finance for Japan's export customers rather than converted into domestic purchasing power, the economic contradictions became unavoidable. For a brief period of time – the years between the onset of the Reagan revolution and the Plaza Accord, i.e., 1981-1985 – the dollars pouring into the coffers of Japan's export champions enabled them to report unaccustomed levels of profitability, even if those dollars did not fully translate into domestic purchasing power. But once the dollar flows lessened with the post-Plaza run-up in the value of the yen, Japan's policy makers were confronted with the reality that the strategy of export-led growth was no longer sufficient to propel the economy forward.

They understood this. A senior Bank of Japan official was quoted anonymously as saying in explaining the bubble: 'We intended first to boost both the stock and property markets. Supported by this safety net – rising markets – export-oriented industries were supposed to reshape themselves so they could adapt to a domestic-led economy'.[18] The Ministry of Finance and Bank of Japan had the tools to steer credit directly into real estate and stock markets.[19] Since Japanese banks lend primarily with the collateral of real estate, soaring real estate prices were both a result of the waves of liquidity pouring into the economy and the means by which that liquidity was transformed into cheap financing.

The deliberate asset inflation of the late 1980s succeeded in postponing a reckoning with the contradiction that lies at the heart of the export-led growth model: that if it succeeds, a country must at some point either reconfigure its economy or, if it wants to keep the model going, transfer purchasing power to its customers. The mechanisms that sparked the Japanese bubble did compensate for a while for the systematic transfer of domestic purchasing power abroad by showering money on households, albeit unevenly. The bubble deceived corporate treasurers into thinking that capital financing was essentially free; companies went on a debt and capital investment binge that bought for Japan the most advanced manufacturing base ever built as well as a lot of fancy headquarters buildings and lavish golf courses.

The bubble provided critical support for the dollar in the wake of the 1987 stock market crash. Like the collapse of Continental Illinois, the crash started in Tokyo when the announcement of the August 1987 trade numbers panicked Japanese fund managers into dumping their holdings of US Treasury securities. A near-halving of the dollar's value since the Plaza Accord had not produced any reduction in the US-Japan bilateral trade imbalance. With the dollar buying fewer than 140 yen, Japanese investments in US Treasuries made earlier in the decade were already well under water. Fund managers expected renewed pressure on the currency and like good traders anywhere, tried to close out their losing positions before they dropped any further. As bond prices fell, yields went up and investors abroad began transferring money out of stock markets into bond markets. The Dow Jones plummeted by nearly 23 per cent in a single day. Fortunately for the dollar and the American markets, however, the Ministry of Finance was able to halt the global stock market collapse by orchestrating a recovery in Tokyo.[20] It followed that by arm-twisting Japanese fund managers to renew their investments in dollar securities; the Bank of Japan re-enforced the arm-twisting by yet more credit creation at rock-bottom interest rates. Credit flowed back into dollar instruments without putting any damper on the Japanese boom which, by the late 1980s, had begun to look like one of the great manias in global financial history.

Asset prices continued to skyrocket, reaching absurd levels. By 1989, the extrapolated land value of Tokyo and its suburbs exceeded that of the entire United States plus the market capitalization of every company listed on the New York Stock Exchange. Meanwhile, the Tokyo Stock Exchange accounted for close to 50 per cent of the market capitalization of the entire world. Even more worrisome to Japan's power-holders than these clearly fantastic prices were the social effects of the bubble. A down payment on a small house now lay far beyond the reach of ordinary middle-class families whose husbands and fathers had formed the foot soldiers of the economic army that had conquered global markets. But people who had title to plots of dirt somewhere found themselves rich beyond their wildest dreams. Social control mechanisms began to break down as youngsters started to disdain the traditional decades of uncomplaining hard work that had formerly been the quid pro quo for economic security. An entrepreneur rumoured to be descended from Japan's pre-modern outcast class deliberately set out to create a labour market and engaged in wholesale, bubble-fuelled bribery to purchase political protection for his business. This ensuing 'Recruit' scandal as it was called after the name of his company, reached to the highest levels of the Japanese power structure, bringing down the government of Prime Minister Takeshita Noboru, another important Tanaka disciple.

The authorities were frightened. The bubble had largely accomplished its purposes. Foreign exchange markets had stabilized, while Japanese industry had used the waves of financing thrown off by the bubble to equip itself with the most formidable manufacturing base ever built. So, beginning on Christmas day 1989 with a steep hike in interest rates, the authorities deliberately set out to take the steam out of the bubble. But they lost control of events. The authorities had had the tools to ratchet up real estate prices. Once prices began to fall, however, they could not stop them. Waves of investment had saddled Japanese companies with debts that they discovered were not 'free' after all. It would take them years to plug the gaping holes this debt opened in their balance sheets.[21] And the Ministry of Finance could not, after all, honour its implicit guarantee to all financial institutions under its purview.

NOWHERE TO TURN?

Despite the increasing stagnation that gripped the Japanese economy in the wake of the bubble's collapse, Japan continued to provide critical support for the dollar and for American hegemony straight through the 1990s. This was most evident at the time of the Mexican peso crisis of early 1995 when it appeared for a while that the US had lost the will and the ability to bail out a country in its own backyard. The passage of NAFTA had led to an unsustainable surge in hot money flowing into Mexico chasing supposed high returns; when these returns proved ephemeral, the money flowed right back out, bringing on a balance of payments crisis.

Bailing Mexico out, however, would require additional funding for the IMF. An unlikely coalition of left Democrats hostile to the IMF and Republicans seeing an opportunity to embarrass the Clinton administration succeeded in blocking passage of legislation to top up the IMF's coffers. Clinton's new treasury secretary, ex-Goldman Sachs co-chair Robert Rubin, found a loophole around the Congressional obstruction. In the process he halted a global run on the dollar as serious as any since 1978. But even when other currencies stabilized against the dollar, the yen continued to soar. By May, it took only 79 yen to buy a dollar, a rate far below what most Japanese exporters needed to cover even their marginal costs – i.e., they were losing money on each sale they made abroad.

The resulting panic in Japan saw the Ministry of Finance go outside the usual order of bureaucratic succession to appoint Sakakibara Eisuke as Director General of the International Finance Bureau, the key official dealing with currency issues. Sakakibara had a well-deserved reputation as a maverick and gadfly, but he got the nod on the basis of his purported relationship with Lawrence Summers, then Undersecretary for International Affairs in the US Treasury (Sakakibara had been a visiting professor in the Harvard economics department when Summers taught there). Sakakibara flew to Washington in June and negotiated with Summers and Rubin what amounted to a quid-pro-quo: American help in bringing down the yen/dollar rate in return for a tacit agreement that Japan would support the market for US Treasury securities.[22] With the Clinton administration at its political nadir in the wake of the 1994 midterm election losses and worried about its re-election prospects, the last thing it needed was a bond market crisis that would send interest rates skyrocketing.

The intervention, staged in August 1995, accomplished its goal of taking the yen/dollar rate back over 100. Rubin masterminded the tactics used to shift sentiment in the foreign exchange markets, but the fire power came from Japan in further waves of liquidity creation. The Clinton administration would also go on to provide political cover for the bail-out package needed to avert a banking crisis in Japan. Bailing out the banks was as politically unpopular in the Japan of 1998 as it would prove in the US of 2008, but after the failure of several financial institutions within weeks of each other in late 1997, there was no choice if a full scale meltdown was to be avoided.

Rubin convinced the President to make a well-publicized telephone call to then-Japanese Prime Minister Hashimoto Ryutaro urging him to do what was necessary. To bail out the banks, the Diet passed the single largest expenditure ever legislated to that point by a government in peacetime.

As the 1990s drew to a close, it became clear that the United States and Japan had evolved a sort of modus-operandi in which Washington and Tokyo would use each other to provide political cover for arrangements needed to keep the global financial order going. There had been a brief period in the late 1980s when the Japanese elite allowed themselves to be seduced by dreams of succeeding the US as the hegemon of the global economy. The events of the 1990s soon disabused them of this notion, however. It was not simply the loss of control after the imploding of the bubble and the inability to restart the engines of growth in its wake. But also the realization that dominance of key upstream components and manufacturing technologies did not, after all, confer the economic leadership that Japan's decision makers had thought was within their grasp. American companies that had barely been heard of twenty years earlier – Microsoft, Intel, Apple, Cisco – emerged as the key pace makers in the 'new' economy growing out of the technological revolutions in computers and telecommunications. For it was no longer so easy to divide 'manufacturing' from 'services' – much of the profits in the new industries came from the bundling and packaging of both.[23]

In this new world, trade conflicts between the US and Japan essentially disappeared. The last serious one had occurred in 1994 over auto parts; Rubin, worried over the effects on the bond market of a visible trade impasse, had persuaded the White House to fold its (quite strong) hand in its efforts to dismantle barriers to sales of American auto parts in Japan. It seemed the two countries were settling into a rough division of economic labor that saw Japan continue to dominate the high-value added end of manufacturing while the US pioneered new industries and packaged new products. Boeing would announce plans for what would become the revolutionary 787 Dreamliner with Japanese companies responsible for the manufacture of the technically sophisticated wing and wingbox. Apple would design and bring on-stream gorgeous new gadgets with the LCD screens and many other high-value added components manufactured by Japanese suppliers.

BUBBLES BREED BUBBLES

But this was not the end of the story. The waves of credit creation undertaken by the Bank of Japan to help bring down the yen in the wake of the Mexican crisis and to stabilize a tottering banking sector directly set the stage for the Asian Financial Crisis of 1998. The Japanese banking system may have been rescued from a complete meltdown, but individual banks, sensitized now to the possibility of failure, were still loathe to lend domestically. The Bank of Japan's credit creation did not spark a domestic investment boom; instead the rivers of cash found their way into the so-called carry trade: yen borrowing by hedge funds and other foreign players with the proceeds swapped into a higher interest currency such as US dollars. From there, much of the money went into emerging markets abroad, in particular into the booming economies of southeast Asia where the tidal waves of credit fuelled unsustainable bubbles in places such as Bangkok.

The bubbles burst. Before the Asian financial crisis would play itself out, Thailand, Indonesia, South Korea, and Russia would see governments fall in the wake of balance of payments impasses. Events would culminate in the collapse of the American hedge fund Long Term Capital Management that threatened to take much of Wall Street with it. But the lessons learned by governments in East and Southeast Asia – both in those countries that had been directly affected and in those countries that had escaped the worst – was never to put themselves in positions again where balance of payments difficulties could bring on political crisis. That meant redoubling efforts to accumulate international reserves – i.e., dollars – with export competitive industries. It was the old Japanese strategy of the 1950s updated to the realities of the new millennium.

This was most obvious – and most significant – in China. China would simultaneously and in defiance of all conventional wisdom rack up both current account surpluses and capital surpluses as foreign investment poured into the country. The inevitable result: a growing horde of international reserves, mostly consisting of direct and indirect claims on the US government. The wall of credit sloshing back into the United States from China and its neighbours permitted the incoming George W. Bush administration to run a repeat of the Reagan revolution. Thanks to Asian appetite for US Treasury securities, the Bush borrowing spree was as politically painless as that of twenty years earlier. Again, cost-free military adventures could be launched with impunity while torrents of cash were channelled by Wall Street into the pockets of the American rich.

Meanwhile, the onset of the new millennium paradoxically granted Japan a temporary reprieve in its attempts to escape the 'policy trap' of its inability to move away from the export-led growth model. Although Japan continued to pile up dollars, the boom in China not only gave Japan a new partner in supporting American hegemony but provided a real path out of the debt hole left behind by the imploding bubble economy of ten years earlier, thanks to Chinese orders for Japanese capital equipment. Cheap Chinese goods smashed many of the trade barriers that had long kept foreign goods out of Japanese stores, meaning that while real incomes remained stagnant for Japanese households, the cost of living fell even faster. And Japan's governing class found in Koizumi Junichiro an answer to Ronald Reagan and the UK's Tony Blair: a slick, media-savvy professional whose talk of reform and sunny, can-do demeanour would divert for a while worries over structural economic pathologies and widening social fissures. Koizumi would serve as prime minister from 2001 to 2006 – the longest period in office since Nakasone. He would be even more obsequious to Washington than Blair. Part of that sycophancy involved a public commitment to reshape the Japanese economy along neoliberal lines.

But while a great deal of neoliberal talk emanated from Koizumi and the people around him, that portion not whipped up directly for Washington's consumption turned out to be largely a cover for loosening the social compact forged in the 1950s. Companies were essentially given the green light increasingly to rely on so-called *fureeta* – temporary workers who did not receive the implied guarantees of economic security that had customarily come with employment at a Japanese company. Koizumi's most famous 'reform' – the overhaul of the Japanese post office including the postal savings system – originated within the Ministry of Finance as an effort to reduce the drain on the Japanese treasury of white elephant spending in rural districts that were losing population. Those who took Koizumi at his word – both Japanese entrepreneurs attempting to introduce genuine markets for corporate control and foreign investors launching takeover bids for what they saw as poorly managed Japanese companies – were almost invariably stymied.[24] Japanese power holders continued to display ambivalence about the transforming power of capitalist relations; they remained unwilling to turn over decisions about the direction of the economy to markets they could not control and did not trust.

THE LEHMAN SHOCK AND THE END OF JAPAN'S EXPORT-LED MODEL?

Koizumi's retirement was followed a few months later by the onset of the subprime crisis in the United States that would lead to the worst financial meltdown since 1931. While Koizumi was still in office, it had been possible politically for Japan to tolerate a continued muddling-through that would presumably have seen the country adjust to a no-growth economy, no longer particularly vital, but with a panoply of cutting edge manufacturing technologies sufficient to ensure it could still pay its way in the world. Japan would continue its role, together with China, in supporting US financial hegemony – perhaps as a kind of sluggish Asian Switzerland – thereby assuring the continuation of the global environment that allowed it to survive, if not notably happily.

But the 'Lehman shock' of September 2008 made this 'muddle through' untenable. With Chinese exports temporarily derailed by the US implosion, Japan's economy went into a tailspin – partly because Chinese orders for Japanese capital equipment plummeted, and partly because Japan's much-vaunted manufacturing supremacy was being challenged like never before. Not a single Japanese semi conductor chip could be found in Apple's hot new iPhone, for example, while the display panels were being made in Korea. The dollars being sent back into the US banking system –whether directly or indirectly via China – were no longer translating into demand for Japanese goods.

In retrospect, doomsayers over the end of the Asian model may have been a trifle premature – China has, in a striking mirror-image of Japan's performance in the mid 1970s, managed to put its economy back on track, stunning much of the world in the process and providing some glimmers of hope to Japan as well. But this was not evident in time to save the LDP from electoral defeat. Koizumi had been succeeded by two colourless LDP hacks, neither of whom had managed to stay in office for more than a year, and finally by an Aso Taro who projected, like Koizumi, a somewhat kooky persona, but without any of Koizumi's savvy or ability to reach the average voter. With Japan's governing apparatus seemingly helpless in the face of the economic meltdown, the LDP was decisively voted out of power in August, 2009.

The election was more significant than many foreign observers realized. The architects of the victory by the Democratic Party of Japan (DPJ) were quite explicit that they were not simply running against the LDP but against the entire governing setup that left significant policy decisions with the bureaucracy – that, in the words of long-time Japan observer Karel van Wolferen, they intended to establish a genuine government.[25] Their success is by no means assured; in fact, the DPJ's first prime minister, Hatoyama Yukio, was forced to resign a scant eight months after he took office.[26] His successor, Kan Naoto, has political roots in the Japanese left, although he and his cabinet may actually be more open to certain capitalist methods than their predecessors, particularly when it comes to encouraging risk-taking by entrepreneurs. The ideal they have in mind for Japan seems to be something along the lines of the most successful northern European social democracies. Measures taken to date indicate that they want to replace the increasingly frayed informal institutions of economic security with explicit mandates.

But whether Japan's new leaders succeed or fail, the days in which Japan acted as a primary supporter for the American-centred global capitalist order have probably ended. If the DPJ succeeds, Japan will become more of a social democracy with money spent on an explicit infrastructure of social welfare rather than being deployed as idle (for Japan) dollars to prop up American demand. And if the DPJ fails, we will probably see a return to bureaucratic control of policy, but with an elite more fragmented than in the past since Japan's political facade will consist not of a single LDP but shifting coalitions of weak parties. This is a political formula for continued economic decline. Whatever the outcome, the household savings rate and the current account surplus are likely to continue falling; meaning simply by the laws of balance of payments accounting that less money will be recycling into dollar markets. And of the sums that Japan does spend overseas, more will be consumed by foreign direct investment as Japan increasingly links itself economically to Asia's new dynamo. A quick drive into central Shanghai from the airport with the lines of Japan-owned factories on the roads makes it evident where Japan is setting its economic sights.

PASSING THE BATON?

China and other Asian countries for their own reasons adopted key parts of the Japanese model, but then found themselves facing many of the same contradictions – in particular, a need to prop up the dollar's hegemony lest they destroy the value of their own holdings and wreck the machinery by which their customers finance purchase of their exports. Indeed, the very emergence of China as such an important overseas prop for the US dollar may be what finally gives Japan the flexibility to begin to walk away from its heretofore central role without toppling the global economic order.

Perhaps China will thus supplant Japan as the key enabler of American financial hegemony. But China is a very different country with a very different history. Oddly enough for an ostensibly Marxist-Leninist polity, it often seems less ambivalent in its embrace of capitalist relations. This may be due to the legitimacy enjoyed by the Chinese government, to return to Anderson's point quoted at the beginning of this essay, a legitimacy Tokyo has lacked for so much of the postwar period because of its obvious subservience to Washington. Indeed, Hung Ho-Fung's contention that Beijing has allowed the emergence of a new and influential class of entrepreneurs and financiers based in coastal China with ties to global capital – a class now too powerful to be thwarted – suggests that China may have become, in his words, 'America's Head Servant'.[27]

But if so, China will not be the kind of servant that Japan has been. Since the contours of the postwar Japanese political economy took final shape in the mid-1950s, Japan's power-holders have acted, as we have seen, almost on auto-pilot, at least with respect to overriding national goals. They have coped with challenges and crises by attempts to recreate inherited certainties. Among other things, that meant deliberate efforts to stymie the growth of an independent class of entrepreneurs and business leaders who might balk at bureaucratic direction. Thus when Tokyo found itself faced with the choice of doing what it took to support a global capitalist order revolving around the US dollar or seeing that order collapse, it could and did take whatever measures were necessary, even if that meant forcing Japan's households to endure steep and chronic declines in the purchasing power of their savings. The bureaucrats did not have to worry about being undermined by powerful capitalists with their own agendas.

China now faces much the same dilemma that Japan began to wake up to some 35 years ago: its economy is now so intertwined with that of the US and it has such a huge position in dollar markets that it cannot walk away from its support for the existing order without doing irreparable damage both to that order and to its own short- and medium-term economic prospects. But China's leaders may be both more conscious of what they are doing than were Japan's and – perhaps – less sure of their instruments of control. This may seem paradoxical since China is an authoritarian, one-party state while Japan is theoretically a democracy whose leaders must answer to an electorate. But the rise of provincial power centres that balk at Beijing's orders, not to mention the swaggering coastal elite of financiers and entrepreneurs that Hung describes, suggests that the Chinese authorities may be less able to emulate the way their Japanese counterparts acted during several crises over the past 30 years: halt runs on the dollar with a few pointed phone calls. Indeed, the very reports that have surfaced in the international press of disputes among China's power holders over currency and monetary policies point to underlying power struggles and raise questions over how and whether they can be resolved, particularly during periods of crisis. [28]

At the same time, the greater awareness of China's leadership of what it is doing and why it is doing it may ultimately prove the critical variable in the perpetuation of American hegemony. Japan's political set-up grew out of a millenia-long tradition of power-holders who pretended they did not exercise power or were doing so in the name of entities that were ultimately figureheads: emperors, shoguns, parliaments; that the policy-makers' right to make decisions that determined how others would live was grounded not in explicit, challengeable authority to adjudicate messy clashes of interest, but part of some ineffable order beyond the reach of politics. That supposed order served to cloak the real loci of power – and indeed forced denial on the power-holders themselves that they were exercising power. As Maruyama Masao wrote in 1946 about Japan's pre-Occupation power structure, 'It was unfortunate enough for the country to be under oligarchic rule; the misfortune was aggravated by the fact that the rulers were unconscious of actually being oligarchs or despots. The individuals who composed the various branches of the oligarchy did not regard themselves as active regulators but as men who were, on the contrary, being regulated by rules created elsewhere.'[29] This fundamental political reality was not in the least affected by the legacy of the Occupation and Japan's ostensible transformation from an oligarchy into a supposedly liberal capitalist democracy. Indeed, the American assumption for Japan of those powers by which a state is commonly recognized – the provision of security and the conduct of foreign relations – if anything served to exacerbate the denial by Japan's policy makers that they had any real control over what they were doing. When they acted reflexively to support the supremacy of the dollar and of American hegemony, they were acting in the manner expected of them – and in the manner they expected of themselves.

China's leaders are under no such illusions. They are perfectly aware of Marx's comment to the effect that 'men make their own history, but they do not make it as they please, that they do not make it under self-selected circumstances, but under circumstances existing already'. The circumstances under which China's leaders are trying to make their own history, to return their country to the pivotal position in human affairs that its very name in Chinese implies (*Chung Kuo*, 'central country') means accepting for the time being the financial hegemony of an unpredictable and even dangerous entity, a United States that has from the inception of their regime posed at least a latent existential threat. They may find themselves, like their forerunners in Tokyo, forced from time to time to support the dollar, even at the cost of foregone purchasing power and a loss of control over certain economic and political outcomes. But they do so with their eyes open.

NOTES

1 Perry Anderson, 'Two Revolutions: Rough Notes', *New Left Review*, 61, 2010, p. 93.

2 See B.C. Koh, *Japan's Administrative Elite*, Berkeley: University of California Press, 1989, esp. p. 254.

3 Andrew Gordon, *The Evolution of Labor Relations in Japan: Heavy Industry, 1853-1955*, Cambridge: Harvard University Press, 1985.

4 Brenner has defined capitalism succinctly as follows: 'the capitalist mode

of production distinguishes itself from all previous forms by its tendency to relentless and systematic development of the productive forces. This tendency derives from a system of social-property relations in which economic units – unlike those in previous historical epochs – must depend on the market for everything they need and are unable to secure income by means of systems of surplus extraction by extra-economic coercion, such as serfdom, slavery, or the tax-office state. The result is two-fold. First, individual units, to maintain and improve their condition, adopt the strategy of maximizing their rates of profit by means of increasing specialization, accumulating surpluses, adopting the lowest cost technique, and moving from line to line in response to changes in demand with respect to supply for goods and services. Second, the economy as a whole constitutes a field of natural selection by means of competition on the market which weeds out those units that fail to produce at a sufficient rate of profit'. Robert Brenner, 'The Economics of Global Turbulence', *New Left Review*, 229, 1998, p. 10.

5 Michael L. Gerlach, *Alliance Capitalism: The Social Organization of Japanese Business*, Berkeley: University of California Press, 1992, chapter four.

6 Textile manufacturers in the Carolinas promised to deliver these two key battleground states into the Republican column in return for a pledge by the Richard M. Nixon campaign to reduce imports from Japan. See I. M. Destler, Haruhiro Fukui and Hideo Sato, *The Textile Wrangle: Conflict in Japanese-American Relations, 1969-1971*, Ithaca: Cornell University Press, 1979.

7 Akio Mikuni and R. Taggart Murphy, *Japan's Policy Trap: Dollars, Deflation, and the Crisis of Japanese Finance*, Washington: The Brookings Institution, 2002, ch. 3.

8 Jacob M. Schlesinger, *Shadow Shoguns: The Rise and Fall of Japan's Postwar Political Machine*, New York: Simon and Schuster, 1997, part one.

9 William Greider, *Secrets of the Temple: How the Federal Reserve Runs the Country*, New York: Simon and Schuster, 1987, ch. 1.

10 The key insider account remains David Stockman, *The Triumph of Politics: Why the Reagan Revolution Failed*, New York: Harper Collins, 1986.

11 See Robert L. Bartley, *The Seven Fat Years and How to Do It Again*, New York: MacMillan, 1992, p. 59.

12 Robert C. Angel, *Explaining Economic Policy Failure: Japan in the 1969-1971 International Monetary Crisis*, New York: Columbia University Press, 1991.

13 Clyde V. Prestowitz, Jr., *Trading Places: How We Allowed Japan to Take the Lead*, New York: Basic Books, 1988, part 2.

14 Hoping to give the ideologically rigid Treasury department of the first Reagan administration an excuse to intervene in currency markets, Fites commissioned a study from Stanford's Professor Ezra Solomon that demonstrated Japan's policies were deliberately keeping the yen's value down. See R. Taggart Murphy, *The Weight of the Yen*, New York: W. W. Norton, 1996 pp. 153-59.

15 The implication was that in this range, bilateral trade problems would largely disappear. Although the remark was attributed to C. Fred Bergsten, his actual

by the end of 1982'. 'What to do about the U.S.-Japan Economic Conflict', *Foreign Affairs*, 60(5), 1982, p. 1069.

16 R. Taggart Murphy, 'Power without Purpose: The Crisis of Japan's Global Financial Dominance', *Harvard Business Review*, March/April, 1989, p. 71-83.

17 Robert Brenner 'What is Good for Goldman Sachs is Good for America: The Origins of the Current Crisis', Center for Social Theory and Comparative History, Institute for Social Science Research, University of California Los Angeles, October, 2009, p. 2.

18 Quoted and translated by Taniguchi Tomohiko, 'Japan's Banks and the "Bubble Economy" of the late 1980s', *Monograph Series Number 4*, Center of International Studies, Program on US-Japan Relations, Princeton University, Princeton, 1993.

19 See the discussion of the mechanics of asset inflation in Mikuni and Murphy, *Japan's Policy Trap*, pp. 145-64.

20 See the account in Murphy, *The Weight of the Yen*, pp. 226-31.

21 Richard C. Koo, *Balance Sheet Recession: Japan's Struggle with Uncharted Economics and its Global Implications*, Singapore: John Wiley & Sons, 2003, esp. p. xi.

22 John Judis, 'A Dollar Foolish', *The New Republic*, 9 December 1996. An account from the Japanese side of the negotiations can be found in 'Sakakibara kyokucho madamada tobidasu "Dai-hogen"', *Shukan Bunshun*, 23 November 1995, pp. 42-5.

23 James Fallows 'China Makes, The World Takes', *The Atlantic*, July/August, 2007, pp. 68-69 discusses the high percentage of the revenues of a given product in today's economy that stem from its branding, design and retailing as opposed to its actual manufacture on the factory floor.

24 R. Taggart Murphy, 'East Asia's Dollars', *New Left Review*, 40, 2006, pp. 54-57 discusses the arrest of a Japanese entrepreneur who took all the neoliberal talk literally.

25 Karel van Wolferen, 'Japan's Stumbling Revolution', *The Asia-Pacific Journal*, 15-2-10, 12 April 2010. This is an English version of an article that originally appeared in Japanese in the March, 2010 issue of *Chuo Koron*.

26 R. Taggart Murphy, 'With Friends Like Us: How the Obama Administration Helped Topple the Japanese Prime Minister', *The New Republic*, 8 June 2010, available at http://www.tnr.com.

27 Hung Ho-Fung, 'America's Head Servant? The PRC's Dilemma in the Global Crisis', *New Left Review*, 60, 2009.

28 See Keith Bradsher, 'China Officials Wrestle Publicly over Currency', *The New York Times*, 25 March 2010.

29 Maruyama Masao, 'Theory and Psychology of Ultra-Nationalism', translated by Ivan Morris, in Masao, *Thought and Behavior in Modern Japanese Politics*, London: Oxford University Press, 1963. Original appeared in Japanese in the May, 1946 issue of *Sekai*.

THE CRISIS IN SOUTH AFRICA: NEOLIBERALISM, FINANCIALIZATION AND UNEVEN AND COMBINED DEVELOPMENT

SAM ASHMAN, BEN FINE AND SUSAN NEWMAN

It is now widely accepted that neoliberalism has entailed a global class project to shift the balance of economic and social power in favour of capital and away from labour. Neoliberalism is complex and uneven, ranging across economic, social and political dimensions, raising doubts over whether it is a legitimate term analytically or strategically. It has varied in time, space and issue, yet perpetuated its own economic and social mythologies – a truly variegated capitalism with corresponding varieties of neoliberalism. Its ascendancy within nation-states (particularly Britain and the US) and international institutions is rooted in the collapse of the postwar boom and ensuing economic crisis of the 1970s, but its establishment as the dominant ideology and policy practice was only possible as part of a broader conjuncture including the collapse of the former USSR, alternative development projects in the South, and retreats by labour and social democracy. In spite of this multi-dimensionality, we would suggest that the nature of neoliberalism cannot be understood without an examination of the processes and influences of what is now commonly, and increasingly, referred to as 'financialization'. Finance has been a critical, even definitive, component and mechanism underpinning and perpetuating neoliberalism.

Financialization as a term is associated loosely with the proliferation of financial markets, institutions and actors that have emerged since the collapse of Bretton Woods. Under this broad term is included the increasing importance of institutional investors; the expanding range of financial activities in the economy; the proliferation of financial services and instruments, and financial institutions and markets, including the now infamous sub-prime mortgages. It has also witnessed huge rewards to those involved in finance, and widening inequalities against previous trends, together with the penetration of finance into ever more areas of economic and social reproduction. This expansion and extension of the financial sector is well documented. The value of financial assets in the US grew from four times GDP in 1980 to ten times in 2007 and the ratio of global financial assets to global GDP has risen threefold from 1.5 to 4.5.[1] Rising incomes from financial investment have lead Martin Wolf to write: 'The US itself looks almost like a giant hedge fund. The profits of financial companies jumped from below 5 per cent of total corporate profits, after tax, in 1982 to 41 per cent in 2007.'[2]

But financialization is much more than simply the proliferation of financial markets and assets. Critically, non-financial companies have diversified into and gained an increasing share of profits from their financial activities, a development accompanied by the increasing financing of investment from retained earnings or borrowing on open markets. In many ways, this dynamic is the opposite of that presented by Hilferding in *Finance Capital*, where he analysed a developing fusion between financial and industrial capital.[3] Instead, financialization (in part) reflects the separation of industrial capital from finance capital in the form of the banks, and the increasing financialization of industrial corporations themselves which, in turn, has induced the refocusing of investment banks towards gaining profits from providing financial services to individuals.[4]

The spreading and individualization of debt, in part to compensate for three decades of stagnant or falling real wages, has become critical to maintaining demand. Consumption is increasingly based on credit, particularly through the use of capital gains in housing as collateral. The growth of personal household debt is extraordinary. In the USA, household debt was 48 per cent of GDP in 1981, in 2007 it was 100 per cent.[5] Financialization, then, is not just about capital, it is about labour. Rising debt has been combined with riches at the top. Income distribution in the US has returned to its peak levels of 1929, with the top 1 per cent of earners taking 23 per cent of income share.[6] We also see the increasing external debt of emerging or middle-income economies. And, while the developing world in particular has not been affected so much directly by contagious toxic assets but by falling demand for exports, foreign direct investment, aid and migrant remittances, nonetheless financialization has been important, as we demonstrate through the case of South Africa, where financial interests have influenced policy and affected class formation. In addition, many commodity markets have become increasingly financialized, with speculation affecting their volatility (not least food and energy). And, critically, we see growth in the world economy led by speculation and a series of speculative bubbles – thus financialization is affecting the rhythm and pace of accumulation.

How do we situate these interconnected developments within Marxist theory? Marx makes two useful distinctions. The first is between interest-bearing capital and other forms of capital, whether they are in production or exchange. And the second is between the real accumulation of capital through the extraction of surplus value in production and the accumulation of fictitious capital – paper claims on surplus value yet to be produced but traded in financial systems. The overall balance between these two forms of accumulation is historically determined, contingent and complex in the light of the portfolio of domestic and international forms it takes.

The neoliberal period has witnessed *both* the subordination of real accumulation to fictitious capital – with the expansion of speculative assets at the expense of real investment – *and* the integration of real accumulation into the realm of interest-bearing capital, resulting in financialized accumulation of a systemic nature. This cannot be separated from developments such as state-led economic and social restructuring, or the spread of privatization, which have further amplified the economic and social importance of financial assets. These developments have been accompanied by broader ideological shifts in politics and identity, with the decline of collective transformative projects and democratic participation and governance increasingly attached to the market and finance, with promotion of citizens as consumers and consumption as the means to self-realization.

The global balance of class forces has thus shifted in two senses: from capital to labour, and from some forms of capital to others. This is not the same as arguing that neoliberalism amounts to the return of a class of rentiers. And while heterodox explanations of the crisis, such as provided by Minsky, have much to offer, they are insufficiently rooted in the class dynamics and political economy of capitalism outlined above.

In sum, financialization:

- reduces overall levels and efficacy of real investment as financial instruments and activities expand at the former's expense, even if excessive investment does take place in particular sectors at particular times;
- prioritizes shareholder value, or financial worth, over other economic and social values;
- pushes policies towards conservatism and commercialization in all respects;
- extends influence, both directly and indirectly, over economic *and* social policy; and
- places more aspects of economic and social life at the risk of volatility from financial instability.

There are other, unforeseen consequences of neoliberalism which have affected the uneven and combined development of capitalism on a world scale. The relaxation of exchange controls has made many economies vulnerable to capital movements and created a pressure to build up high levels of reserves as a safeguard. At a global level, then, we see the USA's enormous balance of trade and payments deficits and, on the other hand, the holding of US dollars as reserves, particularly but far from exclusively by China. The US dollar has not collapsed, despite the country's deficits and minimal interest rates – despite not having adopted the sort of policies inflicted on others with similar deficits. And, whilst financialization is associated with slowdown in general over the period since the end of the postwar boom, there have been pockets of development for those who have sheltered themselves from the more dysfunctional forms of finance, used the state to promote (private) real accumulation, controlled wage increases relative to productivity increase, and found both domestic and international markets to serve. China is the most glaring example now, but the East Asian 'developmental states' preceded it. With some sectoral exceptions around its core and traditional areas of mining and energy, South Africa provides an example of the precise opposite of this form of capitalist development.

HELLO RAINBOW NATION

South Africa is now, 'officially', the most unequal society in the world – though there seems to be a macabre rivalry with Brazil for this status.[7] The poorest 20 per cent of South Africans receive 1.6 per cent of total income while the richest 20 per cent benefit from 70 per cent according to the South African Government's Development Indicators 2009.[8] In the most recent United Nation's Human Development Index of 'wellbeing', South Africa fell one place to 129th out of 182.[9] Before the global economic crisis, South Africa had one of the highest unemployment rates in the world. It now officially stands at 35.4 per cent or one third of the workforce.[10] The continuing relevance of Marx's notion that capital generates and draws upon a reserve army of labour is surely demonstrated by South Africa, though Marx could not have foreseen its members would struggle to survive in the context of the highest levels of HIV infection in the world.[11] This helps explain why, according to the UN, average life expectancy for South Africans is just 51.5 years, even though South Africa is classified as a middle income economy.[12]

How are we to situate these and other developments within a broader analysis of the political economy of South Africa since the defeat of apartheid? We argue that it is necessary to examine the specific form that neoliberalism and financialization have taken in the region, and how wider changes in the world economy and capitalist development have interacted with the legacy of the apartheid past. Global accumulation and its shifts and restructuring are necessarily mediated by the structure of particular economies and forms of class rule. We characterize the system of accumulation in South Africa as a 'Minerals-Energy Complex' (MEC) where accumulation has been *and remains* dominated by and dependent upon a cluster of industries, heavily promoted by the state, around mining and energy – raw and semi-processed mineral products, gold, diamond, platinum and steel, coal, iron and aluminium.[13]

In the context of South African production, financialization has produced a particular combination of short-term capital inflows (accompanied by rising consumer debt largely spent on luxury items) *and* a massive long-term outflow of capital as major 'domestic' corporations have chosen offshore listing and to internationalize their operations while concentrating within South Africa on core profitable MEC sectors. The result, even before the impact of the current crisis, was a jobless form of growth and the persistence of mass poverty for the majority alongside rising living standards for a small minority, including new black elites. Figure one shows annual GDP growth.

Figure 1: Annual GDP growth rate in South Africa 1990-2009

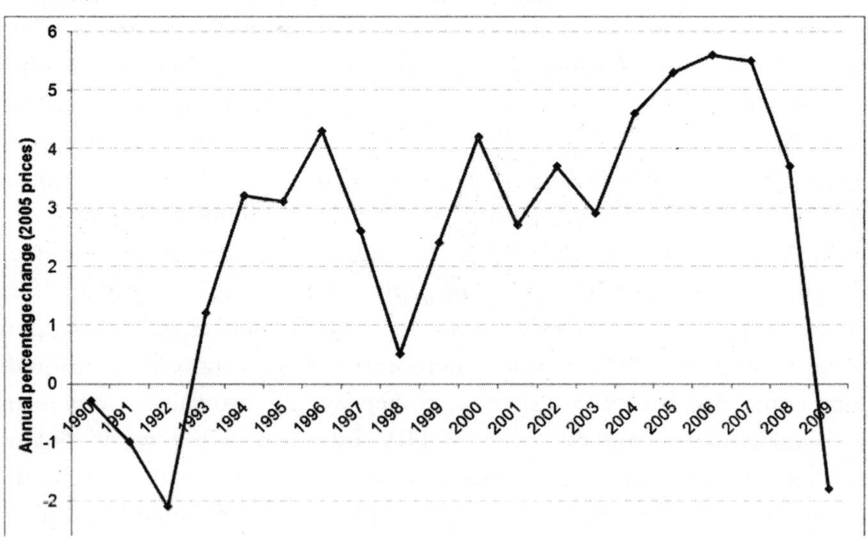

(Source: SARB 2009)

The effect of the crisis in South Africa, like many developing countries, has been felt primarily through falling global demand. In South Africa this has hit mining and manufacturing sectors but has also been accompanied by a steep fall in liquidity and a version of the credit crunch characteristic of Western economies. All of this has only served to intensify inequality with the biggest recession in 17 years yielding:

- The loss of almost 1 million jobs over the course of 2009;
- A 3 per cent fall in GDP between the end of 2008 and mid-2009;
- Output in the mining sector fell by 33 per cent in the final quarter of 2008, the biggest decrease on record;
- A 50 per cent production cut in the car industry in January 2009, the worst ever recorded, according to the National Association of Auto Manufacturers;
- A record 21.6 per cent year-on-year fall in manufacturing production announced in April 2009;
- Total manufacturing production declined by 4 per cent in the fourth quarter of 2009 with the biggest sub-sectors hit hardest: autos, basic chemicals and fabricated metal products. Manufacturing production at the start of 2010 remained below 2005 levels;
- A wholesale collapse in private sector credit extension from the third quarter of 2008 to mid-2009. It has picked up subsequently but growth in credit extended to the private sector was at 1.5 per cent in September 2009, the lowest rate for 43 years;
- Consumer spending shrank by around 5 per cent in the first half of 2009, its biggest contraction for 13 years, producing redundancies across the retail sector;
- The value of South Africa's exports fell by 24 per cent in the first quarter of 2009, increasing pressure on the current account deficit, 7 per cent of GDP;
- A *recovery* in the value of the Rand – the single most traded emerging market currency – by about 20 per cent over the course of 2009.[14]

SYSTEMS OF ACCUMULATION AND THE MINERALS-ENERGY COMPLEX

These short-term and most recent developments are not simply the more or less predictable response to the global crisis. They signal the continuing centrality of mining to the South African economy, something that should come as no surprise from a historical perspective, since mining has long been fundamental to capitalism in the subcontinent. South Africa remains rich in mineral reserves and is the richest nation in the world by 'commodity wealth' according to Citigroup, which estimates its mineral reserves are worth $2.5 trillion.[15] In this light, South Africa's MEC can be understood as a specific instance of a *system of accumulation.* In narrow terms, this can be understood as a core set of industrial sectors which exhibit strong linkages with each other and weak linkages with other sectors. Understood in this narrow sense, this is compatible with technocratic conceptions or possibly 'resource-curse' type arguments, particularly if the notion of the MEC is removed from the broader 'parent' notion of a system of accumulation. In the Marxist frame, however, the idea provides a bridge between the abstract tendencies of the capitalist mode of production and the reality of the production and reproduction of capitalist social relations in specific time and place – i.e. the variations in how the political economy of capitalism is put together and the critical role played by the state in the process.

A system of accumulation develops through the historically contingent linkages which develop between different sections of capital – including finance – and their interaction with the state. These core industries influence the development of other sectors and so indicate a specific form of industrial development. In the case of South Africa's MEC then it is not simply the weight played by the mining and energy sectors but also their determining role throughout the rest of the economy. One merit of this approach is its capacity to conceive of the state and the market as integral parts of a capitalist whole in marked contrast with other approaches, such as those based on notions of the developmental state that, whilst useful as a counter-critique of neoclassical approaches to development, systematically separate and oppose state and market as analytically prior and given.[16]

The MEC has defined the course of capitalist development in South Africa since its minerals revolution of the 1870s, upon which extraction came to be based on the extreme exploitation of black labour, achieved through a system of migrant labour. The discovery of precious metals and minerals produced a rapid inflow of 'English' or 'foreign' capital that quickly established control over the mining industry. Within two decades mining activities accounted for close to 60 per cent of exports from the region. The dominance of mining, and its need for large-scale capital investment (due to deep and dispersed gold deposits) rapidly produced concentration in mine ownership in the hands of six finance houses or producer groups which consolidated their stranglehold over production, distribution and marketing through the Chamber of Mines.[17]

The process was facilitated by an uneasy compromise between Afrikaner political power and foreign economic control and ownership of mining capital. State corporations, especially for steel and electricity, served the

MEC, as did labour control. But policies for diversification of industry out of the core MEC base remained weak. In the 1960s, however, the emergence of an Afrikaner mining house was negotiated (anticipating later black economic empowerment), and certain dysfunctions between large-scale capital and the politics of state intervention were eroded. There was potential for a 'developmental state' sort of strategy. But the 1970s witnessed the collapse of the post-war boom raising prices of both gold and energy (in the wake of the oil crises), thereby consolidating state-conglomerate strategy around MEC core sectors.

This was followed in the 1980s by the gathering crisis of apartheid itself. Yet the effect of sanctions was paradoxical. Exchange restrictions mostly confined domestic financiers to the domestic economy, forcing them to invest in established MEC sectors and acquire the foreign subsidiaries made available by disinvestment. The quantity and range of the conglomerates' holdings multiplied, while the mining industry remained a staple outlet for 'trapped' domestic finance. As a result, the ANC government inherited a highly developed financial system for a middle income country. But rather than channel investment into productive activities and the accumulation of capital stock, investment was increasingly channelled into the acquisition of financial assets under the control of, and/or with close links to, the conglomerates with origins in mining. This pattern not only reflects the general trend in financialization across the globe, but also informed the specific form of restructuring of South African conglomerates since 1994.

Both the apartheid *and* the post-apartheid eras have failed to diversify out of this core base in the MEC, and the strategies pursued by dominant MEC corporations, and their interconnection with and influence over state policy, have continued to be critical in determining the path of economic development. With the central role occupied by the MEC throughout the rest of the economy, manufacturing has thus been confined to a relatively limited number of industries around primary production and has remained weak in the development of capital and intermediate goods sectors – other sectors, especially consumer goods, only surviving through protection. So, whilst 'manufacturing' was the principal contributor to GDP in the 1990s, its sectoral contributions remained closely linked to the mining and energy sectors. The failure to develop light manufactures and other labour-intensive industries has resulted in deeply entrenched levels of unemployment. In 1994, South Africa had an unemployment rate of 20 per cent (31.5 per cent if discouraged work seekers are included) concentrated amongst low- and semi-skilled black workers.[18] This was soon compounded by secular declines in employment across both gold and agriculture.

THE MEC POST 1994: FINANCIALIZATION AND CRISIS

The negotiations to end apartheid were in the event premised upon the achievement of political equality whilst leaving the structure and functioning of the economy intact. Yet, of course, if white capital was to be untouched how was capitalism in South Africa to be de-racialized, never mind decent living standards achieved for the majority? The transitional compromise removed questions of wealth redistribution from the agenda and confined the settlement to narrowly political and constitutional issues, the establishment of bourgeois order, democratic rights and liberal democratic structures. And, whilst white capital for a time thought that the National Party was necessary as a bulwark against the radical demands of the ANC, it quickly became clear that no such assistance was necessary, as the ANC proved itself committed not only to capitalism but to its neoliberal form also. This meant leaving behind the programme of nationalization enshrined in the ANC's own Freedom Charter but also other interventionist policy measures and approaches designed to address the structural legacies of apartheid. White capital, the National Party and the ANC leadership increasingly came together around the pursuit of economic growth through 'competitiveness', faith in private sector investment, liberalization, privatization, Central Bank independence, etc.[19] Zac De Beer's nightmare, that the 'baby of free enterprise' might be 'thrown out with the bathwater of apartheid' – was not to come true.

The shift in part reflected the nature and inherent limitations of national liberation movements. It reflected also changing global conditions and thinking which meant that the National Party itself in its dying years had come to accept neoliberal orthodoxy in its policy prescriptions for the economy. These new conditions meant that white capital sought not only security of property rights and market relations in the new order, but also the right to internationalize and financialize its operations and to act as global 'players'. There was, in addition, both pressure and persuasion from Western governments and international financial institutions which saw a string of ANC economic advisors and leading figures receive training at business schools and international banks in the tenets of neoliberalism and workings of financial markets.[20] Prospective new black capital joined in. And whilst the marginalization of the white far right was a welcome development,[21] the Government's adoption of the non-negotiable Growth, Employment and Redistribution programme (GEAR) in 1996 signalled the crude resolution of any conflict over policy and the full embrace of neoliberalism. GEAR emphasized fiscal austerity, deficit reduction and pegging taxation and expenditure as fixed proportions of GDP. Through GEAR, the Government's stated macroeconomic priorities became the management of inflation, the deregulation of financial markets, tariff reduction and trade liberalization as well as limiting government expenditure. The irony is that while the rationale for these policies was to attract foreign direct investment, their actual effect was to increase the outflow of domestic capital – even while the hoped-for investment inflows failed to materialize.

The period of GEAR saw:

- the overnight abolition of tariff barriers which decimated much (black) labour-intensive manufacturing and increased unemployment;
- the easing of capital and exchange controls, enabling the conglomerates to relocate to the world's leading financial centres, thus increasing their capacity to tap global equity markets, export capital and discipline the state;
- corporate 'unbundling' in which diverse holdings and subsidiaries established during apartheid era have been broken up, sold-off where they are weak or amalgamated where considered to be internationally competitive, thereby nominally reducing conglomerate concentration but increasing concentration within sectors;
- Lack of domestic investment outside core MEC sectors, reinforcing dependence on mining exports and the crisis prone nature of the Rand in light of dependence on short-term capital inflows and permissiveness to outflows;
- Growth of the retail sector as it has expanded into black areas and also of services alongside casualization and informalization, although the informal sector remains small relative to other developing economies.[22]

High interest rates also acted to impede domestic investment. In addition, the high interest rates adopted as the government tightened monetary policy to reduce inflation have attracted an increase in short-term capital inflows into South Africa through the private financial sector.[23] The short-term nature of capital inflows has also affected the time horizons on lending by domestic financial institutions. The vast bulk of these inflows of capital have been channeled towards financial speculation and the extension of private credit to households. Figure 2 shows the expansion of domestic credit since the 1990s. Albeit with a dip in 2002, domestic credit extension increased from less than 60 per cent of GDP in 1994 to just over 85 per cent in 2007. The expansion of credit has not been reflected in increasing physical investment as corporate business enterprises allocate increasing shares of their total investment towards the acquisition of financial assets (Figure 3).

Figure 2. Credit extension and investment as percentages of GDP

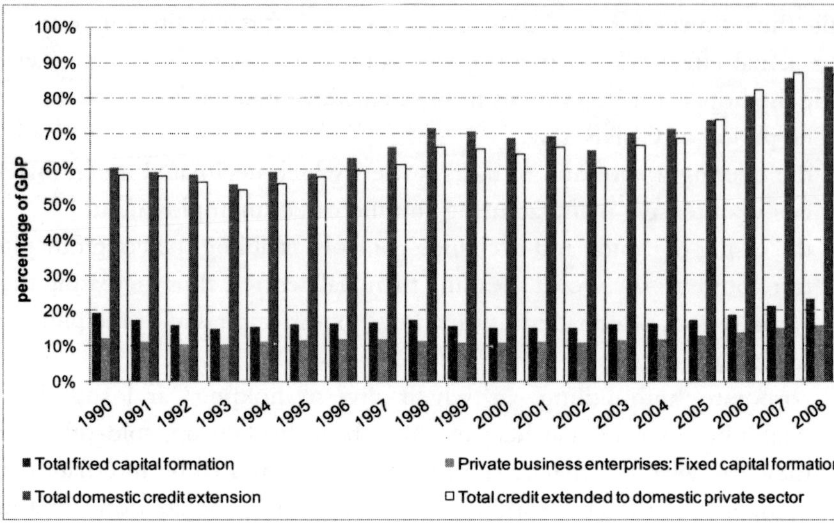

(Source: SARB 2009)

Figure 3. Comparing net capital formation and the net acquisition of financial assets as a proportion of GDP 1970-2007

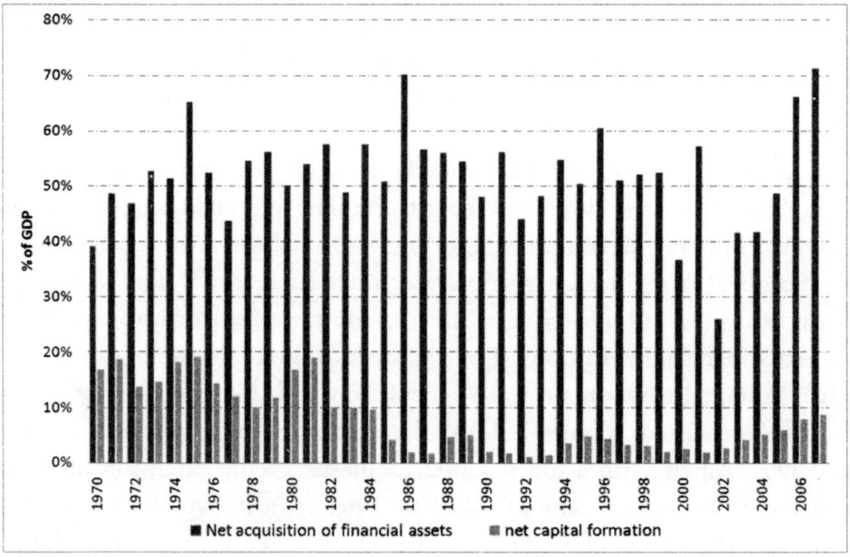

(Source: SARB 2008)

Figure 4. Private Sector Credit Extension by all Monetary Institutions

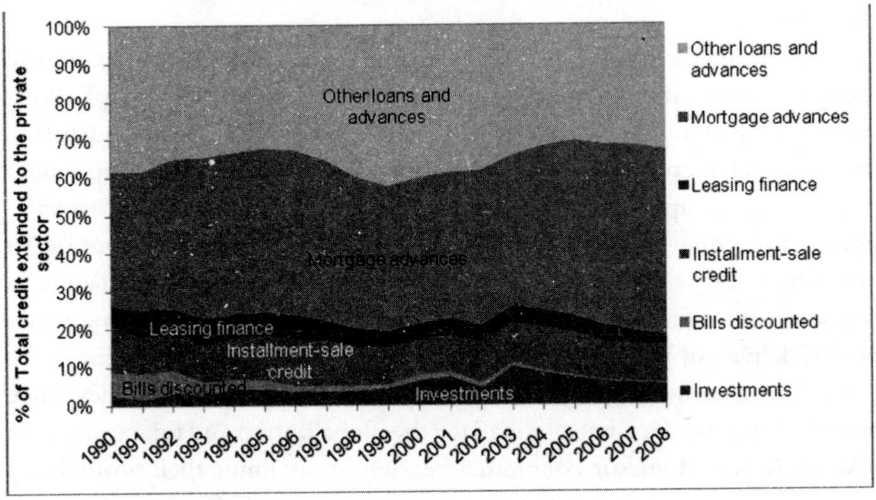

(Source: SARB 2009)

Figure 4 shows a breakdown in the uses of expanded credit to the private sector. Over 90 per cent of domestic credit extension has been channeled into consumption, with mortgage loans making up the highest share, supporting a South African house price bubble. The growth of household debt has underpinned second-home buying, a huge property bubble has emerged with a 389 per cent increase in property prices between 1997 and 2008.[24] In the wake of the collapse of the sub-prime market in the US, South African banks reduced their debt to asset ratios, and South Africans experienced their own credit crunch of sorts. An immediate impact of this credit crunch was an increase in the repossession of cars and homes. The extension of credit for leasing finance contracted by 36.9 per cent between January 2007 and September 2009. Car repossessions increased by 75 per cent in the 12 months prior to July 2008, and banks also struggled to sell repossessed homes.[25]

The expansion of credit had supported a boom in the wholesale and retail sector and also in personal services. Output from the wholesale and retail sector doubled between 2000 and 2007, and the number of jobs increased by over 30,000. But the employment generated in the retail and services sectors has been of low and semi-skilled workers. The subsequent contraction of wholesale and retail and personal services sectors that has taken place with the crisis has lead to large-scale redundancies amongst low paid, low skilled workers alongside the significant job losses in manufacturing. In stark contrast, the financial sector saw a 3.1 per cent increase in employment levels for the same period covering the official onset of the recession in South Africa.

Thus, whilst the crisis has impacted upon the South African economy through traditional transmission mechanisms and its own form of credit crunch, it has done so in ways that remain rooted in its own peculiarities. The financial sector has been the fastest growing in the post-apartheid period, now occupying as much as 20 per cent of GDP or, more exactly, appropriating one fifth of GDP and claiming this to be a contribution to economic activity. Meanwhile, 40 per cent of the population remain entirely without access to financial services of any sort, both directly and indirectly (in jobs delivered) in view of the appallingly low levels of investment.

The broad thrust of economic developments and economic policy since the end of apartheid has been to manage the globalization and financialization of South Africa's domestic conglomerates, whilst sustaining their profitability on core activities within the domestic economy itself. In particular, high interest rates have allowed for short-term capital inflows to compensate for long-term capital outflows, and exchange controls have been successively diminished to prevent the Rand from collapsing at the expense of Rand-denominated capital exports. The consequences for all aspects of economic performance have been significant, not least with fiscal restraint, and levels of investment running around a mere 10 per cent of GDP (whilst calculations of illegal and poorly monitored capital flight run at 20 per cent or more of GDP)!

FINANCIALIZATION AND BLACK INTEGRATION INTO THE RULING BLOC

The ANC's capacity to change South African society has thus been very limited. South Africa remains an extreme case of uneven and combined development: an advanced industrial economy and first world lifestyles exist with abject poverty and unequal social relationships and resource distribution of all kinds. The picture of slow growth, declining investment, rising unemployment, rural degradation, and income and wealth inequality that revealed the key features of the economy towards the end of the 1990s remains little changed over a decade later. The terms of the post-apartheid settlement, the establishment of liberal democracy and political rights alongside economic inequality and with property ownership intact, have been combined with intensive globalization, financialization and corporate restructuring of the economy.

But this has bequeathed to the ANC – within it own narrowing field of political vision – a contradiction: how to develop 'black capitalism' in the context of extreme uneven and combined development, when property rights are unchallenged and redistribution is off the agenda? Segregation and apartheid deliberately restricted the development of black capitalism. The formation and incorporation of a small new black elite in South Africa, often out of former trade union leaders and political activists, has been an important part of the changes which have occurred since 1994. This has involved both intra-capitalist class relations and race relations, with around 10 per cent of the country's top 20 per cent of high earners estimated to be black. 'Black Economic Empowerment' (BEE) deals worth R55 billion were recorded for 2005.[26] However, this new black elite is both highly financialized and often highly dependent upon the state. Its enrichment is notable for involving neither land (other than reallocated mineral rights as opposed to agriculture) nor, in general, productive activity. And, overall, white ownership and domination of the economy remain intact. For example, the proportion of the Johannesburg Securities Exchange market capitalization identified as controlled by 'black-influenced' business groups was 9.6 per cent in 1998, 3.5 per cent in 2002 and 5.1 per cent in 2006.[27]

Its members have derived and benefited from a number of developments. There are individual black managers and executives, nurtured as business has tried to develop a 'black face', but these remain small in number. Estimates for 2005 suggest that of JSE listed companies, under 10 per cent have black executive directors.[28] New black directors frequently sit on many boards and many BEE deals involve the same people again and again. In its initial phase in particular, 'empowerment' was measured through increasing ownership by blacks. Existing white-run conglomerates sold off subsidiary companies and/or shares to black business through deals struck by a host of 'empowerment companies' that often used 'Special Purpose Vehicles' to offer preferential shares to institutional investors (who were paid a dividend linked to the prime lending rate). Black groups, thus, essentially became investment trusts and, as such, were highly vulnerable. Around the time of the Asian financial crisis of 1997/8, falling stock prices and rising interest rates meant many could not repay the loans they had taken out to purchase shares.

From the early 2000s onwards the government moved away from narrow equity ownership criteria to charters for specific industries and more of a 'scorecard' approach encompassing broader criteria, dubbed Broad Based Black Economic Empowerment. Difficulties, however, remain. Concentration of activity upon few firms in specific sectors of the economy means it is difficult for new firms to enter except through acquisition, with the notable exceptions being growing sectors such as mobile telecommunications, media,

IT and healthcare.[29] The privatization and transfer of formerly state assets to black business interests is also a potential area of growth for blacks, in a way not dissimilar to the new elites created by privatization in Russia and elsewhere in Eastern Europe. But the most glaring feature of privatization in South Africa is its limited extent. The telecommunications company TELKOM and the transport giant Transnet are now 'partnerships' with foreign capital and BEE owners. But privatization and class formation seem to clash as goals, given that opportunities within parastatals have proven greater for the new black elite, and white-controlled conglomerates remain shy of funding a privatization programme (as they must at least in part) in deference to shifting their resources abroad.

A major area of growth lies in the granting of state and local government contracts or tenders to black business groups, particularly in the construction industry and also in mineral extraction. Government tenders are worth R120 billion a year. These kinds of deals often reveal the financialized and internationalized nature of the BEE elite. Take the building of the 'Gautrain' for example. This (expensive) express train service now runs between Johannesburg, Pretoria and OR Tambo airport and was built by a South African multinational, the British wing of a Canadian/German multinational and a French multinational brought together by a 'black empowerment company' created specifically for the purpose in a public-private partnership with Gauteng Provincial Government.[30] In this way, many BEE beneficiaries are essentially white even if activities are beneficially black-fronted. This aspect of 'black empowerment' is highly significant, not only in symbolic terms, but in revealing how such 'empowerment' benefits from links with international capital and does not create a productive class within South Africa.

South Africa is obviously not alone in the use of state assets and resources to promote private accumulation. Generations of African exclusion means that political office is highly important to promoting class formation. Corruption is the result, in its many forms, though far less endemic in South Africa than many other post-colonial societies. Yet, in broader terms, black capital remains systemically weak if politically powerful.[31] And so deep contradictions remain for the state – not only how to develop black capitalism when so much white economic power remains but also how to deliver on the inheritance of apartheid, quite apart from 'good governance' and transparency, at the same time as rapid advancement for black elite groups. The effects of the economic crisis have not assisted in resolving such conundrums, but the problems are far more deep-seated.

CONCLUDING REMARKS

The crisis has taken a huge toll on workers and the poor in economic and social terms. It has also led to belt-tightening amongst the middle class. But it has not led to any profound alteration in the structure of economy and society. Business as [un]usual in many ways remains the order of the day, with the deepening of impoverishment and worsening inequalities that barely remain addressed. The political transition from Mbeki to Zuma has involved a degree of recognition of the limitations of GEAR and the neoliberal model, with a (fanciful) debate about whether and how South Africa could become a 'Developmental State' emblematic of this shift. However the record of the Zuma government's first year is poor with little major legislation put in place. Zuma seems content to strive for membership of the BRIC group of nations (to go alongside honorary membership of the G20) – again fanciful given the size of the South African economy – and using the 2010 World Cup both to support such a bid and to act as a repeat of the rugby World Cup (though with much lesser chance of victory). The newly established National Planning Commission and Economic Development Department have, in the space of a year, done little more than name their respective lists of advisors. And any challenge to vested interests, and certainly those of the mining companies, has remained off the agenda. As such, the MEC and its associated command of economic and social life remain pervasive.

These developments need to be located in broader global trends as well as those specific to South Africa and its liberation struggle. The role of global and domestic capital can only be understood if situated in the evolving impact of financialization on the world economy. Globally, the financialization associated with neoliberalism has witnessed the elevation of financial elites, most notably in, but not confined to, the US and the UK. This rise prevails across almost every economic, political, social and ideological indicator. In developing countries, there is the added twist of both creating financial elites and strengthening their roles. This has had a major impact on politics and governance and, correspondingly, policy. It is, after all, what stabilization and structural adjustment have been about over the period of neoliberalism – not just policies but the personnel (with corresponding rewards and interests), institutions and governance to deliver them.[32]

In South Africa, the black elite's incentives to engage in and promote policies for economic and social investments are correspondingly reduced. Paradoxically, then, financialization has the effect of insulating the business and politics of money-making from the imperatives that make it possible – the economic and social reproduction attached to the accumulation of capital. And, by the same token, government is under the command of the

Treasury whose prime result, despite protestations of goals to the contrary in terms of the search for stability and control of inflation, has been to allow for the orderly export of long-term capital. More generally, the extent, nature and mode of policymaking, even where economic and social development has been broached, is marked by acute sensitivity to the need to contain the emergence of alternative politics – public sector provision of housing, for example, brings corresponding organizations and activism for further advance or, at least, resistance against regress, as is overt in the case of free water and electricity in South Africa and the high levels of protests around these.

In the final decades of the twentieth century South Africa brought together the most extraordinarily dislocated combination of forces and trends across time and place. Apartheid offered the most virulent and extreme form of racialized capitalism and, in its final years, had been based in its MEC upon an extraordinarily close collaboration between the state and conglomerate capital, prompting and ultimately delivering a transition highly advantageous to its continuing and shifting imperatives. Yet, the anti-apartheid struggle also spawned a remarkably powerful trade union movement, progressive civil society activism, and a strong left committed to radical change and armed struggle as necessary. In addition, whilst many of these were in freefall or even extinct elsewhere in the world, South Africa's anti-apartheid struggle attracted world-wide solidarity and support on an unprecedented scale (take Palestine as comparator) despite or even because of the uneasy relationship between neoliberalism and democracy and human rights.

In the event, the transition from apartheid has seen the dwindling or dismantling of these progressive forces, and achievements have been desperately disappointing. The significance of the political transition to democracy should not be underestimated, nor the continuing leverage of at least formal commitment to progressive value and politics (compare outcomes in the Middle East or the rest of Africa without unduly homogenising). A President has been deposed in a bloodless coup, with the trade unions still capable of playing a major role in bringing the country to a standstill and shifting personnel, such as the Governor of the Reserve Bank, at the highest levels. But these are token when set against the continuing extremes of inequalities and economic and social deprivations that are most marked, worsening and even sidelined as a normal state of affairs. And whilst there have been shifts in its nature, the MEC and its associated command of economic and social life remain pervasive.

Why has this been so? One answer is to be found in the elevated expectations that are attached to liberation movements that cloak themselves in the doctrines of socialism only to abandon them once more immediate goals of shifts in political regime have been realized. This may now be only of historic interest but is complemented by a second explanation of incorporation of erstwhile progressives through enrichment once in power. The formation of a black elite in South Africa, often out of trade union leaders and political activists, has been a decisive part of the process and has entailed significant intellectual and political retreats and is sickeningly depressing. It has been matched by an equally significant expansion of black employment, opportunities and advancement for at most a minority, primarily through the state, with a corresponding and understandable shifting balance of trade union activity to further material interests as opposed to more fundamental transformative goals, as decline is experienced across the more traditional sources of militancy and organization across mining and large-scale industry.

In the case of South Africa, the intensive globalization and financialization of the economy has involved the corporate restructuring that has enabled incorporation of a black elite. Here the form of enrichment is notable for its lack of productive activity. The black elite's incentives to engage in and promote policies for economic and social investments are reduced to the minimalist imperatives of social, political and ideological containment.

Globally, the first phase of neoliberalism, from the late 1970s to the early 1990s, took the shock-therapy form of the direct state promotion of private capital in general and of finance in particular. The second phase of neoliberalism, still in place if momentarily shaken by the crisis, has involved more extensive and overt state intervention both to sustain financialization and to temper its worst effects, as in public-private partnerships as opposed to privatization. Chronologically, the demise of apartheid coincided with this second phase, bringing the goals of the progressive and interventionist Reconstruction and Development Programme, let alone the Freedom Charter, into conflict with the South African catch-up with the first phase. The adoption of GEAR signalled the brutal resolution of this conflict, not only in that neoliberalism was fully embraced but also the intent of putting the Triple Alliance (of ANC, COSATU and the SACP) under the command and/or outside of government. It is only now, more than a decade later, that the second phase of neoliberalism has been formally endorsed in South Africa just in time to confront the pressing demands of the global crisis.

This commentary suggests that it is inadequate to read off disappointment in the South African trajectory either from the inflexible imperatives of global capitalism or the abject failures and betrayals of domestic politics alone. For one thing, this would leave unexplained why in such favourable conditions for capitalism, it has both suffered a slowdown under neoliberalism and been subject to a crisis that cannot be blamed on the working class and progressive movement demands. Interestingly, however, South Africa is an exception to this, with many commentators blaming high wages, social expenditure and trade union militancy for poor economic performance. It is also essential to situate the role of global and domestic capital and politics in the evolving impact of financialization, whereby the composition of class forces has fundamentally shifted as well as the balance between them and their mode of interaction. Progressive movements and policies are more liable to be marginalized, excluded and repressed than incorporated.

South Africa, then, offers a salient example of the extent to which powerful and progressive movements can be rapidly undone, with the demobilization of civil society, the breaking of strong community organizations and their links with the trade unions and the collapse of much of the left. More hopeful is the renewal of protest, on a huge scale, as a result of anger at government failing to improve or even prioritize basic service delivery to the poorest. The police recorded an average of nearly two 'unrest-related' gatherings a day in the four years to the end of March 2008, and the protests have only increased since. These protests are often disconnected from national political debates, from the radical left, and from a coherent alternative vision. But they point to the vulnerabilities, not only economic, of a system of accumulation which marginalizes so many. For, to the extent that progressive policies can be organized to pursue the meeting of basic needs beyond the barriers of finance, it exposes and challenges the forms of control and power that are inflexible in relation to alternative modes and levels of provision.

NOTES

1 James Crotty, 'Structural Causes of the Global Financial Crisis: A Critical Assessment of the "New Financial Architecture"', *Cambridge Journal of Economics,* 33(4), 2009; José Gabriel Palma, 'The Revenge of the Market on the Rentiers: Why Neoliberal Reports of the End of History Turned out to be Premature', *Cambridge Journal of Economics,* 33(4), 2009.

2 Martin Wolf, 'Why is it so Hard to Keep the Financial Sector Caged', *Financial Times,* 6 February 2008.

3 Rudolf Hilferding, *Finance Capital: A Study in the Latest Phase of Capitalist Development,* London: Routledge and Kegan Paul, 1981 [1910].

4 See Costas Lapavitsas, 'Financialised Capitalism: Crisis and Financial Expropriation', *Historical Materialism,* 17(2), 2009 and Paulo Dos Santos, 'On the Content of Banking in Contemporary Capitalism', *Historical Materialism,* 17(2), 2009. For a critique see Ben Fine 'Locating Financialisation', *Historical Materialism,* 18(2), 2010.

5 Crotty, 'Structural Causes of the Global Financial Crisis'.

6 Robert Wade, 'From Global Imbalances to Global Reorganisations', *Cambridge Journal of Economics*, 33(4), 2009.

7 The comparison with Brazil is important, not least for social policy, as it is widely assumed that the income gap in Brazil has narrowed as a consequence of Lula's policy of providing social grants. Note also that while under-five mortality rates between the richest fifth and the poorest fifth were similar in both countries in the mid-to-late 1990s, namely 66 deaths per 1,000 live births, Brazil appears to be 'well on its way to reaching its Millennial Development Goal target of an average under-five mortality rate of 19 in 2015', but South Africa's target of 20 in 2015 'appears to be out of reach since its average under-five mortality rate has declined only marginally, i.e., from 64 in 1990 to 59 in 2007'. Hannah Bargawi and Terry McKinley, 'Targeting Inequalities in Child Mortality', *Development Viewpoint*, No. 40, Centre for Development Policy & Research, School of Oriental and African Studies, London, October, 2009.

8 The Presidency of the Republic of South Africa, *Development Indicators 2009*, p. 23, available from http://www.thepresidency.gov.za.

9 *The Weekender*, 24th/25th October 2009, p. 1. The UN report is based on data collected in 2007 and so does not reflect the impact of the crisis.

10 *Business Day*, 5 May 2010, p. 1

11 Henry Bernstein 'Globalisation, Neo-liberalism, Labour, with Reference to South Africa', in Alfredo Saad-Filho and Galip Yalman, eds., *Transitions to Neoliberalism in Middle-Income Countries: Policy Dilemmas, Economic Crises, Mass Resistance*, London: Routledge, 2010.

12 *The Weekender*, 24th/25th October 2009, p. 1. The UN also ranks Johannesburg to be the most unequal city in the world.

13 Ben Fine and Zaverah Rustomjee, *The Political Economy of South Africa: From Minerals-Energy Complex to Industrialisation*, Boulder: Westview Press, 1996.

14 *Business Day*, 5 May 2010, p. 1; Gordon Bell, 'Contracts Most Since 1984: GDP Fell Annualised 6.4 per cent', 26 May 2009, Reuters; *Mail and Guardian*, 27 February 2009; '2010/11 - 2012/13: Industrial Policy Action Plan', Department of Trade and Industry, South Africa, February, 2010, p. 13; *Business News*, 30 October 2009, p. 4; *Business Day*, 19 June 2009; *Business Report*, 18 June 2009; *Business Day*, 30 September 2009.

15 *Business Report*, 28 April 2010, p. 1.

16 Samantha Ashman, Ben Fine and Susan Newman, 'The Developmental State and Post-Liberation South Africa', in Neeta Misra-Dexter and Judith February, eds., *Testing Democracy: Which Way is South Africa Headed?*, Cape Town: IDASA Publishing, 2010.

17 Rob Davies, Dan O'Meara and Sipho Dlamini, *The Struggle for South Africa: A Reference Guide to Movements, Organizations and Institutions, Volume One*, Second Edition, London: Zed Books, 1988; Charles H. Feinstein, *An Economic History of South Africa: Conquest, Discrimination and Development*, Cambridge: Cambridge University Press, 2005; Fine and Rustomjee, *The Political Economy of South Africa*.

18 Central Statistical Service, *October Household Survey 1994*, Pretoria: Central

Statistical Service, 1995.

19 For a prescient summary of these processes see Bill Freund and Vishnu Padayachee, 'Post-Apartheid South Africa: The Key Patterns Emerge', *Economic and Political Weekly,* 33(20), 1998.

20 These links continue. In April 2010, just as Goldman Sachs was being accused of defrauding its investors, Tito Mboweni – former trainee at the bank who went on to be Governor of the Reserve Bank – was appointed 'global advisor' to the banking group. *Business Day,* 25 April 2010.

21 The murder of AWB leader Eugene Terreblanche in April 2010 only underlined the weakness of the organized white far right but revealed much about agrarian class relations and working and living conditions for farm workers, drastically hit by liberalization. One of those accused of the murder, a 28-year-old farm worker, alleges Terreblanche regularly defaulted on his R600 a month salary. (By way of comparison, a university lecturer would earn in the region of R20,000 per month.) The second accused, a 15-year-old farm labourer who had worked full time for Terreblanche since the age of 14, declined to apply for bail following his arrest as, according to his lawyer, in jail he is 'sleeping on a bed for the first time in his life. He is also having three meals a day for the first time. He is also studying.' *The Star,* 15 April 2010, p. 1.

22 Neo Chabane, Andrea Goldstein and Simon Roberts, 'The Changing Face and Strategies of Big Business in South Africa: More than a Decade of Political Democracy', *Industrial and Corporate Change,* 15(3), 2006; Freund and Padayachee, 'Post-Apartheid South Africa'; Hein Marais, *South Africa: Limits to Change.* London: Zed, 2001.

23 The financial sector in South Africa is dominated by the 'Big Four' commercial banks: ABSA, First National, Nedcor and Standard Bank. Between them, they provide 95 per cent of the country's retail accounts. The majority of poor black South Africans rely upon informal sector saving and credit associations, co-operatives, burial societies and village banks. See Ralph Hamman, Sanjeev Khagram and Shannon Rohan, 'South Africa's Charter Approach to Post-Apartheid Economic Transformation: Collaborative Governance or Hardball Bargaining', *Journal of Southern African Studies,* 34(1), 2008. The lack of serious detailed analysis of the financial system is compounded by the South African Central Bank, which has turned a blind eye towards the legal export of long-term capital that it has promoted and the illegal that it has induced.

24 Patrick Bond, 'World Economic Crisis: Implications for South Africa', Harold Wolpe Memorial Lecture, University of the Witwatersrand, Johannesburg, 7 May 2009.

25 *Mail and Guardian,* 28 July 2008; *Weekend Argus,* 20 April 2008.

26 William M. Gumede, *Thabo Mbeki and the Battle for the Soul of the ANC,* Second Edition, Cape Town: Zebra Press, 2007.

27 Stefano Ponte, Simon Roberts and Lance van Sittert, 'Black Economic Empowerment, Business and the State in South Africa', *Development and Change,* 38(5), 2007. See also Roger Southall, 'The ANC and Black Capitalism in South Africa', *Review of African Political Economy,* 31(100), 2004.

28 Bill Freund, 'South Africa: The End of Apartheid and the Emergence of the

"BEE Elite"', *Review of African Political Economy,* 34(114), 2007.

29 Ponte, Roberts and van Sittert, 'Black Economic Empowerment'.

30 Freund, 'South Africa'.

31 This acts as a continuing spur to radical nationalist/populist perspectives such as that of ANC Youth Leader Julius Malema, who has important links within government. Thabo Mbeki's brother Moeletsi, in a recent plea for a new African capitalism, also argues that the new black elite are 'a small class of unproductive but wealthy black crony capitalists... ironically, the caretaker of South Africa's deindustrialisation.' Moeletsi Mbeki, *Architects of Poverty: Why African Capitalism Needs Changing,* Johannesburg: Picador Africa, 2009, p. 61.

32 Ben Fine and Dave Hall, 'Terrains of Neoliberalism: Constraints and Opportunities for Alternative Models of Service Delivery', in David McDonald and Greg Ruiters, eds., *Alternatives to Privatization: Exploring Non-Commercial Service Delivery Options in the Global South,* London: Routledge, forthcoming, papers from Municipal Services Project, http://www.municipalservicesproject.org.

DERIVING CAPITAL'S (AND LABOUR'S) FUTURE

DICK BRYAN AND MICHAEL RAFFERTY

Financial derivatives have been identified as the prime suspect in recent financial crises. For those not in the business of derivative analysis, perhaps the first revelation of their potency, and of their capacity to disguise underlying financial exposures, came with the Long Term Capital Management, Enron and WorldCom episodes around the turn of the century. Then came the subprime financial crisis of 2007-8 where 'securitization', a derivative-based process, came to prominence as the global distributor associated with the predatory practice of subprime lending. Credit default swaps betting on corporate insolvency followed. Derivatives seemed to ensure that betting on the misery of others soon became the misery of all. It is hardly surprising that derivatives are widely seen as crisis-laden: financial weapons of mass destruction, as Warren Buffet is so often quoted as describing them.[1]

The label and the reputation may be justified. But presented as explanations they make us jump too quickly to judgment and they miss much. The propensity to depict the global financial crisis in terms of distortion and speculation, with financial derivatives their principal instrument, is, we argue, not fruitful. Indeed, we conjecture that derivatives are not a pathological growth on capitalism – a distortion of some 'true' capitalism. They are integral to capitalism and the expression of its essential property relations and its inventiveness. The contradictions of derivatives are the contradictions of capitalism.

If, in explaining the financial crisis, we go searching for specific flaws within derivatives in terms of their mathematical limitations, their lack of transparency, or their 'toxicity', we are likely to build an analysis of catastrophic inevitability and a politics which is dominated by nostalgia, with the intent to recapture a seemingly safer and more financially innocent era before derivatives. If we rest with such interpretations, it is likely that we will miss the true potency of derivatives both in the recent financial crisis and in the future.

The growth of derivatives trades preceded the financial crisis and was, in aggregate, surprisingly unaffected by the crisis. Their growth looks to be continuing in the aftermath of the crisis. Some argue that this is simply reloading for the next downturn, but Marxism must amount to more than 'shorting the future' (to use the financial term for predicting a downturn). We need to look at how derivatives are shaping capitalism's present and possible future, and situate the current financial crisis within that momentum.

The objective of analysing the 2007-8 crisis is not simply to identify it with a propensity to destruction, to again reveal capitalism's fragility (something which, as Gray notes, is not particular to the left).[2] It is also to look for signs of capitalism's adaptability to build new processes of capital accumulation. Rather than Marx's theories of crisis, this paper is motivated by Marx's 'other' invocation to identify the frontiers of capitalist development and the momentums which drive them. Accordingly, we seek to develop an analysis of how financial and other derivative markets have become integral to contemporary capitalism: a role in which the recent financial crisis, while socially severe, may prove to be analytically more incidental.

In developing this case, we first explore the nature and role of derivatives in a way that identifies how they have become integral to capital accumulation. Specifically, derivatives present new forms of commodities and commodification, opening new frontiers for accumulation in what has conventionally been seen simply as sites of 'circulation'. We then turn to their evolution and the role they played in the global financial crisis. In explaining this role we build the argument that the crisis can be interpreted as a result of the immaturity of derivative markets, rather than, as is popularly held, their over-development. Indeed, derivatives present a site of new potential for capital accumulation. We conclude that the crisis of 2007-08 may well come to be seen a crisis *within* that momentum, rather than a crisis *of* that momentum. Indeed, we argue, the crisis has, if anything, entrenched the momentum. The difference is important not only analytically, but politically too, for it projects a different agenda onto regulatory reform, and a different politics for labour.

WHAT ARE DERIVATIVE MARKETS AND WHY DO THEY MATTER SO MUCH?

There is no simple, universal definition of derivatives, and those advanced in the past have rapidly become redundant as financial markets have evolved.[3] A one-sentence dictionary definition will identify a derivative as an asset or security whose price depends on (or is derived from: hence the etymology of 'derivative') one or more underlying assets. It is a definition which points to the historical way of thinking about derivatives, but it is not a very helpful contemporary definition, certainly if we are seeking to capture a wider social conception of their current role. In any case, it defines only the pricing structure of a derivative, not what a derivative is or does.

Derivatives are conventionally associated with financial products like interest rates and exchange rates, but they apply to many more aspects of society too. Some of these have already been developed in formal financial markets; others remain future possibilities. It is important to conceive of derivatives in a way that includes them all, and thereby create analytical access to these future possibilities.

Derivatives present the logic of deconstructing the social and economic world into ever more precisely defined attributes, each of which can be configured into a measurable (but sometimes contestable and often fragile) instrument to be priced and traded. This logic can be thought of in at least three dimensions:

1. *segmentation*: decomposing the social and economic world into more and more precisely-defined constituent 'elements' or 'attributes'. This is an act of imagination.
2. *quantification*: configuring each element as a measurable entity with attributes of risk, such that each element is in principle comparable with other elements. This turns a contingency of the social and economic world into a recognizable unit of measure, which can be made commensurable with other, different elements or attributes. This is an act of production in the sense that a risk is being consciously configured and calculated.
3. *commodification*: trading each attribute of risk through securities, derivative or insurance markets. This is an act of circulation. The prices at which derivatives circulate remain variable, contingent upon both the prices of underlying assets, and what is innocently termed 'market sentiment' or 'predictions'.

To clarify these three aspects it will be useful to highlight some more general features of derivatives by way of a few leading questions.

What sorts of assets (underlying assets) can have a derivative?

Anything (with asset or commodity-like attributes) that can be independently measured by money (i.e., has a price) or an index could have a derivative. The focus of the derivative is changes in the price/index of the asset (or bundle of assets, as in a security) or the probability of a price or index movement (often referred to as an 'event'). The form of the derivative will then specify how money changes hands as that measurement goes up or down. Commonly-traded derivatives address interest rates, exchange rates and oil price movements, but more recently-developed derivatives address such things as credit default risk, house price movements or temperature changes.[4]

Securities, while not simply derivatives, have a critical derivative dimension. Securities are bonds issued on the basis of assets and the expected income streams associated with those assets. Mortgage backed securities are bonds in which the purchaser of the bond acquires an income stream linked to a bundle of mortgages. The derivative dimension is that the buyer of the security has acquired an exposure to the performance of an asset (mortgage repayments) but without owning the underlying asset (the mortgages or houses themselves). The price of the security therefore varies with the rate of repayment of mortgages, not with house prices per se.

An essential dimension of derivatives, therefore, is that they involve competitive positions on directions and degrees of change. As many facets of economic and social life change, and in ways that might be measured, the potential for innovation in derivative products is enormous. The potential depends essentially on whether there can be an independent (verifiable) measure of change (so that markets cannot be readily manipulated) and whether there would be enough demand for the product to make a derivative market profitable to operate.[5]

What is involved in the ownership of a derivative?

A derivative gives ownership of a financial exposure to the performance of the underlying asset: a right to buy or sell or to a payment when the price/index of the underlying asset changes. In this sense a derivative is a contingent claim, because its price will depend – is contingent – on future circumstances. But, and this is critical, it involves no (necessary) ownership of the underlying asset. With an oil future or option, one is not buying/selling a barrel of oil (the underlying asset), although that could be the ultimate intended consequence, but buying/selling exposure to changes in the price of a barrel of oil (the contingency).[6] With weather derivatives, to take another example, there can be no ambiguity about the underlying 'asset' being traded: markets trade an indexed measure of rainfall or temperature or frost, but one cannot buy and sell the weather itself. In this light also we can understand a mortgage-backed security as a having derivative-like elements. The owner of the security owns a monetary exposure to the performance of a bundle of mortgages: that is, there is ownership of repayments on the mortgages; not ownership of the mortgages themselves.

Ownership of exposure to the performance of assets without ownership of the underlying asset has two particular advantages. First, it creates a leveraged exposure to the underlying asset: it is a cheap way of participating in the returns that come with ownership. Second, it makes transfers of this kind of ownership simple: it is much easier to trade ownership of an oil derivative contract than to transfer ownership of a barrel of oil. By making transfers of risk ownership simple, derivatives also make it possible to separate or combine different risks together into new 'synthetic' products. It is this ability to make assets fungible (to blend attributes of capital) that has helped make derivative markets so liquid. The focus of derivative ownership, therefore, is intense price competition on the performance of capital, but freed from the impediments of either physical or legal asset ownership.

Who trades derivatives?

Derivatives are generally associated with prices or indices whose movement is not readily predictable, but where those movements can have widespread or otherwise significant financial consequences. There are some who fear the price or index going down, and some who fear it going up. If their fears are significant, then investors may be willing to purchase a financial instrument to have the fears abated. And there will be still others, usually depicted as 'speculators', who want to take on bets about the price or index movement.

Derivatives are, therefore, integrally tied to risk – although strictly speaking to both risk and uncertainty. It is well understood that to make profits, there must be risks. But companies (and individuals) face all sorts of risks. Some they are happy to hold, for they are integral to entrepreneurial strategy (or, for individuals, integral to life experience). But other risks are not wanted. Indeed, all corporations (and individuals) would sell off (neutralize) some risks, and be prepared to pay to do so, at least up to a certain price. And someone must be on the other side of these contracts. They may be a party with a symmetrically opposite risk, or they could be investment banks, hedge funds or sovereign wealth funds, looking to earn a premium for taking on that exposure.

As such, most derivative products are associated with businesses where there are profit consequences of price/index movements. To look at who is trading these products, the Bank for International Settlements (BIS) Triennial survey of Foreign Exchange and Derivative Markets gives some broad insight. The last published survey, for 2007, shows that the share of trades undertaken by big banks[7] had fallen from 60 per cent in 1998 to 38 per cent in 2007, while the share undertaken by 'other financial institutions' has grown from 20 per cent to 43 per cent of turnover.[8] Central to the 'other financial institutions' category are pension funds and hedge funds (addressed shortly).

Securities, in particular, have emerged as a significant source of private debt growth. Between 1990 and 2008 asset-backed securities made up 43 per cent of private debt in the advanced capitalist economies, with an annual growth rate of 19 per cent. Corporate bonds, conversely, made up just 8 per cent of corporate debt, with an annual growth rate of just 6 per cent.[9] Hence those wanting debt-exposure to corporations are gravitating towards securities rather than corporate bonds, and corporations themselves are increasingly drawing on securities rather than financial institutional lending to raise debt. Beyond the corporate securities lie a raft of other asset-backed securities and collateralized debt obligations. These securities have been purchased by two primary categories of investors: investment banks, pension funds and hedge funds[10] on the one hand and the sovereign wealth funds of the surplus economies of Asia and the Middle East on the other.[11]

As we will consider shortly, these products are not entirely internal to the corporate and financial world. The process of securitization draws households into the mix, albeit as providers of income streams for securities rather than as market traders.

How are derivatives priced?

The critical technical issue is how to price risk: at what price is unwanted risk worth retaining because it is too expensive to sell; at what price is risk worth buying? Historically, these were calculations based largely on experience and intuition, but since the 1980s these are issues that have been thought of in markets as formal, technical problems, with technical solutions. Along with actuarial data, the Black-Scholes options pricing model was thought to have provided the solution.[12] Two ever-present problems, however, have been made stark by the recent financial crisis. First, when a buyer acquires a calculated risk, an incalculable uncertainty goes along with it. When markets become volatile, and there is an atmosphere of unfamiliarity, incalculable uncertainties are more likely to be revealed.[13] Second, markets trade not just current risk, but expectations of future risk, and hence expectations of where the risk calculations are likely to go. McKenzie argues that once the formula was put into practice by derivative traders, it ceased to operate as a predictor of price, and became a benchmark from which price varied.[14] In effect, the pricing of risk will tend to run ahead of the technical calculations, as traders seek to beat or at least anticipate the market's next moves.[15]

If derivatives are produced and involve ownership, they must be commodities. What sorts of commodities are derivatives?

Derivatives are commodified risk. However, the conception of 'risk' as a commodity stretches the popular understanding of a commodity, especially where that popular conception is (still) conceived as physical output produced in a factory. Indeed, this contrast is often at the basis of the argument that there is something 'unreal' or 'fictitious' about derivatives. The argument itself has a lineage going back at least to the development of the joint stock company, when the idea of a fictitious legal entity (the 'corporation') becoming an owner of capital was similarly questioned.[16] Contrary to this popular conception, we contend that derivatives are both real and integral to accumulation, albeit also objects of speculation. Hence, there is a need to grapple with the logic of derivatives in order to understand accumulation more generally, including the circuit of industrial capital (the stylised 'factory' model of accumulation). Two points are pertinent here.

First, the circuit of industrial capital starts with money capital in the form of credit or equity. But the interest rate on the credit and the price of equity changes in uncertain ways over time,[17] and hence with ramifications for the share of produced surplus that must go to the lender or investor. The sale of output generates revenue, but perhaps in a currency of unknown value at the time of payment. There are risks of disruptions of all sorts to the production process and risks of shifts in consumer demand. Contingency is central, and to omit it from a depiction of the nature of industrial capital involves not an abstraction from, but idealization of, market processes. It is the idealization of an equilibrium model.

Second, in the circuit of industrial capital, exchange value is thought of as embodied in commodity output, and when the commodity is sold for final consumption, it leaves the sphere of competition. In the case of a derivative, competition is embodied in the substance of the product: the exchange value is located in what the product does, or what it sets in motion, and what it sets in motion is competitive calculation. In the case of car insurance, to take a simple example – a product with option-like dimensions – the insurer faces costs of repairing smashed cars plus their administration costs. To that they seek to add a certain rate of profit. But for a consumer, the value of the commodity purchased is not a certain amount of repairs but the *right* to repairs (the right to set production in motion) should your car get damaged. The commodity output is a contingent claim on production. With a different sort of derivative, such as a security based on the income stream of household electricity payments, the existence of the security means that the payment for electricity by households is not simply an act of consumption, constituting the end of a process of electricity production and distribution. Here the payment itself becomes the basis of a traded product and the security stays in circulation. Hence, unlike the depiction of a circuit of industrial capital, where commodity output 'leaves' the sphere of capital, derivative commodities remain in circulation. We have elsewhere called them 'meta-commodities' but equally they may be thought of as 'meta-capital' because of their capacity to blend across the circuit of capital as a whole.[18]

Why might derivatives be central to understanding accumulation?

Framed as distinctive sorts of commodities, there is an inclination to cast derivatives analytically at the margin: as conceptually different and functionally marginal, and hence also as dispensable. The propositions above, however, point in quite a different direction. The distinctiveness of derivatives is that they can create new sites for accumulation, and new ways of disaggregating and re-aggregating circuits of capital. They facilitate the imagination of vast ranges of novel commodities, which, once conceived and produced, seem to have almost insatiable demand. The key to this imagination is that things we have formerly thought of as singular, total entities can be decomposed into constituent dimensions, with each dimension then conceived as a discrete risk, and hence as a discrete risk-based commodity. A loan, once conceived simply as credit, is now decomposed into interest rate risk, foreign exchange risk and default risk. Interest rate risk can be broken down into, for example, the risk of divergence between different base rates for calculating variable interest rates (e.g. LIBOR or the US prime rate) (basis risk); risks of prepayment of loans (options risk), risks of changing differences between short-term and long-term interest rates (yield curve risk), and so on. Each of these risks can be priced discretely and traded at a rate of billions of dollars a day. And each of these risks can be decomposed into multiple subsets, opening possibilities of new products, tailored more and more precisely.

At issue is whether this process of segmentation, quantification and commodification can be constituted as a contribution to accumulation in the sense of creating new value, or is simply a redistribution of the surplus (created in the 'real' economy). A full engagement with this issue is beyond the scope of our analysis, although it can be readily contended that there are elements of both. But if the growth of derivatives is seen *simply* as redistribution of the surplus, we miss the momentum that is driving the formation of new derivative products and the specific form these innovations are taking. Framed in this way, derivatives can be posed as opening up new frontiers of accumulation which are generally located within already existing activities, but giving those activities new commodified dimensions.

Loans have long existed, but decomposing loans into commodified risk attributes is a new invention. Moreover, what can be done for loans can be done for many facets of economic and social life. We may debate whether these initiatives actually make life better, just as we could debate the merits of advertising or many facets of the legal industry. Derivative market development is conceived within an agenda of precision of calculation: an agenda that is integral to the logic of capital. The effect is to extend the calculus of finance and risk into wider social domains, and this, perhaps, is the underlying dynamic of what is being called 'financialization'. From this perspective, we can look at how derivatives have evolved in the recent past and may potentially develop as expressions of this calculative logic.

THE RISE OF FINANCIAL DERIVATIVES

Derivatives on money

Derivatives relating to commodity production and trade have a long history. The era of financial derivatives awaited the last third of the 20th century. Prior to then, many sorts of insurance markets developed rapidly in the 19th century, but commodity money in the form of gold and/or silver saw fairly stable exchange rates, and hence no demand for exchange rate hedging. Similarly, modest use of debt by industrial capital and moderate changes in interest rates saw little need for interest rate derivatives. The same could be said, broadly, of the post-Second World War Bretton Woods Agreement, where fixed exchange rates and national capital controls occluded the development of financial derivatives: both the need and the legal conditions. Indeed, many forms of derivative began life or were resurrected as an attempt to escape the constraints of national capital controls, and in so doing contributed to the de facto breakdown of the Bretton Woods regime.

Derivatives relating to money (currencies and interest rates) emerged from the 1970s. From the formal end of the Bretton Woods Agreement in 1971, the world's exchange rates progressively floated, many national capital controls were lifted and international price stabilisation schemes were abandoned. The free-market economists, who provided the intellectual foundations to floating rates and open capital markets, had argued that floating rates would be stable because they would reflect 'fundamental value': roughly, the 'real' performance of each national economy. This performance would change gradually and accordingly exchange rates would shift only slowly. It is a conception of markets that was, no doubt, misconceived theoretically but, more critically, it played out empirically quite differently. Foreign exchange markets were not stable: indeed they became highly volatile and beyond prediction. Moreover, the concurrent growth of Eurofinance markets meant that borrowing and lending was occurring at a rapidly-increasing rate across nations, and at interest rates and exchange rates that differed from those of 'official' markets.

The combination of volatile exchange rates and increasing development of global debt markets saw the growth of foreign exchange and interest rate derivative markets to provide private hedging against these new exposures to the uncertain future value of different forms of money. Increasingly, the precise modes of calculation they required and generalized also revealed opportunities for arbitrage across spatially differentiated markets. Developments in computer technology and the 'science' of derivative pricing models were integral to this expansion.

Accordingly, from the early 1980s markets trading financial derivatives grew rapidly. They grew as sites of hedging, where capital could trade the risks and uncertainties of future exchange rate and interest rate movements – movements that could have profound impacts on profitability. As highly liquid markets trading price exposures not underlying assets, derivatives provided fertile space also for speculation. Not just hedge funds, but industrial corporations and financial institutions too have, on an increasing scale, maintained financial divisions through which they trade in open positions, all with varying success. How large a proportion of the market is made up of speculation is difficult to measure. Hedge funds are widely castigated for their role as speculators. It is worth recalling that, although they have been growing rapidly since around 2002, in 2006 they still held only 2.5 per cent of all funds under management.[19] Yet as active traders, hedge funds account for significantly more than 2.5 per cent of transactions – the figure in some markets has been as high as 50 per cent of transactions.[20]

The growth of derivative markets from 1987 to 2009 is shown in Figure 1. It shows data for the three largest derivative products: derivatives on money (interest rates and currencies), credit derivatives and equity derivatives. They are shown as a measure of the value of outstanding contracts at year end.[21] The figure shows an aggregate rapid rate of growth to a value of almost $415 trillion in 2009. Despite popular predictions in the height of the crisis that derivatives generally had turned toxic, we see that they continued to grow, albeit at a slower rate. Credit derivatives are a notable exception, to be considered shortly.

Figure 1

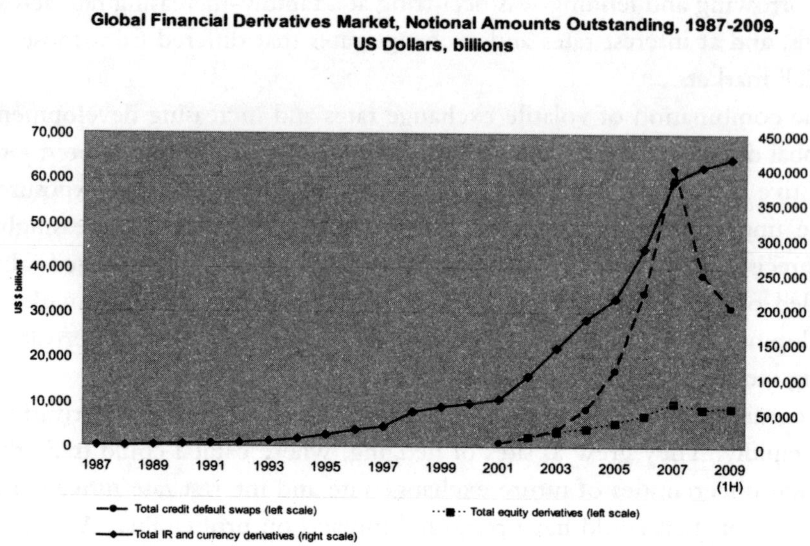

Source: IDSA[22]

With the most critical risk for the global expansion of capital relating to the uncertain value of money across space and time (exchange rates and interest rates),[23] it is not surprising that the predominant trading activity and growth over the past 3 decades has been of derivatives on money: interest rate and exchange rate futures, options and swaps.[24] Indeed, so great is the dominance of derivatives on money that in Figure 1 it has been necessary to present money derivatives on a different scale from the other derivative forms. In 2007, for example, the outstanding value of derivatives on money (almost four hundred trillion dollars) was 6 times the value of credit derivatives and almost 40 times the value of equity derivatives. By 2009, with credit derivatives halving, that dominance was even greater.

Derivatives on money are reasonably straightforward. But our earlier definition(s) of derivatives were framed so as to engage innovation in the way the logic of derivatives is applied to wider social and economic life. While interest rate and exchange rate derivatives remain quantitatively dominant, there were concurrent developments in other forms of derivatives. These were the acts of segmentation, quantification and commodification we referred to earlier. They have become more conspicuous and extravagant in the imagination of new ways to identify and segment risk. In financial markets where institutions are looking for yield and to diversify asset portfolios, these new products were especially attractive. We can classify them in two categories: derivatives on assets and derivatives on income streams, although many derivative products work to blend these attributes.

Derivatives on assets

As technology in financial markets developed, it became simpler to invent and list new products on financial exchanges. In addition to their traditional role, initially in commodity futures and options and then money derivatives, existing exchanges such as *Eurex* and the *Chicago Mercantile Exchange* have more recently introduced derivatives markets for a broader range of products, mainly involving the reinvention of everyday things as financial assets to be traded. There has been a growth in derivative markets for equities, the weather, metal prices, energy prices, real estate and macroeconomic indicators such as wage movements, and a vast range of indices which measure certain characteristics of each of these, and composite attributes of combinations of them.[25] In addition, over-the-counter brokers, working mainly in investment banks, have imagined and compiled all sorts of risk trades between particular parties with unique but tradeable risks.

The emergence of each of these new products can be explained in terms of providing hedging facilities against direct risk exposures – for example, energy providers have an exposure to temperature, farmers to frost, industry to wage trends. More broadly understood, these new risk products provided a means for portfolio diversification.

Credit derivatives, especially credit default swaps (CDS) are critical in this regard and warrant particular attention because of their sudden expansion and their prominence before and during the global financial crisis (see Figure 1). Credit derivatives involve trades on the likelihood of a credit event (essentially, an inability to repay a loan). They became the fastest growing derivative product between 2001 and 2007,[26] and their collapse in 2008 was at the centre of the insolvency of leading investment banks.

Unlike many of the new products listed above, credit derivatives are constructed both for long-term purposes (essentially for institutions to hedge credit risks) and the short term, where they are traded actively as part of diversified asset portfolios. In a standard credit derivative, the 'protection seller' receives regular payments from the 'protection buyer' but, in return, the former has to guarantee to the latter particular agreed payments in the case of default or some other incapacity to pay.

Within this process, credit default swaps were initially developed for hedging purposes. Banks would use credit default swaps to hedge their loan books and their exposures to securitizations. Relieved of repayment/default risk, a bank's lending activity effectively becomes a straight play on interest spreads. Industrial corporations also found them effective. Two corporations with quite different default risks (for example, one in agriculture, the other in electronics) could swap an exposure to each other's default risks and thereby diversify their individual risks. In CDS markets, this hedging takes place predominantly through what are called 'single-name instruments'. They are often contracts lasting multiple years.

From around 2004 credit derivatives rapidly spread beyond that direct hedging role. Because a derivative allows for a price exposure to a default without the need for ownership of (direct exposure to) a default event, credit derivatives could be held in the asset portfolio of third parties, unrelated to the default event. To meet this demand by third parties, credit derivatives developed into forms more appropriate to third party portfolios, such as credit-linked notes and portfolio correlation products.[27]

These products also came to be applied to a wider range of 'events' and to securitized obligations. They involve what are called 'multi-name instruments'. In essentially the same process that applied in the 'originate-to-distribute' models now familiar in relation to mortgage-backed securities and other CDOs, multi-name credit derivatives involve either products where a diverse range of credit risks are bundled together, tranched, credit-rated, and sold into global financial markets or products based on trading a credit default index. In effect, these multi-name credit derivatives became just another asset class within a diversified portfolio.[28] They were anticipated to generate an attractive return and their price would predictably cycle differently to that of other asset classes. In a sense, the specific risk exposures it attached to was secondary to the fact that it was different from other products and hence associated with diversification of risk.

It is notable that, despite their 'bad press' in the global financial crisis, the subsequent decline in CDS transactions has been modest. In 2009, the notional amounts outstanding in credit default swaps markets was still around 2006 levels, for both single-name and multi-name products.[29] No doubt, credit derivatives showed in a stark way what is inherent in all derivatives: that the commodification of risk permits diversification of risk portfolios, and feeds the search for yield. With diversification comes more widespread exposure to any particular risk, such that where risks are dramatically mispriced, the possibility of contagion increases dramatically. Nonetheless, they are playing a functional role for capital in providing facilities for hedging credit risk and in portfolio diversification.

Derivatives on income streams

Derivatives on income streams, as distinct from derivatives based on changes in asset values or events, are generally styled as securities, and the process as securitization. They actually have a long history – longer than financial derivatives proper – but they have not historically been framed as derivatives.

Indeed, it could be said that the global financial crisis has brought them to prominence as derivatives, for it is precisely their derivative dimension that was central to the crisis. This specific issue will be considered shortly.

As with derivatives on newly-conceived assets, derivatives on income streams started growing in the 1980s, especially through state-issued securities, but by the 1990s private label securities were growing. Figure 2 shows global private-label securities issuance between 2000 and 2009 for the primary categories of securities: asset-backed commercial paper (ABCP) (used by corporations to bring forward payments on receivables); asset backed securities (ABS); mortgage-backed securities (MBS) and collateralized debt obligations (CDO and CDO^2).[30] In aggregate they grew from almost nothing in the early 1990s to $1.3 trillion in 2000 and $4.7 trillion in 2006, but slumped to $1 trillion in 2009. Since 2000 most of the growth and subsequent decline in security issuance has been in mortgage backed securities and collateralized debt obligations (CDOs).

Figure 2

Global Private Label Securitization, 2000-2009, by Type (billion US dollars)

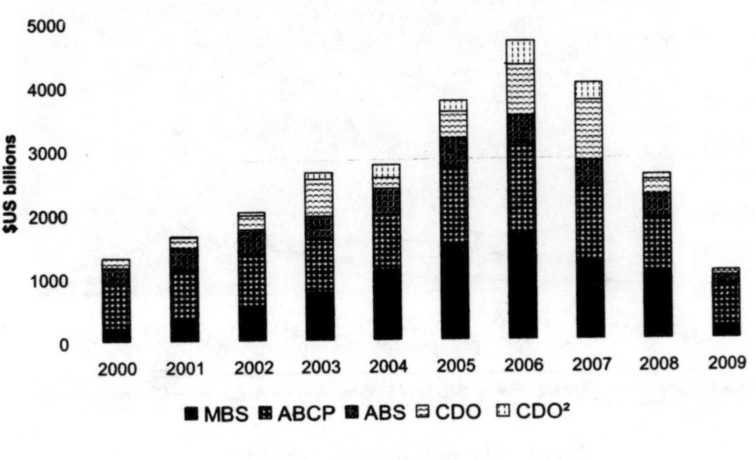

Source: IMF[31]

Apart from mortgages, what sorts of income streams have formed the basis of securities issuance? Moody's lists the following class of assets on which asset-backed securities are built: 'aircraft leases, home equity loans, auto loans and leases, manufactured housing, credit card receivables, small business loans, dealer floor plan loans, student loans, equipment loans and leases, franchise loans, time share loans, health care receivables, and tobacco settlements'.[32]

Figure 3 shows evidence from the United States between 1996 and 2010 on the issuance of the major securities listed by Moody's. The figure shows starkly the rapid growth of home equity security issuance from 2000 to 2007, by which time they comprised 65 per cent of all security issuance. In the financial crisis, home equity security issuance fell from a 2006 peak of $483 trillion to just $2 trillion in 2009.[33] Figure 3 shows also the dominance of securities based on income streams generated directly from households: home equity, auto loans, credit card loans and, especially from 2001, student loans. Indeed, the category of 'other' in Figure 3, representing forms of security issuance not backed directly by household incomes, has been remarkably minor throughout the period.

Figure 3

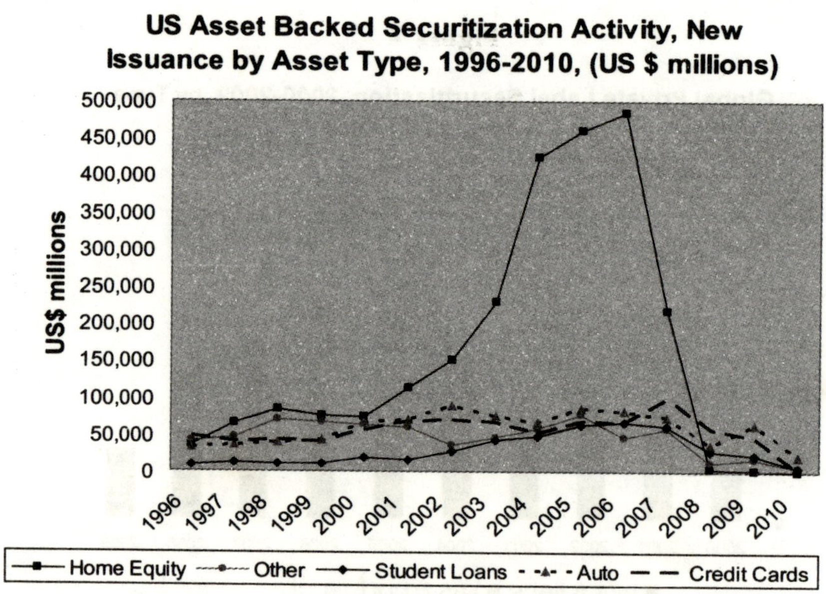

Source: Thomson Reuters, SIFMA[34]

The growth of household borrowing, as the foundation for the rapid growth of securities until 2007, is now well understood as a combination of two factors. First was the existence of stagnant or falling real wages which led to the growth of working-class demand for borrowing in order to sustain living standards.[35] Second was predatory marketing practices by money lenders, especially towards economically vulnerable groups.[36] Together, these two factors were complementary, at least for a brief era in securities markets. The 'originate-to-distribute' model of the securities industry meant that a key risk of loans to households, the risk of non-repayment, could be passed on from the loan originator to the security buyer: there was no need for due diligence on the part of the loan originator so long as there remained market demand for the associated securities.[37] The issue of who was buying the securities, and why, will be considered shortly.

The Moody's list above nominates not just households as objects of securitization, but a range of other assets too which generate reliable income streams. In particular, utilities such as airports (and aircraft), roads, electricity, water, telecommunications and health industry income became the objects of new financial calculation. These 'infrastructure' and 'quasi-monopoly' assets, so called because they have relatively stable cash flows and low correlation with economic cycles,[38] were reconfigured so that their (presumed) reliable revenue streams could be sold into financial markets in return for lump-sum (plus interest) payments: they were securitized. The owner of a toll road, for example, could sell into financial markets a product which provided an income stream based on the rate of toll payments.

The derivative aspect of securities, to reiterate, is that they involve selling off an income stream (or a claim contingent on future events), but without selling off the (underlying) asset that generates the income stream. In the case of toll roads, the owner of the security owns the income stream from the toll roads but without owning the roads themselves. In the case of mortgage-backed securities, the owner of the security owns the stream of interest payments on mortgages, but does not own the mortgages themselves, and hence has no claims on the houses that sit under the mortgages.

For the issuer of the security, the benefits of securitization come from transforming future – and therefore to some degree uncertain – income (tolls, electricity bill payments, student loan repayments) into guaranteed and up-front revenue (the sale price of the security), and selling off the risks of the revenue stream. It permits them to build more toll roads, more electricity supply and give more loans than if they had to await full repayment. For the purchaser of the security, they gain exposure to a tradable asset that is likely to give a better rate of return than bank deposits or Treasury bonds, and it gives them a diversification of risks without having to own underlying assets. Such securities became alternatives to buying treasury bonds: many of them rated AAA, and so presumed to be just as (or almost as) secure, but with higher rates of return.

The critical technical question is how much risk is attached to these securities, and the risk-return calculation required to price them. We know from the well-documented history of mortgage-backed securities and explanations of the global financial crisis that the issuers of securities often either did not realize, or sought to hide, the 'real' risks.[39] It is also clear that credit rating agencies and other market gatekeepers such as audit firms and investment banks, whose specialist role was to make such calculations, got it disastrously wrong.[40]

Framed in terms of the accuracy of pricing of risk, and who knew and did not know about product quality and inappropriate credit ratings, the analysis gives focus to moral and market failure. This, in turn, opens up policy agendas about strategies to make these markets more transparent, with agendas of product disclosure and consumer protection.[41] But those agendas avoid engagement with the reasons that these markets grew the way they did. A politics based on understanding how financial markets are evolving, and the potentials that might lie therein for labour, must explore these reasons rather than privileging an (essentially conservative) agenda of simply containing the operation of financial markets.

PORTFOLIO DIVERSIFICATION AND THE SEARCH FOR YIELD

What explains the rapid growth, especially from the 1990s, of forms of derivatives based on product innovation pertaining to new asset types and income streams? We have already considered the growth of household debt combined with new acts of imagination and technological innovation, facilitated by a lax regulatory environment. We might frame these as supply side factors. There were demand side factors, too: the surpluses being accumulated in the sovereign wealth funds of Asia and the Middle East and the hedge funds employed by the super-rich and also increasingly by pension funds. They were all looking for products in which to hold their wealth. Specifically, this demand side focus points to capital's search for yield and the associated strategy of risk diversification.[42]

The precipitating factor was low interest rates and hence low rates of return on sovereign debt. The Reserve Bank of Australia (RBA) noted in 2004:

> With interest rates on low-risk investments falling to low levels in many countries, investors have sought to maintain yields by moving into higher-risk assets such as corporate debt and emerging market debt. As they have done so, credit spreads on these assets have declined, which means that investors are receiving less compensation for the risk they are taking on.[43]

In a similar vein, the Governor of the Bank of England observed in 2007:

> This desire for higher yields could not be met by traditional investment opportunities. So it led to a demand for innovative, and inevitably riskier, financial instruments and for greater leverage. And the financial sector responded to the challenge by providing ever more sophisticated ways of increasing yields by taking more risk.[44]

In explaining this shift, the role of hedge funds and sovereign wealth funds has been prominent.[45] The RBA had identified in 2004 that 'the low interest rate environment may also have encouraged a shift in investments towards hedge funds as, in the past, hedge funds have achieved higher average returns than traditionally managed investments, albeit in exchange for greater risk'. The search for yield generated diversification. 'Hedge funds appear to be having trouble maintaining their rate of return as their typical investment plays have become "crowded". This in turn has caused some hedge funds to seek a wider range of investment opportunities and to take on more risk.'[46] Evidence also points to sovereign wealth funds, in the search for yield, increasingly placing reserves with hedge funds, along with growing investments in derivatives and asset-backed securities.[47]

The search for yield provides a critical explanation of the pursuit of higher risk. But, of itself, it is limited in explaining financial innovation. After all, the appetite for profits and preparedness of capital to take risks is not new. Two further elements in this explanation are needed.

First, the innovation of new sorts of financial products has to be understood in the context of the recognition that the world lacks any 'objective' financial anchor. With exchange rates and interest rates volatile, cash itself being necessarily denominated in a particular currency embodies significant risks. With interest rates on US Treasury bonds pushed to low levels, their rate of return was not compensating for the risk of a volatile dollar: a risk amplified by declining US macroeconomic indicators. With no safe (risk free) way in which to hold assets, the response of investors was to diversify, and, moreover, to go looking for assets whose prices would cycle differently from the stock market and other, more standard, products. Trading in derivatives and securities became the predictable response and, as we will consider shortly, investment in household income streams (securities based on mortgage and other loan repayments) provided a new site for investment opportunities.

Second, the acquisition of derivatives as part of the strategy of diversification itself generated an innate search for yield. Whereas a bond (say a treasury bond) is an asset that generates a rate of return (an interest stream), derivatives are different. As an exposure to the performance of an asset, their price varies with the performance of the underlying asset, or that performance in relation to the performance of another asset/index. But they generate no rate of return in themselves. Derivatives are not assets to which a rate of return attaches, but assets in which a competitively calculated rate of return is embedded. As contracts of capital commensuration, the search for yield (and its inherent calculus) is innate.

Framed in terms of diversification and derivatives' innate search for yield, there is a momentum in accumulation that exists beyond bubbles and lax regulation. If diversification is driven, at least in part, by the absence of a safe store of value, then we must ask whether the purchase of exotic derivative products should be cast as speculation, or as a manifestation of the absence of a stable unit of value? If the search for yield is innate within the structure of derivatives, is that search to be cast in a framework of 'speculation', with all its moral connotations and regulatory implications, or as integral to the emergent system of calculation?

DERIVATIVES AND THE POLITICS OF THE CRISIS

Concerns about risk management failure, lack of market transparency, speculation and bailing out the rich have brought forth a range of regulatory agendas inclined to tame speculation and excess, and return finance to a subordinate role in the economy. There are calls for the utilities functions of banking to be separated out from the 'gambling' functions, taxes on financial transactions and on financial sector salaries.

None of these sorts of agendas goes inside the logic of derivatives and seeks to build a perspective based on reading the momentum within capital that, while precipitating the global financial crisis, remains an on-going feature of, and site of innovation in, contemporary capitalism. On the contrary, the recent recovery in derivative turnover is being widely interpreted as a rebuilding of speculative positions and creating the preconditions for the next crash.

The issue here is not an opposition to markets being made transparent or financial salaries being made modest, but that these agendas look to the flaws of finance and financial management, not to the transformations and contradictions that financial innovation brings. They frame a response to the crisis in terms of creating an environment in which finance is secondary to 'real' production – indeed, they often even hark back to an idealized conception of capitalist economy before the rise of derivatives. But the dichotomy between the 'real' and the 'financial' is functionalist at best and contrived and ahistorical at worst: it is unsustainable analytically and unenforceable in regulation.

The derivative form of capital is not an aberration: it is changing capitalism in critical ways, for it gives fluidity to that which has always aspired to be flexible; where to be fixed is to be competitively vulnerable. But fluidity is the enemy of regulation. Swaps permit one form of asset to be made to appear as another form, so short-term finance can be made to appear long-term: so-called speculative transfers can be made to appear like long-term investments. As assets which give exposure to competitive performance but without ownership of the performers, derivatives change the concept of ownership in capitalism. Derivatives are breaking down the difference between equity and debt, and hence what it means to 'own'. The class of capital appears as much less personal (the bloated capitalist) and even institutional (the large corporation) than Marxists would generally like to think. 'Who does labour confront when it confronts capital?' was always a difficult question to specify, but it has become more complex. Labour now confronts a competitive system of calculation, which we name as 'capital'.

Moreover, labour itself is being incorporated into capital in new ways, not just via the workplace discipline that comes with intensified competitive calculation, but via the process of securitization. Some have sensed this new development, but have cast it in terms of growing household debt, with the appropriation of interest payments out of labour's income being treated as a further 'take' on surplus value.[48] But this is not the critical aspect of the development, and it is certainly not new: labour has paid interest (and rent, a similar appropriation from wages) for thousands of years. The critical development is the recasting of labour as the provider of income streams for securities, to facilitate asset diversification and the search for yield. The rapid growth of mortgage, auto, credit card and student loans, as well as contracts on telephones, energy and health care, all provide the raw materials on which securities are built to meet the demands of global investors. Indeed, as Robert Shiller noted in 2003:

> Far more important to the world's economies than the stock markets are wage and salary incomes and other non-financial sources of livelihood such as the economic value of our homes and apartments. That is where the bulk of our wealth is found.[49]

Labour's expenditures are now even more integral to capital's profitability and its risk management strategies than when Keynes nominated effective demand as a critical category of policy. The conditions of working-class life – the need for multiple income households; the needs of old age, education, health, and others – are re-configured so as to privilege the payments that will form the basis of securities. The question – 'What is the class of labour?' – now increasingly needs to be framed in terms of systematic risk shifting that comes with financial innovation. The International Monetary Fund captured a key dimension of this process when it described households as the financial system's 'shock absorbers of last resort'.[50]

From the perspective of capital, labour is not just a labouring class producing surplus value. Labour is now also cast by capital as an 'asset class': not in the sense of the 'ownership society' promoted by President Bush, but an object of portfolio investment that sits alongside other asset classes like equities, bonds and credit derivatives. In the search for yield and diversification, the household and its wage income represents new opportunities for capital's profitable asset holding. In particular, working-class aspirations of home ownership were, in the lead-up to the crisis and subsequently, a particularly attractive investment for capital. With housing treated by workers as a place to live (from labour's perspective, an illiquid asset), there was the anticipation that investing in labour's desire to retain its home was likely to be safer than many investments. The widespread availability of AAA rated mortgage-backed securities seemed to vindicate this perception.

History now shows that labour as an asset class was not well risk-managed by capital or the state. From around 2003 the lending was over-extended, and households took out loans that were unlikely to be repaid: the now-familiar story of 'sub-prime' and 'originate-to-distribute'. Significant parts of labour failed to deliver the repayments which formed the income streams of the mortgage-backed securities. The prices of many securities were destined to tank. By 2007, a cycle of foreclosures was underway and the holders of mortgage-backed securities began losing money rapidly. In important respects, therefore, it was labour, and its failure as an asset class, not its power as a working class, that triggered the global financial crisis.

Contra the position that 'labour was not to blame for the financial crisis', we argue that there is a need to focus directly on labour's role in the crisis. It is through this focus that we can find the power of organized labour beyond its advocacy of state regulation. Indeed, in understanding the power of labour in the context of finance, there is a clear parallel with the labour process. Just as the worker cannot be separated from their labour power – part of what constitutes labour as a distinctive and critical input into production – so the worker cannot be separated from the risks attached to their loan repayments. With this inseparability comes political capacity. Unlike all other inputs into production or forms of asset, labour expresses the capacity to resist inside production and inside finance. Capital's vulnerability to labour in production is also its vulnerability to labour in finance.

Capital's aspiration is for investment outlets which tap into the incomes of labour but which keep labour compliant. Such investments cannot be both sustainable and also based on the short- or medium-term impoverishment of labour via the extraction of unsustainable interest payments – what Lapavitsas has termed 'financial expropriation'.[51] This was capital's – and the state's – recent error in the incorporation of labour into global finance via securitization. Capital's need is for a sustainable working class that will participate actively in financial markets and provide long-term product to meet the demand of securities markets. Various regulatory agenda follows to protect capital from itself, including agendas for market transparency.

To protect capital from labour's failure as an asset class requires that labour be better risk-managed. Financial literacy coupled with consumer protection constitutes a particular response from states, on behalf of capital, for addressing labour as a source of financial crisis. For capital, workers (and households) must be made to perform more effectively as financial entities, capable of meeting capitals' requirements of an asset class. For capital itself, the focus turns to new products that might be sold to labour as protection against the vicissitudes of financial markets: products such as real-estate futures markets and income and pension insurance. For the state, policy focus has turned to financial literacy. Programmes of financial literacy are being presented as beneficial for workers, so that they might better pursue their own self interest. But the effect is to create labour as a more reliable asset in which to invest. The International Monetary Fund, amongst others, stated the agenda clearly:

> Overall, the transfer of risk from the banking sector to nonbanking sectors, including the household sector, appears to have enhanced the resiliency and stability of the financial system – mainly by widely dispersing financial risks, including throughout the household sector. Policymakers may now need to take the next logical step by helping households to improve on their financial education and to obtain quality advice and products necessary to manage their financial affairs. In fact, there is a growing consensus, in both the public sector and the financial services industry, on the importance of promoting the financial education of households.[52]

The possibility of achieving the aspired-to financial literacy is dubious.[53] It is hard to disagree with the conclusions of Schuberth and Schurz who, in a review of the effects of financial literacy, contend that 'the primary purpose of financial literacy programs is to discipline the uninformed poor how to behave in a way that makes public regulation obsolete and enables the solution of problems by market forces'.[54] But our concern in this context is not whether financial literacy will make markets more efficient and workers more prudent, but that the agenda aims to re-build labour in the image of capital.

The implications for labour open up as a response to this scenario. The agenda developed in this paper points to a focus on the process of commodification of risk, and the incorporation of labour into capital's risk-shifting agenda: an agenda which presents as the 'other side' of derivative growth from the 1980s, expressing that growth as a defeat of labour as well as an innovation of capital.

Framed this way, the alternative politics is conceived in resistance to risk shifting: a struggle for public housing, public pensions and public education; not better practices in the process of lending and securitization of mortgages and tuition fees, or greater prudence in the investment of workers' savings. This is, of course, not a new agenda. Indeed, it may appear as both age-old and as highly state-centred. But, in the current era, such stands represent not a defence of the state (for states themselves are integral to the risk-shifting process) but an attack on capital's new frontier of accumulation. The alternative meaning, therefore, is to give everyday struggles a global context and impact. Moreover, an awareness of the commodification of risk (and derivatives as commodities) reminds us that all struggles against risk shifting, be they over wages and working conditions or pensions, mortgage repayments and bank fees are all struggles in the site of capitalist production.

Labour can learn from the financial crisis that it is integral to this frontier of accumulation. Its failure to perform at this frontier (a failure to keep repaying loans) was the catalyst of the global financial crisis: it showed the potency of labour, albeit unintended. We find, through financial innovation, that capital needs labour, and in new and urgent ways.

The decline of manufacturing and the rise of finance is not the end of labour as a class, but the possibility of its reinvention. This implies the need to go beyond class organization in the sense of trade unions that obtain more individual incomes for workers and labour parties that obtain the same via transfer payments. It suggests the need to think about a shift to class organizations that concentrate on winning class benefits in the form of universal goods and collective services not based on the expenditure of individual incomes or borrowing to obtain them. This involves moving towards decommodifying social relations, including labour power itself. This is the essential political agenda of resistance to the derivative form.

NOTES

We would like to thank the editors for their extensive and penetrating comments on earlier drafts of this paper and to participants at the *Socialist Register* workshop in Toronto in February 2010 for their input. Nick Coates also provided valuable comments. We wish to thank Tobias Adrian and Andy Jobst for assistance in sourcing data on securitization.

1 Behind Buffet's rhetorical flourishes about derivatives, Berkshire Hathaway is an active user of derivatives, and not simply as 'hedging' instruments. Even when he was warning about derivatives Buffet explained that 'At Berkshire, I sometimes engage in large-scale derivatives transactions in order to facilitate certain investment strategies'. More recently, in response to observations about the company's extensive derivatives trading he noted somewhat less allegorically, '[w]e've used derivatives for many, many years. I don't think derivatives are evil, per se, I think they are dangerous… We use lots of things daily that are dangerous, but we generally pay some attention to how they're used.' Cited in Alex Crippen, 'Democrats Reject Warren Buffet's Bid for Derivatives Exemption', CNBC, 26 April 2010, available at http://www.cnbc.com.

2 John Gray, *Black Mass: Apocalyptic Religion and the Death of Utopia*, London: Allen Lane, 2007.

3 Dick Bryan and Michael Rafferty, *Capitalism with Derivatives: A Political Economy of Financial Derivatives,* London: Palgrave Macmillan, 2006, pp. 64-5.

4 The sorts of objects that can and do have derivatives attached is evolving rapidly. For example, the Chicago Mercantile Exchange has traded hurricane futures since 2007. See http://www.cmegroup.com/trading/weather/hurricanes/hurricane.html. In 2003 the Pentagon briefly ran what became known as a terrorism futures market, before it was shut down following political pressure. See, for example, Karl Hulse, 'Pentagon Prepares a Futures Market on Terror Attacks', *New York Times*, 29 July 2003. Whether these novel forms of derivative are integral to accumulation, or incidental and merely speculative, is an issue we will consider shortly.

5 John Parsons, 'Bubble, bubble, how much trouble: Financial markets, capitalist development and capitalist crises', *Science and Society*, 52(3), 1988; Bryan and Rafferty, *Capitalism with Derivatives*, ch. 2.

6 It may or may not lead to a change of ownership of a barrel of oil itself, according to the specificities of the contract, but usually these contracts are settled in cash.

7 The BIS has a category called 'reporting dealers', which are the large institutions on which banking data are based.

8 The other 20 per cent is non-financial institutions: essentially corporations and states. See Dick Bryan, 'The Global Foreign Exchange Market: An Interpretation of the Bank for International Settlements' Survey of Foreign Exchange and Derivatives Market Activity, 2007', *Global Society*, 22(4), 2008.

9 McKinsey Global Institute, *Global Capital Markets: Entering a New Era*, McKinsey & Co., 2009, p. 25.

10 In 2006, 47 per cent of all issued CDOs were purchased by hedge funds, although they generally purchased the senior tranches. Banks and insurance companies, while less exposed to CDOs generally, were more heavily weighted to the lowest, so-called 'equity' tranches. See: International Monetary Fund, *Global Financial Stability Report*, October 2007, p. 15; and House of Commons, *Treasury Committee Report on Financial Stability and Transparency*, London: The Stationery Office Limited, 2008, p. 24.

11 The International Monetary Fund, *Global Financial Stability Report*, October 2007, pp. 48-9 estimated that in 2006 sovereign wealth funds were worth between $2 trillion and $3 trillion and were growing at a rate of almost $1 trillion per annum.

12 The Black-Scholes options pricing model was the basis of the awarding of the 1997 Nobel Prize for Economic Sciences to two of its authors, Myron Scholes and Robert Merton. (Black, by then deceased, was thereby not eligible for the award). Its essential insight was to provide the formula to calculate the price of an option on any underlying asset, and it did so via a descriptive formula that could calculate the value of these synthetic securities from existing asset and bond prices and their volatilities.

13 These events may be thought of as the limitations of pricing risk in terms of formalistically-conceived probabilities, or in terms of 'fat tails' in distributions, such as are the focus of Nassim Nicholas Taleb, *The Black Swan: The Impact of the Highly Improbable*, New York: Random House, 2007.

14 Donald McKenzie, *An Engine, Not a Camera: How Financial Models Shape Markets*, Cambridge: MIT Press, 2006.

15 This is Keynes' depiction of stock markets trading on psychology – on popular opinion of popular opinion – only now expressed as popular opinion about future technical calculation. The pricing of risk is therefore never a precise exercise.

16 Bryan and Rafferty, *Capitalism with Derivatives*, ch.4.

17 Even fixed interest rates change in reference to the prime rate.

18 Bryan and Rafferty, *Capitalism with Derivatives*, p. 154, and following Geoffrey Kay, 'Abstract Labour and Capital', *Historical Materialism*, 5, 1999, pp. 1272-76.

19 Gabriel Galati and Adrian Heath, 'What drives the growth in FX activity? Interpreting the 2007 triennial survey', *BIS Quarterly Review*, December 2007, p. 72.

20 The Bank of England estimates that hedge fund trading activity accounted for around 40 to 50 per cent of daily turnover on the New York Stock Exchange

and London Stock Exchange in 2005. Bank of England, *Financial Stability Report*, April, 2007, p. 36 and House of Commons, *Treasury Committee Report*, p. 11. We are indebted to Photus Lysandrou for pointing us to these sources, and have drawn on his analysis at other parts of this paper. For a summary version, see Photis Lysandrou, 'The root cause of the financial crisis: a demand-side view', Economists' Forum, *Financial Times*, 24 March 2009, available at http://blogs.ft.com.

21 The figure shows both exchange-traded and over-the-counter (OTC) derivatives. Comparing values of the two markets is difficult, for the former emphasises turnover of short-term contracts, while the latter emphasises amounts outstanding on long-term contracts. Showing this figure as 'amounts outstanding' reflects the dominance of OTC markets. See Bryan, 'The Global Foreign Exchange Market', for an explanation. For the level of aggregation presented in this figure, the detailed problems of measurement can be left aside.

22 International Swaps and Derivatives Association (ISDA) Market Survey historical data, 2009, available at http://www.isda.org.

23 Perhaps it is now inappropriate to conceive of exchange rates as relating to money across space. The reduction of national capital controls after 1971 served to break the link between currency and nationality, for most currencies had developed off-shore markets. But the proposition will be nonetheless clear.

24 The product categories themselves are not entirely unambiguous, for the one derivative can have multiple attributes. Nonetheless, the major agency of data collection, the Bank for International Settlements, classifies derivatives by a measure of primary attribute.

25 See, for example, the listings of the CME at http://www.cmegroup.com.

26 The Bank for International Settlements triennial survey of foreign exchange and derivative markets shows that in 2007 the outstanding value of credit derivative contracts was $51 trillion. Between 2001 and 2004, the notional value of credit derivatives outstanding increased sixfold, and between 2004 and 2007 the value increased a further twelvefold. Bank for International Settlements (BIS), *Triennial Central Bank Survey of Foreign Exchange and Derivatives Market Activity in 2007 – Final Results*, Basel: BIS, 19 December 2007, available at http://www.bis.org.

27 Lehman Brothers, 'The Lehman Brothers Guide to Exotic Credit Derivatives, 2004', available at http://www.investinginbonds.com.

28 David Mengle, 'Credit Derivatives: An Overview', *Federal Reserve Bank of Atlanta Economic Review*, 92(4), Fourth Quarter 2007, pp. 12-13.

29 Bank for International Settlements, *BIS Quarterly Review*, December 2009, p. 23.

30 A CDO^2 is a CDO for which the collateral is another CDO.

31 International Monetary Fund, *Global Financial Stability Report*, October 2009, p. 84, available at http://www.imf.org.

32 Moody's.com, 'Products and Services: Asset Backed Securities Research', available at http://www.moodys.com.

33 More recent data indicate that by late 2008 there was a significant turnaround in these markets. The BIS reported that international debt securities issuance increased 30 per cent over 2008, almost all of it in the second half. Bank for International Settlements, *BIS Quarterly Review*, March 2009, p. 23, available at http://www.bis.org. In particular, US mortgage-backed securities issuance in 2009 was up 51 per cent from 2008, with the familiar big banks back in the market as issuers. Almost 90 per cent of this 2009 issuance was by government-sponsored enterprises Fannie Mae, Freddie Mac and Ginnie Mae, but Bank of America and Goldman Sachs, too, were back issuing mortgage-backed securities (See 'UPDATE 2-U.S. mortgage bond issuance jumped in 2009', *Reuters*, 31 December 2009, available at http://www.reuters.com). In Britain, Lloyds started issuing mortgage-backed securities in September 2009 (See 'Lloyds Plans to Issue Mortgage-Backed Securities', *Wall Street Journal*, 22 September 2009, available at http://online.wsj.com).

34 The Securities Industry and Financial Markets Association (SIFMA), US ABS Issuance 1996 - May 2010, available at http://www.sifma.org.

35 Leo Panitch and Sam Gindin, 'The Current Crisis: A Socialist Perspective', *The Bullet*, 142, 30 September 2008, available at http://www.socialistproject.ca.

36 Elvin K. Wyly, Mona Atia, Holly Foxcroft, Daniel J. Hammel and Kelly Phillips-Watts, 'American Home: Predatory Mortgage Capital and Spaces of Race and Class Exploitation in the United States', *Geografiska Annaler B*, 88(1), 2006.

37 Malcolm D. Knight (General Manager, Bank for International Settlements), 'Some reflections on the future of the originate-to-distribute model in the context of the current financial turmoil', Speech at the Euro 50 Group Roundtable on 'The future of the originate and distribute model', London, 21 April 2008, available at http://www.bis.org.

38 'Debate: Infrastructure – A new asset class?', *Euromoney*, June 2006, available at http://www.euromoney.com.

39 The US Securities and Exchange Commission's prosecution of Goldman Sachs over its knowing creation of flawed securities is a conspicuous case in point.

40 There is now an extensive literature on the role of credit ratings agencies. See House of Commons, *Treasury Committee Report*, ch. 7 for a concise summary.

41 Knight, 'Some reflections'.

42 Lysandrou, 'The root cause of the financial crisis'; House of Commons, *Treasury Committee Report*.

43 Reserve Bank of Australia, 'Statement on Monetary Policy', November 2004, p. 24, available at http://www.rba.gov.au.

44 Mervyn King (Governor, Bank of England), Speech at the Northern Ireland Chamber of Commerce and Industry, Belfast, 9 October 2007, pp. 2-3, available at http://www.bankofengland.co.uk.

45 House of Commons, *Treasury Committee Report*, p. 11.

46 Reserve Bank of Australia, 'Statement on Monetary Policy', p. 25.

47 Claudio Borio, Gabriel Galati and Adrian Heath, 'FX reserve management: trends and challenges', *BIS Papers No. 40*, May 2008, available at http://www.bis.org.

48 For example, Costas Lapavitsas, 'Financialised capitalism: Crisis and financial expropriation', *Historical Materialism*, 17(2), 2009.

49 Cited in A. Leyshon and N. Thrift, 'The Capitalization of Almost Everything: The Future of Finance and Capitalism', *Theory, Culture and Society*, 24(7-8), 2007, p. 97.

50 International Monetary Fund, *Global Financial Stability Report*, April 2005, p. 89, available at http://www.imf.org.

51 Lapavitsas, 'Financialised Capitalism'.

52 International Monetary Fund, *Global Financial Stability Report*, April 2005, p. 5.

53 I. Erturk, J. Froud, S. Johal, and A. Leaver, 'The Democratisation of Finance? Promises, Outcomes and Conditions', *Review of International Political Economy*, 14(4), 2007.

54 Helene Schuberth and Martin Schurz, 'Rewards for the Rich, Rhetoric for the Poor? Financial Governance Mechanisms for the U.S.', ONB Workshop Series No. 1, Paradoxes of Financial Systems, Vienna, 2004, p. 133.

CANNIBALISTIC CAPITALISM: THE PARADOXES OF NEOLIBERAL PENSION SECURITIZATION

SUSANNE SOEDERBERG

Workers have become increasingly dependent on the economic performance of corporations for the value of their retirement savings as pension funds across the OECD area have ramped up investment in corporate stocks and bonds. This phenomenon, known as pension securitization and wrapped in the discourse of the 'empowerment' of the worker as a shareholder, has become a defining and highly problematic feature of the neoliberal era.[1] Neoliberalism – and, by extension, securitization – needs to be understood not as an end state but as an ongoing and contradictory process aimed at deepening and widening the marketization of society.[2] This process demands that the manifestations of crises of capital accumulation, including struggles that threaten to delegitimize neoliberal rule, be absorbed or displaced, spatially and temporally. It also necessitates that states and capitalist classes continually engage in the construction, naturalization and social reproduction of highly paradoxical neoliberal accumulation strategies such as pension securitization.

Cannibalistic capitalism captures the processes by which workers' savings in the form of pension funds *feed off* both their own increased indebtedness *and* that of other workers, a condition driven largely by stagnant real wages and unemployment. As has especially been evidenced in the US, which shall be the focus of this essay, due to the dependence of pension funds on high-risk investments, their investment strategies mutilate the value of pension savings with the advent of more frequent and deeper financial crises that serve to wipe out gains made during a speculative run. Instead of serving to weaken cannibalistic capitalism, crises have had the effect of deepening neoliberalisation by allowing financial corporations and their shareholders (which include pension funds) to prey on those dispossessed workers, who, in the absence of a safety net, strive to maintain basic living standards through the credit system.

We may see cannibalistic capitalism as a form of financial fetishism that involves the '*illusion of securitization*', or what Pierre Bourdieu observed as the attempt to construct and propagate (among social actors, including pension fund beneficiaries) a fundamental belief in the value of the stakes and of the game itself.[3] Put differently, illusions of securitization capture the machinations involved in creating a belief that individuals will gain not only more economic freedom but also greater economic rewards by relying on the market as opposed to the government. Financial fetishism arises from the representation and discourse of the financial markets in reified terms in which social relationships appear as relations between 'things', i.e., workers voluntarily sell their labour power in exchange for money. On this view, financial markets are represented as separate from the so-called 'real' economy, and are thereby rendered as relatively 'unreal' or highly abstract.

Key features of financial fetishism aid the implementation and reproduction of securitization. Financial fetishism creates a cult of professional (read: scientific) expertise, wherein formal tools and technical knowledge are deemed valid, objective, infallible and true – unquestionably worthy of both our trust and our money. This technical and exclusionary knowledge in turn facilitates two important illusions necessary for the success of securitization. On the one hand, workers are intentionally kept in the dark as to how their investments increase in value. That is, financial fetishism obfuscates the linkages between workers' exploitation (and the exploitation of the natural environment) and interest income. In the financial system, money is largely represented as growing on trees. In addition, by presenting risk as a purely economic phenomenon, financial fetishism voids social content, especially class power, from the dominant discourse.

On the other hand, this depoliticised representation of financial markets has facilitated the rise of market populism, or the marketization of resistance, which is used to define workers as shareholders and draw them into channelling their frustrations into marginal forms of participation as shareholders in corporate governance. Market populism frames the market as more democratic than the state largely due to the stimulus of competition, in which consumers and shareholders can exercise 'real' power, while at the same time contending that deregulated markets can serve people more effectively and efficiently, primarily through the mechanism of shareholder activism.

It is critical to understand the securitization of pension savings and the increased reliance of workers on financial markets as a result of complex forms of struggles between workers and capitalists, mediated by the state.[4] Generally speaking, the dependence of labour on the market has been accomplished through ongoing and intensifying attempts to discipline workers – both inside and outside the reserve labour army. This occurs in two ways. First, through structural violence taking the form of physical coercion (e.g., prisons), or what Loïc Wacquant refers to as the 'criminalization of poverty'; second, through economic coercion (e.g., the dereliction of labour law, deregulation of employment, retraction of collective protections, and so forth).[5] In contrast to the call for 'less government' that is inherent to financial fetishism, the need for 'big government' to facilitate the marketization of labour is justified by labour's place in the so-called 'real' economy.

> The same parties, politicians, pundits, and professors who yesterday mobilized, with readily observable success, in support of 'less government' as concerns the prerogatives of capital and the utilization of labour [and their old age savings], are now demanding, with every bit as much fervour, 'more government' to mask and contain the deleterious social consequences, in the lower regions of social space, of the deregulation of wage labour and the deterioration of social protection.[6]

As forms of state intervention, financial fetishism and the marketization of labour reveal that securitization, and its intensification in the form of cannibalistic capitalism, is neither a natural nor neutral phenomenon. Cannibalistic capitalism serves the capitalist class in at least three interlocking ways. First, due to their reliance on Wall Street, workers (i.e., 'Main Street') have a strong stake in the preservation of the system that exploits them because the destruction of the capitalist system entails the annihilation of their savings. Second, with each crisis, dispossessed workers become increasingly reliant on the credit system, thus exposing themselves to the disciplinary, demobilizing, and individualizing tendencies of debt (collection agencies, bond rating agencies, prisons, courts, and so forth). Third, workers have been relegated to the ever-growing reserve army of underemployed and unemployed labour.[7] This, in turn, serves to erode solidarity, weakening collective action against the class-based and capitalist nature of securitization.

CONSTRUCTING NEOLIBERAL PENSION SECURITIZATION

An initial wave of what might be called primary pension securitization can be traced back to the 1960s and refers to the raising of finance (debt) through the issuance of securities (e.g., equity holdings in the form of stocks) in the stock markets. This intensified in the 1980s with the neoliberal state's attempt to shift labour's demand for social security to the market.[8] As a market-oriented form of political domination, neoliberalism emerged as a response to the late 1970s crisis of overaccumulation, which manifested in stagflation, unemployment, and high levels of social discontent. As David Harvey explains, neoliberal attempts to overcome barriers to capital valorisation were marked by two related trends. First, stock values became more of a guiding force of economic activity. Second, the gap between money capital earning dividends and interest on the one hand, and manufacturing or merchant capital looking to gain profits on the other was increasingly narrowed.[9]

The American state in particular facilitated, naturalized and reproduced these trends by encouraging private retirement savings through more market-linked, defined-contribution plans, such as Individual Retirement Accounts[10] and 401(k) plans, thereby attempting to remove or decrease the more secure defined-benefit schemes. At the same time, pension funds sought to deal with the limits of overaccumulation by investing in riskier instruments, most notably corporate equities, which yield higher returns than fixed-income securities (e.g., fixed-rate government bonds). The total assets of pension funds that gravitated to corporate stocks grew from 35.1 per cent ($871 billion) in 1980, to 41.3 per cent ($4 trillion) in 1993, to 47.3 per cent ($6.7 trillion) by 1997, to 49.5 per cent ($8.6 trillion) by 2008.[11] Over this time, a social reality was constructed in which workers increasingly acquired a strong stake in the preservation of securitization, including the corporations in which their pension funds held assets.

By the late 1990s more and more pension funds across the globe had also become heavily engaged in secondary securitization, which involves the pooling and repackaging of existing loan assets into securities that are, in turn, sold to investors, such as pension funds.[12] Secondary securitization exposed workers' savings to ever-riskier investment instruments, e.g., credit derivatives, as well as high-risk asset classes such as hedge funds and private equity firms. With the advent of the 2007 sub-prime fiasco, pension funds in the OECD area, especially those with the largest equity holdings (e.g., Ireland, the United States, Australia, and the United Kingdom), lost $5.4 trillion of their total asset value of $27.8 trillion.[13] Since the 2008 financial crisis, secondary securitization has, in some cases, intensified rather than abated.[14]

The state's role in facilitating secondary forms of securitization was ramped up in 1999, when the US government came to the aid of institutional investors by dismantling one of the cornerstones of the New Deal: the Glass-Steagall Act of 1933. In replacing Glass-Steagall with the Gramm-Leach-Bliley Financial Services Modernization Act, the US government removed the firewall between bankers and brokers and therewith the longstanding restriction that commercial banks could receive no more than 10 per cent of their income from the securities markets. The official justification for removing this firewall was to 'allow consolidation in the financial sector that will result in efficiency gains and provide new services for consumers'.[15] A key feature of this strategy involved asset-backed securities (ABS). Basically, ABS describes a practice of bundling or pooling a stream of future repayments (e.g., consumer debt in the form of credit cards, student loans, mortgages, etc.) to provide the basis for the issue and payment of interest and principles on securities.[16] While asset securitization has been practiced since the 1970s, it has risen to dizzying and dangerous heights since the late 1990s and played a key role in the implosion of the overly-leveraged hedge fund Long Term Capital Management, as well as the bursting of the high-tech bubble in the early 2000s and the sub-prime mortgage calamity of 2007.

The significance of financial fetishism re-emerges here with the representation of ABS and credit derivatives as rational, efficient, and natural (evolutionary) outcomes of a maturing (as opposed to the 'immature' markets found in the Third World), and thus increasingly sophisticated, financial system. The alleged infallibility of securitization – that is, selling the obligations to investors in return for a fresh infusion of money that can be used to make more loans – rests on socially constructed trust in the scientific knowledge and management of risk through, for example, risk-based pricing. Elvin Wyly et al. note that the doctrine attached to this mechanism seems to falsely equate financial innovation with democratized access to capital (other people's money).[17]

Table 1 demonstrates the allocation of pension fund assets among corporate equities, banks and hedge funds, and other investments. As labour's deferred wages and salaries entered Wall Street, securitization continued to deepen and widen. Surplus capital also continued to expand in the area of consumer credit, as beleaguered workers sought to maintain living standards by borrowing heavily. In just seven years (2002-2009), the rate of consumer debt to income rocketed to 40 per cent, doubling the rate of the mid-1970s and making the credit card industry the most profitable financial service in the US.[18] At the end of 2008, with 70 per cent of US families holding credit cards, Americans' credit card debt reached $972.73 billion, up 1.12 per cent from 2007.[19]

Table 1
Pension Fund Asset Allocation, 1999-2008*
(in $ billions)

Year	Total Assets	$ Equity	% Total Assets	$ Bonds	% Total Assets	$ Other Assets, e.g. Hedge Funds and Equity Firms	% Total Assets
1999	8,329.6	3,941.8	47.3	1,948.4	23.4	2,015.6	24.2
2000	8,208.7	3,987.3	48.6	1,764.7	21.5	2,061.2	25.1
2001	7,541.3	3,714.2	49.3	1,708.2	22.7	1,771.0	23.5
2002	6,912.2	3,159.4	45.7	1,714.6	24.8	1,694.4	24.5
2003	8,391.8	4,188.2	49.9	1,855.2	22.1	2,006.6	23.9
2004	9,191.1	4,714.0	51.3	1,928.5	21.0	2,221.3	24.2
2005	9,683.9	5,028.4	51.9	1,960.6	20.2	2,347.3	24.2
2006	10,768.5	5,564.3	51.7	2,062.6	19.2	2,780.7	25.8
2007	11,313.8	5,599.7	49.5	2,187.4	19.3	3,146.8	27.8
2008	8,590.2	3,576.5	41.6	2,217.1	25.8	2,440.2	28.4

* I have excluded the category of 'cash items', due to their negligible amounts, which hover around 4 per cent to 5 per cent over the above timeframe.

Source: The Conference Board, *The 2009 Institutional Investment Report: Trends in Asset Allocation and Portfolio Composition*, New York: The Conference Board, 2009, p. 14.

Both the primary and secondary waves of securitization represent the social reproduction of neoliberalisation in two ways. First, securitization constructs a social reality in which workers, through their pension savings, have a strong stake in the preservation of securitization, including the corporations in which they hold assets. That is, labour becomes dependent on new forms of capital accumulation based on higher levels of risk (always defined in financial not social terms). More fundamentally, workers become dependent on a system that exploits them because they know that the destruction of the capitalist system entails the obliteration of their savings, although, as we will see below, the erosion of pension savings occurs regardless in cannibalistic capitalism.[20]

Second, securitization represents the social reproduction of neoliberalism through what Marx referred to as fictitious capital. For Marx, fictitious capital represents capital that is either not backed by any commodity transactions, or that which is produced whenever credit is extended in advance, in the anticipation of future labour as a counter-value, as it is in the cases of sovereign debt and ABS.[21] The value of fictitious capital is determined by the price for which credit is sold and speculates on 'as-yet-unproduced' surplus value. For Marx, only investment in production – as opposed to investment in interest-generating fictitious capital – can create surplus value: 'if no real accumulation, i.e., expansion in production and augmentation of the means of production, had taken place, what good would there be from the accumulation of debtor's money claims on…production?'[22]

The tendency to deepen and widen the securitization of pension fund savings may be seen as a sign of overaccumulated capital, an attempt to expand and reproduce capitalism through the credit system, which has historically involved strategies of speculation, fraud, and predation. As Marx reminds us, while the credit system has the potential to resolve imbalances to which capitalism is prone, it can do so only at the price of internalizing these contradictions. Thus, the incessant need for more intensified forms of speculation, fraud, and predation is, in part, naturalized and reproduced through financial fetishism and structural violence over labour – the hallmarks of cannibalistic capitalism.

An understanding of the durability and paradoxes of neoliberal pension securitization and the new union activism in the wake of the financial crisis needs to be informed by the corporate governance doctrine, which reveals the ways in which market dependence shapes the political understandings and actions of workers.

CORPORATE GOVERNANCE AND CANNIBALISTIC CAPITALISM

The credit system and fictitious capital are integral to a state-supported strategy to deal with the limits and crises of capital accumulation. Today's cannibalistic capitalism feeds off workers' debt, annihilates pension savings (when asset bubbles burst) and opens new fields for securitization strategies to increase workers' dependence on the market. One of the more revealing aspects of the accumulation and disciplinary strategy of cannibalistic capitalism is the class dynamics of market incomes.

On the one side, investment banks such as J.P. Morgan and Goldman Sachs paid out enormous bonus packages in 2009 linked to record profits. Both were bailed out in various ways by public funds that will eventually be recouped from income and other taxes on workers; and both continue to be supported by generous public policies to prop up corporations such as capital-gain tax advantages, lack of consumer protection in credit markets, limited transparency, lax anti-trust law enforcement, and so forth. The political rhetoric that encourages workers' engagement in 'corporate governance' is silent on these issues.

Workers, on the other side, have paid a high social cost. Since the second wave of securitization in the late 1990s, the fastest-growing and largest group of conscripts to the reserve labour army has been the 'suburban poor'.[23] The new economic environment catapulted many workers further into debt, encouraging new forms of fictitious capital in the form of securitized debt. The high-risk, junk mortgage loans that many workers entered into, and so revealing of the processes of cannibalistic capitalism, have been particularly devastating for the most vulnerable groups of the working class – older workers close to retirement and members of racially marginalized communities.[24] In the aftermath of the 2007 sub-prime crisis, official poverty rates shot up to their highest levels in a decade.[25]

In the wake of the sub-prime fiasco, the continued resort to neoliberal policy measures and the continued dependence of accumulation on the credit system suggests that cannibalistic capitalism still characterizes this period. Pension funds, for instance, are engaging in the same risky investment behaviour that got them into financial crisis. Table 1 reveals that there has been some movement away from equity holdings; pension fund assets have shifted to largely unregulated and highly leveraged hedge funds and equity firms. According to key observers, these have remained the investment vehicle of choice for pension funds allocating capital to 'alternative investments' in order to recoup the $5.4 trillion in losses from the 2007 meltdown (of which only $1.5 trillion was regained as of 2009).

The decision by pension funds to invest in riskier portfolios at this moment raises concerns on at least two counts. First, the lack of regulation and high leverage of hedge funds encourage riskier investments, but have not necessarily resulted in better performance on returns than other types of investments (although hedge fund managers are making billions of dollars in fees). Second, the riskier investment portfolios of pension funds do nothing to compensate for the income distribution inequities of the existing pension system for workers, while at the same time expanding the flow of funds into the private financial system.[26] Moreover, the increased reliance on the credit system encourages pension funds to pursue ever-higher forms of risk, necessitated to increase returns via securitization in good times but also during times of economic downturn. In contrast to the high-risk strategy of the private pension industry, the US Social Security Trust Fund experienced a positive return of 5.1 per cent during the 2008 crisis due to its conservative investment portfolio of, mainly, bonds.[27]

There has been a false, depoliticised dilemma being offered to pension fund beneficiaries to make up for the losses incurred by securitization. Workers, especially from the public sector, are being told that the only way to restore retirement earnings is by contributing more to their pension savings through their current wages and/or pursuing higher risk portfolios in equity financing firms and hedge funds, and other highly speculative venues. This Hobson's Choice reflects the deepening of the exploitative relationship between Wall Street and Main Street, including the class-led attempt to establish securitization as a natural, inevitable and rational preference.[28]

Financial securitization, whether with respect to pension portfolios or other issues, cannot be isolated from issues of struggle and power. However, contesting securitization, and the market dependence it creates for workers, has too often embraced its illusions, in what can be referred to, not without irony, as a marketization of resistance that depoliticises and de-classes struggles. A prominent example is with regard to the securitization of pension funds, and the way that the 'corporate governance doctrine' has been taken up by some union activists.[29]

The corporate governance doctrine emerged in the 1980s alongside the development of the neoliberal state and its key encouragement of financial fetishism and the marketization of labour. This period led to the first wave of securitization, and a parallel growth in discontent among many shareholder groups regarding corporate restructuring and malfeasance, with the most spectacular being the Savings & Loan crisis of the late 1980s. This discontent encouraged a burst of shareholder activism, which took the form of market populism.

It was in this populist context that the corporate governance doctrine emerged, with its dominant definition based on agency theory developed in neoclassical economics.[30] Within modern forms of corporate organization, managers are seen as the 'agents' of shareholders (known in agency theory as 'principals'), and are therefore expected to engage in activities that maximize value to shareholders by increasing the market price of shares. Ensuring that managers remain accountable to shareholders by maximizing value is the cornerstone and defining feature of Anglo-American forms of corporate governance, and explains how the ever-sharper separation of the formal owners of corporations in shareholding from the managers who control corporate assets is reconciled in practice.[31] Corporate governance is primarily concerned with understanding and providing solutions to this 'principal-agent problem' by ensuring that the interests between principals (shareholders) and agents (managers and the board of directors) are aligned. The doctrine of corporate governance comes to stand for both the unity of institutions, processes and practices that shape the way shareholders, directors and management interrelate within the corporation, and as a framework for conceptualizing and legitimating these relationships.

Within the organizational terrain of the corporate governance doctrine, political resistance to corporate activities is framed by – and thereby limited to – a seemingly democratic and formal exchange between those who own (principals) and those who control (agents). The extent and content of the interaction between shareholders and management is, moreover, legally prescribed by the rules of allegedly neutral government bodies such as the Securities and Exchange Commission (SEC). Shareholder activism usually takes the form of proxy voting, dialogue with management and, although rarely, divestment.

The corporate governance doctrine can be seen as a form of financial fetishism that shields hierarchies of power and wealth and evades the exploitative elements within corporations. It suggests that corporations lack any built-in structure of authority and power rooted in capitalism.[32] Thus, the corporate governance doctrine acts to contain principal-agent tensions within legal frameworks while depoliticising struggles within the bounds of a supposedly impersonal market. The doctrine serves to re-focus political discontent into market-based terms such as excessive executive pay packages, discrimination policies, and disclosure devoid of any considerations of class and capitalist-state relations. Two examples of how the corporate governance has come to serve the illusion of securitization are telling: the 'new activism' around unions as shareholders, and the 'equal access' proposal for stakeholders to gain positions on Boards of Directors, each of which helps to explain how cannibalistic capitalism is naturalized, neutralized and reproduced.

The 'new activism' here refers to a strategy for the revival of trade unions not in terms of their role as workers, but as 'active shareholders' in corporate governance issues. Union organizations, union-based pension funds, individual union members and labour-oriented investment funds have all become increasingly cognizant of their powers as 'owners' of vast sums of pension fund capital. Some commentators refer to this as 'labour's capital'.[33] Unlike traditional forms of union activism, which rely on mobilizing around collective bargaining demands, the new shareholder activism focuses on ensuring that good corporate governance practices are met by way of proxy voting, dialogue and negotiation with management and other shareholders.[34] While the discourse of labour shareholder activism is not new, its current incarnation is distinct given its centrality to the corporate governance doctrine. Indeed, this activism mirrors the phenomenon of some 'ethically mandated' institutional investors challenging corporate power within market structures through, for instance, a corporate social responsibility framework.[35]

By flexing their financial clout through shareholder oversight and influence on corporate decision-making, proponents of this new activism believe that unions will make more inroads in securing workers' interests than by using older strategies to change corporate behaviour.[36] Labour shareholder activism has assumed different forms such as economically targeted investments, social screening and shareholder advocacy initiatives. But the main strategy to effect change in publicly held corporations has been shareholder advocacy through proxy proposals.[37] Maureen O'Connor notes that union-led activism largely involves submitting precatory (advisory) shareholder proposals.[38] During the 2006 proxy season, for instance, corporations faced more than 200 shareholder proposals from major union-sponsored pension funds. These proposals dealt with corporate governance and largely focused on executive pay and board accountability, however, as opposed to broader social issues.[39]

In their bid to use shareholder rights to influence managers, unions have sought to align themselves with other shareholders – itself a reflection of the interdependency brought about by securitization. This alignment has been facilitated by appeal to the broader – and common – concern of protecting shareholder value. As such, the economic best interests of beneficiaries are privileged over specific claims that could further the interests of workers as a whole. Some commentators have gone so far as to suggest that the success of union led shareholder campaigns is dependent on downplaying social issues. As one observer notes:

> Indeed, past voting patterns clearly indicate that shareholder resolutions that are brought forward because of their appeal to shareholders with special interests generally do not pass. Shareholder resolutions that focus on social or labour issues generally fail, while those that have attracted majority support are the ones that are viewed by professional money managers as clearly serving shareholder value.[40]

In other words, by remaining within the *form* of financial fetishism, the new activism is limited by the overriding goal of profit maximization in the corporate governance framework. The illusion of securitization under cannibalistic capitalism of relying on market mechanisms is therein validated and reproduced. Yet, the new activism has failed to bring about substantive social welfare gains, as evidenced by stagnant real wages, the steady erosion of workers' rights, and the general decline of the average real pension benefit by one-third since the 1980s.[41]

The danger of union activists adhering to the corporate governance doctrine is that it depoliticises power relations that are central to the workings of the corporation and obscures their impact on the wider social environment. Depoliticisation of resistance occurs in at least two ways. On the one hand, resistance to current practices is recast in exclusionary terms of shareholder activism; those who do not directly own enough shares of corporations cannot contest its policies, power or behaviour. On the other hand, political resistance is constrained within financial codes and economic laws that are used to shift the contestation of corporate power, and the particular exploitative relationships formed by securitized pension funds, to the apolitical realm of the market.

In the wake of the Enron collapse in 2001 and many subsequent debacles, appeals to the corporate governance doctrine surged as shareholders, led by the new activists, sought to correct the lack of board independence from management by asking the SEC to revise its rules to allow for an easier and direct process for shareholders to nominate candidates for a company's board of directors – a mechanism formally known as the 'Proposed Election Contest Rules' (hereafter: equal access). The aspect of equal access that is of central concern pertains to the ability of shareholders to nominate their candidates for seats on the board of directors.[42] In theory, shareholders are, under the present system, legally permitted to place their own board candidate on the proxy. This, however, can only be achieved through a costly and burdensome proxy contest.[43] The minimum expense of such a bid is typically $250,000. Thus, in practice, management has the upper hand, as they are able to draw on corporate coffers to oppose the candidacy. Due to these barriers, there is effectively only one candidate for each board seat, which is hand selected by company management. Shareholders are not permitted to vote against this candidate, all they can do is withhold their vote. As one observer notes, 'The height of irony is that a candidate nominated by management needs only one vote to secure a place on the board of directors, even if an overwhelming majority of shareowners oppose the nominee.'[44]

The pushback that soon developed against the equal access proposal reveals not only the 'illusion of securitization' but also what is at stake when corporate governance becomes politicised. In July 2007, when the first rumblings of the sub-prime crisis could be detected, the SEC offered two alternative proposals to mediate the mounting disputes around equal access, both of which had the effect of silencing shareholder voice. First, the SEC proposed that a minimum of 5 per cent ownership in a corporation would be required if a shareholder wished to sponsor proxy resolutions. To put this number in perspective, according to ownership data of the top 25 publicly listed corporations only a handful of major financial corporations, such as Berkshire Hathaway, Barclays Global Investors, Fidelity Management & Research, hold over 5 per cent of shareholdings in the largest 25 publicly-listed corporations in the US.[45] Second, the SEC proposed that shareholders either be limited or prohibited in their ability 'to nominate members of corporate boards'.[46] The Social Investment Forum, a formidable alliance of 500 shareholders and shareholder groups in the US, vehemently opposed both proposals.

The SEC was originally expected to reach a resolution regarding equal access during the 2008 proxy season. However, aside from clarifying its position regarding rules permitting management's exclusion of certain shareholder proposals related to the election of directors,[47] the SEC has not undertaken any major ruling on the equal access proposal well into 2010. This is the case despite the rhetoric of the Obama administration across the sub-prime mortgage crisis demanding better oversight and accountability of financial corporations.

It should come as no surprise that several conservative interest groups, think tanks and business organizations, including the Business Roundtable, a highly influential lobby group of CEOs of leading companies in the US, have strongly advised the SEC to reject the equal access proposal on the grounds that it will not serve shareholder interests because of the presence of 'collateral objectives' linked to special interest groups – read: trade unions.[48] As Lucian Bebchuk observes, citing the Roundtable position, some institutional investors, particularly the more active union and state pension plans – the same groups that spearheaded the equal access proposal[49] – 'can be expected to put forward and vote for shareholder election proposals to advance "special interests of their own that are unrelated to the openness of the proxy process"', such as wages, unionization and benefits, and environmental protection.[50]

The following excerpt of a letter penned by the Competitive Enterprise Institute, and addressed to the SEC in opposition to the shareholder access proposal, is worth quoting at length, as it reveals the underlying capitalist motivations for continued support of the corporate governance doctrine.

> Through pension funds, labour unions and other *anti-market interest groups* have significant stakes in major corporations as well as entrepreneurial new firms. *A shareholder access rule would allow*

> *them and other activists to achieve through the board nomination process what they have been unable to accomplish through the political process.* [...] The implications go far beyond unions. Everything on the anti-market political wish list from Kyoto-like carbon restrictions, to auto emissions standards, to prescription drug price controls, to animal rights activism, to interfering with defense contractors to advance foreign policy objectives would be possible. *These initiatives, whatever their merits, belong in the political arena, not in corporate boardrooms where the focus should be on maximizing shareholder value.*[51]

In contrast to these sentiments, union activists need to *delegitimize* – as opposed to participate in – the representation of corporations as apolitical entities that possess a 'natural right' both to make profits in the interests of shareholder value and to place the goal of profits and value above 'mere' social and the environmental concerns.

THE ILLUSIONS OF CORPORATE GOVERNANCE

Despite the ongoing paradoxes inherent to the securitization of pension savings, including the recent sub-prime crisis, neoliberal forms of domination have deepened and consolidated. This can be readily seen in the marketization of resistance through the corporate governance doctrine. The doctrine depoliticises and declasses struggles, especially during times of crisis, but also deepens two key components of cannibalistic capitalism: financial fetishism and the marketization of labour.

The actions of the US government, as well as global responses to the crisis as with the G20 Summits, confirm these trends.[52] Following the ideological contours of corporate governance, a major focus of popular discontent in the US has been the $700 billion in government bailouts channelled through the Troubled Assets Relief Program (TARP), and the record bonuses drawn by TARP recipients. President Obama and his government have played into electorate anger with tactics that appeal to the seemingly democratic sentiments of corporate governance. Through the proposed financial tax, for instance, Obama plans to 'get back "every single dime" that taxpayers put into bailing out the financial companies. Those firms can afford to pay the fee because of Wall Street's [in the words of Obama] "massive profits and obscene bonuses."'[53]

While the enormous profits and outsized bonuses of Wall Street *are* unjustified – even during boom times – and should be subject to taxation, the state's illusory demonization of banks, while actively supporting the banking system and reproducing cannibalistic capitalism, distorts the reality and the complexity of the uneven and exploitative class relationship between Wall Street and Main Street, between financial capitalists and workers. Obama's response, as with the attempts of the G20 Summits to strengthen the global financial architecture, need to be understood as class-based strategies to ensure new domains for the securitization of pension savings.[54] Such seemingly innocuous and technical paradigms as corporate governance falsely empower workers as shareowners. In fact, workers' security has been made – in the present as well as in the future – more dependent on their own exploitation through cannibalistic capitalism.

Any effective political alternative to this will have to break with the (futile) goal of aligning the interests of Wall Street with Main Street. It must transcend the bounds of corporate governance and the new activism being taken up by some union activists by reconnecting the production and reproduction of cannibalistic capitalism with financial fetishism and the marketization of labour. For too long, discussions around finance, particularly around the fashionable term 'financialization', have avoided theorizing the growing, albeit complex, connection between workers, the bourgeois state, pension funds, the credit system, and corporate power. This void has contributed to the ongoing effects of individualization and marketization on the working classes. These have narrowed the scope for radical, collective political action through working-class organization. As pension fund beneficiaries, workers and unions need to find ways not only to repoliticise the corporate governance doctrine and expose its capitalist nature, but also to move our struggles outside its bounds, beyond a system in which the concern for profits and interest-based revenue become both the means and the end of challenging corporate power.

NOTES

1 This essay develops themes covered in Susanne Soederberg, *Corporate Power and Ownership in Contemporary Capitalism: The Politics of Resistance and Domination*, London: Routledge, 2010.

2 Jamie Peck and Adam Tickell, 'Neoliberalizing Space', *Antipode*, 34(3), 2002, pp. 380-404.

3 Pierre Bourdieu, *The Social Structures of the Economy*, Cambridge: Polity Press, 2005.

4 See, for example, Kim Moody, *Workers in a Lean World*, London: Verso, 1997.

5 Loïc Wacquant, *Punishing the Poor: The Neoliberal Government of Social Insecurity*, Durham: Duke University Press, 2009.

6 Peck and Tickell, 'Neoliberalizing Space', p. 389.

7 Pierre Bourdieu, *Acts of Resistance: Against the Tyranny of the Market*, New York: New Press, 1998, p. 98.

8 For more information about the socialization of securitization in the context of the so-called 'Ownership Society', see Soederberg, *Corporate Power and Ownership*.

9 David Harvey, *A Brief History of Neoliberalism*, Oxford: Oxford University Press, 2005, p. 32.

10 An Individual Retirement Account is defined as a 'tax-deferred retirement account for an individual that permits individuals to set aside money each year, with earnings tax-deferred until withdrawals begin at age 59-and-a-half or later (or earlier, with a 10 percent penalty)'. For further information, see: http://www.investorwords.com/2641/IRA.html.

11 The Conference Board, *The 2009 Institutional Investment Report: Trends in Asset Allocation and Portfolio Composition*, New York: The Conference Board, 2009, p. 14. For more discussion on this, see Soederberg, *Corporate Power and Ownership*.

12 P. W. Feeney, *Securitization: Redefining the Bank*, London: St. Martin's Press, 1995.

13 The Conference Board, *The 2009 Institutional Investment Report*.

14 OECD, *Pension Markets in Focus,* October 2009, Issue 6, Paris: OECD.

15 Robert Pollin, *Contours of Descent: U.S. Economic Fractures and the Landscape of Global Austerity*, London: Verso, 2003, p. 32.

16 'The process of ABS involves the transfer of a pool of relatively homogeneous assets from the lender (originator or issuer) to a special purpose vehicle (SPV). The SPV, which typically has trust status under the law, finances the transfer of these assets through the issue of tradable securities. ABS is a particular form of "off-balance sheet" accounting, whereby assets are isolated, repackaged and sold on the capital markets, and liabilities are thus reduced.' Paul Langley, 'Financialization and the Consumer Credit Boom', *Competition & Change,* 12(2), 2008, p. 137.

17 E. Wyly, M. Moos, D. Hammel, and E. Kabahizi, 'Cartographies of Race and Class: Mapping the Class-Monopoly Rents of American Sub-prime Mortgage Capital', *International Journal of Urban and Regional Research*, 33(2), 2009, pp. 332-54.

18 Arthur MacEwan, 'Inequality, Power, and Ideology', in *The Economic Crisis Reader*, Boston, MA: Dollars & Sense, 2009, pp. 5-15.

19 'Credit card statistics, industry facts, and debt statistics', available at http://www.creditcards.com. R.D. Manning, *Credit Card Nation: The Consequences of America's Addiction to Credit*, New York: Basic Books, 2000.

20 Harvey, *Limits to Capital*, London: Verso, 1999.

21 Ibid., p. 266

22 Ibid., p. 269.

23 Elizabeth Kneebone and Emily Garr, 'The Suburbanization of Poverty: Trends in Metropolitan America, 2000 to 2008', Washington: The Brookings Institution, 2010.

24 Wyly et al, 'Cartographies of Race and Class: Mapping the Class-Monopoly

Rents of American Sub-prime Mortgage Capital', pp. 332-54.

25 MacEwan, 'Inequality, Power, and Ideology', p. 1.

26 Arthur MacEwan, 'Hedge Funds', in *The Economic Crisis Reader,* Boston: Dollars & Sense, 2009, p. 93.

27 OECD, *Pension Markets in Focus.*

28 For a critique of the construction of 'Main Street', see Soederberg, *Corporate Power and Ownership.*

29 Ibid.

30 Eugene F. Fama, 'Agency problems and the theory of the firm', *Journal of Political Economy*, 88(2), 1980, pp. 288-307.

31 Michel Aglietta and Antoine Reberioux, *Corporate Governance Adrift: A Critique of Shareholder Value*, Cheltenham: Edward Elgar, 2005.

32 Paddy Ireland, 'Corporate Governance, Stakeholding, and the Company: Towards a Less Degenerate Capitalism', *Journal of Law and Society*, 23(3), 1996, pp. 287-320.

33 Archon Fung, Tessa Hebb and Joel Rogers, eds., *Working Capital: The Power of Labor's Pensions*, New York: Cornell University Press, 2001.

34 Maureen O'Connor, 'Labor's Role in the Shareholder Revolution', in F. Archon, T. Hebb, and J. Rogers, eds., *Working Capital: the Power of Labor's Pensions*, New York: Cornell University Press, 2001, pp. 67-92.

35 Peter F. Drucker, *The Unseen Revolution: How Pension Fund Socialism Came to America*, New York: Harper & Row, 1976.

36 Stewart J. Schwab and Randall S. Thomas, 'Realigning Corporate Governance: Shareholder Activism by Labor Unions', *Michigan Law Review*, 96, 1998, pp. 1018-94.

37 Regulations detailing the shareholder proposal process are available at the Securities and Exchange Commission's website: http://www.sec.gov.

38 O'Connor, 'Labor's Role'.

39 Barry Burr, 'Union funds champs of proxy season', *Pensions & Investments*, 5 February 2007.

40 Lucian A. Bebchuk, 'The Business Roundtable's Untenable Case Against Shareholder Access', *Harvard Law and Economics Discussion Paper,* No. 516, Cambridge: Harvard Law School, 2005, p. 7.

41 David M. Brennan, '"Fiduciary Capitalism", the "Political Model of Corporate Governance", and the Prospect of Stakeholder Capitalism in the United States', *Review of Radical Political Economy,* 37(1), 2005, pp. 39-62.

42 Proxy cards allow shareholders to vote at a meeting, whether or not they decide to attend. For further information, see the statement on proxy cards at http://www.pgecorp.com.

43 Proxy contests arise when a dissident shareholder or group distributes its own proxy materials separate from management's proxy materials. Both groups then wage an active solicitation campaign to persuade shareholders to vote their respective proxy cards.

44 William Baue, 'The Key to Director Independence: Equal Access to Corporate Board Elections', *SocialFunds*, 1 April 2003.

45 The Conference Board, *The 2007 Institutional Investment Report: Trends in Asset*

Allocation and Portfolio Composition, New York: The Conference Board, 2007.

46 Social Investment Forum, '2005 Report on Socially Responsible Investment Trends in the United States – 10 Year Review', Washington: Social Investment Forum, 2006.

47 Securities and Exchange Commission, 'Shareholder Proposals Relating to the Election of Directors', 6 December 2007, available at http://www.sec.gov.

48 See Letter from Henry A. McKinnell, Chairman, Business Roundtable, to Jonathan Katz, Secretary, Securities and Exchange Commission, 22 December 2003. Available at http://www.sec.gov.

49 The equal access proposal was put forward by the American Federation of State, County, and Municipal Employees Pension Plan (AFSCME), a major, union-sponsored pension plan representing the largest union for workers in the public service. It has subsequently been supported by a broad range of shareholder interests including the California Public Employees' Retirement System (CalPERS) and the Council of Institutional Investors (CII), which represents $3 trillion in shareholder assets.

50 Bebchuk, 'The Business Roundtable's Untenable Case', p. 7.

51 Competitive Enterprise Institute, '"Shareholder Access" Harmful to Shareholders, Groups Say', 7 February 2007, available at http://cei.org, my emphasis.

52 Susanne Soederberg, 'The Politics of Representation and Financial Fetishism: The Case of the G20 Summits', *Third World Quarterly*, 31(4), 2010, in press.

53 'Obama Tax May Cost JPMorgan, Bank of America $1.5 Billion Each', *Bloomberg Businessweek,* 14 January 2010, available at http://www.businessweek.com.

54 See, for example, Soederberg, 'The Politics of Representation and Financial Fetishism'.

CRISIS *IN* NEOLIBERALISM OR CRISIS *OF* NEOLIBERALISM?

ALFREDO SAAD-FILHO

The banks are fucked, we're fucked, the country's fucked.
Anonymous British cabinet minister[1]

This rather perceptive assessment of the implications of the current crisis for the United Kingdom (and a good many other countries) is more candid and insightful than the twaddle of many mainstream journalists, economists and politicians, who proclaim the virtues of the 'free market' while blaming an unholy coalition of unhinged bankers, shifty borrowers and incompetent regulators for the disaster.[2] In order to save neoliberalism from itself, the free marketeers have nationalized some of the largest financial institutions in the world, socialized financial market risks and pumped huge amounts of public money into the economy. The rhetorical gyrations justifying this frenzy have been ideological in the worst possible sense: they are deliberately misleading representations of reality, concocted to confuse the audience and stultify the opposition. In contrast, Marxian assessments of the crisis, being grounded upon the realities of accumulation and located within systemic analyses of the class relations under neoliberalism, suggest that this is not a crisis of (de)regulation but, instead, a *systemic crisis in neoliberal capitalism*. It is not, yet, a crisis *of* neoliberalism.

NEOLIBERALISM AND FINANCIALIZATION

Neoliberalism is the mode of existence of contemporary capitalism. This system of accumulation emerged gradually, since the mid-1970s, in response to the transformation of the conditions of accumulation accompanying the disarticulation of the Keynesian-social democratic consensus, the paralysis of developmentalism and the implosion of the Soviet bloc.[3] In essence, neoliberalism is based on the systematic use of state power, under the ideological guise of 'non-intervention', to impose a hegemonic project of recomposition of the rule of capital at five levels: domestic resource allocation, international economic integration, the reproduction of the state, ideology, and the reproduction of the working class. These are summarily described below in order to locate the contradictions leading to the current crisis.

Under neoliberalism, state capacity to allocate resources intertemporally (the balance between investment and consumption), intersectorally (the composition of output and investment) and internationally (the articulation of capitalist production and finance across borders) has been systematically transferred to an increasingly globalized financial sector in which US institutions play a dominant role.[4] Resource control has given the financial institutions a determining influence upon the level and composition of investment, output and employment, the structure of demand, the financing of the state, the exchange rate and the patterns of international specialization in most countries. The extended influence and resourcing of finance has supported the development of a whole array of new instruments, the rapid expansion of purely speculative activities and, inevitably, the explosive growth of rewards to high-ranking financiers.[5]

Financialization and the restructuring of production are underpinned by the transnationalization of circuits of accumulation, which is commonly described as 'globalization'. These developments have recomposed the previous 'national' systems of provision at a higher level of productivity at firm level, created new global production chains, reshaped the country-level integration of the world economy, and facilitated the introduction of new technologies and labour processes, while compressing real wages.[6] Finally, financialization has also supported the reassertion of US imperialism.[7]

Financialization is not a distortion of a 'pure capitalism' or the outcome of a financial sector 'coup' against productive capital. It is, rather, a structural feature of accumulation and social reproduction under neoliberalism. In this sense, 'finance' includes not only the banks and institutional investors (pension funds, mutual funds, hedge funds, stockbrokers, insurance companies and other firms dealing primarily with interest-bearing capital), but also the financial arm of industrial capital, whose profitability increasingly depends on financial engineering. The constitutive role of finance in the capital relation under neoliberalism has allowed it to appropriate an increasing share of the profits extracted by the non-financial corporate sector. This process has played a major role in the polarization of incomes under neoliberalism.[8]

Even before the current crisis, the notion that finance mobilises and allocates resources efficiently, drastically reduces systemic risks and brings significant productivity gains for the economy as a whole was untenable.[9] Not only did the expected acceleration of growth through financial and capital account liberalization fail to materialise in most countries but, instead, finance-induced crises have become more frequent.[10] Conversely, the growth accelerations in the age of neoliberalism have been largely unrelated either to changes in financial sector regulations or capital account liberalization. An alternative interpretation is more plausible: regardless of these limitations, financialization plays a pivotal role in contemporary capitalism because it supports the transnationalization of production, facilitates the concentration of income and wealth and supports the political hegemony of neoliberalism through continuing threats of capital flight. The power of finance has become especially evident during the current crisis, when several governments were compelled to rescue large institutions and, in some cases, entire financial systems at huge cost to the public. Even more strikingly, these revived institutions immediately started demanding budget cuts because of the alleged 'unsustainability' of the fiscal position of states that, nominally, 'own' some of the largest banks in the land.[11] Never in economic history has so much trouble and expense been rewarded with such effrontery.

FINANCIALIZATION AND SOCIAL DISCIPLINE

Neoliberal financialization has imposed specific modalities of social discipline upon key social agents. These include the state (the need to enforce restrictive welfare policies and contractionary monetary and fiscal policies under the continuing threat of fiscal, exchange rate or balance of payments crisis), industrial capital (global competition promoted by the state and facilitated by finance), and the financial sector itself (competitive international integration under a US-led regulatory umbrella). However, unquestionably the most stringent forms of discipline have been imposed upon the working class.

Hundreds of millions of workers have been forcibly incorporated into transnational circuits of accumulation during the last three decades, greatly increasing competition between individual capitals and between (and within) national working classes. The global restructuring of production, accompanied by regressive legal, regulatory and political changes, have transformed the patterns of employment in most countries and facilitated the imposition of restrictions to the wages, subsidies, benefits, entitlements systems and other non-market protections that had been introduced under various interventionist regimes. These technological, economic, legal and political shifts have drastically narrowed the scope for resistance against neoliberal capitalism.

At another level, social discipline has been imposed through the financialization of the reproduction of the working class, most remarkably by means of the housing market boom and the expansion of personal credit in the last two decades. These offered highly profitable lines of business for many financial institutions and became an important mechanism of social integration, especially in the US and UK. Under their chronically straitened circumstances, partly because of the disappearance (or the export) of millions of traditionally relatively well-paid skilled jobs and their replacement by less well-paid service jobs and, partly, because of the retrenchment of the welfare state, many workers were drawn into systematic borrowing while their conditions of employment deteriorated. In these circumstances, it is unsurprising that many households became either chronically indebted or increasingly reliant on asset price inflation, or both, in order to meet their reproduction needs.[12] For example,

> [T]here has been a 74 per cent increase in health insurance premiums for the average US family with health care coverage, which has led to 29 million American adults incurring unsecured consumer loans to make up for the gap between medical coverage and actual costs... [U]nsecured debt has also become an important contributor in granting access to university education... [M]iddle-income households are [also] using mortgage debt to supplement the lack of funding for basic education as many families now opt to pay a premium for purchasing houses within a good school catchment area... In addition to medical bills and education... a large portion of middle- and low-income households use unsecured debt as a safety net or to fund daily living expenses... [M]iddle-income households are incurring ever greater levels of debt to maintain the historically constructed notion of the American middle-class standard of living.[13]

Many households reacted to the neoliberal reforms by maxing out their credit cards and turning their homes and retirement pensions into virtual cash machines in order to bypass the stagnation of wages and the retrenchment of public welfare provision.[14] However, pressures for timely repayment based on the threat of losing homes, cars and reputations helped to push many debtors into financial difficulties, including the need for long working hours in multiple jobs with precarious employment rights, rising stress levels and, inevitably, a declining propensity to engage in political or industrial militancy.

Unsurprisingly, financialization has supported a significant rise in the rate of exploitation foremost seen in a corresponding decline in the wage share of national income in most countries. In the US, for example,

> From 1979-2004 the [income] share of the top 5 percent of households rose from 15.3 percent to 20.9 percent while that of the poorest 20 percent fell from 5.5 percent to 4.0 percent ... [I]ncome growth has been particularly concentrated at the very top. In 2000 and again in 2005 the richest hundredth of one percent... of families in the United States received 5 percent of total income, a level that had been not been reached previously since 1929. During the 1950s and 1960s the share received by the top 0.01 percent was between 1 percent and 1.5 percent of total income.[15]

Similarly, in the UK,

> [The] top 0.05 per cent of the population had seen its share of national income decline ... from 1937 till the 1970s ... but by 2000 its share was *higher* than it had been in 1937. And the very rich got richer faster than the merely wealthy. In the 1980s, every group in the top tenth of taxpayers increased their share of national income, but in the 1990s the increase in the share of the top tenth was *all* accounted for by the top 0.1 per cent ... [T]he average ratio of CEO-to-employee pay was 47 in 1999; ten years later it was 128.[16]

Personal credit was also a key macroeconomic policy tool. Every time the US and UK economies slowed down as, for example, in the late 1990s, after the dotcom bubble and after 9-11, their central banks lowered interest rates and encouraged remortgaging and the accumulation of unsecured debt in order to prop up demand. These policies have been referred to as 'asset price Keynesianism',[17] because, to some extent, private deficits replaced the role of public sector deficits in macroeconomic stabilization. This policy was temporarily successful, and demand induced by home equity extractions added approximately 1.5 per cent per year to the rate of growth of US GDP between 2002 and 2007. Suggestively, this was just about the difference between US and Eurozone growth rates during that period.[18]

The significance of personal debt for social reproduction under neoliberalism does not support the right-wing view that the current crisis was caused by the profligacy of poor US and UK households. Nor does the left-populist claim that the indebted workers were merely victims of structural forces hold up. The analysis above *does*, however, imply that the crisis was the outcome of an unsustainable process of neoliberal financialization, perverse changes in labour market structures and regressive shifts in the provision of the means of subsistence, underpinned by limited macroeconomic policy tools and propped up by deeply ideological claims about 'competition' and 'individual choice'. The crisis also shows that it is impossible to eliminate poverty by lending to the poor: poverty has many causes, but insufficient access to credit is not one of them.

It is also impossible to stabilise complex economies over long periods through the manipulation of mass credit, above all because the material limitations in their ability to repay eventually must restrict the working class's borrowing capacity. Consequently, *in extremis*, their debts may have to be nationalized, inflated away or legislated out of existence. But this happens only exceptionally: under normal circumstances, excess debt leads only to individual penury and social degradation.

NEOLIBERALISM'S CONTRADICTIONS

The neoliberal system of accumulation is structurally unstable at five levels. First, the sheer weight of finance in the economy, facilitated by technological developments that reinforce financial innovations and speed financial transactions, and by regulatory liberalization, determines that accumulation under neoliberalism has often taken the form of financial (bubble-like) cycles which eventually collapse with destructive implications and requiring a state-sponsored bailout. These cycles include: the international debt crisis of the early 1980s, the US savings & loan crisis of the 1980s, the stock market crashes of the 1980s and 1990s, the Japanese crisis of the late 1980s, the crises in several middle income countries at the end of the twentieth century, and the dotcom, financial and housing bubbles of the 2000s, culminating with the current global meltdown. It is also striking that the business model of neoliberalism's beacon enterprises is, often, based primarily on plunder and fraud, across a spectrum ranging from Enron to Bernard L. Madoff Investment Securities. Although these crises and a succession of large-scale bankruptcies demonstrate the irrationalities of accumulation under neoliberalism, the illusion of prosperity was supported by the Fed's apparent ability to coordinate the clean-up operations while sustaining growth in the dynamic centre of the world economy.

Second, the latest cycle was predicated on a seemingly bottomless appetite for credit by households and the state, which provided outlets for the commodities and the fictitious capital produced by the global corporations. However, growing household consumption was sustainable only while rising house prices conjured up the equity which could be withdrawn through new loans and remortgages.[19] It would eventually become impossible to service rising debts with stagnant household incomes – especially if interest rates had to rise in order to prick asset bubbles or keep inflation low. Rising house prices also depended on the flow of mortgage credit by the financial institutions, which was, in turn, reliant on US and UK policies to promote speculative capital inflows, buy-to-let swindles (in the UK) and predatory subprime lending (in the US) allegedly in order to 'expand home ownership'.[20] These loans were sliced up and traded repeatedly among the financial institutions, generating staggering fortunes in the process.[21] However, when swelling losses threatened to overwhelm the financial sector, governments swiftly collectivized risks, nationalized the imperilled institutions and plugged the sector's balance sheet with endless quantities of newly minted cash.

Third, the cycle required a continuing flow of financial resources to the US and the UK to buy shares, T-bills, mortgage-based securities and real estate. These funds were converted into tradable financial assets, allowing the intermediaries to extend credit in the domestic economy. Evidently, these transfers are ultimately unsustainable because the US and UK cannot expect to be permanently subsidized by cheap goods *and* cheap finance supplied by the rest of the world. Nevertheless, these resource flows temporarily supported the claim that the finance-driven restructuring of capitalism had been successful, and that the US and UK were consistently doing 'better' than the economies which embraced neoliberalism a little more reluctantly (especially Japan and the Eurozone). These performance differences in the years preceding the crisis helped to legitimize neoliberalism, and to disguise the fact that the so-called 'Great Moderation' was largely founded on unsustainable debt-led growth supported by misaligned exchange rates.[22]

Fourth, macroeconomic stability, predictable central bank policies, hands-off financial regulation, the Basel II framework and 'mark to market' accounting rules increased the economy's vulnerability to swings, shocks and confidence crises. They created incentives for rising leverage and for an increasing reliance by the financial institutions on short-term wholesale funding rather than retail deposits. Leveraging and the creation of liquidity through the transformation of debt into tradable papers boosted asset prices which, in turn, encouraged further leveraging, in a kind of Ponzi process. Conversely, when liquidity fell highly leveraged financial institutions had to cut their balance sheets rapidly, contributing to the severity of the crisis.

Fifth, it was expected that securitization would increase the resilience of accumulation by transferring risk to those better able to hold it. However, in reality the financial institutions lost the incentive to evaluate risk because their papers were being traded immediately, while the buyers relied on meaningless credit ratings to disguise their ignorance.[23] The ensuing flood of securities silently destabilized global finance.[24] In sum, although the trigger for the crisis was the collapse of subprime mortgages in the US, there were several weak links along the chain: the recycling of US and UK current account deficits, the rate of accumulation of personal debt, the relationship between consumption and interest rates, the fragility of the balance sheets of the large financial institutions and their structured investment vehicles, the need for low inflation and predictable changes in interest rates, and so on.

In this sense, the current crisis exposes the limitation of financialization as the driver of global accumulation. The contradictions underlying the crisis indicate that this is a *systemic crisis in neoliberalism*, but it is *not a crisis of neoliberalism* because, although the reproduction of the system of accumulation has been shaken, it is not currently threatened by a systemic alternative.

NOT MOVING FORWARD

The financial collapse delivered a stunning blow to the neoliberal consensus, as was aptly illustrated by Alan Greenspan's confession of 'shocked disbelief'.[25] *The Economist* was nothing less than apocalyptic:

> [E]conomic liberty is under attack and capitalism … is at bay … but those who believe in it must fight for it … In the short term defending capitalism means, paradoxically, state intervention. There is a justifiable sense of outrage … that $2.5 trillion of taxpayers' money now has to be spent on a highly rewarded industry. But the global bailout is pragmatic, not ideological … If confidence and credit continue to dry up, a near-certain recession will become a depression, a calamity for everybody.[26]

For a few weeks in 2008 global capitalism seemed to bleed uncontrollably, as losses reportedly climbed towards US$ 40 trillion or, alternatively, 45 per cent of the world's wealth.[27] Several states nationalized key financial institutions, guaranteed deposits and financial investments, cut interest rates and implemented expansionary fiscal policies and so-called 'quantitative easing' to support finance, aggregate demand and employment. It is impossible to calculate the cost of these initiatives. They included central bank purchases of temporarily worthless financial assets, which may gain value as the global economy stabilises, 'Keynesian' initiatives to protect employment, which partly pay for themselves through additional tax revenues and reduced social security transfers, and a significant amount of borrowing to fund regular spending, which became necessary because of the crisis-driven decline in taxation. These measures were unsurprising: they reflect, on the one hand, the post-Great Depression consensus that aggressive expansionary policies can avert a deflationary spiral, and, on the other, the neoliberal claim that financial sector stability is paramount.

Heavy state spending and the socialization of losses and risks stemmed the haemorrhage of bank capital and postponed the collapse of some large manufacturing conglomerates, especially the old US automakers. However, they did not revive bank credit, and their huge costs have triggered severe fiscal problems especially in the US, UK, peripheral European economies and fragile Gulf states. As Joseph Stiglitz put it,

> [T]he very actions that saved the economies of the world have presented a new problem for fiscal policy, as questions are being raised about governments' ability to finance their deficits. There are speculative attacks against the weakest countries, which find themselves caught between a rock and a hard place ... The financial markets that caused the crisis – which in turn caused the deficits – went silent as money was being spent on the bailout; but now they are telling governments they have to cut public spending. Wages are to be cut, even if bank bonuses are to be kept.[28]

Despite their *tactical* proficiency, instantly coming up with trillions of dollars to support the banks and shore up the global economy, the neoliberal bourgeoisies and their paid economists have demonstrated a staggering lack of *strategic* imagination. Even the most promising recovery scenarios offers only slow growth, a decade of austerity and a wave of unemployment which may last for an entire generation. The emerging consensus is that the system of accumulation can be fixed with a little financial regulation, marginal exchange rate adjustments, a rebalancing between exports and domestic demand in Germany and East Asia, and austerity for wages and public consumption in the UK and eventually in the US. These cosmetic changes are unlikely to rebalance the global economy or make much of a contribution to managing the ongoing restructuring of accumulation. Their simplicity is symptomatic of the mainstream's superficial understanding of the crisis; they point to a slow and very bumpy recovery, with the emergence of deep financial, fiscal, exchange rate and unemployment crises in one country after another, and over a long period of time.

Most recovery plans bypass the need for an alternative mechanism of social integration, fail to recognise that the manipulation of personal debt will be insufficient to stabilise demand and employment, and ignore the fact that the contraction of credit, wages and pensions and the need for fiscal retrenchment will compromise long term demand growth. Although state spending has plugged the gap during the crisis, this is unsustainable without significant changes in taxation and the distribution of income, but these are not currently on the cards.[29] Recovery plans also presume that contractionary fiscal policies are essential to protect state credit ratings in the short-run and avoid inflation in the long-run, and envision that, after the return of 'normal' conditions, the manipulation of interest rates should become once again the most prominent macroeconomic policy tool. That is, the neoliberal camp essentially expects the global system of accumulation to get back to its pre-crisis state (plus or minus some marginal tinkering) after a prolonged and rather costly period of instability.[30]

Even more alarmingly, although many proposals to address the crisis and prevent a repeat have been aired, three years after the onset of the crisis and two years after the collapse of Lehman Brothers very little of substance has actually happened. The ideas on the table or being discussed in the world's legislatures include a devaluation of the dollar to help rebalance the US economy, a coordinated set of higher inflation targets to erode public debts while preventing explosive capital movements to low inflation countries,[31] the taxation of bank assets and financial transactions, a review of supervisory agency responsibilities, the prohibition of certain types of short-selling, regulatory changes requiring the financial institutions to prepare 'living wills' and/or buy insurance against possible failure, and rules to increase capital requirements countercyclically, constrain leveraging and speculation, ban proprietary trading, restrict the hedge funds and cap bonuses. Other suggestions include stricter regulation of the credit rating agencies, increased transparency in derivatives trading (for example, through the creation of centralized exchanges), and stronger consumer protection against predatory lending.[32]

However, no significant macroeconomic adjustments have taken place yet, and the financial institutions have been lobbying ferociously against any attempt to curb their operations. They argue that the US and UK should not deliberately maim a large industry in which they have a comparative advantage, and that taxation or regulation would lead to the mass exodus of banks, hedge funds and traders to Switzerland, Singapore or the Gulf.[33] Their well-funded campaign is only part of the problem.

Macroeconomic adjustments have been hamstrung by a number of major economic challenges that remain in place. A first is the conflicting pressures on the dollar (it must fall to help correct the US current account deficit, but it tends to rise whenever there is uncertainty elsewhere, especially in the systemically important countries or the Eurozone); China's parallel unwillingness to let its currency appreciate is a second. Structural contradictions within the Eurozone are a further difficulty: between surplus and deficit countries; between entrenched monetary conservatism and the need to deploy expansionary policies to address the crisis in the smaller countries; and – more fundamentally – between monetary unification and continuing fiscal fragmentation.

A fourth obstacle is the extraordinarily inflexible monetary policy apparatus that has remained in place to lock in low inflation.[34] Its rigidities are compounded by significant monetary policy differences between the US, Japan, the UK and the Eurozone. For example, the first two do not have legally binding inflation targets to raise, the UK cannot act in isolation, and the ECB has been built to enforce low inflation, and its governance structure makes it difficult to change course.[35] Complications of a different order would arise if inflation rose too fast in certain countries, because governments would be compelled to limit their fiscal stimuli and raise interest rates, potentially stalling the recovery.

Finally, another set of difficulties concerns reaching legislative agreement about how to tax the financial sector, set capital requirements, dismantle institutions that are too big to fail (and, therefore, that have in-built incentives to behave recklessly), and unscramble players' incentives (bonuses are outrageously high in the good times, and absurd when the financial sector refuses to lend even though it is being propped up by the state). These difficulties are especially visible in the debates surrounding the financial market reform bill in the US Congress. In conclusion, the largest economic crisis since 1929 has demonstrated that transferring control of capital to finance fosters speculation and systemic instability and does not improve macroeconomic performance. Yet, the institutional imperatives of reproduction of neoliberalism make it difficult for governments to introduce a new economic policy framework.

COMING OUT OF LEFT FIELD

Although the left has been severely weakened by the neoliberal onslaught, it should seek to intervene in the current debates offering democratic policy alternatives defending jobs, salaries, pensions and welfare standards, improving the quality of investment, protecting the environment, and seeking to turn the current crisis *in* neoliberalism into a *crisis of neoliberalism*.[36] These proposals can be framed, initially, along two axes.

First, no concessions should be offered on jobs, pensions or welfare. Those who benefitted disproportionately from the good times, and whose greed caused the crisis, should pay for it. Besides, offering concessions to protect individual employers or countries will only intensify the continuing race to the bottom under neoliberalism.

Second, the left can demand the takeover of the financial system and its transformation into a public utility. This can be justified at two levels. On the one hand, the economic argument for profits is that they encourage capitalists to invest wisely in order to multiply their capital and avoid losses. However, if the financial sector is unproductive and if its losses must be socialized, especially when they are large, there is no justification for profits in this sector. On the other hand, governments have given huge sums of money to the banks, but the banks are refusing to lend. The banks are not interested in low-risk-low-return operations, and they have to rebuild their reserves. This bottleneck is helping to perpetuate the crisis. Such a 'catch-22' is unavoidable given the institutional structure of the financial system, the imperatives of competition, and the constraints imposed by the crisis.

Nationalization without (further) compensation will cut this Gordian knot. Ideally, it should be supplemented by closing down the hedge funds and other institutions trading only between themselves and performing no productive service for the economy, pegging bankers' compensation to civil servants' salaries, imposing capital controls and centralising currency trading, abolishing the secondary markets for public securities, and creating a democratically accountable management structure for the financial sector. If the state runs the banks according to public policy goals, it will not have to accommodate short-term profitability; the banks will no longer be involved in socially destructive businesses, and society can be more certain that there will be no financial crises or bailouts in the future. At a strategic level, nationalization is important because the ownership of financial assets is at the core of the reproduction of capitalism today. Paradoxically, this is also the weakest social relation both economically and ideologically now, and a mass campaign to nationalize finance could destabilise the class relations at the core of neoliberalism.

It goes without saying that state ownership of finance does not signal the abolition of capitalism. The state had full ownership or significant control of finance in France and Iceland until a few years ago, and in Brazil and South Korea under their respective military dictatorships. Legal ownership can help, but what really matters are the objectives of government policy and which class and other interests are served by the financial institutions. As opposed to financial system-led systems, state-led co-ordination of economic activity is potentially more advantageous for the working class because the state is the only social institution that is at least potentially democratically accountable and that can influence the pattern of employment, the production and distribution of goods and services and the distribution of income and assets at the level of society as a whole.

In addition to the financial reforms sketched above, a democratic economic strategy can focus on the expansion of two complementary areas: the sectors producing goods and services for the workers and the poor (and where production is, often, relatively labour-intensive, as in construction and non-durable consumer goods), and the sectors that can help to relax the balance of payments constraint in deficit or vulnerable countries. They can be prioritised through the adoption of policies enforcing capital controls, maintaining exchange rates compatible with current account balance, avoiding domestic and external debt, introducing accommodating fiscal and monetary policies and rising tax ratios, and securing investment in public and environmentally sustainable goods. All these goals are compatible with a green investment strategy, which, especially in the large economies, has become imperative in order to avoid global environmental collapse.

Left mobilisation along these lines will not be welcomed by the neoliberal elite. The left should have no illusions that there is an 'antagonistic' relationship between production and finance under neoliberalism simply because financial gains are, by definition, deductions from the surplus value extracted by industrial capital. This principle is too abstract to support a political alliance between the left and the industrial – or the 'national' – bourgeoisie. Industrial capital is *materially* committed to the reproduction of neoliberalism, and the expectation that industrial capitalists will suddenly decide to follow Keynesian, developmentalist or democratic economic policies drastically misunderstands contemporary capitalism.[37]

This essay has argued that neoliberalism is a material form of social reproduction and social rule encompassing the structure of accumulation, international exchanges, the state, ideology and the reproduction of the working class, and which is compatible with a wide variety of policies under a supposedly 'free-market' umbrella. This totality has been destabilized by the crisis, and the neoliberal consensus is attempting to restore the *status quo ante* as much as possible. This goal is grounded in the realities of social reproduction, and supported by the class alliances which structure, and benefit from, neoliberalism.

In sharp contrast with these stabilizing goals, the destabilization of neoliberalism is a project of the radical left, and the spectrum for alliances at the top is very limited. Conversely, the scope for alliances at the bottom of the world's society is, potentially, unlimited. A left strategy to transcend neoliberalism must be based on mass political movements transforming the state and the processes of socio-economic reproduction and political representation – that is, imposing a new system of accumulation, including a new configuration of the economy and more equal distributions of income, wealth and power.

If the global working class remains passive the crisis will be resolved through an increase in the rate of exploitation. The default position in capitalism is that the workers are not only penalised disproportionately by crises; they must also compensate the capitalists for their losses.[38] This is partly because of the way in which capitalist economies absorb and process adverse shocks and, partly, because the workers are, by definition, closer to the edge of survival and have much greater difficulty turning changing circumstances to their advantage. This makes it essential to reinforce the distributional aspect of economic policy during the crisis by strengthening the links between economic and social policies in order to protect the vulnerable when they need it most (at a minimum, through the imposition of an extraordinary 'crisis tax' on the rich and on large corporations), while, at the same time, imposing progressive structural changes in the current modality of economic and social reproduction.

In sum, the alternative for the workers is to push the cost of the crisis on to the capitalists through a campaign for the takeover of the financial system and the democratization of finance, which would contribute to the destabilization of neoliberalism. Large-scale mobilizations depend on the left's ability to imagine an alternative future including the values of democracy, solidarity, satisfaction of basic needs and environmental sustainability. They can draw inspiration from the historical struggles for the limitation of the working day, for public health and education, for citizenship rights, and for the extension of democracy, in which the tireless work of millions of left activists has been essential to bring significant gains for the majority.

NOTES

1. *The Guardian*, 19 January 2009.
2. For example, George Osborne and Jeffrey Sachs suggest that: 'Blaming our predicament on financial markets… ignores the awkward truth that governments have enabled, if not enthusiastically promoted, recklessness, through chronic deficits and lax financial regulation'. 'A Frugal Budgetary Policy Is The Better Solution', *Financial Times*, 15 March 2010, p. 15; and also 'Capitalism at Bay', *The Economist*, 16 October 2008.
3. See Alfredo Saad-Filho, 'Introduction', in Saad-Filho, ed., *Anti-Capitalism: A Marxist Introduction,* London: Pluto Press, 2003; Alfredo Saad-Filho and Deborah Johnston, eds., *Neoliberalism: A Critical Reader*, London: Pluto Press, 2005; and Alfredo Saad-Filho and Galip Yalman, eds., *Neoliberalism in Middle*

Income Countries: Policy Dilemmas, Economic Crises, Forms of Resistance, London: Routledge, 2010.

4 See, for example, Leo Panitch and Sam Gindin, 'Global Capitalism and American Empire', in *Socialist Register 2004*; Leo Panitch and Martijn Konings, eds., *American Empire and the Political Economy of Global Finance,* London: Palgrave, 2009; and Chris Rude, 'The Role of Financial Discipline in Imperial Strategy', in *Socialist Register 2005*.

5 For a detailed analysis of financialization in the US, see Greta Krippner, 'The Financialization of the American Economy', *Socio-Economic Review*, 3(2), 2005.

6 See David Kotz, 'The Financial and Economic Crisis of 2008', *Review of Radical Political Economics*, 41(3), 2009; and Susan Watkins, 'Shifting Sands', *New Left Review*, 61, 2010.

7 See the *Socialist Register 2004* and *2005*.

8 For example, and including only a subset of what has been defined as 'finance': 'In 2002, the [narrow financial] sector generated an astonishing 41 per cent of US domestic corporate profits… Average pay in the sector rose from close to the average for all industries between 1948 and 1982 to 181 per cent of it in 2007'. Martin Wolf, 'Cutting Back Financial Capitalism is America's Big Test', 15 April 2009, available from http://www.ft.com. Also see: John Bellamy Foster and Hannah Holleman, 'The Financial Power Elite', *Monthly Review*, 62(1), 2010 and Kotz, 'Financial Crisis'.

9 These conclusions are undeniable. For example, '[It] is hard to argue that the new [financial] system has brought exceptional benefits to the economy generally. Economic growth and productivity in the last 25 years has been comparable to that of the 1950's and 60's, but in the earlier years the prosperity was more widely shared'. Paul Volcker, 'Remarks at the Economic Club of New York', Transcript available from http://www.econclubny.org.

10 See Carmen Reinhard and Kenneth Rogoff, *This Time is Different*, Princeton: Princeton University Press, 2010; and J. Stiglitz, *Freefall: America, Free Markets, and the Sinking of the World Economy*, London: Allen Lane, 2010.

11 For a particularly egregious example, see 'Moody's Warns US Over Credit Rating Fears', *Financial Times*, 4 February 2010, p. 17.

12 Needless to say, millions of working- and middle-class households have profited from financialization and asset inflation by refinancing their mortgages under more advantageous conditions or purchasing goods and services that would otherwise have remained beyond their reach. Although no generalisation across the working class is possible, there is incontrovertible evidence that large numbers of workers and members of the middle-class (however defined) have become chronically financially distressed during the last twenty years (see below).

13 Johnna Montgomerie, 'The Pursuit of (Past) Happiness? Middle-class Indebtedness and American Financialisation', *New Political Economy*, 14(1), 2009, pp. 16-18.

14 'In 2002… [the gross equity extracted from housing in the US] leaped up to equal about 8 percent of disposable personal income, and from 2004-06 they

were in the range of 9-10 percent of disposable personal income. These huge extractions from home equity, which would not have been possible in the absence of the rapid runup in home prices, represented additional spendable funds beyond households' disposable income'. Kotz, 'Financial Crisis', p. 312.

15 Ibid., p. 310.

16 Stefan Collini, 'Blahspeak', *London Review of Books*, 8 April 2010, p. 31.

17 See, for example, Robert Brenner, 'Interview on the Current Crisis', 29 January 2009, available at http://www.hani.co.kr; and Christian Marazzi, *The Violence of Financial Capitalism*, Los Angeles: Semiotext(e), 2010, pp. 34-35.

18 Marazzi, *Violence,* p. 35.

19 'By the summer of 2007 housing prices had risen by 70 percent corrected for inflation since 1995. At its peak in 2007, the housing bubble created an estimated $8 trillion in inflated new housing wealth, out of total housing wealth of $20 trillion, or 40 percent of housing wealth'. Kotz, 'Financial Crisis', p. 311.

20 For a review of Alan Greenspan's ideologically-driven support for the property boom, see 'Greenspan's view', *Le Monde diplomatique - English Edition*, January 2009, available from http://mondediplo.com.

21 For a detailed study of remunerations in the financial sector, see Lucian Bebchuk, Alma Cohen and Holger Spamann, 'The Wages of Failure: Executive Compensation at Bear Stearns and Lehman 2000-2008', Working Draft, 22 November 2009, available from http://www.law.harvard.edu/faculty/bebchuk.

22 For a starry-eyed overview of the 'Great Moderation', see Ben Bernanke, 'Remarks at the meetings of the Eastern Economic Association', Washington, 20 February 2004, available from http://www.federalreserve.gov. For a review of the US experience, see Leo Panitch and Sam Gindin, 'Finance and American Empire', in Panitch and Konings, eds., *American Empire*.

23 'The proposition that sophisticated modern finance was able to transfer risk to those best able to manage it has failed. The paradigm is, instead, that risk has been transferred to those least able to understand it'. Martin Wolf, 'Seeds of Its Own Destruction', 9 March 2009, available from http://blogs.ft.com.

24 For an engaging account of the transformations of finance during the last two decades, see Gillian Tett, *Fool's Gold: How Unrestrained Greed Corrupted a Dream*, London: Little, Brown & Co., 2009.

25 'Testimony of Dr. Alan Greenspan to the Committee of Government Oversight and Reform', 23 October 2008, p. 2.

26 *The Economist*, 'Capitalism at Bay'.

27 See Alan Greenspan, 'Equities Show Us The Way to a Recovery', *Financial Times*, 30 March 2009, p. 13; Gillian Tett, 'Lost Through Destructive Creation', *Financial Times*, 9 March 2010 and 10 March 2010, available from http://www.ft.com.

28 Joseph Stiglitz, 'The Non-Existent Hand', *London Review of Books*, 22 April 2010, pp. 17-18.

29 'The current economic upheaval demonstrates that access to credit is no replacement for real wage growth and adequate social protection. As such,

political interventions to stem the current financial crisis need to address the chronic liquidity and impending solvency problems faced by the household sector... [due to] the huge stock of unsecured debt that must be serviced at the same time as asset prices are falling... Moreover, these households may no longer be able to continue funding consumption through debt if consumer credit dries up. What is more, undoubtedly households will be left footing the bill for the US government's multiple [bank] bail-out packages... Whether through increased income taxes or further reductions in government services, households are expected to face their own adversity while being relied on to jump-start the economy'. Montgomerie, 'The Pursuit of (Past) Happiness?', pp. 18-19.

30 For the IMF's current views of the road to recovery, see: Dominique Strauss-Kahn, 'World Can Grow Faster With Right Policies', *IMF Survey Magazine: In the News*, 5 June 2010; and John Lipsky, 'The Road Ahead for Central Banks: Meeting New Challenges to Financial Stability', Speech at a High-Level International Conference on Central Banks and Development of the World Economy: New Challenges and a Look Ahead, 18 June 2010, both available from http://www.imf.org

31 See Tim Leunig, 'Coordinated Inflation Could Bail Us All Out', *Financial Times*, 16 February 2009, p. 11.

32 See Olivier Blanchard, 'The Crisis: Basic Mechanisms, and Appropriate Policies', IMF Working Paper 09/80, April 2009, and Martin Wolf, 'Why Cautious Reform Of Finance Is The Risky Option', *Financial Times*, 28 April 2010, p. 13.

33 These threats of mass exit are hollow because the state, in these rival financial centres, does not have the resources to support and, if necessary, bail out the relatively aggressive institutions which might want to be based there.

34 See Alfredo Saad-Filho, 'Monetary Policy in the Neoliberal Transition', in Robert Albritton, Bob Jessop and Richard Westra, eds., *Political Economy and Global Capitalism*, London: Anthem Press, 2007.

35 See Thomas Palley, 'Europe's Debt Crisis and Keynes' Green Cheese Solution', 23 May 2010, available from http://blogs.ft.com.

36 For an overview of left proposals, see http://www.peri.umass.edu/safer. Pro-poor (democratic) economic policy alternatives to neoliberalism are reviewed in Arthur MacEwan, *Neo-liberalism or Democracy?*, London: Zed Books, 1999, and Alfredo Saad-Filho, 'There is Life beyond the Washington Consensus: An Introduction to Pro-Poor Macroeconomic Policies', *Review of Political Economy*, 19(4), 2007.

37 See the following defence of the City of London by the director-general of the Confederation of British Industry (CBI): 'The City is a vital part of the UK, not a "bloated excrescence" that unbalances the economy, the CBI director-general said yesterday… Richard Lambert said the City benefited the nation as a whole… Mr Lambert said that in a free society "it is not the job of a politician – or, for that matter, of a regulator – to argue that a particular form of activity is or is not of social value"'. See: 'CBI Chief Defends City as Vital to UK', *Financial Times*, 4 September 2009, p. 2.

38 'Over the past three quarters, America has seen national income rise by $200bn ... but profits have increased by $280bn while wages have fallen by $90bn. In Britain, where recovery has been slower, national income has grown by £27bn since the middle of last year; higher profits have accounted for £24bn of the rise. Wages have risen by £2bn'. See: Larry Elliott, 'So Much For The Spring of Discontent', *The Guardian*, 29 March 2010, p. 26.

THE CRISIS, THE DEFICIT AND THE POWER OF THE DOLLAR: RESISTING THE PUBLIC SECTOR'S DEVALUATION

KARL BEITEL

The fallout from the subprime debacle has brought to the fore, once again, the role of the state in the management and containment of crisis. The stakes involved in this debate, for both capital and progressive social movements, are potentially enormous. Even ardent defenders of neoliberalism concede that the proximate cause of the current downturn was Wall Street's own speculative excesses that culminated a nearly two-decade-long deregulation of finance. The problem facing leading sectors of US business and finance is that the resulting reliance on public expenditure to sustain rates of return on private investment poses a threat to the ideological legitimacy of the neoliberal project. A growing chorus of voices is raising concerns over the supposedly deleterious effects of rising government deficits on the long-term growth potential of the US, as well as the threat posed to the international status of the dollar. It is no surprise that proponents of liberalization, including defenders in the Obama administration, have moved to limit meaningful discussion over the content and scope of ongoing government intervention.

Among the many tasks facing the left everywhere, those facing the US left are especially urgent and daunting. Given that attacks on the alleged failure of government were central to the ideological construction of neoliberalism, challenging the devaluation of the public sector is a necessary first step to opening space for the discussion of alternatives. In the most immediate sense, what is at stake is defending the living standards and employment prospects of tens of millions of unemployed workers. This requires countering claims regarding the alleged inflationary effects of government deficits, as well as claims that debt-financed government spending leads to the 'crowding out' of private investment. Doing so likewise requires clarifying what is really at stake in arguments regarding the relation of deficits to the dollar's international reserve currency status. Deficit spending need not involve any inflationary increase in the money supply. Nor do deficits lead to an automatic crowding out of private sector investment. The real issues at stake in the debate over deficits are efforts to defend and perpetuate a set of political-economic arrangements that benefit powerful private interests, particularly capital invested in the global circuits of finance. As we shall see, deficits do in fact pose a problem for capitalists. Particularly during periods of acute crisis, deficits are required to offset faltering rates of investment and profits. At the same time, deficits raise the possibility of government expenditure being used to provide direct benefits to popular constituents. For capital, this raises the spectre of government actions running counter to their own perceptions of economic self-interest. Underlying the growing alarm over deficits is a demand that the present (and any future) US government demonstrate its commitment to placing the interests of wealthy investors over and above the wellbeing and health of its popular classes.

Challenging the hegemonic consensus should not be misinterpreted as implying that deficits represent a panacea for stagnation or falling rates of return on investment. Nor is it our task, as socialists, to propose more 'efficient' means for managing the current crisis. Rather, the debate over government intervention is inseparable from the struggle to open the political space to pose meaningful questions about the efficiency of markets, the class interests served by present policy initiatives, and the viability of more progressive and egalitarian alternatives.

DO DEFICITS REALLY CAUSE INFLATION?

The contemporary critique of deficits draws upon some variant of the still influential monetarist strand of economics. Reduced to its essentials, the argument linking deficits to inflation rests on the assertion that government deficits lead to an 'exogenous' injection of bank reserves into the monetary circuit. Banks respond by seeking to lend these reserves out, leading to the creation of additional deposits. Banks that hold these deposits are in turn encouraged to issue more loans, expanding the money supply and hence total expenditure to a degree that far exceeds the rate of growth of output. This process of monetary expansion is what allegedly causes the inflation in the prices of goods and services.[1]

This argument fundamentally misrepresents the relation between the money supply and prices. Government deficits are not, in general, the cause of excess liquidity or an excessive expansion of bank deposits. Nor does the US government compete for an existing pool of savings, driving up interest rates and depressing the rate of private investment. While it is true that the Treasury finances deficits through 'credits' from the Federal Reserve, any additional liquidity pumped into the money market can be reabsorbed and extinguished through the issue of new government securities, or through 'open market' and 'reverse repo' operations conducted by the Federal Reserve. Further, because the issue of new government debt essentially 'borrows back' reserves created through the initial government payment, it is inaccurate to claim that the government competes for a fixed sum of investment-seeking savings. On the contrary, government borrowing functions to mop up any excess liquidity created by the initial financing of the government deficit.[2]

Contrary to the orthodox argument, the correct starting point is that the money supply – means of payment created through extension of credit – adjusts to the requirements of the production and circulation of the total commodity product. Increases or decreases in the money supply – purchasing power held in the form of deposits – are not the principal cause of increases or decreases in the prices of *produced* goods and services. Nor are prices set by 'money chasing goods'. On the contrary, firms set prices by imposing markups over and above per unit costs, or some variant of administered, or full cost, pricing. Changes in output prices reflect changes in unit costs – i.e. wages, direct inputs, overhead, and interest – as well as changes in firms' demanded profits as reflected in the markup.

If the rate of profit is falling, due to a fall in the output-to-capital ratio, firms may attempt to protect their existing profit margins by increasing the markups applied on per unit costs.[3] Changes in the money supply are not the cause of this type of inflationary dynamic. On the contrary, the role of banks in the price-setting process is that of providing the necessary purchasing power to allow firms to realize, or monetize, their demanded profits. It is true that households can spend using demand deposits created by the initial government payment. However, this will induce a rise in prices only if the economy is operating at or near full employment, or if this additional nominal demand is absorbed by a firm's decision to increase markups in lieu of increasing employment and output. The correct relation is thus not that an increase in money supply leads to higher prices. Rather, higher prices necessitate a greater volume of circulating means of payment.

The money supply is in this sense fully endogenous to the capital circuit, with the volume of means of payment adjusting to the needs of capitalists to purchase labour power and other inputs to the production process and to ensure the turnover of the commodity product (subject to lenders decisions to ration, or otherwise limit, the supply of credit. This basic dynamic is entirely independent of the level of the government deficit. Nor do government deficits undermine the ability of the Fed to siphon excess liquidity out of the inter-bank market to regulate the overnight interest rate (see footnote 2). This is why, as seen in the Figures for the US, Japan and Germany in the appendix to this essay, we find essentially no correlation between higher deficits and either inflation or higher interest rates in the major developed capitalist countries over recent decades.

DEFICITS AND INVESTOR CONFIDENCE

Orthodox critics of government deficits might concede some of the points argued above, given the lack of empirical evidence linking deficits to either higher inflation or lower profits. Even if these points are conceded, however, critics of government deficits can still raise what is perhaps the most substantial argument regarding the need for governments to exercise fiscal restraint. This is the claim that higher deficits will at some point undermine investor 'confidence' in the policy choices of the offending government. Once the issue is stated as such, the reason for the loss of confidence is ultimately of secondary importance. The proximate cause can be fear over inflation, the alleged crowding out effect of private investment, anxiety over the longer-term threat of higher taxes (this is often a prime issue of concern), or simply a crisis of confidence once some tipping point in the acceptable ratio of total sovereign debt to GDP is breached. Once this point is reached, the result is the well-known sequence that begins when the collapse of confidence triggers capital flight as investors dump the bonds and other investments denominated in the currency of the offending government. Bond prices and exchange rates both plummet. This increases long-term interest rates and, via the depreciation of the exchange rate, increases the prices of imported goods and services.[4] Higher interest rates and rising inflation further undermine confidence, depressing investment. This induces a contraction in employment and output. Capital flight accelerates, leading to even higher inflation. Eventually, the government is forced to boost interest rates to defend the currency and re-attract investment. Once investors are satisfied that the government is sufficiently committed to the principles of 'sound finance' – i.e., fiscal restraint, imposition of limits on social expenditure and wages, and restraint on taxes – capital returns and inflation abates. The restoration of business confidence in turn provides a renewed stimulus to the restoration of a higher rate of investment.

Clearly, the concern over deficits is in large part a question of the confidence creditors have in the policies of the debtor government. Stating matters as such, however, begs the question – confidence in what? We have already seen that a deficit does not directly induce either higher inflation or the crowding out of private investment. Nor is the concern that rising US deficits threaten the spectre of sovereign default. On the contrary, because the US can borrow in its own currency, it can always pay off maturing obligations by simply issuing more dollars. Such is the nature of the seigniorage privilege: any sovereign government can always meet any and all repayment obligations by simply issuing more cheques, provided only that bondholders have 'lent' to this state in the currency of the debtor government. When investors, including foreign central banks, purchase the debt of the US government, capitalists (both foreign and domestic) and central banks have effectively replaced a claim on the Federal Reserve – the banking branch of the US government – with a claim on the Treasury Department – the spending and taxing branch of the central government. When the bond matures, investors can always demand repayment in dollars, thereby re-converting the form of the outstanding liability from the debt of the US central government back into dollar reserves that serve as means of payment on the international market. However, given that these funds (reserves) would generally be reinvested, creditors typically agree to roll over maturing debt at the interest rate then prevailing on the secondary market.

By so agreeing to defer perpetually the point of final settlement, bondholders are in effect granting to the US an open-ended line of credit that, for all practical purposes, can be treated as potentially 'infinite'. If wealthy investors and foreign central banks are going to extend the US an essentially open-ended line of credit, they want to feel assured that the US will not abuse this confidence by acting in ways seen as inimical to their own class interests. Therein lies the *real* source of elite anxiety over deficits. Capital is simultaneously dependent upon and threatened by its own reliance on government deficits and the seigniorage privileges exercised by central governments able to borrow in their own currencies on the international market. On the one hand, government expenditures are essential to sustaining growth and accumulation, and are primary sources of firm's realized profits that are typically either invested in financial instruments or distributed in the form of dividends to households. At the same time, deficits pose a potential threat to capital in revealing the latitude of governments to pursue progressive, even potentially socialist, programmes and initiatives.

There are no technical constraints on the ability of the US government to, for example, allocate an additional $1 trillion to urban reinvestment initiatives over and above existing spending commitments. The US government could institute a policy of full employment by embarking on a publicly led programme of infrastructure investment to create a more environmentally sustainable form of urban development. Further, the latitude of the central government to determine the level and allocation of taxes means that imposing higher taxes on wealthy households can always be used to reduce the deficit. Clearly, any significant redirection of the scale and content of government spending towards expanding social programmes (such as health care and public employment) and the launching of a state-initiated, government-controlled programme of 'green' infrastructure investment would pose significant threats to the major political-economic advances achieved by capitalist owners over the past three decades. This is why any potential expansion of government expenditure that expands benefits to workers will be rigorously policed and resisted.[5]

The debate over the relation between government deficits and 'confidence' must therefore by understood as code for the demand that the US maintain a docile and disciplined workforce, stable prices, a climate favourable to generous and steady yields on financial investments, regulatory forbearance, and restraint on taxes. For global investors, including American finance, confidence is about the demonstrated commitment to preserving the major policy advances achieved by the top tiers of the capitalist class over the last three decades – i.e., financial deregulation and liberalization, reduced taxes, the enhanced power wielded by financial owners over corporate management via mergers and leveraged buyouts, 'free trade' agreements that have pried open formerly protected markets, and an open-ended commitment to socialize losses. Similarly, what is being signalled in statements by the Obama administration regarding its commitment to ensure cost-neutrality of any increase in social spending commitments is a publicly transmitted, ideologically coded discourse regarding the fealty of the US to act as pre-eminent guardian of the dominant propertied interests. Concerns over rising prices, the crowding out of private investment, the 'job-destroying' impact of imposing higher taxes on distributed profits and the capital gains of capitalist households, and the threat posed to long-term prosperity by 'excessive' regulation of Wall Street will all be mobilized as needed to preserve and defend these elite prerogatives.

At root, the debate over the 'acceptable' level of the deficits is about the perceived commitment of the US political class to act as the pre-eminent guardian of the dominant propertied interests. This applies not only to those interests in the US, but insofar as the American state continues to serve capitalism's 'global superintendent', to capitalists headquartered in Japan and Western Europe.[6] Certainly this requires US commitment of military power to insure the security of foreign direct investments, funding for which is rarely the subject of serious constraints due to its effect on public deficits. This was one of the lessons of the Reagan period – the US can readily expand the deficit so long as it does so in a manner congruent with securing and defending the broader, system-wide interests of the most transnationalized sectors of the capitalist class. Hence, the US – particularly under a Democratic administration – must signal its ongoing commitment to uphold corporate and investor rights to markets and profits over and above the social entitlements of popular constituents. It must defend the principle of multilateral 'free trade' agreements that establish the right to own and dispose of foreign assets and repatriate profits without limit. And, perhaps most critical in the current context, the US must demonstrate its commitment, and ability, to balance price control with ongoing access to cheap credit to avert massive devaluation of capital invested in over-valued, over-leveraged circuits of global finance.

CAN INVESTORS PUNISH THE US GOVERNMENT?

The critical link in the claim that the US must limit social expenditures to appease the anxieties of the investor class is the assertion that governments that fail to maintain a sufficiently competitive business environment must contend with the threat of capital flight. Certainly smaller governments, particularly countries that cannot borrow in their own currencies on the international market, face something very akin to veto power over their policies. In relation to the major capitalist states, particularly those that issue currencies that serve as international means of payment and international reserves, matters are more complex. There is a significant disagreement at present regarding the ability of the dollar to sustain its present international reserve currency status.[7] While the dollar's status is certainly in question over the long-term, the fact is that it has no significant challenger at present, and thus will continue to occupy its de facto role as international reserve currency in the coming decade. This implies that there are limits on the degree to which global investors can wield veto power over policy choices solely through the conduit of the private market – i.e., solely through decisions to buy and sell the debt of the US government. We therefore require a more nuanced understanding of the relation between the 'imperatives' of liberalized finance and the policy choices available to governments issuing currencies that serve as international means of payment and reserve store-of-wealth.

What the story of financial liberalization tends to elide is that, while market integration has certainly enhanced the power of mobile finance, capital is equally constrained by the need for an international means of payment required to lubricate the circuits of international trade and finance, and the need for a highly liquid, yield-bearing asset that serves as a 'safe haven' reserve claim-on-wealth. This requirement can be solved in three ways. The first is to constitute the international monetary system on a commodity basis, with gold serving as the standard of value and the ultimate means of international settlement (even if rarely used as such in actual international payments). The second would be a global central bank able to issue and manage an international means of payment organized through a clearing union that would provide countries with some type of drawing rights, subject to various provisions and conditionalities.

The third – and current – arrangement is to constitute the international system on a pure 'fiat money' basis, with the world's dominant state issuing the currency unit that serves as the de facto unit of account (vehicle currency), means of payment, and reserve claim-on-value. While the dollar presently serves as the world's pre-eminent international means of payment, this arrangement is inherently problematic. For one, the dollar, being a non-convertible currency, cannot serve as an *absolute* standard through which the exchanges rates of all other currencies are measured. Nor do payments by US 'residents' (governments, firms, and households) using dollars constitute a means of *final* international settlement, as trade deficits have their corollary in an increase of the aggregate debt of the US to the rest of world. The problem here is not that the US is likely to default on what amounts to a massive – and growing – 'promissory note'. Rather, the issue is that, in the absence of gold convertibility, this massive dollar overhang raises the spectre of devaluation of the purchasing power of the dollar on the international market.[8] The questions thus become: first, why do foreign central banks and global banking corporations presently continue to accept and hold dollars, as opposed to yen or euros; and second, what would undermine such willingness to continue to purchase and hold the debt of the US government?

Foreign demand for the dollar cannot be understood in the way the 'neo-chartalist' (state-based) approach to money would account for demand for dollars inside the US: that is, merely as the expression of the legal capacity to impose taxes and designate the money-unit that must be used by the general public for payment of said taxes owed to the central government.[9] Such powers do not extend outside the territory under the sovereign authority of the central government. Nor does the Federal Reserve have the power to impose reserve requirements on foreign banks. Hence a disjunction arises in a global market environment between the need for an international means of payment and the fact that money-units are still primarily issued and managed on a national-territorial basis. The question remains, therefore, why is the dollar, and the debt of the US government, the world's pre-eminent reserve claim-on-value, as opposed to the yen or the euro?

THE POWER OF THE DOLLAR

Powerful systemic forces continue, for now, to underpin international demand for dollars as means of payment and international reserve. Most obviously, accumulation in much of Europe and East Asia remains inextricably tied to the US market. The dollar is similarly the vehicle currency for the invoicing of the international oil trade. Foreign producers, and central banks, thus have little choice but to continue to accept and accumulate dollars. When foreign central banks recycle dollars back into the US capital account, they do so knowing this tends to lower the long-term US interest rate, supporting US demand for their products and sustaining their exporters' profits. Willingness to hold dollars is the quid pro quo of a symbiotic and mutually beneficial arrangement wherein foreign exporters gain access to the world's largest market while the US is assured that foreigners will continue to purchase Treasury bonds sold on the international market.

The status of the dollar is further buttressed by the still formidable position of the US multinationals, which still continue to control a significant share of international trade and investment. As powerfully argued by Ellen Frank, this creates demand for the home currency, given both the large share of US multinational assets denominated in dollars and the fact that these corporations will prefer to borrow and invoice payments – including the distribution of profits to shareholders – in dollars.[10] Equally critical to the system of market support buttressing the dollar is the power and global reach of Wall Street and the presence of US offshore banking affiliates located in the London-centred Euromarkets. US multinational banks have the distinction of having their 'home' deposit and asset base located within the world's largest domestic market. US banks are positioned in the 'nexus' between the US Treasury and the Federal Reserve, which confers privileged access to the world's deepest and most liquid domestic bond market and, via their offshore affiliates, the London-based Euromarkets. The unrivalled depth and liquidity of the US bond and money market, and the extremely large base of dollar-denominated assets and deposits may be leveraged through the platform provided by the London Euromarkets to expand and consolidate the global reach, and dominance, of American finance.

Despite having been tarnished by the recent crisis, Wall Street continues to define the cutting edge investment strategies for private finance. US investment banks still retain leading positions in international bond underwriting and providing merger and acquisition advice. The centrality of the dollar is further buttressed by the role of hedge funds and private equity firms that collect and manage the savings of the US capitalist class, which constitutes one of the world's largest nationally-based, yet globally-scaled, pools of yield-seeking finance. All these factors position Wall Street as the critical link between the US and the international financial market, thereby reinforcing the role of the dollar as the international reserve currency supported by the sovereign guarantee of the world's most powerful government.

The structural underpinnings of the dollar are further buttressed by the fact that it has no viable challenger at present. It is very clear today how overstated was all the talk of the 'threat' posed to the dollar by the emergence of the euro a decade ago.[11] As Figures II and III in the appendix to this essay show, there has been no fundamental rebalancing of the composition of official foreign reserves away from dollars in favour of euros; indeed, adjusting for changes in the exchange rate, foreign central banks have actually increased their holdings of dollars relative to euros on a unit-for-unit basis.

While diversification of foreign exchange reserves into euros could in principle still take place, multiple factors presently mitigate against the likelihood of the euro and the ECB supplanting the present status of the Treasury-Fed 'complex'. For one, the preference for the dollar reflects, in part, the 'fractured sovereignty' that characterizes the monetary integration of Europe. In the monetary sphere, the EU can, for practical purposes, be regarded as a single country for which the euro serves as money-of-account and means of payment. Control over fiscal policy, by contrast, remains vested at the level of sovereign national governments subject to influence by popular constituents. The result is a structural disarticulation between the procedures that sustain and reproduce the euro as a monetary unit vested within a multinational institution – the ECB – and the national legislative sphere within which governments retain authority over public finances. The ECB thus has no counterpart in the form of a single, nationally-controlled Treasury analogous to the case of the US Treasury-Federal Reserve. Because no single state wields sovereign authority over the territory in which the euro functions as unit of account, the euro lacks the support of a single, unified, and highly liquid sovereign debt market. Hence, we have the anomaly of a single currency unit 'norming' what amounts to a highly fragmented set of sovereign debt markets characterized by very different political and social dynamics.

The euro thus has run into trouble based on what was always a problematic attempt to treat the debt of a small peripheral country like Greece as if it were the same as the debt of the large powerful economies of Germany and France. The terms of the Maastricht Agreement and the founding articles under which the ECB was established attempted to resolve this contradiction by stipulating a rule-based policy framework that inscribed principles of fiscal probity into member countries' public budgets. The fallout of the 2010 Greek crisis has revealed the underlying fissures and weaknesses inherent in the institutional arrangements that support the monetary unification of Europe. Although major European governments did eventually agree to a €750bn bailout package for distressed governments (subject to harsh conditionalities), the decision-making process evidenced a lack of any clear centre of political-economic leadership able to balance defence of rentier-managerial prerogatives with the type of pragmatic adjustments made necessary in times of crisis.

Moreover, the response to the Greek crisis revealed enduring tensions between the major EU governments, particularly divergences in the strategic orientations of the German and French political leadership. Despite shared commitment to the principle that fiscal adjustment must be ultimately be borne by the popular classes through welfare reductions, France's current political leadership is more willing to tolerate higher deficits to provide needed government stimulus. Germany, by contrast, remains Europe's most rigorous adherent to the principle of balanced budgets, for both historical reasons (the lingering memories of hyper-inflation and, more recently, the costs associated with East German integration), and due to the configuration of political forces inside Germany that underpins the unwillingness to be the 'bail-out agent' for greater Europe. This was seen, for instance, in the harsh conditions demanded by the Merkel government for German participation in any member-country bailout, raising questions concerning whether it is feasible to reconcile such ideological adherence to the principle of a balanced budget with the need for a more pragmatic approach to crisis management.[12] This suggests the potential for a chronic, and potentially deepening, crisis of governance that does not bode well for the long-term future of monetary integration in Europe.[13]

Most importantly, European elites share an insistence that social austerity is the only viable longer-term means available for shoring up confidence in the euro. This reveals the degree to which the regulatory architecture of the euro, as currently constituted, embodies a deflationary, profoundly anti-labour, bias. This is perhaps the central social contradiction inherent in the euro project. On the one hand, the euros' status as an international currency rests upon the ongoing commitments of member governments that remain nominally accountable to popular constituents. Conversely, any deepening of the crisis will intensify demands for social and fiscal retrenchment to secure market confidence in the ongoing viability of a united Europe. This policy is not without its dangers. For one, austerity measures can result in a more overt politicalization of public budgets, as they reveal the profoundly pro-rentier, pro-managerialist bias of the underpinnings of the EU-euro project. Moreover, it is difficult to simply annul entitlements to social welfare that reflect long histories of social compromise and class struggle. The class problem, from the vantage point of capitalist owners, is that popular classes can refuse the imposition of austerity and reductions in the living standards required to send the requisite signals of European governments willingness – and capacity – to appease the prerogatives of private finance. If such measures were successfully resisted, this could have equally profound repercussions on international confidence in the current regulatory configuration of Europe.

Whatever the outcome of the current crisis in the Eurozone, what does seem certain is that the underlying weaknesses of the euro will serve to reinforce, at least for the time being, the international reserve currency status of the dollar. Investors are simply unwilling to extend the same confidence never to default that they currently extend to the American government to European states. It is the sovereign debt of the US, not that of Germany or France, which remains the closest thing to a risk-free asset currently traded on the international market. For all these reasons, the euro and debt of the German and French governments are unlikely to usurp the role of the dollar or the debt of the US government as international means of payment and lubricant of the world market.

China potentially represents a more viable long-term threat to established US predominance in the realm of international finance. Much discussion has transpired regarding whether China will eventually ascend to superpower status and challenge the US for global hegemonic dominance. Bracketing for the moment the question of China's long-term ascendance to dominant power status, it is clear that significant obstacles exist to the emergence of the renminbi as a global alternative to the dollar over the next decade. For one, transforming the renminbi into an international reserve currency would require a massive increase in the world renminbi supply. To do so, China would have to run sustained trade deficits, or organize a massive outflow of renminbi on its capital account in the form of renminbi-denominated loans, direct investment, and purchases of financial assets. Further, for the renminbi to function as a major reserve store-of-wealth, China could need to insure the existence of a sufficient stock of renminbi-denominated bonds that would be freely traded on the global market. China would be required to shift to full and free convertibility on its capital account, leaving foreigners free to buy and sell renminbi (and government bonds) in any desired amount. Finally, China would have to instil confidence among international investors regarding the central government's unswerving commitment to liberalization of the capital account backed by a credible commitment to never default.

These conditions are unlikely to be met over the next ten-year period. China's export capital continues to derive significant benefits from undervaluing the renminbi relative to the rate likely to prevail if the renminbi was allowed to freely float on the open market. There is ample reason to anticipate China will move with caution towards full liberalization of its capital account, as doing so would effectively cede control over the long-term interest rate to foreign holders of renminbi-denominated debt. Further, given the renminbi's current lack of reserve status, there are limits on the willingness of foreigners to accept the renminbi as a medium of international settlement. Nor do the Chinese Central Bank and Treasury have the technical and institutional infrastructure in place that is required to manage the renminbi as a reserve currency on an international basis. China's banking sector lacks the vast global reach of the US Treasury/Fed/Wall Street complex, and has no domestic counterpart to the vast liquidity and depth of the US bond market. Chinese banks presently have limited ability to underwrite new issues on the international bond and equity markets, and lack any meaningful institutional presence in the London-based Euromarkets. Nor are foreign investors likely to put the same degree of trust in China's commitment never to default as they presently do in the commitment of the US government. For all these reasons, over the short-to-medium term China has neither the desire nor the capacity to launch the renminbi as a serious international alternative.[14]

Discussions regarding the eventual formation of the East Asian currency union must similarly be evaluated with caution. While East Asia is characterized by deepening trade and investment integration, long-standing tensions in the Sino-Japanese relationship would appear to rule out any near-term currency union.[15] Moreover, China's international standing benefits from continued use of the renminbi as vehicle currency and means of payment in bi-lateral trade agreements. Beijing has to date given little indication of willingness to sacrifice national development goals in the interests of regional unity. Equally importantly, neither Japan nor China possesses the technical capacity at present to establish the full set of market infrastructure and regulatory supports that is a key prerequisite for currency union. In short, East Asia has no counterpart to Germany and the Bundesbank that provided the critical political and technical leadership in forging the terms of monetary integration in Europe.[16] Nor are ASEAN countries likely to opt for full-fledged currency union with China anytime soon, given inevitable Chinese domination of the terms of such unification. While expansion of the Chaing Mai Initiative and Asian Bond Fund will continue to facilitate deepening of regional capital markets, and could thus lay the basis for monetary union, such an eventuality presently appears some way off.

Proposals to shift to an international currency based on some variant of standard drawing rights (SDRs) are largely empty simply because this is not a real possibility at present. Institution of a Keynesian-type 'bancor' unit of account and medium of international settlement would impose severe restrictions on the currency policy prerogatives on the major capitalist governments. Despite floating a proposal for a greater role for SDRs as the medium of international settlement, it is doubtful China would actually accept the terms of such an arrangement. For one, China would be required to allow the renminbi to appreciate to eliminate the surplus on its current account. It would similarly be required to finance the drawing rights of countries running persistent deficits. Clearly the US would never accept such an arrangement. Nor would Japan and Europe elites readily cede control over their exchange rate to a global clearing bank. Recent proposals by the Chinese Central Bank regarding SDRs are in fact a demand that the US safeguard the international value of the dollar that serves as China's basic reference point for managing the price of the renminbi on the global market.

These considerations highlight a critical point. In the absence of a world currency issued by a world central bank, the dollar's status as reserve currency is required to reconcile the need for a global means of payment within an international economy wherein currencies are issued and regulated on an essentially national-territorial basis (the euro being a type of intermediate case). US trade deficits continue to supply the means of payment that lubricate the international circuits of trade and finance. US fiscal deficits supply the basic asset – the debt of the US government – that serves as the pre-eminent store of claims on value convertible on demand into the currency – the dollar- that functions as international means of payment. The credibility of the implicit guarantee to always pay any and all maturing obligations allows the US to issue the IOU that, for all practical purposes, is treated as a nearly risk-free asset on the international market. No other state, including the leading powers of Europe, can offer a similar guarantee at present.

In sum, there are compelling grounds for assuming the dollar will continue to occupy a privileged place in the realm of international finance over the coming decade. Both the self-interest of other leading capitalist states and the systemic need for a viable international means of payment and reserve claim on value will continue, over the near term, to underpin the dollar's reserve role on the international market. Foreign governments will chafe over US abuse of its seigniorage privileges. Concerns will be raised about the long-term viability of this set of international financial arrangements, including threats to shift some portion of world trade away from the dollar. These threats could one day certainly be realized. For now, however, it appears there are no real alternatives to the depth and size of the US securities market and the preeminent positions of Wall Street and London as nerve centres of global finance.

These considerations certainly do not rule out the possibility of a dollar crisis in the coming decade. What they suggest, however, is that other leading governments would intervene to support the dollar in the event of a major currency crisis, galvanizing multilateral support with the spectre of potentially catastrophic global consequences if the Fed was forced to impose higher interest rates to fend off a speculative attack on the dollar. In contrast to the 1979-1985 period, when the Fed was able to use high interest rates to crush organized labour and restore international confidence in the dollar, the US and global economy remains saddled with a staggering level of debt. In the current environment, increasing interest rates would be likely to result in massive asset deflation and plunge the world into deep recession.[17]

All this adds impetus to the demand issuing from the leading sectors of global finance for the US to act as prudent guardian of the prerogatives of the capital-owning class: limit social expenditure, prevent 'excessive' regulation of financial markets, demonstrate continued support for liberalization, and provide de facto blanket guarantees to major banks in the event of a system-level crisis while refusing to contemplate any significant increase in taxes on the incomes and assets of capitalists. Warding off policy initiatives perceived as threats to class power and privilege has assumed renewed urgency given the tarnished legitimacy of the post-1980 model of deregulated, hyper-leveraged finance. Doing so requires constant vigilance to limit debate over the range of policy choices actually available. The powerful evocation of the threat of a dollar crisis is primarily a means of rallying the US population around the need to curtail social expenditures in the name of preserving American financial prerogatives.

A progressive alternative to the current system of dollar-based international finance is certainly needed – nowhere is this truer than in the Global South. In the interim, the left must question 'belt-tightening' arguments that primarily serve the interests of those that occupy the commanding heights of global finance. Rejection of orthodoxy is both analytically sound and a necessary, albeit partial, step in composing an intellectual framework of counter-hegemonic opposition to the still-prevailing neoliberal, pro-market consensus. There are no technical reasons why the US – and other major sovereign governments – cannot sustain significantly higher deficits then at present. Raising taxes on wealth-owning households can be used to reduce deficits over the longer-term, and the policy autonomy of states can be supported through the re-imposition of capital controls – always the ultimate anathema of international finance.

The more general point is that policy choices are never strictly constrained by the impersonal imperatives of globalization or the operation of economic processes at the level of the international market. The rules of international finance are socially constructed, and hence can be changed to serve a very different set of social imperatives and interests. Nor are states constrained by the imperatives of balanced budgets. Certainly in the case of the major sovereign governments, seigniorage privileges allow for implementation of social programmes directly benefiting workers that run counter to the interests of owners. Aspirations for greater economic security, for stable income and employment, and for sustainable long-term infrastructural investment need not be sacrificed at the sacrosanct altar of 'sound finance'. Reclaiming the ideological terrain from the centre-right must begin with a categorical, unequivocal rejection of the orthodox claims concerning the negative impacts of deficits. The real issue at stake is what set of social and class interests are to be served by existing arrangements.

THE LIMITS OF DEFICITS

Arguing that class interests and elite prerogatives, as opposed to the 'laws' of economics, underlie the debate over deficits does not imply that state spending can, in itself, resolve barriers to accumulation rooted in falling rates of profit and persistent underinvestment. Deficits can offset a fall in the rate of return on existing investments insofar as the decline reflects a fall in final demand linked to insufficient private investment. Deficits are far more limited in their ability to offset a deterioration in the supply-side determinants of the rate of profit – i.e., a fall in the output-to-capital ratio not offset by a sufficient increase in the share of profits in total income. Similarly, deficits can, for a time, compensate for a cyclical fall in output and employment. However, without a far more comprehensive socialization of investment, government stimulus is far less able to remedy the longer-term secular decline in the rate of net investment that appears endemic to developed capitalist economies.

This raises the spectre that long-term underaccumulation and higher unemployment leading to higher debt obligations of sovereign governments will define the real nature of any looming sovereign debt crisis. Global investors, including the largest central banks, will either have to adjust to a long-term increase in the acceptable level of sovereign debt that, particularly if tied to expenditures that directly benefit popular constituents, runs counter to ruling interests and prerogatives. Barring this, capitalist owners, via representatives in the major political parties, will have to attempt to impose a wrenching downward adjustment on government budgets. Imposing such reductions will be problematic, given demographic pressures driving higher pension and health care outlays, political resistance to cuts in social insurance by the popular classes and, particularly critical for capitalists, the role of deficits in sustaining profits in the face of faltering rates of net investment.

Of course, those that own and manage the global corporate accumulation apparatus will not agree, solely on the basis of maintaining social cohesion and consensus, to higher taxes on distributed profits. Nor can the US (or Europe) readily shift the burden of adjustment onto the developing world in a manner analogous to the sovereign debt crisis of 1979-89. In short, outside of East Asia, capital in the developed 'core' of North America, Japan, and Western Europe appears to have fewer 'external' options at present for displacing the crisis and creating conditions favourable to the shift toward a more investment-centred regime of development. If so, this suggests that a steady rise in the debt of sovereign governments will be a defining characteristic of the unfolding of any long-term 21st century accumulation crisis.

STRATEGIES FOR THE LEFT

What then are the political and strategic implications for the US left in the coming period? The deep basis of support for the dollar as the basic pivot of global finance, ongoing coordination of policy amongst the major central banks, *and* the lack of a viable alternative to the dollar, all speak to a more flexible policy space than is typically implied in much of the writing on global finance by the left over the last decade. How all these dynamics will play out is impossible to predict. What seems clear, however, is that the level and composition of government budgets will be a critical terrain upon which social forces will seek to advance their opposing interests. This raises the question of how the broadly-defined left can attempt to strategically engage these developments in the coming decade. Clearly, the current balance of forces in unfavourable for advancing a left-progressive, much less socialist, project. But by forcefully rejecting arguments regarding the negative effects typically attributed to government deficits, we can start to carve out a space for developing a challenge to the still-prevailing dominance of the neoliberal, pro-market, hegemonic consensus. The use of deficit expenditure to protect income security and increase direct employment can be linked to calls for reductions in military budgets and higher taxation on capitalist households. Equally critical, it is incumbent on the left in the developed capitalist world to support transformation of the rules governing international finance through capital controls; calls for a global clearing union; an enhanced role for regional development banks to support multilateral trade agreements in the Global South; and arrangements to allow smaller governments to fix repayment of debt in their home currency unit-of-account.[18]

Our ability to press such demands will ultimately depend on the level of political development and independence of popular forces. That is why, to open space for developing an independent left-progressive politics, the first step is to engage in immediate, concrete struggles that provide direct benefits to working-class constituents. At the same time, it is necessary to link such demands to building a broader-based, multi-sector, anti-imperialist, and ultimately anti-capitalist, popular alliance. Obviously, capitalists will rigorously resist any change in existing financial arrangements as constituting infringements upon their by now taken-for-granted power and prerogatives. Such is the terrain of any future political engagement over the level and composition of government budgets. The radical 'kernel' of Keynesian intervention today lies in the contribution it can make to revealing the latitude that contemporary governments have to pursue progressive, potentially socialist, spending initiatives. This can allow socialists to point towards the possibility of a deepening socialization – and democratization – of investment. It is incumbent on us, as radical intellectuals, to reveal how struggles to defend the value of the public sector and to expand public employment in the face of capitalist crises can call forth initiatives that prefigure post-capitalist, potentially socialist, alternatives.

APPENDIX

Figures Ia, b, and c show the annual change in government deficits, the annual inflation rate, and the 10-year interest rate for Japan, Germany and the US respectively. We find no evidence of any relation between higher deficits and inflation. Nor is there any clear link between deficits and the long-term interest rate.

Figure Ia: Japan, 1986-2009

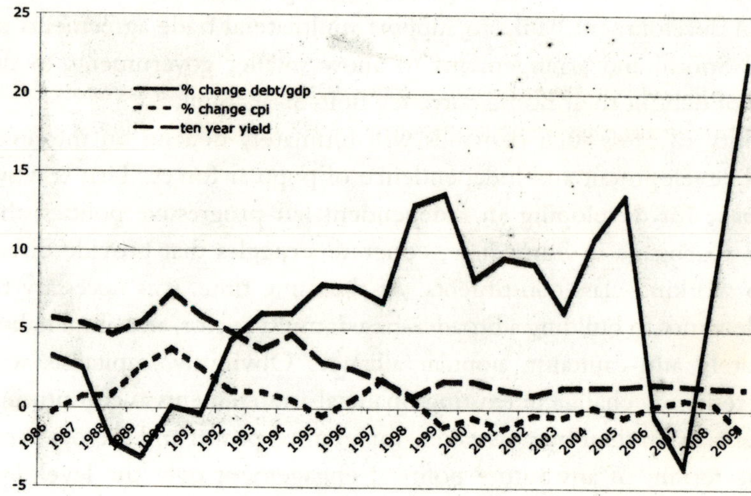

Sources: World Economic Outlook (IMF) and Bank of Japan.

Figure Ib: Germany, 1986-2009

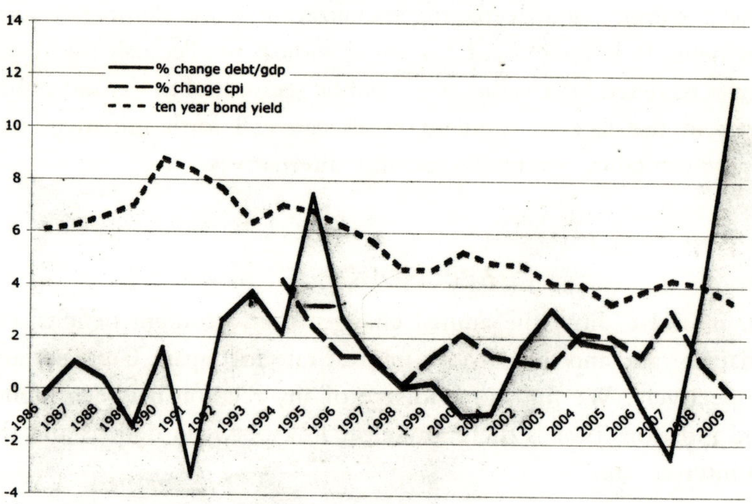

Sources: World Economic Outlook (IMF) and Bundesbank.

Figure Ic: US, 1986-2009

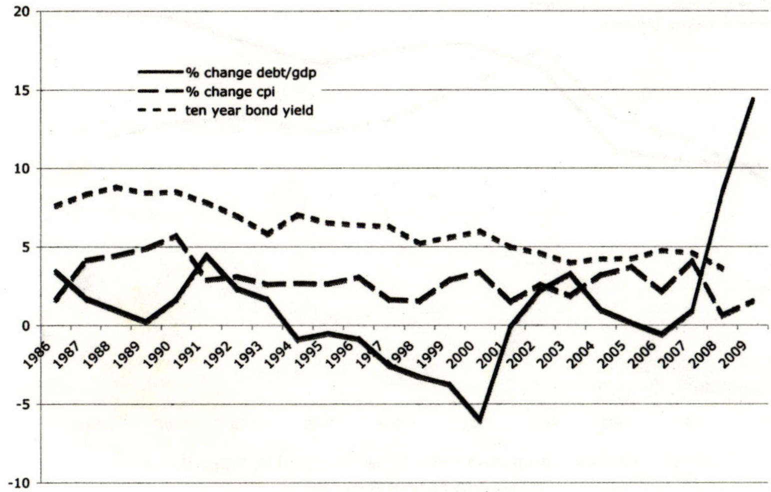

Sources: World Economic Outlook (IMF) and Federal Reserve Bank.

Figure II: Dollar Share of Official Reserves

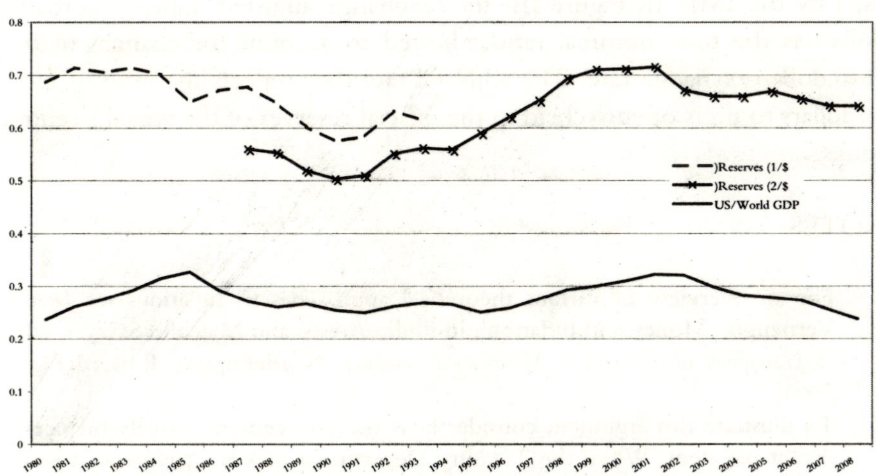

Sources: Currency Composition of Official Foreign Exchange Reserves and World Economic Outlook (IMF).

Figure III: Ratio of Euro/Dollar of Official FX

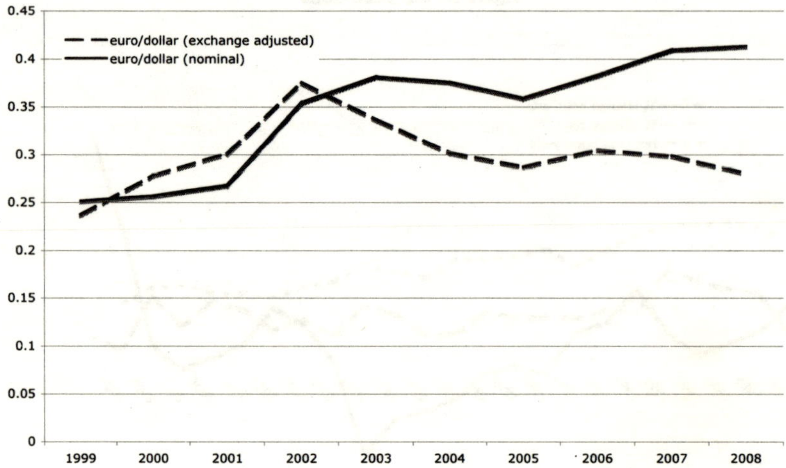

Sources: Currency Composition of Official Foreign Exchange Reserves (IMF) and Federal Reserve.

Note: in Figure II, the two different lines for the percentage of dollars in official reserves are due to different recoding and accounting methodologies used by the IMF. In Figure III, the 'exchange adjusted' ratio of euros to dollars is the total nominal ratio adjusted to account for changes in the euro:dollar exchange rate. The adjusted rate thus reflects the ratio of units of dollars to units of euros held in the official reserves of the world's central banks.

NOTES

1 For an overview of various theoretical approaches to inflation, see Matias Vernengo, 'Money and Inflation', in Philip Arestis and Malcolm Sawyer, eds., *A Handbook of Alternative Monetary Economics*, Northampton: Edward Elgar, 2006.

2 To illustrate this argument consider how the government actually finances a deficit payment. When the Treasury Department makes a payment, it issues a check or, more commonly today, makes a direct electronic deposit into the bank account of the payment recipient. The recipient's bank credits the payee's account, while simultaneously sending a signal to the Federal Reserve informing the central bank of receipt of this Treasury-issued check or electronic deposit. The Fed credits the account held by this bank at the Federal Reserve with reserves of an equal amount. Banks finding themselves in possession of reserves created by the deficit-generated deposit will typically seek to lend these reserves out, primarily on the short-term inter-bank money market at the lending rate set by the Federal Reserve (the federal funds rate). The Fed and

Treasury uses various mechanisms such as open market operation, reverse repo agreements, and payment of interest on deposits held at the Federal Reserve to drain liquidity from the inter-bank money market, thus allowing the inter-bank market to clear at the target rate set by the Federal Reserve. See Randall Wray, *Understanding Modern Money: The Key to Full Employment and Price Stability*, Northampton: Edward Elgar, 1998, pp. 74-94.

3 See Michal Kalecki, *Theory of Economic Dynamics: An Essay on Cyclical and Long-Run Changes in Capitalist Economy*, London: Allen and Unwin, 1954, pp. 11-27; Alain Lipietz, *The Enchanted World: Inflation, Credit, and the World Crisis*, London: Verso, 1985, pp. 107-129; Augusto Graziani, *The Monetary Theory of Production*, Cambridge: Cambridge University Press, 2003, pp. 96-113.

4 This is the channel through which a crisis of confidence triggered by deficits can lead to higher prices, appearing to confirm claims that deficits cause inflation. It is necessary, however, to distinguish between direct effects of government deficits on money supply and prices and a rise in prices due to a decision to punish the offending government,

5 For a class analysis of the neoliberal project, see Gérard Duménil and Dominique Lévy, *Capital Resurgent: Roots of the Neoliberal Revolution*, Cambridge: Harvard University Press, 2004; David Harvey, *A Brief History of Neoliberalism*, Oxford: Oxford University Press, 2005; and Greg Albo, Sam Gindin, and Leo Panitch, *In and Out of Crisis: the Global Financial Meltdown and Left Alternatives*, Oakland: PM Press, 2010.

6 Leo Panitch and Sam Gindin, 'Superintending Global Capital', *New Left Review* 35, 2005.

7 Radical analyses of enduring strength are found in Leo Panitch and Sam Gindin, 'Finance and American Empire' in *Socialist Register 2005*; and Ellen Frank, 'The Surprising Resilience of the U.S. Dollar', *Review of Radical Political Economics*, 35(3), 2003. For a more pessimistic view see Giovanni Arrighi, 'Hegemony Unraveling – I', *New Left Review*, 32 2005 and 'Hegemony Unraveling – II', New *Left Review,* 33, 2005. Orthodox sceptics include Barry Eichengreen, *Global Imbalances and the Lessons of Bretton Woods*, Cambridge: MIT Press, 2007; and Fred Bergsten, 'The Dollar and Deficits', *Foreign Affairs*, 88(6), 2009.

8 This contradiction is inherent in the use of a non-convertible fiat money possessed of a relative value as the de facto international unit of account and means of payment. See David McNally, 'From Crisis to World Slump: Accumulation, Financialisation, and the Global Slowdown', *Historical Materialism*, 17(2), 2009.

9 Pavlina Tcherneva, 'Chartalism and the Tax-driven Approach to Money', in Philip Arestis and Malcolm Sawyer, eds., *A Handbook of Alternative Monetary Economics*, Northampton: Edward Elgar, 2006.

10 Frank, 'The Surprising Resilience of the U.S. Dollar'.

11 David N. Gibbs, 'Washington's New Interventionism', *Monthly Review*, 53(4), 2001; and Barry Eichengreen, *The Dollar and the New Bretton Woods System*, 2004, available at www.econ.berkely.edu.

12 See Adam Tooze, 'The Message From Berlin that Europe Failed to Grasp', *Financial Times*, 5 May 2010; and Quentin Peel, 'Merkel Struggles to Justify the

Deal at Home', *Financial Times*, 12 May 2010.

13 Arrangements between the ECB and member governments functioned to undermine the ability of smaller countries such as Greece to offer credible guarantees not to default. Further, the Articles limit access to overdraft accounts by member governments with unfunded deficits – i.e. debits in these government's accounts held at the regional central banks that have not been redeemed through the sale of new securities on the capital market. Moreover, the Articles of the European Central Bank appeared to forbid central bank direct purchases of newly issued government debt - although this was finally ignored as the crisis worsened through the spring of 2010.

14 Bilateral trading arrangements using the renminbi, not the dollar, as vehicle currency and means of payment, if eventually linked to the growing presence of Chinese banks on the international market, could lay the basis for the full liberalization of China's capital account. This could, over time, transform China's role as provider of liquidity to the world market.

15 The US has exploited Japanese anxiety over China's global re-emergence through security arrangements that integrate Japan into the umbrella of a regional US-led protectorate. The effect is to drive a wedge between any possible China-Japan rapprochements that would be a necessary prerequisite to the construction of a framework of consensual regional leadership outside the US imperial orbit. China's pursuit of an independent defence policy similarly rules out any move towards more comprehensive regional integration along lines similar to that which occurred in Europe under the aegis of the NATO compact.

16 See Injoo Sohn, 'East Asia's Counterweight Strategy: Asian Financial Cooperation and Evolving International Monetary Order', G-24 Discussion Paper No. 44, UNCTAD, Geneva, March 2007.

17 To reiterate – the dollar is not immune from a crisis of confidence. Because the dollar does not constitute a stable monetary standard, an international disturbance could well occur in the coming decade. Rather, the argument here is that there are no technical constraints on the US ability to run higher deficits at present, nor is there an objective 'tipping point' when the debt-to-GDP ratio becomes structurally unsustainable. The dollar's future will be determined by international geo-politics and class struggle, not by immutable 'laws' of economics. Further, global capital has no exit strategy or alternative, which is why other major governments and central banks would support the dollar in the event of a crisis.

18 See Jane de Arista, 'U.S. Debt and Global Imbalances', *International Journal of Political Economy,* 36(4), 2007-8.

FROM RESCUE STRATEGIES TO EXIT STRATEGIES: THE STRUGGLE OVER PUBLIC SECTOR AUSTERITY

GREG ALBO AND BRYAN EVANS

The ongoing drama of the global financial crisis has continually shuffled lead characters and taken unexpected turns in plot. It opened as a liquidity crisis in exotic high-risk sub-prime mortgages concentrated in speculative urban development projects in the US in mid-2007. But by fall 2008, it had evolved into a general solvency crisis for the American and British financial systems with the startling collapses of Lehman Brothers, Black Rock, AIG and many other bed-rock financial institutions. The possibility of systemic financial contagion erupting could not be ruled out of bounds. Indeed, in the whirl of financial turbulence, smaller countries on the northern periphery of Europe – and almost immediately in Ireland, whose 'Celtic Tiger' economic model had partaken in all the hype about the efficacy of liberalized financial market – began to suffer wholesale collapses of their banking systems and severe economic slowdowns. From there, the freezing up of money markets from the panicked de-leveraging of financial institutions and corporate borrowers across the core capitalist countries meant that new investment and global trade collapsed. By 2009, the financial crisis had mutated into a general economic contraction with no corner of the world market untouched.

The massive 'rescue strategies' to stop the death spiral of collapsing markets that followed – backstopping mortgage markets, injecting capital into bank's balance sheets, and radical shifts in monetary and fiscal policies toward expansionary positions – retrieved emergency forms of state intervention not seen for decades. As a consequence, government budgetary positions moved sharply into deficit over 2009-10; they are forecast to remain in the red for the foreseeable future. In the space of three years, the largest financial crisis in history had morphed into an unparalleled crisis of the public sector.

In countries on the southern European periphery, deemed to be suffering from structural problems of competitiveness and under the straightjacket of EU restraints on activist industrial policies, a full-blown sovereign debt crisis erupted, with Greece the focal point.

The public sector crisis is now taking concrete form in the planning and implementation of so-called 'exit strategies' from the emergency fiscal measures to offset the demand shocks from the crisis. Although there remain serious concerns over the pace of return to the neoliberal orthodoxy of balanced budgets in the midst of still stagnant economies, calls for public sector austerity are coming from both the political right and social democratic parties. But the key agitators are the international agencies co-ordinating global capitalism – the IMF, OECD and the EU, with the gatherings of the G20 playing a crucial facilitating role. As the central apparatus charged with financial matters, and with a long record of monitoring and imposing the disciplines of neoliberal policies on national states, the IMF has gone so far as to suggest that two decades of 'fiscal adjustment' – read long-term austerity – might well be in order as an appropriate 'debt stabilization strategy'.[1]

In 2010 the crisis entered a new phase of intense political struggle over which classes will pay for the exit strategy. Given the sheer variety of exit strategies and the uneven forms of resistance being waged, this essay begins by offering a general perspective on the politics of austerity in the current conjuncture, analyzing the nature of struggle over public sector cuts, including what it means for a further neoliberal restructuring of the state in the core capitalist countries. It will then undertake an examination of the political conflict over exit strategies in four key cases – the US, the UK, Ireland and Greece. Finally, it will turn to reflect on the overall political terrain for public sector fronts of resistance to the cuts.

EXIT STRATEGIES AND NEOLIBERALISM

There has been a great deal of confusion about state policy during the crisis. The most common interpretation, even in many Marxist accounts, has been to suggest that states initially rediscovered Keynesianism and recovered power vis-à-vis markets as part and parcel of their rescue strategies to control market instabilities; but now the state is regressing and losing power as it implements neoliberal strategies of austerity at the insistence of financial markets. Posed in this way, the analysis is quite misleading. It leaves the impression that the move to fiscal austerity represents a weakening of the state relative to market actors, and current political struggles need to be oriented toward re-establishing a 'strong state' to sustain the stimulus measures and to ensure that a regulatory regime to 'repress' finance is adopted. State intervention cannot be gauged by the level of expenditures or size of fiscal deficit; by no means are these direct indices of the capacity for intervention into the economy. In particular, they tell us nothing about the form the interventions take, the kinds of class strategies being advanced, and what alternate strategies must confront. The politics of the cuts need to be assessed, not in the crude terms of more state or more market, but with respect to state power and market disciplines, their political viability and class strategies.[2] The overall aim of economic policy is always to uphold the general conditions for capital accumulation; and it does so by ensuring labour-power is available for exploitation and that capitalist control over money and credit creation is maintained.[3] This requires the establishment of specific market and financial disciplines that constrain both the state and market actors. These disciplines are the indirect effect of general policy frameworks, budgetary decisions and modes of administration.

In the current crisis, the economic policies deployed in both rescue and exit strategies have been designed to stabilize and sustain a liberalized financial system. This crucial parameter for state policy has been from the outset, first, that the private banking system be salvaged and sustained, irrespective of how much 'moral hazard' this causes; and second, that systematic restructuring of the financial sector as a whole be avoided if at all possible. Since the crisis was triggered by the massive volume of debt that could not be absorbed within the private financial system, this always meant 'socializing' bad loans by the state taking them on, whether by 'stranding' the debt on the balance sheets of central banks, or by taking the bad debt directly into the public accounts, or by temporary nationalizations. (The full public ownership of the banking system has, of course, been ruled out of the bounds of acceptable policy options, even if the case had popular appeal and strong theoretical backing.)[4] As in past financial crises, the crucial policy questions have turned around 'distributional conflicts': the 'haircut' that the financial sector would take for the bad loans and the new taxes they might face; the distribution of the public debt burden between taxes and long-term bond flotation; and the allocation of cuts between state activities.[5]

The instability of the recovery in 2010 is very much related to the precarious balance sheets of a great many banks, as new 'stress tests' still suggest a great deal of weakness. Market disciplines in the financial sector are, therefore, only slowly being re-imposed. Many of the emergency state measures for the financial sector have remained in place, with the astonishingly low interest rates for borrowing from central banks and the associated loose monetary policy being the most visible, and yet banks continue to be reluctant to lend. This has shaped a crucial component of the general exit strategy of avoiding government writedowns of private bank debts. The financial sector is seen as simply not able to accommodate the banks fully paying up. Whatever 'haircuts' may at some time be negotiated with the financial sector, particularly for some of the more desperate cases of sovereign default risks, this is not remotely a general policy orientation for the capitalist core as a whole.[6] On the contrary orthodox banking precepts are being resuscitated especially in the financial markets which rate, buy and sell government bonds, to reassert the pre-eminence of financial disciplines over government finances.[7]

But it is a complete nonsense to see this in terms of some objective measure of a state 'living beyond its means'. It is the product of a particular ruling-class strategy to impose austerity on the working classes and on the public sector to pay for the financial crisis. It arises from the reassertion of the financial and market disciplines of neoliberalism. In contrast to everyday perceptions, the exit strategies represent a powerful and interventionist economic policy on the part of capitalist states to try to restore 'market regulation', very much along the lines of the always extensive state intervention and regulation to this end throughout the neoliberal era, as well as to reproduce, more generally, the political relations that have constituted capitalist states in this era.

The attempt to return to neoliberal financial disciplines is reasserting a further distributional dynamic that is framing the exits to austerity. The payment of debt is partly to come out of tax revenues from growth resulting from the driving up of exports via attacking the wage and regulatory components of unit labour costs. It is also to occur from a net transfer from the state sector, drawn from income support programmes, the incomes of public employees and public asset sales, to the capitalist sector through debt and interest payments, in the context of an overall decline in the level of government expenditures. The consequences of this fiscal strategy is quite transparent: the working classes, directly through wage repression to boost international competitiveness, and indirectly through tax increases and public sector cuts, should pay for the crisis and for the restoration of the economic viability of capitalist control over the financial system.

This logic is embedded in the concrete forms that fiscal strategies for the state sector are taking. In aggregate, the neoliberal 'golden rules' for limits on government borrowing over the business cycle are being restated as the overarching budgetary guideline. In practice, this translates into deficit and debt targets in the transition to austerity. Following positions already emerging in the EU and from IMF advisories, the Toronto G20 communiqué forwarded targets (with some variations for different countries and zones) of cutting budgetary deficits in half by 2013, and phasing in reduction of gross debt as a per cent of GDP by 2016.[8] In terms of taxation, the exit strategies are consistent with core neoliberal positions: an emphasis on shifting the burden of taxes away from capital toward workers, with the weight of tax increases skewed toward VAT taxes; and the only modest efforts at financial taxes are often negated by plans for further corporate tax cuts. Nowhere does an exit strategy advance anything like a systematic 'crisis tax' levied on accumulated wealth and high incomes.

A reorganizing of state apparatuses is also evident in the strengthening of neoliberal administrative modes and the primacy given to 'cuts' across all branches of the state. Fiscal control is often taking the form of a 'specialized administrative apparatus' such as the British 'Office for Budget Responsibility',[9] to oversee the cuts, with special sanction enforced by the state executive and a capacity to probe departmental budgets. Such bodies bear some resemblance to the review boards and commissions set up in the first phase of neoliberalism in the 1980s.[10] But not only are the current cuts more severe, there are some important administrative differences. The new fiscal control apparatuses are being given greater powers over departments; tend to be more insulated from parliamentary oversight; have greater freedom to bypass public sector unions and challenge collective agreements; and are mandated to explore asset sales, commercialization and other modes of administration of policies. Given President Obama's difficulties with Congress, especially significant in this respect was his establishment in 2010 of the National Commission on Fiscal Responsibility and Reform, followed by his appointment as the new director of the White House Office of Management and Budget of Clinton's old budget director, Jack Lew (whose main qualification was having brokered deals with Republicans in Congress when Clinton 'ended welfare as we know it').

A number of characteristic neoliberal administrative norms go along with such enhanced capacities for fiscal control.[11] The bulk of deficit reduction is to come from expenditure cuts as opposed to tax increases; public sector wage freezes or cuts are to be directly legislated if concessions cannot be negotiated; government employment levels are to be lowered via layoffs, contracting-out, flexibilizing the labour process and even mass off-shoring of work; pension plans for public employees are to be constrained; and cuts are to be implemented such that the branches of the state supporting welfare, public education and cultural activities are disproportionately rolled-back, while departments facilitating accumulation are marginally hit, and the coercive apparatuses largely maintain their budgets.

The Toronto G20 communiqué boasted that '[w]hile the global economic crisis led to the sharpest decline of trade in more than seventy years, G20 countries chose to keep markets open to the opportunities that trade and investment offer'. And now 'fiscal consolidation plans... are essential to sustain recovery, provide flexibility to respond to new shocks... and avoid leaving future generations with a legacy of deficits and debt'.[12] The political tensions over the pacing of the exits were given expression in the G20's contradictory call for 'growth-friendly fiscal consolidation' – too much austerity could damage the recovery, and yet a failure to cut deficits could harm growth and investor confidence. This unwieldy compromise reflects deeper contradictions in the politics which have underpinned neoliberalism and in the global coordination of the world market.

From its origins, the neoliberal project has rested upon raising the rate of exploitation, a massive restructuring and internationalization of capital, and financialization. State power and administration were reformed to sponsor and reinforce these particular market imperatives. The transformations re-established capitalist profitability, but raised problems of realisation of the increased value being produced. This contradiction figured at the national level in increased social inequalities with the over-consumption of the highest income strata on the one hand, and the resort to higher levels of debt by the working classes to try to sustain relative living standards on the other. At the level of the world market, with all countries driven by this 'competitive austerity' to export-led growth, the US acted as consumer of last resort, aided by the role of the dollar in currency markets and the depth and inventiveness of its credit markets. The austerity strategies being adopted, as many Keynesian and Marxist critics rightly point out, are designed to cause a further decline in the wage share and further reliance on export-led growth, with the sources of new net effective demand quite uncertain, except to return to the same credit markets and US imbalances that laid the conditions for the financial crisis.

The spectrum of conservative and social democratic parties adopting some form of austerity strategy has been all but encompassing. Moreover, the inertia in the political alignments in the capitalist core has a parallel in the international correlation of forces. In the wake of the crisis, an unprecedented degree of coordination between states sprang forward in the expanded form of the G20 Washington meeting of 2008 and agreement on a global fiscal stimulus. But the austerity exits have again raised the quandary of rebalancing the world market between surplus and deficit zones in international trade. This is a dilemma that has spanned the neoliberal epoch, and bred competitive rivalries in the world market. The uncertainty of how to resolve this contradiction reflects underlying national political arrangements and class alliances re-enforced by neoliberal policies. It underlies the distinct possibility of a long period of stagnation, and the IMF's prognosis of permanent austerity for the public sector.

Three points of dissent, raised by Keynesian critics in particular, continue to receive attention – the timing of the exits in the business cycle, their emphasis on structural adjustment, and the lack of significant adjustment of global imbalances. The three criticisms are clearly linked, all pivoting around a stampede to the exit before the crisis has fully receded and new sources of accumulation and world demand have appeared. First, the fear of 'inappropriate timing' is that the move to exit strategies in monetary and fiscal policies may be too soon, given the fragility of the recovery. Since the loan portfolios and reserve positions of banks have yet to fully stabilize and private investment remains insufficient to drive a new round of accumulation, there plainly are substantial risks of a slide back into recession unless fiscal stimulus is maintained. Second, it is argued that the exit strategies rely too extensively on wage and labour market flexibility and cuts in social transfers, while mobilizing extensive resources for the financial sector. The effort to re-establish the pre-eminence of monetary policy and interest rates in economic regulation comes with the cost of a huge asymmetry in the distributional burden of the exit.

Finally, the turn to austerity is seen as far too uncoordinated, with the large export zones, Germany in the EU and China in East Asia especially, cutting back from fiscal stimulus in a way that leaves, in aggregate, the world market in the exact place before the crisis began – still far too dependent on the battered US consumer markets. Indeed, current debate looks like nothing so much as the discussions of a 'rotating Keynesianism' between the triad of the US, Germany and Japan from the mid-1970s through the 1980s. The dilemma, then as now, is of breaking from the US as 'consumer of last resort', and a realignment of the quasi-fixed exchange rates between the US dollar, the Euro and, now, the Yuan. Led by Germany, the EU zone has converted to austerity and weak internal demand (compounded by the structural current account surpluses of Germany), a weaker Euro and export competitiveness; while East Asia remains too locked into its own export-oriented development models to cope with problems of surplus capacity, enormous labour reserves and 'weak' internal demand. The US, for its part, is calling for a quite implausible doubling of its exports as a central part of its policies for fiscal sustainability. There is indeed every reason to suggest a return to the global imbalances that existed before the crisis, but in much more adverse, inferior conditions.[13] This lies behind the cautions of the Obama Administration at the Toronto G20, and especially its criticisms directed at Germany and China that they were not doing enough to assist in global rebalancing in pulling back on stimulus and realignment of currencies. And they are the basis of concerns – and often alarm – of a range of liberal and left economists that the austerity exits may well engender a collapse into a 'third depression'.[14]

Yet given the current class configurations, the political viability of a 'centre-left' alternative of a government-led Keynesian stimulus as the basis for building an alternative to neoliberalism is, at best, tenuous. For a period after the onset of the crisis, increased government spending could be funded by borrowing and a loose monetary policy, but it was always clear that eventually there would have to be a turn to taxation and struggles over distribution. With all the exit strategies rejecting a 'repression' of finance, the capacity to tax the capitalist class is further eroded by attempts to increase 'international competitiveness'. The taxation demands also compete with attempts to increase private investment, and also run up against fears they will add to the constraints on consumption from the de-leveraging of household debt and declining incomes. Yet the even less ambitious project of supporting an alternate fiscal policy through a strategy of 'shared austerity', of spreading the work and taxing the working class to sustain the public sector while allowing overall inequalities to increase, is no less tenuous. It depends upon holding a very large political coalition together, anchored in broad sections of the working classes. The main political struggles from below are primarily directed at alleviating the worst impacts of austerity, without for the most part advancing strategies to take on other, more ambitious, objectives.

The political coalitions supporting neoliberal austerity have been remarkably resilient, with the social democratic left failing to advance an alternate coalition and programme. It is difficult to identify a case where the financial crisis has led to a crisis in the power bloc – between finance and industry, between big and small capitals, between regional centres – apart from forwarding alternate tactical agendas. It is equally hard to uncover systematic differences in approach between conservative, liberal and social democratic governments beyond the subtleties that have marked neoliberalism out from social liberalism.[15] Even in the European peripheries, where general strikes have broken out across the spring and summer of 2010, there has not been anything approaching a parliamentary crisis from political deadlock, or a crisis in the social democratic parties, amidst the passage of radical austerity packages.

THE CUTS AND PUBLIC SECTOR STRUGGLES

The United States: one-sided class war

While the US has not suffered the worst effects of the economic crisis spawned by its own financial sector, it has been at the centre of the global financial crisis. US GDP fell from a pre-crisis growth rate of 2.7 per cent in 2007 to a -2.4 per cent rate by the end of 2009. From its 2007 level of 4.6 per cent, unemployment shot up through 2009, and by May 2010 the national unemployment rate had reached 9.7 per cent. When the level of underemployment is included, what Americans call 'The Great Recession' had hit over 17 per cent of the US labour force with various degrees of 'measured' unemployment.[16]

The massive $800 billion Federal stimulus program, in the form of the American Recovery and Reinvestment Act of 2009 launched by the Obama Administration, has generated heated debate over how much it contributed to the burden of public debt as part of the US recovery strategy.[17] But even this level of federal state expenditure (in which the stimulative stance was designed to be sustained through 2010) could not offset the extensive cutbacks at the state level, which various estimates suggest actually pushed the national economy to contract by 0.5 per cent of GDP in 2009. From the outset of the crisis, American budgetary politics have been focused equally on the battles over austerity at the state level (and, in turn, the budgetary cuts of US cities, where radical new experiments in market modes of administration are emerging). This is occurring before anything like the American exit to austerity at the national level has been clarified.

Since the summer of 2008, 231,000 state and local government jobs have been lost and it is projected that at least a further 900,000 public and private sector jobs could be lost if the fiscal crisis gripping America's subnational governments is not arrested. No less than 33 states are still facing budget shortfalls of 20 per cent or more in 2010; and all states combined are running an aggregate deficit of 30.2 per cent of total budgetary requirements.[18] Even a brief tally of the public sector carnage is disquieting: as many as 25 states are in the process of cutting support to primary and secondary education; 34 states are cutting support to state owned colleges and universities; 26 states have implemented hiring freezes; 13 states have begun laying off workers; and 22 states have cut public sector wages and salaries.[19]

The last thirty-years of American history can all too easily be characterized as a one-sided class war where the ruling class has strolled from victory to victory, amidst the political and ideological disorganization of the working class. As a consequence, the degree of polarization in American incomes has been shocking. A recent analysis of data from the Congressional Budget Office found that over the period 1979 to 2007 the concentration of income in the top 1 per cent of American households moved to the greatest level it has been since 1928, driven by dramatic growth in the after-tax incomes of America's wealthiest households.[20] Between 1992 and 2007 alone the income of the top 400 households grew by an astonishing 476 per cent, not least due to a dramatic one-third decline in the tax rate on the wealthiest, while median family after-tax income rose by only 13.2 per cent.[21] But even such modest income 'growth' between 1992 and 2007 appears robust in comparison to the decline in per capita income by 2.6 per cent on average between 2008 and 2009. In California, Connecticut, New York, Arizona, Nevada, Wyoming, Texas, Florida, Georgia, and Minnesota, the decline exceeded 3 per cent.[22]

Despite rising unemployment, state cutbacks and a trade union movement cowered by the depth of the crisis, there have been a few notable examples of resistance. This has been especially so in California, where the fiscal crisis is particularly acute, the assault on public services most aggressive, and where Republican Governor Arnold Schwarzenegger's proposed $12.4 billion in cuts will result in the loss of 331,000 jobs (perversely, the largest number of these are in health and human services programmes that bring in federal matching funds).[23] What initially sparked the mobilization of resistance was a decision by the University of California to raise tuition fees by 32 per cent. Public sector unions, and particularly those representing teachers, have been at the forefront of attempting to build a common front of resistance to austerity. Besides unions, the front has included a wide range of community and immigrant groups, as well as an extensive range of users of public services. With access to post-secondary education narrowing, questions of class, race and gender – especially of hard-hit Afro-American communities and increasingly politicized Latinos – have been a crucial dimension to the struggle. An unprecedented coalition of students and workers was forged to counter the attacks on affordable higher education. This included large scale organizing of marches, teach-ins, strikes, and building occupations. There are, as well, some inklings of a political agenda that goes beyond labour economism to entertain a more transformative politics.

The attack on public education moved the California Federation of Teachers (CFT) to organize a 'March 4 Day of Action' in 2010 that mobilized teachers and allies across California to picket and express opposition to cuts to education and other public services. The following day the 'March for California's Future' began a 48 day, 250-mile journey to the state capital of Sacramento. The CFT understood the need to build a broader coalition and was joined by the Service Employees International Union (SEIU), the American Federation of State, County and Municipal Employees (AFSCME) and ACCE (Alliance of Californians for Community Empowerment – previously ACORN). The objective of the march was popular education seeking to clarify for the general public what forces and past decisions caused the budget crisis, develop an understanding of the effect of budget cuts on all Californians, and identify alternative solutions, including the need for progressive tax policy.

A new campaign and coalition, the *Fight for California's Future*, led by the CFT, seeks to extend resistance struggles to cuts in social services, health care, and community amenities such as public parks.[24] What has been emerging through the struggle is a more ambitious agenda across many sectors of the movement: broadening the social wage to include free public education – pre-school through to and including post-secondary; a restoration of all public sector cuts and an expansion of public services; full citizenship rights for immigrants; among others. Also, the March 4 Day of Action went beyond California, with students, teachers and union activists in 32 states participating in demonstrations against austerity measures.[25]

The most promising union campaigns in the US have been those which sought to broaden their appeal by speaking to issues and struggles of all working-class people – organized and unorganized – by politicizing and transforming the legalistic confines of North American collective bargaining systems. Yet, as inspiring as many of these examples of public sector common fronts of resistance to date are, they tend too often to be isolated, sporadic and without a full political understanding or organizational depth to confront what they are up against. As a result, the best examples of militant community organizing, such as POWER in San Francisco or the Miami Workers Center, tend to be concentrated in particular communities in urban centres, without any comparable state-wide or national presence. The fidelity to the Democratic Party still prevails among much of the union leadership and progressives, though it is now threadbare as a constructive alliance, and has lost its grip over much of the rank-and-file workforce. Bill Fletcher has expressed the impasse of US labour well: 'Our unions suffer from a profound conservatism, a failure to recognize the kinds of changes that are going on, and therefore our need for a visionary movement.'[26] It is this kind of insight into what ails US labour that activists elsewhere also need to pay heed to.

Britain: bettering Thatcherism

Even before the financial crisis materialized in 2007, Britain's New Labour Government had been endeavouring to eliminate public sector jobs and cap pay. In the depths of the crisis in 2009, and even as GDP contracted by nearly 5 per cent and projections for 2010 foresaw an anemic 1.2 per cent growth rate, the Gordon Brown government announced that contributions to public sector pensions would be cut by £1 billion per year through to 2011 and public sector pay increases would be yet further constrained to 1 per cent (on the assumption that inflation was growing faster).[27] These initial steps were meant to control a fiscal deficit that had shot up to 11.3 per cent of GDP in 2009 (with gross debt at 72.3 per cent of GDP). In the first quarter of 2010, the number of unemployed in Britain surpassed 2.5 million, the highest since 1994, pushing the national unemployment rate to 8 per cent, and in some regions to as high as 14 per cent.[28] When during the 2010 election campaign, Gordon Brown argued that Tory proposals for immediate and massive public sector cuts would risk a depression, this was at odds with what his Chancellor of the Exchequer, Alistair Darling, had stated just weeks before the election was called, when he seemingly boasted that Labour's planned exit to austerity included public spending cuts that would be 'deeper and tougher' than Thatcher's cuts of the 1980s.[29]

On May 24, 2010, the new Conservative Chancellor of the Exchequer, George Osborne, introduced the first phase of the new Conservative-Liberal Democrat coalition government's programme of public expenditure austerity with the promised cuts that appeared to top Darling's reactionary boast. The cuts fell disproportionately on education, employment programmes, child trust funds and transfers to local government. The first casualties were to be an estimated 30,000 to 60,000 public sector workers who would pay for the speculation of British bankers with their jobs.[30] This was followed by the June 22 budget, which set out to reduce permanently public expenditure by £32 billion per year until 2014-15 and to reduce public sector borrowing from 4 per cent of GDP in 2009-10 to 1.1 per cent by 2015-16.[31] As a consequence, public sector employment is forecast to fall by at least 500,000 to 600,000 positions over the period of austerity.[32] Treasury analysis of the 'dis-employment' effect of the budget leaked to *The Guardian* suggested that unemployment could rise by 1.3 million.[33]

The punitive austerity of the new government has been enthusiastically greeted not only by City of London bond traders but also by the Confederation of British Industry: 'Just as private sector firms had to take strong action to cut costs during the recession, so too must the public sector. We believe there is still considerable scope to make even greater savings by re-engineering public service delivery.'[34] For the CBI, public pensions are unsustainable, a lower minimum wage for youth and apprentices is required, and the public sector workforce needs to be subjected to the flexibilization strategies that have worked so well for the profitability of business, reflecting the British Chambers of Commerce's consistent contention that the UK is 'becoming increasingly uncompetitive due to the rising cost of labour'.[35]

Britain's ruling class has been thoroughly cohesive in seizing the opportunity to turn a crisis of financial capitalism into a crisis of the public sector and an unprecedented challenge to public sector workers. The British union and working-class movements have proven much less capable, and certainly far more fragmented and divided, in response. In part, this is explained by an enduring commitment to the Labour Party despite a decade of 'New Labour' government which took up where Thatcher left off, and often went a few steps further with respect to the marketization and privatization of public services.

Notwithstanding the defensive politics of the Trade Union Congress, public sector workers have been at the forefront of resisting public sector austerity. All the main unions in the public sector have been engaged in a myriad of campaigns and fronts to defend workers and public services. This was already highlighted by the first national strike by teachers in 21 years in early 2008, followed a few months later by the two largest unions in the UK – Unison and Unite – leading 500,000 local government workers in England, Wales and Northern Ireland in a two-day industrial action. In another example, since 2007 workers at the Royal Mail, represented by the Communication Workers Union (CWU), have contended with efforts to flexibilize their work through contracting out, expanded use of part-time work, and the application of new technologies. In September 2009, a strike ballot won more than 75 per cent of votes in favour of industrial action and set in motion a series of nation-wide actions that lasted through to March 2010, when an agreement was reached with important job security commitments won (but the new coalition government will now revive New Labour plans to partially privatize Royal Mail).[36] And under the militant leadership of Mark Serwotka, the Public and Commercial Services Union has led a series of strikes against austerity since 2004, including twice bringing out more than 200,000 workers in March 2010.

These have all been, notably, sectoral struggles by unions that have not been able to break through to new levels and forms of class struggle. The People's Charter for Change launched in March 2009 by a coalition of leading figures on the left of the Labour Party and the broader left (including Tony Benn, Ken Loach, Billy Bragg, Suresh Grover, Peter Tatchell, and even the former footballer Gordon Taylor, as well as MPs John McDonnell, Alan Simpson, Jeremy Corbyn and George Galloway, and union leaders Bob Crow. Paul Kenny and Tony Woodley). The Charter set out an alternative political agenda including the nationalization and democratization of finance; full employment; a reduction in working hours; raising the minimum wage to 50 per cent of the median hourly rate; the building of 3 million affordable homes; an end to privatization initiatives and to bring privatized entities back into public ownership; and improvement in pensions.[37] Although it was billed as a 'massive petition campaign', it failed to make much impact in 2009. The Trade Union Congress voted to back the Charter only when Britain's largest union, Unite, explicitly endorsed it (its leader, Tony Woodley, was one of the original signatories) and it was made clear that the Charter was being advanced not as an alternative to the Labour Party, but rather as a platform of policies to be campaigned for within the party. Predictably, at the 2009 Labour Party conference reference to the Charter was sparse, as it stood in stark contrast to the Brown government's policies.

But leading up to the general election, and as a challenge to the anti-public services consensus of business and all three major parties, the Trade Union Coordinating Group, comprised of an eclectic grouping of eight unions which came together in March 2010 to plan a 'programme of resistance', re-endorsed the Charter, with RMT (National Union of Rail, Maritime and Transport Workers) leader Bob Crow pointing to the general strikes in Greece and Portugal as positive examples for British workers.[38] This promising appearance of a potential pole of resistance to austerity emerging within the British working class, with the tentative building of some elements of a public sector common front, explicitly anti-neoliberal in its approach, was soon deflated when the leading left Labour figure behind the Charter, John McDonnell, could not secure enough nominations from fellow MPs to stand in the Labour leadership contest. It would still appear that the trade union leadership – and indeed many sections of the broader left in Britain – is incapable of getting out from under the dead weight of New Labour's dismal project.

Ireland: social partnership for austerity

The scope and depth of the Irish financial crisis was second only to Iceland's among OECD countries and, consequently, the politics of shifting the burden of paying for the crisis to the public sector has been that much more acute. In 2006, the year before the crisis exploded, Ireland's GDP grew at a solid 6 per cent. By 2008, however, the 'Celtic Tiger' was no longer roaring: it shrank by 3.0 per cent and by a further 7.1 per cent in 2009; and growth is projected to be, at best, negligible for 2010. Some 25 per cent of homes in Ireland have been threatened with foreclosure through the crisis.[39] The price of underwriting the losses in the financial sector required the Irish state to spend 10 times more per capita than did the US on its financial sector bail-out.[40] Whereas in 2006 unemployment stood at 4.5 per cent, by the first quarter of 2010 it had tripled to 13.2 per cent.[41] Indeed, an unprecedented 16 per cent of private sector jobs have been destroyed. As a consequence, the budgetary deficit hit 14.3 per cent of GDP in 2009, and this pushed gross government debt to 70.3 per cent of GDP.

With the adoption of the Euro ruling out the traditional route of currency devaluation in economic crises, the Fianna Fáil government of Brian Cowen, following the OECD's advice, instead pursued a brutal 'internal devaluation' – a neoliberal euphemism for wrenching policies of wage concessions and public sector austerity, while framing the problem as one of the declining international competitiveness of the 'Irish nation' due to high wages and government expenditures. Within the course of 14 months beginning in October 2008 the government delivered three crisis budgets to the Dáil each marking a successive escalation of efforts to underwrite the crisis by shrinking public services and attacking public sector jobs and incomes. When the first of the wide-ranging cuts to education and health services were proposed, it was met by a series of demonstrations: starting with one by 25,000 pensioners and students in Dublin followed by the largest anti-government mobilization in three decades when 120,000 protested in Dublin on February 21, 2009; and culminating, a few days later, in industrial action by public servants in opposition to a pension levy that would effectively cut their pay. A movement for a national general strike was underway. But just as a major common front seemed to be surging forward, it was called off when the Labour Party refused to support it. April's emergency budget then sought to address a further 4.5 billion euro erosion in public finances through additional income tax increases. By now popular anger at public sector cuts and tax increases to cover the financial debacle was such that in early June gains were made in the European Parliament elections not only by the Labour Party but also by the Socialist Party, while the People Before Profit Alliance and the Workers Unemployed Action Group scored strong victories in the local elections held at the same time.[42]

By the end of 2009 the political divisions intensified, and the two-decade long 'social partnership' between unions and big business organizations looked to be breaking apart. The private sector unions' resistance to the Irish Business and Employers' Confederation's determination to amend the 6 per cent pay increase agreed to in August 2008 led the latter to entirely withdraw from the concertation agreement.[43] At the same time, negotiations between the government and the public sector unions over how to reduce the public service wage bill by 1.3 billion euros in 2010 broke down on December 4, 2009 (a general public sector strike that had been scheduled for December 3 was successfully derailed under the mistaken belief that a settlement was at hand). In ending the negotiations, Prime Minister Cowen contended that there was no alternative to pay cuts. The December 9 budget was unequivocal in shifting the cost of the crisis onto the public sector and its workers. More than 4 billion euros in cuts were involved, including reducing public sector wages by 7 per cent and social benefits by 4.1 per cent (despite the growing army of unemployed), as well as cancelling front-line services and capital investment projects.[44]

With the Teachers' Union of Ireland calling the budget a declaration of war on public services, and the Civil Public and Services Union (representing the lowest paid public sector workers) taking a series of highly effective strike actions in January 2010 against the budget measures (disrupting everything from passport services to health administration), it appeared overall that working-class militancy was ascending. This was cut short, however, when the trade union leadership proposed that unions would cooperate in the restructuring of public services in return for rescinding the pay cuts. This, in effect, signalled their desire to return to concertation as way of managing the Irish austerity exit. The Services, Industrial, Professional and Technical Union (SIPTU) responded to concerns being voiced in the media that union actions might lead to a political crisis and destabilization of the government by explicitly stating that industrial action had no purpose other than to spur negotiations. And the public sector unions unilaterally agreed to a four week moratorium on industrial action to allow the government time to consider whether or not it would restart negotiations.[45] The de-escalation by the union leadership meant that planned strikes by teachers, hospital workers, civil servants and other public sector workers were, in the course of events, abandoned.

On March 30 the unions and government arrived at the 'Croke Park Deal'. The Deal effectively meant that public sector unions were endorsing massive public sector jobs losses (up to 18,000 was the number being mooted) in exchange for the Cowen government's commitment that none of the job losses would be involuntary and that there would be no further pay cuts. The government remained steadfast, however, that existing job cuts would remain, and left open the possibility of reversing pay cuts only for the lowest paid.[46] Despite a measure of opposition from civil service and teachers' unions, the Irish Congress of Trade Unions urged acceptance on the grounds that even if an ongoing industrial relations 'war' was taken up, it would not change the 'external factors that are influencing the situation'.[47] On May Day, SIPTU President Jack O'Connor suggested that although the unions could defeat the government, such a victory would still leave debt and the financial markets to be addressed, while Croke Park afforded the 'public service considerable influence in the partnership process'.[48] The Irish union leadership thus clings to its corporatist 'social partnership' as a junior supplicant within the Irish state, even while Irish capital has rejected it. Readmission to the processes of concertation became the priority for much of top leadership cadres. The door opened for a public sector common front was slammed shut.

Greece: crisis and resistance

The most militant and organized opposition to austerity to be found anywhere in Europe is found on the streets of virtually every Greek city and town. In 2007, before the depth of the financial crisis was coming to be understood and felt, there were a mere five strikes in all of Greece. Today, it is virtually impossible to keep count of the steam-roller of working-class actions. Since the government announced it would move toward austerity in the early part of 2010, there have been five 24 hour general strikes (February 24, March 11, May 5, May 20 and June 29). These have presented the highest profile mobilizations, but there have been hundreds of small actions at the local and sectoral levels.

The tremendous fiscal stress which Greece faces is not because of a particularly severe recession relative to other European states. In 2007, Greece's economy was growing at a healthy 4.5 per cent, and GDP continued to expand at a modest 2 per cent through 2007. In 2009, GDP in Greece fell 2 per cent but this was half the 4 per cent decline for the Eurozone as a whole.[49] The economic contraction put the Greek deficit at 13.5 per cent for 2009, and gross debt at 119.0 per cent of GDP.

The source of the deficits and public debt is not, as in Ireland and Britain, a consequence of the collapse of the Greek banking system; nor is it the absurd view that the Greek welfare state and the services it delivers are too generous (it is military spending that is disproportionately high). The problems stem from the relations between the state and the Greek ruling classes, and its regressive and narrowly designed tax regime. While Greek corporate taxes are set at 25 per cent and the EU average is just below that, the real taxation level on Greek corporations is far below the nominal level as well as below the EU average.[50] This is an aspect of several enduring features skewing the public sector: rampant corporate tax evasion; structures of corruption leading to over-pricing of public investments and contracts with the private sector; the inconsistent collection of VAT; and a wide range of business activities including profits from the sale of Greek stocks, income from ships and shipping, and capital gains from the sale of a family business, left entirely tax exempt. The result is that Greece has one of the lowest levels of tax revenue in the Euro zone. Between 1991 and 2006, total revenues to the government averaged 37.9 per cent of GDP compared to 45.3 per cent within the Eurozone as a whole.[51] In other words, the fiscal crisis is a product of widespread tax evasion and avoidance, especially by the country's ruling class. Bringing tax revenues in line with the EU average would largely resolve the budgetary crisis.

But as Greece has become the main battlefield for the European neoliberal exit strategy, the social democratic PASOK government of Prime Minister George Papandreou, under great external pressure and, like Ireland, without the option of currency devaluation as a member of the Eurozone, presented an 'Economy Protection Bill' in March 2010 which outlined 5 billion in cuts. This was followed by the 'Stabilization Programme' that was adopted by the Greek National Assembly in May, opposed only by the Communist Party (KKE), the Coalition of the Radical Left (SYRIZA), and several deputies of the ruling PASOK. Overall, the austerity programme was projected to cause the economy to shrink by a further 3.7 per cent in 2010 and by 2.5 per cent for 2011, even as official unemployment in Greece rose to over 12 per cent (from 8.3 per cent in 2007), with the OECD suggesting that unemployment in 2011 will hit over 14 per cent.[52] As in other structural adjustment programmes, the cuts meet the 'conditions' incorporated into the Greek 'fiscal consolidation plan' as part of the EU/IMF 110 billion euro Stabilization Programme for Greece (with the EU also putting in place an additional 440 billion euro in the European Financial Stability Facility).

For the public sector, the cuts are staggering: pay is immediately cut by 7 per cent and frozen for the next five years; cuts in vacations and other bonuses (which together make for a 20 per cent pay cut); contract and temporary workers in the public sector are to be terminated; for every five retirements from the public sector, only one replacement hire will be allowed; and a huge number of state corporations including Olympia Airlines, water companies, electricity producers, public transport, the post office and ports are to be wholly or partially privatized. Another central target is the Greek pensions system for all workers: the retirement age is to be raised from 55 to 60 for women and for men the retirement age will be based on some measure of life expectancy; when one does retire, the pension will no longer be based on the final year of work but rather on a calculation that will be based on the worker's lifetime earnings; and the number of years of work to qualify for a full pension rises from 37 years to 40. These changes are expected to result in a 45 to 60 per cent reduction in pension benefits for all Greek workers. In terms of other changes, private employers are granted greater flexibility to terminate workers, and the minimum salary for youth and the long-termed unemployed is cut by 40 per cent. While VAT is increased from 21 to 23 per cent (following on a prior increase by PASOK which had already raised it from 19 per cent), and a slew of other indirect taxes are also increased, the corporate tax rate will be brought down by 1 per cent annually to 20 per cent by 2014. The bitter irony of the Greek austerity programme being implemented by PASOK is that it will shrink the incomes of the people who actually pay taxes and thus will exacerbate the shortfall in government revenues, while cutting the taxes on the capitalists who extensively avoid paying taxes.

The May 5 general strike, called in immediate response to the introduction of the austerity programme in the National Assembly, brought 300,000 protestors out into the streets of Athens, with both the Communist Party and the independent left party SYRIZA highly mobilized in organizing the turnout, while the leaders of the Greek General Confederation of Labour (which brings the private sector unions together) were roundly criticized by the new unions of precarious workers in a myriad of service occupations for their reluctance to oppose the austerity. Militancy has been expressed as well in a growing number of occupations, including at Olympic Airlines, garbage collection centres, bank branches, and offices of pension funds, local government, the Employment Ministry, and even of the EU in Greece.[53]

It is by no means clear whether this remarkable opposition to austerity can be sustained and deepened. SYRIZA's attempts to develop the ideological and organizational capacities for resistance through neighbourhood and workplace struggle committees may be important elements in establishing an organizational structure capable of resisting the government. But this may falter in face of the stifling orientation to the old-style top-down 'popular front' that still marks the KKE's politics, together with the close alignment to PASOK of much of the trade union leadership, although whether PASOK can survive as a party is an open question today given the growing rift with its working-class base and the government's embrace of police repression against demonstrators. What is clear is that the outcome of the struggle underway in Greece will have implications throughout the continent.

THE LEFT AND THE POLITICS OF AUSTERITY

The inability of the liberal and social democratic centre – certainly at the level of political forces – to advance an alternative exit strategy to neoliberal austerity needs to be incorporated into the calculations of the socialist left. So does the fact that the current fiscal crisis does not at all correspond with a crisis of the state rather than the entrenchment of neoliberal forms of administration and budgetary policy. Above all it is necessary to come to terms with the resilience of political alliances within ruling classes at the national and international levels, on the one hand, and the inability of working classes and the socialist left to address its own organizational crisis and marshal an anti-capitalist programme, on the other. To be sure, the left needs to be alert to several forces that have been prominent across the range of struggles that have emerged: public sector workers facing layoffs and wage concessions, coping with reduced quality of services, or fighting privatization; community groups, social agencies and users dependent upon public services; and the union and social movement activists and radical left that have distanced themselves from social democracy. These are, more or less, the social movements and strata that have been struggling to form an anti-neoliberal alliance and an alternate organizational practice out of the crisis of the left for two decades. With the hardening of the political right and the centre-left either tracking the austerity exit or failing to offer a plausible alternative, a new political opening is emerging in the common fronts of resistance to austerity.

It is also necessary for the left to take into account how abjectly the austerity exits expose the degree to which the existing political parties and the senior state administration do not represent the 'general interest' or a plausible stance of 'neutrality' toward financial capital. The political dominance of financial capital at the heart of the state, often directly in the political executive and senior levels of administration, in forming the exit strategies, candidly shatters illusions of the 'impartiality' and 'economic necessity' of neoliberal market disciplines and state autonomy. The efforts of ruling blocs to mobilize the 'national-popular' imagery of the nation – 'saving the Greek nation', 'a strong Wall Street is a strong America', 'the British people pulling together' – in support of the rescue and exit strategies lack credibility among ordinary citizens. The sheer falsity of these claims provides space at the ideological level for alternate interpretations of the crisis, the cuts and, more fundamentally, of capitalist democracy.

The common fronts of resistance to the cuts have thus been able to present themselves to some extent at the axis of a division between 'the people' and the 'banks and the state' in the general strikes, mass demonstrations and an array of other direct actions such as office and plant occupations. There have, of course, been huge differences in the ability to sustain these political actions, as the examples above have shown. Yet the political space has been opened for anti-austerity fronts to deepen and unite political struggles of public sector workers, user groups and the wider left, even if only by initially campaigning around the distributional question of who should pay for the crisis. In implementing austerity and expanding neoliberal modes of administration, the parliamentary parties, the political executive and senior administration have objectively set themselves against public sector workers over the form of state administration, work intensification and pay, the quality of service delivery and democratic accountability. User and community groups are, in turn, directly impacted by the level, quality and availability of public service provision. This should provide more and more opportunity for linking these struggles, for example, between transit workers and riders; between settlement workers and migrants; between library workers and readers; and so forth.[54]

Struggles that begin as defensive mobilizations about the level of service, the attack on wages and the distributional inequities of austerity will quickly come face to face with the broader neoliberal exit agenda. This should allow democratic struggles over the legitimacy of the austerity programmes to contest neoliberal discourses, and indeed its administrative programme. These struggles can resonate with questions of social justice and community control; and they can help foster the construction of political alliances where services are delivered across widely dispersed places. The political challenge is to generate organizational linkages so that struggles for community control can fuse with struggles over the state from bases both inside and outside the state, at various scales of political struggle.

But it should by now be evident that the fronts of resistance confront a still-powerful neoliberal state and a power bloc vigorously advancing its interests nationally and internationally. This makes it crucial to offer systematic critiques of the failings of capitalism and develop visions of and programmes for socialist alternatives. Some of these were beginning to take shape in the first phase of the crisis – around green jobs, seizing and converting shutdown plants, deepening collective provision in the 'caring sectors', worktime reduction and many others. New strategies were also emerging in terms of finance, pivoting around bank nationalization, and from there to unhinging government finance from private bond markets, and forming new mechanisms for implementing capital controls.[55]

These types of visions and programmes need to be anchored in the concrete struggles of public sector workers and communities, and linked to national struggles at the summit of the state over the political legitimacy and the distributional impacts of the austerity exits. This approach would dispense with the false juxtaposition – itself a reflection of the crisis of the left – of struggling inside the state and over parliaments at the national level or outside the state and in the streets at the community level. Rather, the anti-austerity struggle has to be waged on two fronts: inside the state and at its summits where political power is concentrated and the agenda of neoliberalism is being advanced; and in public sector workplaces and communities where struggles over the cuts can be directly contested and alternate forms of administration and control explored.[56]

No economic crisis follows an exact script. Who would have foretold that, three years after the American working class started failing to meet mortgage payments on their piece of the American Dream in 2007, general strikes would erupt across Europe in the spring of 2010 over public sector cuts and form the fulcrum point of the crisis? And more soberly: who would have thought that the greatest bout of financial turbulence in the history of capitalism would only expose more than ever the political vacuum that has been left by the defeats of militant trade unionism and socialist politics in the late 20th century? But taken together, these two realizations may yet clarify what needs to be done.

NOTES

1 IMF, *Fiscal Monitor: Navigating the Fiscal Challenges Ahead*, Washington: IMF, May 2010, p. 30. Also see: IMF, *Exiting from Crisis Intervention Policies*, 4 February 2010; IMF, *Strategies for Fiscal Consolidation in the Post-Crisis World*, 4 February 2010; and Bank of International Settlements, *The Future of Public Debt: Prospects and Implications*, BIS Working Papers, No. 300, March 2010.

2 The focus here is on the fiscal imbalances from the crisis, and not the longer term structural pressures on the public sector placed on revenues from neoliberal policies. Nor is the focus on the tendency for social needs to grow as capitalism develops and thus placing socialization pressures on the state. This is the case with education, healthcare, daycare, and so on. This latter contradiction has been handled under neoliberalism by various forms of privatization, commercialization, subsidization and elimination. On the origins of this fiscal crisis see the classic works: James O'Connor, *The Fiscal Crisis of the State*, New York: St. Martin's Press, 1973; Ian Gough, *The Political Economy of the Welfare State*, London: Macmillan, 1979.

3 Suzanne de Brunhoff, *The State, Capital and Economic Policy*, London: Pluto Press, 1976; Nicos Poulantzas, *State, Power, Socialism*, London: Verso, 1978.

4 Greg Albo, Sam Gindin and Leo Panitch, *In and Against the Crisis: The Left and Strategic Alternatives*, Oakland: PM Press, 2010, pp. 109-14; Willem Buiter,

'Time to Take the Banks into Full Public Ownership', *Financial Times*, 16 January 2009, available at http://blogs.ft.com.

5 Carmen Reinhart and Kenneth Rogoff, *This Time is Different*, Princeton: Princeton University Press, 2009. A punchier assessment is: Rick Wolff, 'Austerity: Why and for Whom?', *MRZine*, 4 July 2010, available at http://www.monthlyreview.org/mrzine/.

6 Nouriel Roubini and Stephen Mihm, *Crisis Economics*, New York: Penguin Press, 2010, ch. 7.

7 See the essay by Karl Beitel in this volume as well as Yeva Nersisyan and Randall Wray, 'Deficit Hysteria Redux?', *Real-World Economics Review*, 53, 2010.

8 'The G-20 Toronto Summit Declaration', 26-27 June 2010, p. 3, available at http://g20.gc.ca.

9 Michael Burke, 'Fake Independence of the "Office for Budget Responsibility"', *Socialist Economic Bulletin*, 15 June 2010, available at http://socialisteconomicbulletin.blogspot.com. President Obama established the National Commission on Fiscal Responsibility and Reform in February 2010.

10 Donald Savoie, *Thatcher, Reagan, Mulroney: In Search of a New Bureaucracy*, Toronto: University of Toronto Press, 1994; CSE State Group, *Struggle over the State: Cuts and Restructuring in Contemporary Britain*, London: CSE Books, 1979.

11 KPMG International, *Tough Choices Ahead: The Future of the Public Sector*, Ottawa: KPMG, 2009, available at http://www.kpmg.com; Christoph Hermann and Jörg Flecker, eds., *Privatization of Public Services: Impacts for Employment, Working Conditions, and Service Quality*, London: Routledge, forthcoming; B. Guy Peters and Jon Pierre, eds., *Politicization of the Civil Service in Comparative Perspective: The Quest for Control*, New York: Routledge, 2004.

12 'The G-20 Toronto Summit Declaration', pp. 5, 2.

13 Martin Wolf, 'Three Years On, Fault Lines Threaten World Economy', *Financial Times*, 14 July 2010.

14 Paul Krugman, 'The Third Depression', *New York Times*, 27 June 2010; George Stiglitz, *Freefall*, New York: W.W. Norton, 2010; and, more critically, Özlem Onaran, 'Fiscal Crisis in Europe or a Crisis of Distribution?', SOAS, Research on Money and Finance, Discussion Paper, No. 18, 2010.

15 Indeed, the 'fiscal workout' by the social democratic government in Sweden in the 1990s, after its banking crisis, is generally invoked as a model for the austerity exits. Papandreou in Greece and José Zapatero's Socialist Party in Spain have been in the forefront of imposing public sector cuts, without exploring alternate strategies or fostering political mobilizations.

16 Bureau of Labor Statistics, *Household Data – Historical, Employment Status of the Civilian Non-institutional Population 16 years and over, 1970 to Date*, available at http://www.bls.gov; *Regional and State Employment and Unemployment Summary*, 21 May 2010; Economic Policy Institute, *Economy Track*, available at http://www.economytrack.org.

17 This pushed the general government deficit for the US for 2009 to 11.0 per cent , and gross debt to 83 per cent of GDP. These figures are drawn from:

OECD, *Economic Outlook*, No. 87, Paris: OECD, May 2010, p. 83 and Annex 32.

18 See the Center on Budget and Policy Priorities studies: Michael Leachman, Eric Williams and Nicholas Johnson, *Failing to Extend Fiscal Relief to States Will Create New Budget Gaps, Forcing Cuts and Job Loss in at Least 34 States*, June 2010; *Slideshow: The State Budget Crisis and the Economy*, June 2010; and Elizabeth McNichol and Nicholas Johnson, *Recession Continues to Batter State Budgets,* May 2010. These studies available at http://www.cbpp.org.

19 Rick Wolff, 'Economic Crisis Hits States and Municipalities', *The Bullet,* No. 268, 2 November 2010, available at http://www.socialistproject.ca.

20 Arloc Sherman and Chad Stone, *Income Gaps Between Very Rich and Everyone Else More Than Tripled in Last Three Decades*, Center on Budget and Policy Priorities, 25 June, 2010, p. 1.

21 Mitchell, Lawrence, *Where Has All the Income Gone? Look up*, Economic Policy Institute, 3 March 2010, available at http://www.epi.org; and Andrea Orr, *At the Top: Soaring Incomes, Falling Tax Rates*, Economic Policy Institute, 7 April 2010, available at http://www.epi.org.

22 Bureau of Economic Analysis, US Department of Commerce, *News Release: State Personal Income 2009*, 25 March 2010, Table 1; and *Per Capita Personal Income, Personal Income, and Population, by State and Region*, 2008-2009, available at http://www.bea.gov.

23 Ken Jacobs, Laurel Lucia and T. William Lester, 'The Economic Consequences of Proposed California Budget Cuts', Center for Labor Research and Education, University of California, Berkeley, 2010, available at http://laborcenter.berkeley.edu.

24 'Fight for California's Future', California Federation of Teachers, available at http://www.cft.org; Adam Hefty, 'What's Next After March 4?', *Against the Current*, 146, 2010.

25 None of these actions, however, were as dramatic as the struggle over public sector cuts and higher education that has held political centre stage in Puerto Rico. There political conflicts over budgetary cuts were punctuated by a one-day general strike on October 15, 2009, and continuing political strife. The general strike itself was led by public sector unions who mobilized 200,000 workers for a demonstration in San Juan. The strike was in response to the threat from the governor that 12 per cent of the Puerto Rican public workforce would be laid-off in an effort to address a $3.2 billion budget deficit, and to the use of 'economic emergency' powers to override collective agreements and existing labour laws that prohibit unjustified termination of public employees. Public sector fightbacks continued in 2010, including at the 11 campuses of the University of Puerto Rico, where a two month student strike unfolded over cutbacks and tuition hikes. See Roberto Ramos-Perea, 'Explosive Political Situation in Puerto Rico', *America Latina en Movimiento*, 30 June 2010, available at http://alainet.org.

26 David Bacon, 'Labor Needs a Hard Left Turn: Interview with Bill Fletcher', Centre for Labor Renewal, 21 July 2005, available at http://www.centerforlaborrenewal.org.

27 Thomas Prosser, 'Social partners react to planned public spending cuts', *European Industrial Relations Observatory*, 18 January 2010, available at http://www.eurofound.europa.eu.

28 John Hilary, 'Cuts: who's paying for the financial crisis?', *The Guardian*, 16 May 2010. Eurostat, 'Real GDP Growth Rate', available at http://epp.eurostat.ec.europa.eu.

29 Larry Elliot, 'Alistair Darling: We will cut deeper than Margaret Thatcher', *The Guardian*, 25 March 2010.

30 'Cutting now remains a risk to recovery', *The Independent*, 14 May 2010.

31 HM Treasury, *Budget 2010*, 22 June 2010, pp. 1-2, available at http://www.hm-treasury.gov.uk.

32 Office for Budget Responsibility, HM Treasury, 'OBR Forecast: Employment', 30 June 2010, available at http://budgetresponsibility.independent.gov.uk. There is also a great deal of speculation about how many civil service jobs will be 'off-shored' as part of the cuts: Nicolas Timmins, 'Call to Send Civil Service Jobs Offshore', *Financial Times*, 2 May 2010.

33 Larry Elliot, 'Budget will cost 1.3m jobs – Treasury', *The Guardian*, 29 June 2010.

34 Julia Kollewe, 'Spending Cuts: City reaction', *The Guardian*, 24 May 2010.

35 See Prosser, 'Social Partners'; and John Millington, 'Business Club Signs up to Tory Cuts Drive', *Morning Star*, 16 March 2010.

36 Tim Webb, Zoe Wood, Nicholas Watt and Patrick Wintour, 'Vince Cable plans new attempt to privatise Royal Mail', *The Guardian*, 20 May 2010.

37 'The People's Charter', available at http://thepeoplescharter.org.

38 John Millington, 'Eight unions join forces to combat cuts', *Morning Star*, 7 March 2010.

39 Ronan Lyons, 'Is Ireland in a jobs recession or a jobs depression?', 12 October 2009, available at http://www.ronanlyons.com.

40 Morgan Kelly, 'Burden of Irish debt could yet eclipse that of Greece', *The Irish Times*, 22 May 2010.

41 Eurostat, 'Real GDP Growth Rate' and 'Unemployment Rate by Gender, Total', available at http://epp.eurostat.ec.europa.eu.

42 Finance Department, 'Summary of Supplementary Budget Measures', 2009, available at http://www.budget.gov.ie; Michael Parsons, 'Workers' group stages comeback in Clonmel', *The Irish Times*, 9 June 2009.

43 The concertation of national level collective bargaining or 'social partnership' emerged in 1987 in response to the economic crisis of the 1980s. From that point forward, a corporatist, multipartite system of bargaining extended into the framing of economic and social policy. The trade-off embedded within the process was between taxes and wages and has led critics of the process to contend that rather than improving working class social and economic conditions it has instead contributed to and legitimated relative wage and income inequality, as well as comparatively high levels of poverty and low levels of expenditure on public services.

44 'Lenihan says "worst is over" as 4bn euro in cuts unveiled', *The Irish Times*, 9 December 2009.

45 Martin Wall, 'Unions defer dispute escalation for one month', *The Irish Times*, 16 February 2010.

46 'Public Service Pay Deal', *The Irish Times*, 31 March 2010; Civil Public and Services Union, 'CPSU Executive Unanimously recommends Members to reject Draft Agreement', 12 April 2010, available at http://www.cpsu.ie.

47 Charlie Taylor, 'ICTU defends public sector deal', *The Irish Times*, 2 April 2010.

48 Marie O'Halloran, 'Union head warns of "pyrrhic victory"', *The Irish Times*, 3 May 2010.

49 Eurostat, 'Real GDP Growth Rate' and 'Unemployment Rate by Gender, Total'.

50 Eurostat, 'Taxation Trends in the European Union', Press Release, 28 June 2010, available at http://europa.eu; Sofia Lampousaki, 'INE/GSEE Presents Economic and Employment Outlook for 2009', *European Industrial Relations Observatory*, 16 December 2009, available at http://www.eurofound.europa.eu.

51 Michael Burke, 'EU calls for Greek population to tighten belts to support wealthy Greek tax dodgers', *Socialist Economic Bulletin*, 19 February 2010, available at http://socialisteconomicbulletin.blogspot.com.

52 IMF, *World Economic Report: Rebalancing Growth*, Washington: IMF, April 2010, Table 2.4; OECD, 'Greece', *Economic Outlook*, No. 87, May 2010.

53 George Yorgos, 'The Struggle intensifies in Greece', *Socialist Worker*, 31 March 2010, available at http://socialistworker.org.

54 Hilary Wainwright, *Public Service Reform… But Not as We Know It*, East Sussex: Picnic, 2009.

55 For examples: Philip Arestis and Malcolm Sawyer, 'The Future of Public Expenditure', *Renewal*, 17(3), 2009; *A Progressive Program for Economic Recovery and Financial Reconstruction*, Political Economy Research Institute, 2009; ITUC, 'Global Union Statement: Take Action on Jobs to Sustain the Recovery', June 2010, available at http://www.ituc-csi.org.

56 Michael Lebowitz, *The Socialist Alternative: Real Human Development,* New York: Monthly Review Press, 2010, pp. 115-6, 164-5.

THE CENTRE CANNOT HOLD: REKINDLING THE RADICAL IMAGINATION

NOAM CHOMSKY

On February 18, 2010, Joseph Andrew Stack crashed his small plane into an office building in Austin Texas, hitting an IRS office, committing suicide. He left a Manifesto explaining his actions.[1] It was mostly ridiculed, but it deserves much better, I think.

Stack's manifesto traces the life history that led him to this final desperate act. The story begins when he was a teenage student living on a pittance in Harrisburg, Pennsylvania near the heart of what was once a great industrial centre. His neighbour was a woman in her 80s, surviving on cat food, the 'widowed wife of a retired steel worker. Her husband had worked all his life in the steel mills of central Pennsylvania with promises from big business and the union that, for his 30 years of service, he would have a pension and medical care to look forward to in his retirement. Instead he was one of the thousands who got nothing because the incompetent mill management and corrupt union (not to mention the government) raided their pension funds and stole their retirement. All she had was social security to live on'; and Stack could have added that there have been concerted and continuing efforts by the super-rich and their political allies to take even that away on spurious grounds. Stack decided then that he couldn't trust big business and would strike out on his own, only to discover that he couldn't trust a government that cared nothing about people like him but only about the rich and privileged; or a legal system in which, in his words, 'there are two "interpretations" for every law, one for the very rich, and one for the rest of us'. A government that leaves us with 'the joke we call the American medical system, including the drug and insurance companies [that] are murdering tens of thousands of people a year,' with care rationed largely by wealth, not need. All in a social order in which 'a handful of thugs and plunderers can commit unthinkable atrocities ... and when it's time for their gravy train to crash under the weight of their gluttony and overwhelming stupidity, the force of the full federal government has no difficulty coming to their aid within days if not hours.' And much more.

Stack tells us that his desperate final act was an effort to join those who are willing to die for their freedom, in the hope of awakening others from their torpor. It wouldn't surprise me if he had in mind the premature death of the steel worker that taught him about the real world as a teenager. That steel worker didn't literally commit suicide after having been discarded to the trash heap, but it's far from an isolated case; we can add his and many similar cases to the colossal toll of the institutional crimes of state capitalism. There are poignant studies of the indignation and rage of those who have been cast aside as the state-corporate programs of financialization and deindustrialization have closed plants and destroyed families and communities. They reveal the sense of acute betrayal on the part of working people who believed they had fulfilled their duty to society in a moral compact with business and government, only to discover that they had been only instruments for profit and power, truisms from which they had been carefully protected by doctrinal institutions.

There are striking similarities in the world's second largest economy, investigated by Ching Kwan Lee in her penetrating inquiry into Chinese labour.[2] Lee draws the close comparison between working-class outrage and desperation in the discarded industrial sectors of the US and the fury among workers in what she calls China's rustbelt -- the state socialist industrial centre in the northeast, now abandoned by the state in favour of state capitalist development of the southeast sunbelt. In both regions Lee finds massive labour protests, but different in character. In the Chinese rustbelt workers express the same sense of betrayal as their counterparts here, but in their case betrayal of the Maoist principles of solidarity and dedication to development of the society that they thought had been a moral compact, only to discover that whatever it was, it is now a bitter fraud. In the sunbelt, the workers lack that cultural tradition and still rely on their home villages for support and family life. They denounce the failure of authorities to live up to even the minimal legal requirements of barely liveable workplace conditions and payment of the pittance called salaries. According to official statistics there were 58,000 'mass incidents' of protest in 2003 in one province of the rustbelt, with 3 million people participating. Some 30-40 million workers who were dropped from work units 'are plagued by a profound sense of insecurity,' arousing 'rage and desperation' around the country, in Lee's words.[3] She expects that there may be worse to come as a looming crisis of landlessness in the countryside undermines the base for survival of the sunbelt workers, who lack even a semblance of independent unions, while in the rustbelt, workers do not have anything like the civil society support that often exists here in the United States. Both Lee's work and the studies of the US rustbelt make clear that we should not underestimate the depth of moral indignation that lies behind the furious and often self-destructive bitterness about government and business power.

We find something similar in rural India, where food consumption has sharply declined for the great majority since the neoliberal reforms were partially implemented, while peasant suicides are increasing at about the same rate as the number of billionaires, amidst accolades for India's fabulous growth. Fabulous growth for some, that is – but not so attractive for the workers transferred to India to reduce labour costs by IBM, which now has three-fourths of its work force abroad.[4] *Businessweek* calls IBM the 'quintessential American company,' not inappropriately: it became the global giant in computing thanks in large part to the unwitting munificence of the US taxpayer, who also substantially funded the IT revolution on which IBM relies along with most of the rest of the high tech economy – mostly under the pretext that the Russians are coming.

There is much excited talk these days about a great global shift of power, with speculation about whether (or when) China might displace the US as the dominant global power, along with India – which, if it happened, would mean that the global system would be returning to something like what it was before the European conquests. Their recent GDP growth has indeed been spectacular. But there is more to say. In the UN human development index, India retains its place near the bottom, now 134th, slightly above Cambodia, below Laos and Tajikistan. China ranks 92nd, a bit above Jordan, below the Dominican Republic and Iran. By comparison, Cuba, under harsh US attack for 50 years, is ranked 52nd, the highest in Central America and the Caribbean, barely below Argentina and Uruguay. India and China also suffer from extremely high inequality, so well over a billion of their inhabitants fall far lower in the scale. Furthermore, an accurate accounting would go beyond conventional measures to include serious costs that China and India cannot long ignore: ecological, resource depletion, and others.

The speculations about a global shift of power overlook something that we all know: nations divorced from the internal distribution of power are not the real actors in international affairs, a truism brought to our attention by that incorrigible radical Adam Smith. He recognized that the principal architects of power in England were the owners of the society, in his day the merchants and manufacturers, who made sure that policy would attend scrupulously to their interests however 'grievous' the impact on the people of England and worse, the victims of 'the savage injustice of the Europeans' abroad: British crimes in India were the main concern of an old-fashioned conservative with moral values.

To his modern worshippers, Smith's truisms are ridiculed as 'elaborate theories of how world history was being manipulated by shadowy corporatist/ imperialist networks,' one of the tragic legacies of the '60s, to quote New York Times thinker David Brooks;[5] actually the '70s, 1776 to be exact.[6] One of many illustrations of how the intellectual and moral level of today's 'conservatism' compares to what its heroes understood full well.

In the interests of full disclosure, I should mention that Brooks identifies me as the villain who adopts Adam Smith's heresy.

Bearing Smith's radical truism in mind, we can see that there is indeed a global shift of power, though not the one that occupies centre stage: a shift from the global work force to transnational capital, sharply escalating during the neoliberal years. The cost is substantial, including the Joe Stacks of the US, starving peasants in India, and millions of protesting workers in China, where labour share in national income is declining even more rapidly than in most of the world.

In their very illuminating work, Martin Hart-Landsberg and Paul Burkett observe that China plays a leading role in the real global shift of power, having become largely an assembly plant for a regional production system.[7] Japan, Taiwan, and other Asian economies export parts and components to China, and provide most of the advanced technology. Much concern has been aroused by the growing US trade deficit with China, but less noticed is the fact that the trade deficit with Japan and the rest of Asia has sharply declined as the new regional production system takes shape. The *Wall Street Journal* illustrates with a Sloan Foundation study (2007) that 'found that only $4 of an iPod that costs $150 to produce is made in China, even though the final assembly and export occurs in China. The remaining $146 represents parts imported to China.'[8] The *Journal* concludes that if only the value added by manufacturers in China were counted, the real US-China trade deficit might by reduced by as much as 30 per cent while the US trade deficit with Japan would rise by 25 per cent. US manufacturers are following the same course, providing parts and components for China to assemble and export, mostly back to the US.

For the financial institutions, retail giants, ownership and management of manufacturing industries, and sectors closely related to this nexus of power, all of this is heavenly. Not for Joe Stack and many others like him.

To understand the public mood it is worthwhile to recall that the conventional use of GDP to measure economic growth is highly misleading. There have been efforts to devise more realistic measures, such as the General

Progress Indicator, which subtracts from GDP expenditures that harm the public (crime, pollution, etc.) and adds estimated value of authentic benefits (volunteer work, leisure, etc.). In the US, GPI has stagnated since the 1970s, though GDP has increased, the growth going into very few pockets. That result correlates with studies of social indicators, the standard measure of health of a society. They tracked economic growth until the mid-1970s, then began to decline, reaching the level of 1960 by 2000 (the latest figures available). The correlation with financialization of the economy and neoliberal socio-economic measures is hard to miss, and not unique to the US by any means.

It's true that there is nothing essentially new in the process of deindustrialization. Owners and managers naturally seek the lowest labour costs; efforts to do otherwise, famously by Henry Ford, were struck down by the courts, so now it is a legal obligation. One means is shifting production. In earlier days the shift was mostly internal, especially to the southern states, where labour could be more harshly repressed. Major corporations, like the US steel corporation of the sainted philanthropist Andrew Carnegie, could also profit from the new slave labour force created by the criminalization of black life after the end of Reconstruction in 1877, a core part of the American industrial revolution, continuing until the Second World War. It is being reproduced in part during the recent neoliberal period, with the drug war used as a pretext to drive the superfluous population, mostly black, back to the prisons, also providing a new supply of prison labour in state or private prisons, much of it in violation of international labour conventions. For many African-Americans, since they were exported to the colonies life has scarcely escaped the bonds of slavery, or sometimes worse.

In the ultra-respectable *Bulletin of the American Academy of Arts and Sciences*, we can read that the 'prison system in America has grown into a leviathan unmatched in human history,' making the US 'the home to the largest custodial infrastructure for the mass depredation of liberty to be found on the planet,' mostly black, a product of the past 30 years, as is the fact that the US 'leads the world not only in incarceration rates but in executive compensation,' facts that are increasingly recognized to be linked, a Harvard Business School professor points out, as is the fact that the US is lagging far behind much of the world, particularly China but Europe as well, in green technologies.[9]

It is easy to ridicule some of the ways in which Joe Stack and others like him articulate their very genuine and just concerns, but it's far more appropriate to understand what lies behind their perceptions and actions, and particularly, to ask ourselves why the radical imagination is failing to offer them a constructive path while the centre is very visibly not holding, and those who have real grievances are being mobilized in ways that pose no slight danger, to themselves and others.

Stack's manifesto ends with two evocative sentences: 'The communist creed: From each according to his ability, to each according to his need. The capitalist creed: From each according to his gullibility, to each according to his greed'.

Stack minces no words about the capitalist creed. We can only speculate about what he meant by the communist creed that he counterposed to it. It's not unlikely that he regarded it as an ideal with genuine moral force. If so, that would not be too surprising. Some of you may recall a poll in 1987, on the bicentennial, in which people were given a list of statements and asked which they thought were in the Constitution. At that time, no one had a clue what was in the Constitution, so the answer 'in the Constitution' presumably meant: 'so obviously correct that it must be in the Constitution'. One statement that received a solid majority was Joe Stack's 'Communist creed'.[10]

I qualified the comment with the phrase 'at that time'. Today, a segment of the population memorizes and worships the Constitution – the words at least. The Tea Party has produced its catechism for political candidates: one requirement is that they must agree to scrap the tax code and replace it with one no longer than 4,543 words -- to match the length of the Constitution, unamended.[11] Only some amendments share this holy status, particularly the Second under the recent interpretation by the Supreme Court reactionaries, but the First Amendment is more questionable because of what it might be taken to imply about separation of Church and State. Meanwhile, Texas announced its new textbook requirements, which apply to the whole country because of the size of the Texas market.[12] Jefferson was cut from the list of those who inspired 18th and 19th century revolutions, replaced by Thomas Aquinas, Calvin and Blackstone. The decision reflects the distaste for Jefferson because, among other heresies, he coined the phrase 'separation between church and state'. For today's version of conservatism the US is a Christian country, something like the Islamic Republic of Iran, or the Jewish State of Israel. In that connection, Golda Meir is listed as required learning for children, but no Hispanics. Along with normal racism, that reflects the curious amalgam of extreme anti-Semitism and support for Israel among right-wing religious sectors. Such matters are of no slight significance when we try to look ahead.

The anti-tax extremism of the Tea Party movement is not as immediately suicidal as Joe Stack's desperate action, but it is suicidal nonetheless, for reasons that need no elaboration. California today is a dramatic illustration. The world's greatest public system of higher education is being dismantled. Governor Schwarzenegger says he'll have to eliminate state health and welfare programs unless the federal government forks over some $7 billion, and other governors are joining in. At the same time a powerful states rights movement is taking shape demanding that the federal government not intrude into our affairs – a nice illustration of what Orwell called 'doublethink': the ability to hold two contradictory ideas in mind while believing both of them, practically a motto for the times. California's plight results in large part from anti-tax fanaticism. It's much the same elsewhere, even in affluent suburbs.

Encouraging anti-tax sentiment has long been a staple of the business propaganda that dominates the doctrinal system. People must be indoctrinated to hate and fear the government, for good reasons: of existing power systems, the government is the one that in principle, and sometimes in fact, is answerable to the public and can impose some constraints on the depredations of private power; the corollary to 'getting government off our backs' is groaning beneath the even greater weight of unaccountable private tyrannies. But business anti-government propaganda has to be nuanced: business of course favours a very powerful state that works for Adam Smith's principal architects, today not merchants and manufacturers, but multinationals and financial institutions. Constructing this internally contradictory propaganda message is no easy task. Thus people have to be trained to hate and fear the deficit, a necessary means to stimulate the economy after its destruction at the hands of the dominant financial institutions and their cohorts in Washington. But at the same time the population must favour the deficits, almost half attributable to the growing military budget, which is breaking records, and the rest predicted to overwhelm the budget thanks to the cruel and hopelessly inefficient privatized health care system, a gift to the insurance companies and big Pharma.

Despite such difficulties, the propaganda tasks have been carried out with impressive success. One illustration is the public attitude towards April 15, when tax returns are due. Let's put aside for the moment the thought of a much more free and just society. In a functioning democracy of the kind that formally exists, April 15 would be a day of celebration: we are coming together to implement programs that we have chosen. Here it is a day of mourning: some alien force is descending upon us to steal our hard-earned money. That's one graphic indication of the success of the intense efforts of the highly class-conscious business community to win what its publications call 'the everlasting battle for the minds of men,' and like even the most vulgar propaganda it has grains of truth that the Joe Stacks perceive.

Another stunning illustration of the success of propaganda, with considerable import for the future, is the cult of the killer and torturer Ronald Reagan, one of the grand criminals of the modern era, who also had an unerring instinct for favouring the most brutal terrorists and murderers around the world, from Zia ul-Haq and Gulbuddin Hekmatyar in today's AfPak to the most dedicated killers in Central America to the South African racists who killed an estimated 1.5 million people and had to be supported because they were under attack by Nelson Mandela's ANC, one of the 'more notorious terrorist groups' in the world, the Reaganites determined in 1988. And on and on, with remarkable consistency. His grisly record was quickly expunged in favour of mythic constructions that would have impressed Kim il-Sung. Among other feats, he was anointed as the apostle of free markets while raising protectionist barriers more than any postwar president – probably more than all others combined – and implementing massive government intervention in the economy. He is hailed as the grand exponent of small government and of law and order. Government grew relative to GDP during his years in office, while he informed the business world that labour laws would not be enforced, so that illegal firing of union organizers tripled under his supervision. His hatred of working people was exceeded perhaps only by his contempt for the rich black women driving in limousines to collect their welfare checks.

There should be no need to continue with the record, but the outcome tells us a lot about the intellectual and moral culture. For President Obama, this monstrous creature was a 'transformative figure'. At Stanford University's prestigious Hoover Institution, he is revered as a colossal figure whose 'spirit seems to stride the country, watching us like a warm and friendly ghost'.[13] We arrive in Washington at Reagan International Airport – or if we prefer, at John Foster Dulles International Airport, honouring another prominent terrorist commander. His achievements include installing the torture regime of the Shah and the reign of the most vicious of the terrorists of Central America, whose exploits reached true genocide in the highlands while Reagan praised the worst of the mass murderers, Rioss Montt, as 'a man of great personal integrity' who was 'totally dedicated to democracy' and was receiving a 'bum rap' from human rights organizations.[14]

Painfully to record, many of the Joe Stacks whose lives the 'warm and friendly ghost' was ruining join in the adulation, and hasten to shelter under the umbrella of the power and violence that he symbolized.

All of this evokes memories of other days when the centre did not hold. One example that should not be forgotten is the Weimar Republic: the peak of western civilization in the sciences and the arts, also regarded as a model of democracy. Through the 1920s the traditional liberal and conservative parties that had always governed the Reich entered into inexorable decline, well before the process was intensified by the Great Depression. The coalition that elected General Hindenburg in 1925 was not very different from the mass base that swept Hitler into office eight years later, compelling the aristocratic Hindenburg to select as Chancellor the 'little corporal' he despised. As late as 1928 the Nazis had less than 3 per cent of the vote. Two years later the most respectable Berlin press was lamenting the sight of the many millions in this 'highly civilized country' who had 'given their vote to the commonest, hollowest and crudest charlatanism'.[15] The centre was collapsing. The public was coming to despise the incessant wrangling of Weimar politics, the service of the traditional parties to powerful interests and their failure to deal with popular grievances. They were drawn to the forces dedicated to upholding the greatness of the nation and defending it against perceived threats in a revitalized, armed and unified state, marching to a glorious future, led by the charismatic figure who was carrying out 'the will of eternal Providence, the Creator of the universe', as he orated to the mesmerized masses. By May 1933 the Nazis had largely destroyed not only the traditional ruling parties but even the huge working-class parties, the Social Democrats and Communists, along with their very powerful associations. The Nazis declared May Day 1933 to be a workers' holiday, something the left parties had never been able to achieve. Many working people took part in the enormous patriotic demonstrations, with more than a million people at the heart of Red Berlin, joining farmers, artisans, shopkeepers, paramilitary forces, Christian organizations, athletic and riflery clubs, and the rest of the coalition that was taking shape as the centre collapsed. By the onset of the war perhaps 90 per cent of Germans were marching with the brownshirts.

The world is too complex for history to repeat, but there are nevertheless lessons to keep in mind, and even memories. I am just old enough to remember those chilling and ominous days of Germany's descent from decency to Nazi barbarism, in the words of the distinguished scholar of German history Fritz Stern, who tells us that he has the future of the United States in mind when he reviews 'a historic process in which resentment against a disenchanted secular world found deliverance in the ecstatic escape of unreason'.[16]

That is one possible outcome of collapse of the centre when the radical imagination, though powerful at the time, nonetheless fell short.

The popular mood today is complex, in ways that are both hopeful and troubling. One illustration is attitudes towards social spending on the part of those who identify themselves in polls as 'anti-government'. A recent scholarly study finds that by large majorities, they support 'maintaining or expanding spending on Social Security, child care, and aid to poor people' and other social welfare measures, though support falls off significantly 'when it came to aid to blacks and welfare recipients'. Half of these advocates of reducing the role of government believe 'that spending is too little [on] assistance to the poor'.[17] In the population as a whole, majorities, in some cases substantial, feel the government is spending too little to improve and protect the nation's health, and on Social Security, drug addiction, and child care programs – though again, there is an exception on aid for blacks and welfare recipients, partly a tribute to Reaganite thuggery, I suspect.

The results give some indication of what might be achieved by commitments even far short of the radical imagination, and of some of the impediments that will have to be overcome for these and much more far-reaching purposes.

The Massachusetts election in January 2010, which undermined majority rule in the Senate, gives some further insight into what can happen when the centre does not hold and those who believe in even limited measures of reform fail to reach the population. In the election to fill the seat of the Senate's 'liberal lion', Ted Kennedy, Scott Brown ran as the 41st vote against health care, which Kennedy had fought for throughout his political life. A majority opposed Obama's proposals, but primarily because they gave away too much to the insurance industry. Much the same is true nationally.

One interesting feature was the voting pattern among union members, Obama's natural constituency. Of those who bothered to vote, a majority chose Brown. Union leaders and activists reported that workers were angered at Obama's record generally, but particularly incensed over his stand on health care. As one reported, 'He didn't insist on a public option nor a strong employer mandate to provide insurance. It was hard not to notice that the only issue on which he took a firm stand was taxing benefits' for the health care won by union struggles, retracting his campaign pledge.[18]

There was a massive infusion of funds from financial executives in the final days of the campaign. That was one part of a broader phenomenon, which reveals dramatically why Joe Stack and others have every reason to be disgusted at the farce that they were taught to honour as democracy.

Obama's primary constituency in the 2008 election was financial institutions, which have gained such dominance in the economy since the '70s. They preferred Obama to McCain, and largely bought the election for him. They expected to be rewarded, and were. But a few months ago, responding to the rising anger of the Joe Stacks, Obama began to criticize the 'greedy bankers' who had been rescued by the public, and even proposed some measures to constrain their excesses. Punishment for his deviation was swift. The major banks announced prominently that they would shift funding to Republicans if Obama persisted with his offensive rhetoric.

Obama heard the message. Within days he informed the business press that bankers are fine 'guys'. He singled out for special praise the chairs of the two leading beneficiaries of public largesse, JP Morgan Chase and Goldman Sachs, and assured the business world that 'I, like most of the American people, don't begrudge people success or wealth', such as the huge bonuses and profits that are infuriating the public. 'That's part of the free market system,' Obama continued; not inaccurately, as 'free markets' are interpreted in state capitalist doctrine.[19] His retreat however was not in time to curb the flow of cash to help gain the 41st seat.

In fairness, we should concede that the greedy bankers have a point. Their task is to maximize profit and market share, in fact that's their legal obligation. If they don't do it, they'll be replaced by someone who will. These are institutional facts, as are the inherent market inefficiencies that require them to ignore systemic risk. They know full well that this oversight is likely to tank the economy, but such externalities are not their business, and cannot be, for institutional reasons. It is also unfair to accuse them of 'irrational exuberance', to borrow Alan Greenspan's brief recognition of reality during the tech boom of the late '90s. Their exuberance was hardly irrational: it was quite rational, in the knowledge that when it all collapses, they can flee to the shelter of the nanny state, clutching their copies of Hayek, Friedman, and Rand. The same is true of the Chamber of Commerce, the American Petroleum Institute, and the rest of the business leaders who are running a massive propaganda campaign to convince the public to dismiss concerns about anthropogenic global warming – with great success; those who believe in this liberal hoax have reduced to barely a third of the population. The executives dedicated to this task know as well as the rest of us that the liberal hoax is real, and the prospects grim. But they are fulfilling their institutional role. The fate of the species is an externality that they must ignore, to the extent that market systems prevail.

Returning to the very instructive Massachusetts election, the major factor was voting patterns. In the affluent suburbs, voting was high and enthusiastic. In the urban areas, heavily Democratic, voting was low and apathetic. The headlines were right to report that voters were sending Obama a message: the message from the rich was that we want even more than what you are doing for us. And from the rest, the message was Joe Stack's: in his words, the politicians are not 'the least bit interested in me or anything I have to say', though very much interested in the voices of the masters. Doubtless there was some impact of the populist image crafted by the PR machine ('I'm Scott Brown, this is my truck', 'regular guy', nude model, etc.). But this appears to have had only a secondary role. The popular anger is real and entirely understandable, with the banks thriving thanks to bailouts and many other gifts from the nanny state while the population remains in deep recession. Even official unemployment is at 10 per cent and in manufacturing industry at the level of the Great Depression, with one out of six unemployed, and with few prospects for recovering the kinds of jobs that are lost as the economy is being reshaped.

National polls reveal much the same phenomenon. A recent survey, conducted in March 2010, shows a 21-point enthusiasm gap between the parties, with 67 per cent of Republicans saying they are very interested in the November elections, compared with 46 per cent of Democrats.[20] In a major shift from the norm, by a 10-point margin registered voters with the highest interest in the November elections said they believe the Republicans are better at dealing with the economy, a combination of a solid Republican (mostly affluent) sector and disillusioned Democrats. Half of Americans would like to see every member of Congress defeated in the election, including their own representative. The public conception of democracy is almost as negative as that of the business world, which is now lobbying fiercely to ensure that even shareholders should have no say in choice of managers, let alone stakeholders, the workforce and communities; though some liberals are seeking to find '"a fair position" that straddles the divide between companies and shareholders,' as the *Wall Street Journal* puts it, implicitly recognizing the decision of the courts a century ago that the corporation is identical to the management.[21]

It is true that there was a stimulus, much too small but it had an effect – saving over 2 million jobs according to the Congressional Budget Office. But the perception of the Joe Stacks that it was a bust is not without basis. Over a third of government spending is by states, and the decline in state spending approximated the federal stimulus, so the aggregate fiscal expenditure stimulus was flat, according to a study by the prestigious National Bureau of Economic Research.[22]

The centre is clearly not holding, and those who are harmed are once again shooting themselves in the foot. The immediate consequence in Massachusetts was a vote to block the appointment of a pro-union voice at the NLRB, which has been virtually defunct since Reagan's successful war against working people. That is what can be expected in the absence of constructive alternatives.

Do these exist? Let's have a look at the industrial heartland, in Ohio, where GM continues to close plants. In March 2010, Louis Uchitelle of the New York Times, one of the few journalists who pays attention to labour issues, reported from the scene of one recently closed plant. He writes that President Obama 'never sought to reopen the factory even after the federal government became controlling shareholder in GM during the auto bailout. What he has done instead is try to ease some of the pain by sending an ambassador as a salve for the community's wounds, offer[ing] hope and aid' – the aid mostly suggestions.[23] Meanwhile another Ambassador, Secretary of Transportation Ray LaHood, was in Spain, dangling the prospect of federal stimulus money for Spanish firms to produce the high speed rail facilities that the US badly needs, and that could surely be produced by the highly skilled work force that is reduced to penury in Ohio.[24] Joe Stack's experience in Harrisburg again.

In 1999, as a Republican Congressman, LaHood introduced a bill that would have provided federal financing for transportation infrastructure. It would have authorized the Treasury to provide $72 billion a year in interest-free loans to state and local governments for capital investments, including investment in transportation infrastructure, not borrowing the money but issuing US notes, much as Lincoln did to finance the Civil War and as FDR did during the Great Depression. Today's LaHood is approving federal stimulus money to go to Spanish firms for the same purpose.[25] Another sign of how the centre has been shifting to the right in the past 40 years.

The radical imagination should suggest an answer. The factory could be taken over by the workforce with the support of the communities that are left desolate, and converted to production of high speed rail facilities and other badly needed goods. The idea is not particularly radical. In the 19th century, it was intuitively obvious to New England workers that 'those who work in the mills should own them,' and the idea that wage labour differed from slavery only in that it was temporary was so common that it was even a slogan of Lincoln's Republican party. During the recent years of financialization and deindustrialization there have been repeated efforts to implement worker and community takeover of closing plants. The ideas not only have immediate moral appeal to the affected workforce and communities, but should be quite feasible with sufficient public support. And far-reaching in their implications.

For the radical imagination to be rekindled and to lead the way out of this desert what is needed is people who will work to sweep away the mists of carefully contrived illusion and reveal the stark reality, and to be directly engaged in popular struggles that they sometimes help galvanize. What we need, in short, is the late Howard Zinn, a terrible loss. There won't be another Howard Zinn, but we can take to heart his praise for 'the countless small actions of unknown people' that lie at the roots of the great moments of history, the countless Joe Stacks who are destroying themselves, and maybe the world, when they could be leading the way to a better future.

NOTES

1 For the full text of Joseph Stack's statement, see "The inquisition is still alive and well today'. Text of denunciation of American tax system by alleged pilot in Texas crash', 18 February 2010, available at http://www.msnbc.msn.com.

2 Ching Kwan Lee, *Against the Law: Labour Protests in China's Rustbelt and Sunbelt*, Berkeley: University of California Press, 2007.

3 Ibid., p. 5, 6.

4 Peter Coy, Michelle Conlin and Moira Herbst, 'The Disposable Worker', *Bloomberg Businessweek*, 7 January 2010.

5 David Brooks, 'The Wal-Mart Hippies', *New York Times*, 5 March 2010.

6 The year Adam Smith' *The Wealth of Nations* was published.

7 Martin Hart-Landsberg and Paul Burkett, *China and Socialism: Market Reforms and Class Struggle*, New York: Monthly Review Press, 2005.

8 John W. Miller, 'Some Say Trade Numbers Don't Deliver the Goods', *Wall Street Journal* , 27 March 2010.

9 Glenn Loury, 'The Challenge of Mass Incarceration in America'; Rakesh Khurana, 'Challenges to Business in the Twenty-First Century: The Way Forward'; Richard Meserve, et al., 'On the Future of Energy'; all found in *Bulletin of the American Academy of Arts and Sciences*, 63(2), Winter 2010.

10 Frank A. Bennack, Jr., *The American Public's Knowledge of the US Constitution: A National Survey of Public Awareness and Personal Opinion. A Hearst Report*, New York: The Hearst Corporation, 1987.

11 Kate Zernike, 'Tea Party Avoids Divisive Social Issues', *New York Times*, 12 March 2010; Bernie Becker, 'A Revised Contract for America, Minus "With" and Newt', *New York Times*, 14 April 2010.

12 James McKinley, 'Texas Conservatives Win Curriculum Change', *New York Times*, 12 March 2010.

13 A quote from the recent book by Hoover fellows Martin and Annelise Anderson, *Reagan's Secret War: The Untold Story of His Fight to Save the World From Nuclear Disaster*, New York: Crown Publishers, 2009, p. 395.

14 Jennifer Schirmer, *The Guatemalan Military Project: A Violence Called Democracy*, Philadelphia: University of Pennsylvania Press, 1988, p. 33.

15 *Berliner Tageblatt*, quoted in Peter Fritzsche, *Germans into Nazis*, Cambridge: Harvard University Press, 1999.

16 Fritz Stern, Acceptance speech upon receiving the Leo Baeck Medal at the 10th annual dinner of the Leo Baeck Institute, November 14, 2004.

17 General Social Survey (GSS) from the National Opinion Research Center.

18 Jane Slaughter, 'Anger over Health Care Bill Creates Uncertain Future', *Labor Notes*, 20 January 2010.

19 Quotes from his interview with BusinessWeek, 'Obama's Corporate Messaging', *Bloomberg Businessweek*, 10 February 2010.

20 Bruce Drake, 'Democrats' Dilemma: Health Care Vote and the "Enthusiasm Gap"', 16 March 2010, available from at http://www.politicsdaily.com.

21 Kara Scannell, 'Proxy Plan Roils Talks on Finance Rules', *Wall Street Journal*, 17 March 2010.

22 Joshua Aizenman and Gurnain Kaur Pasricha, 'On the ease of overstating the fiscal stimulus in the US, 2008-9', NBER Working Paper 15784, February 2010.

23 Louis Uchitelle, 'For Auto Towns, Emissary Is Ambassador of Hope', *New York Times*, 5 March 2010.

24 Thomas Catan and David Gauthier-Villars, 'Europe Listens for US Train Whistle', *Wall Street Journal*, 29 May 2009; Joan Lowy And Matt Leingang, "Stimulus Watch: Foreign firms eye Obama rail plan", *Seattle Times*, 21 July 2009.

25 See for example the case of funds awarded to Wisconsin: Tom Held and Tom Daykin, 'Doyle, mayors laud high-speed rail plan', 28 January 2010 and Larry Sandler, 'Wis. high-speed rail work could start soon, LaHood tells Kohl', 4 March 2010, both available at http://www.jsonline.com.

ALSO AVAILABLE FROM LEFTWORD

SOCIALIST REGISTER 2010

Morbid Symptoms

Health under Capitalism

Editors: Leo Panitch, Colin Leys

978-81-87496-91-5, pp. xiv+325, paperback

Health care today is the object of struggle between commercial forces seeking to make it a field of capital accumulation, and popular forces fighting to keep it – or make it – a public service with equal access for all. This volume focuses on the historical, economic, social and political determinants of health under capitalism.

Contents: Colin Leys: Health, health care and capitalism; Hans-Ulrich Deppe: The nature of health care: commodification versus solidarity; David Coburn: Inequality and health; Rodney Loeppky: Certain wealth: accumulation in the health industry; Kalman Applbaum: Marketing global health care: the practices of big pharma; Marie Gottschalk: US health reform and the Stockholm syndrome; Christoph Hermann: The marketisation of health care in Europe; Pat Armstrong and Hugh Armstrong: Contradictions at work: struggles for control in Canadian health care; Paula Tibandebage and Maureen Mackintosh: Maternal mortality in Africa: a gendered lens on health system failure; Robert Albritton: Between obesity and hunger: the capitalist food industry; Lesley Henderson: Medical TV dramas: health care as soap opera; Julie Feinsilver: Cuban health politics at home and abroad; Shaoguang Wang: China's double movement in health care; Mohan Rao: 'Health for all' and neoliberal globalisation: an Indian rope trick; Meri Koivusalo: The shaping of global health policy; Sanjay Basu: Building a comprehensive public health movement: learning from HIV/AIDS mobilisations; Julian Tudor Hart: Mental health in a sick society: what are people for?

SOCIALIST REGISTER 2009

Violence Today

Actually Existing Barbarism

Editors: Leo Panitch, Colin Leys

978-81-87496-79-3, pp. viii+277, paperback

Is this a new age of barbarism? The scale and pervasiveness of violence today calls urgently for serious analysis of:

- the 'war on terror' and counter-insurgencies;
- terror and counter-terror;
- suicide bombings and torture;
- urban gang warfare; and
- the persistence of chronic violence against women.

Such violence entails human tragedies on a scale comparable to those of the two world wars. The fact that millions of people are living in fear of violent death is an appalling indictment of the nirvana of global capitalism that now prevails.

The opening essay offers an overview of the scale and variety of contemporary violence while also taking up once again the question of socialism versus barbarism. Other essays analyse the nature and roots of paradigmatic cases of violence around the world. And several of the concluding essays deal, from various different standpoints, with the still important question of whether violence has any place in socialist strategy in the context of today's actually-existing barbarism.

CONTRIBUTORS: Samir Amin, John Berger, Henry Bernstein, Michael Brie, Vivek Chibber, Ruth Wilson Gilmore, Philip Green, Barbara Harriss-White, Steffen Jensen, Sofiri Joab-Peterside, Colin Leys, Tania Murray Li, Ulrich Oslender, Leo Panitch, Dennis Rodgers, Lynne Segal, Joe Sim, Steve Tombs, Achin Vanaik, Anna Zalik

SOCIALIST REGISTER 2008

Global Flashpoints

Reactions to imperialism and neoliberalism

Editors: Leo Panitch, Colin Leys

978-81-87496-75-5, pp. xiv+362, paperback

New forces of resistance have emerged to both American imperialism and neoliberalism. But how far do these forces represent a progressive alternative? This volume surveys the key flashpoints of resistance today.

The main arena of resistance to imperialism is the Middle East. Six essays explore the ambivalent nature of Islamic anti-imperialism, and the West's crucial role in making it so significant, as well as the different forms it takes as a political creed; and they provide particular insight into the relationship between religion and politics today in Iraq, Palestine and Turkey.

Resistance to neoliberalism has been seen most clearly in the 'pink tide' in Latin America. Seven essays evaluate the potential – or lack of it – for a 21st century socialism across the region, and especially in Venezuela, Bolivia, Mexico, and Argentina; while an interview with João-Pedro Stédile, leader of Brazil's Landless People's Movement, provides a unique perspective on class struggles in that country.

Three further essays look at recent reactions to neoliberalism and imperialism elsewhere – in Eastern Europe, in France, and in the heart of empire, the United States itself. The volume concludes with a symposium: three leading left economists analyse neoliberalism as a global regime of social and political control, and critically examine the left's response to it.

CONTRIBUTORS: Bashir Abu-Manneh, Gilbert Achcar, Aijaz Ahmad, Gregory Albo, Sabah Alnasseri, Elmar Altvater, Edur Velasco Arregui, Yildiz Atasoy, Asef Bayat, Emilia Castorina, Ana Esther Ceceña, Wes Enzinna, Marta Harnecker, Raghu Krishnan, Margarita López Maya, Kim Moody, William Robinson, Richard Roman, Alfredo Saad-Filho, João Pedro Stédile, G.M. Tamás, Adrien Thomas

SOCIALIST REGISTER 2007

Coming to Terms with Nature

Editors: Leo Panitch and Colin Leys

978-81-87496-69-4, pp. xvi + 363, paperback

This volume develops a better eco-socialist understanding of contemporary capitalism, and advances the kind of politics that could lead to an ecologically sustainable as well as a democratic socialism. Beginning with a leading filmmaker's vivid images of the crisis, seventeen essays address:

How capitalism is capable of finding new fields of accumulation in nature
The significance of capitalism's historic dependence on fossil fuels
Why renewable energy is neglected by 'New Labour' in Britain
Environmental effects of China's growth
Eco-Populism and environmental degradation in Africa
How globalized capitalist agriculture is destroying the ecosphere
The truth about the Kyoto Protocol
Water, power and money
How capitalism profits from waste
The contradictions of consumerism
The world-wide conflicts generated by the environmental crisis
The limits of 'eco-localism' and 'market ecology'
Party-building for eco-socialists: lessons from the German Greens
The eco-socialist case for democratic planning

CONTRIBUTORS: Greg Albo, Almar Altvater, Henry Bernstein, Achim Brunnengräber, Daniel Buck, Elinor Harriss, Barbara Harriss-White, Minqi Li, Brenda Longfellow, Michael Löwy, Joan Martinez-Alier, Philip McMichael, Costas Panayotakis, Jamie Peck, Heather Rogers, Neil Smith, Erik Swyngedouw, Dale Wen, Frieder Otto Wolf, Philip Woodhouse

SOCIALIST REGISTER 2006

Telling the Truth

Editors: Leo Panitch and Colin Leys

pp. 296, paperback

Fifteen leading writers explore the problem of truth and the lack of it in thirteen original essays on: the cynical state; 'capitalist democracy'; the 'business community'; 'welfare reform'; 'law and order'; the media and the Iraq war; global poverty statistics; development economics; the politics of theatre; academic postmodernism; socialists and the problem of class; the history of truth.

CONTRIBUTORS: Atillio A Boron, Terry Eagleton, Barbara Ehrenreich, Ben Fine, Doug Henwood, Michael Kustow, Colin Leys, Robert W McChesney, David Miller, Frances Fox Piven, Sanjay G Reddy, John Sanbonmatsu, G M Tamas, Elisa Van Waeyenberge, LoicWacquant

Talking About Trees

Science, Ecology and Agriculture in Cuba

Richard Levins

978-81-87496-63-2, pp. 169, hardcover

"Levins' writing is compelling, as always, and makes a valuable contribution to our thinking about a sustainable alternative to the rapacious globalization ravaging the planet today."

Vijay Prashad

Understanding dynamic complexity is the central scientific problem of our time. We need to look at science itself as an object of study, a historically developed way of producing knowledge that creates a rich mix of insights and confusions. Our approach needs to be partisan, rejecting the notion that feeling is the enemy of reason or that a commitment to human well-being is an enemy of objectivity.

Richard Levins, an ex-tropical farmer turned Harvard University ecologist, biomathematician and philosopher of science, gives us his first book since the hugely influential *The Dialectical Biologist*. He argues for a good, combative, perceptive scientific method that is more reflective of the complex, dynamic world in which we live and more supportive of precautionary decisions.

Talking About Trees ranges widely, from personal narratives to theoretical discussions on the need for the precautionary principle in science. Levins offers a strong critique of the industrial-commercial pathway to development; in its place he promotes an alternative development pathway that emphasizes economic viability with equity, ecological and social sustainability and empowerment of the dispossessed.

RICHARD LEVINS is John Rock Professor of Population Sciences, Harvard School of Public Health, Harvard University, Boston, MA. He is author, along with Richard Lewontin, of *The Dialectical Biologist*, Harvard University Press, 1985.

The Darker Nations

A Biography of the Short-lived Third World

Vijay Prashad

978-81-87496-67-0, pp. 384, paperback

"At a time when the politicians and ideologues of the Washington Consensus appeal to former colonies to free themselves from history, Vijay Prashad stubbornly carries on, recalling a past without which it is impossible to understand the present."

Tariq Ali

"The Third World was not a place," argues Vijay Prashad. "It was a project." This book is a paradigm-shifting history of both a utopian concept and global movement—the idea of the Third World. *The Darker Nations* traces the intellectual origins and the political history of the attempt to knit together the world's impoverished countries in opposition to the United States and Soviet spheres of influence in the decades following World War II, as nation after nation across Asia, Africa and South America gained political independence from colonial rule.

Traversing continents, Vijay Prashad's fascinating narrative takes us from the birth of postcolonial nations after World War II to the downfall and corruption of nationalist regimes. A breakthrough book of cutting-edge scholarship, it includes vivid portraits of Third World giants like Jawaharlal Nehru, Egypt's Nasser, and Indonesia's Sukarno—as well as scores of extraordinary but now-forgotten intellectuals, artists, and freedom fighters. *The Darker Nations* restores to memory the vibrant though flawed idea of the Third World, whose demise, Prashad ultimately argues, has produced a much impoverished international political arena.

VIJAY PRASHAD is a prolific writer and the author of several books, including four for LeftWord Books. He teaches at Trinity College, Connecticut, USA.

Capital

Volumes I, II, III

Karl Marx

978-81-87496-94-6, pp. 768 + 564 + 960, hardcover

Karl Marx's classic work reissued in a beautifully bound hardcover boxed set from LeftWord.

Volume I
A Critical Analysis of Capitalist Production
Translated from the third German edition by Samuel Moore and Edward Aveling and edited by Frederick Engels
978-81-87496-95-3, pp. 768, HC

Volume II
A Critique of Political Economy
The Process of Circulation of Capital edited by Frederick Engels
978-81-87496-96-0, pp. 564, HC

Volume III
A Critique of Political Economy
The Process of Capitalist Production as a Whole edited by Frederick Engels
978-81-87496-97-7, pp. 960, HC